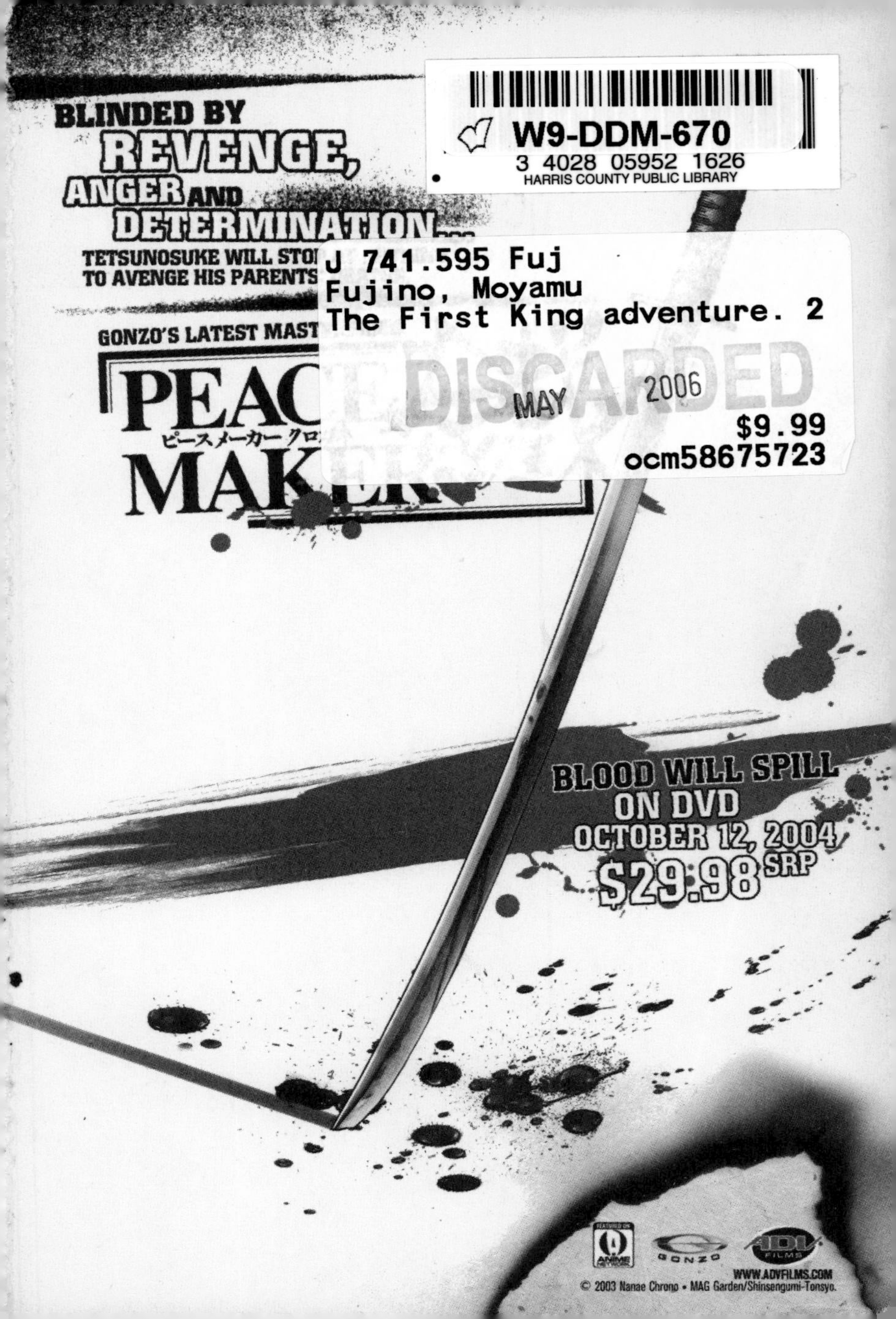
BLINDED BY
REVENGE,
ANGER AND
DETERMINATION...
TETSUNOSUKE WILL STO
TO AVENGE HIS PARENTS
GONZO'S LATEST MAST
PEAC
ピースメーカー
MAK
BLOOD WILL SPILL
ON DVD
OCTOBER 12, 2004
$29.98 SRP
WWW.ADVFILMS.COM
© 2003 Nanae Chrono • MAG Garden/Shinsengumi-Tonsyo.

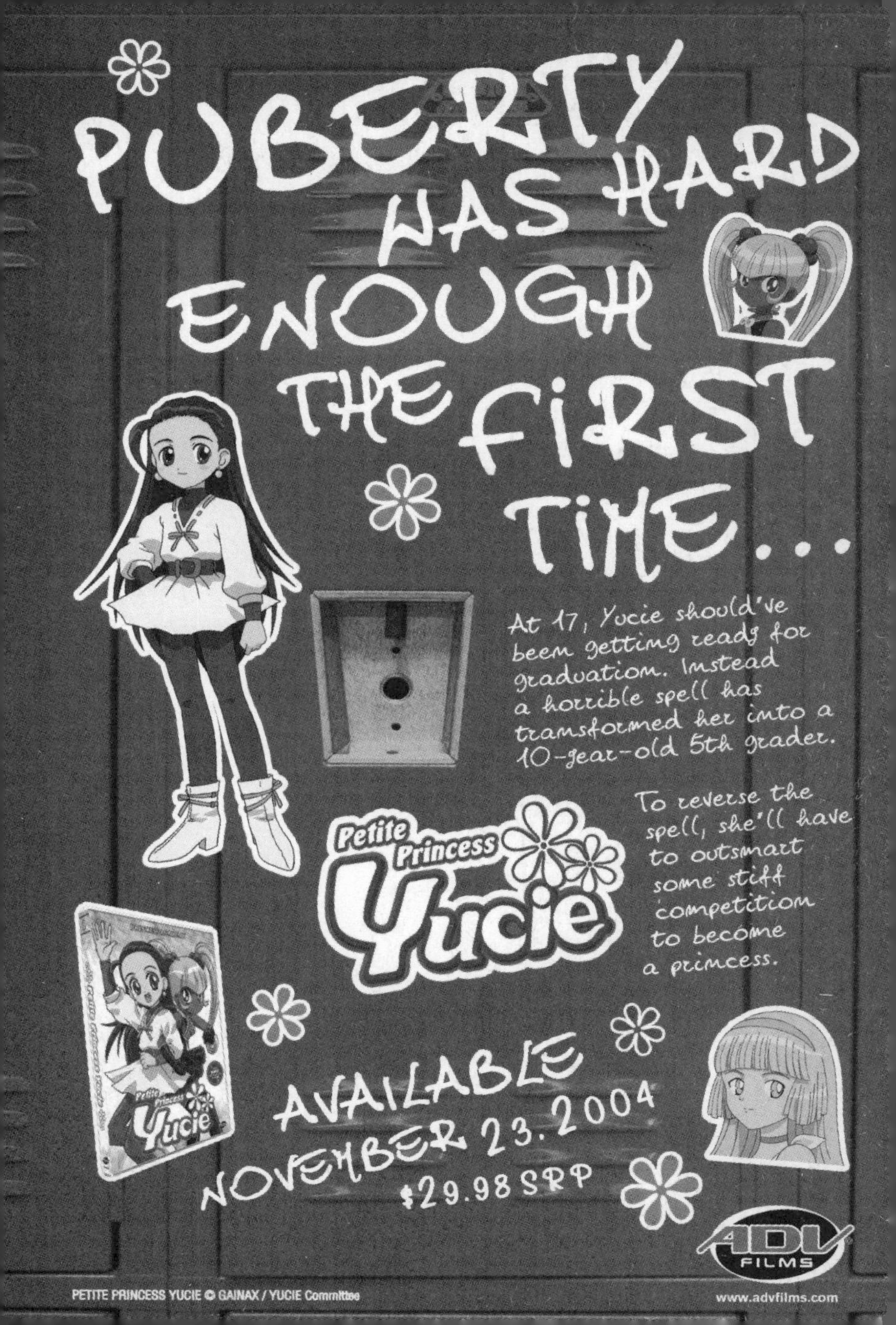
PUBERTY WAS HARD ENOUGH THE FIRST TIME...
At 17, Yucie should've been getting ready for graduation. Instead a horrible spell has transformed her into a 10-year-old 5th grader.
To reverse the spell, she'll have to outsmart some stiff competition to become a princess.
Petite Princess Yucie
AVAILABLE NOVEMBER 23, 2004
$29.98 SRP
ADV FILMS
PETITE PRINCESS YUCIE © GAINAX / YUCIE Committee
www.advfilms.com

Dancing Queen

IN A MAGICAL WORLD, SHE FINDS THE GRACE TO LAND HER PRINCE

Art
Mizuo Shinonome
Story
Ikuko Itoh & Jun-ichi Satoh

PRINCESS TUTU

THE HIT SHOJO MANGA
IS ALSO AN ANIME SERIES —
BOTH FROM ADV!

www.adv-manga.com

THE ADVENTURE CONTINUES IN

the First King Adventure 3

Young Prince Varumu has accepted his destiny as the ruler of the magical kingdom of Tiltu, and he continues the trial that will one day make him King. With the fleeting help of Leanne Phaigrey Drown, he must search for the master of the crystal ball in hopes of collecting another symbol, but it won't be an easy pact to make. And with new competition closing in on the Prince's potential partners, the race for the crown begins in *The First King Adventure* Volume 3.

COMING SOON FROM ADV MANGA!

www.adv-manga.com

LETTER FROM THE ADV MANGA TRANSLATION STAFF

Dear Reader,

On behalf of the ADV Manga translation team, thank you for purchasing an ADV book. We are enthusiastic and committed to our work, and strive to carry our enthusiasm over into the book you hold in your hands.

Our goal is to retain the spirit of the original Japanese book. While great care has been taken to render a true and accurate translation, some cultural or readability issues may require a line to be adapted for greater accessibility to our readers. At times, manga titles that include culturally-specific concepts will feature a "Translator's Notes" section, which explains noteworthy references to the original text.

We hope our commitment to a faithful translation is evident in every ADV book you purchase.

Sincerely,

Javier Lopez
Lead Translator

Kay Bertrand

Brendan Frayne

Amy Forsyth

the First King Adventure 2

© Moyamu Fujino 2003
All rights reserved.
First published in 2003 by MAG Garden Corporation.
English translation rights arranged with MAG Garden Corporation.

Translator **KAY BERTRAND**
Lead Translator/Translation Supervisor **JAVIER LOPEZ**
ADV Manga Translation Staff **AMY FORSYTH AND BRENDAN FRAYNE**

Print Production/Art Studio Manager **LISA PUCKETT**
Pre-press Manager **KLYS REEDYK**
Sr. Designer/Creative Manager **JORGE ALVARADO**
Graphic Designer/Group Leader **GEORGE REYNOLDS**
Graphic Artists **HEATHER GARY AND NATALIA MORALES**
Graphic Intern **MARK MEZA**

International Coordinators **TORU IWAKAMI,
ATSUSHI KANBAYASHI AND KYOKO DRUMHELLER**

Publishing Editor **SUSAN ITIN**
Assistant Editor **MARGARET SCHAROLD**
Editorial Assistant **SHERIDAN JACOBS**
Editorial Intern **MIKE ESSMYER**

Research/Traffic Coordinator **MARSHA ARNOLD**

Executive VP, CFO, COO **KEVIN CORCORAN**

President, CEO & Publisher **JOHN LEDFORD**

Email: editor@adv-manga.com
www.adv-manga.com
www.advfilms.com

For sales and distribution inquiries please call 1.800.282.7202

ADV MANGA™ is a division of A.D. Vision, Inc.
10114 W. Sam Houston Parkway, Suite 200, Houston, Texas 77099

English text © 2005 published by A.D. Vision, Inc. under exclusive license.
ADV MANGA is a trademark of A.D. Vision, Inc.

ISBN: 1-4139-0225-1
First printing, February 2005
10 9 8 7 6 5 4 3 2 1
Printed in Canada

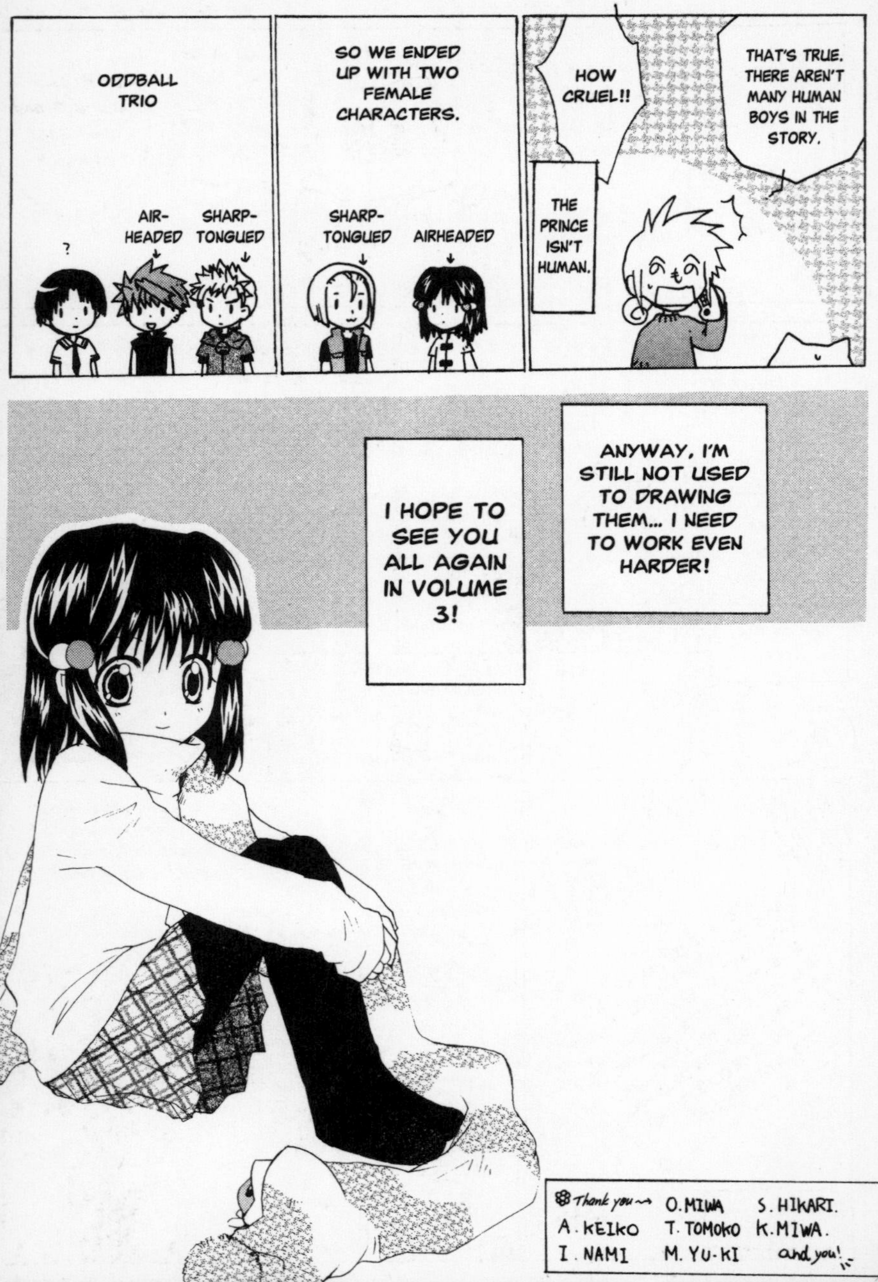
ODDBALL TRIO
?
AIR-HEADED
SHARP-TONGUED
SO WE ENDED UP WITH TWO FEMALE CHARACTERS.
SHARP-TONGUED
AIRHEADED
HOW CRUEL!!
THAT'S TRUE. THERE AREN'T MANY HUMAN BOYS IN THE STORY.
THE PRINCE ISN'T HUMAN.
ANYWAY, I'M STILL NOT USED TO DRAWING THEM... I NEED TO WORK EVEN HARDER!
I HOPE TO SEE YOU ALL AGAIN IN VOLUME 3!
Thank you~ O.MIWA S.HIKARI.
A.KEIKO T.TOMOKO K.MIWA.
I.NAMI M.YU-KI and you!

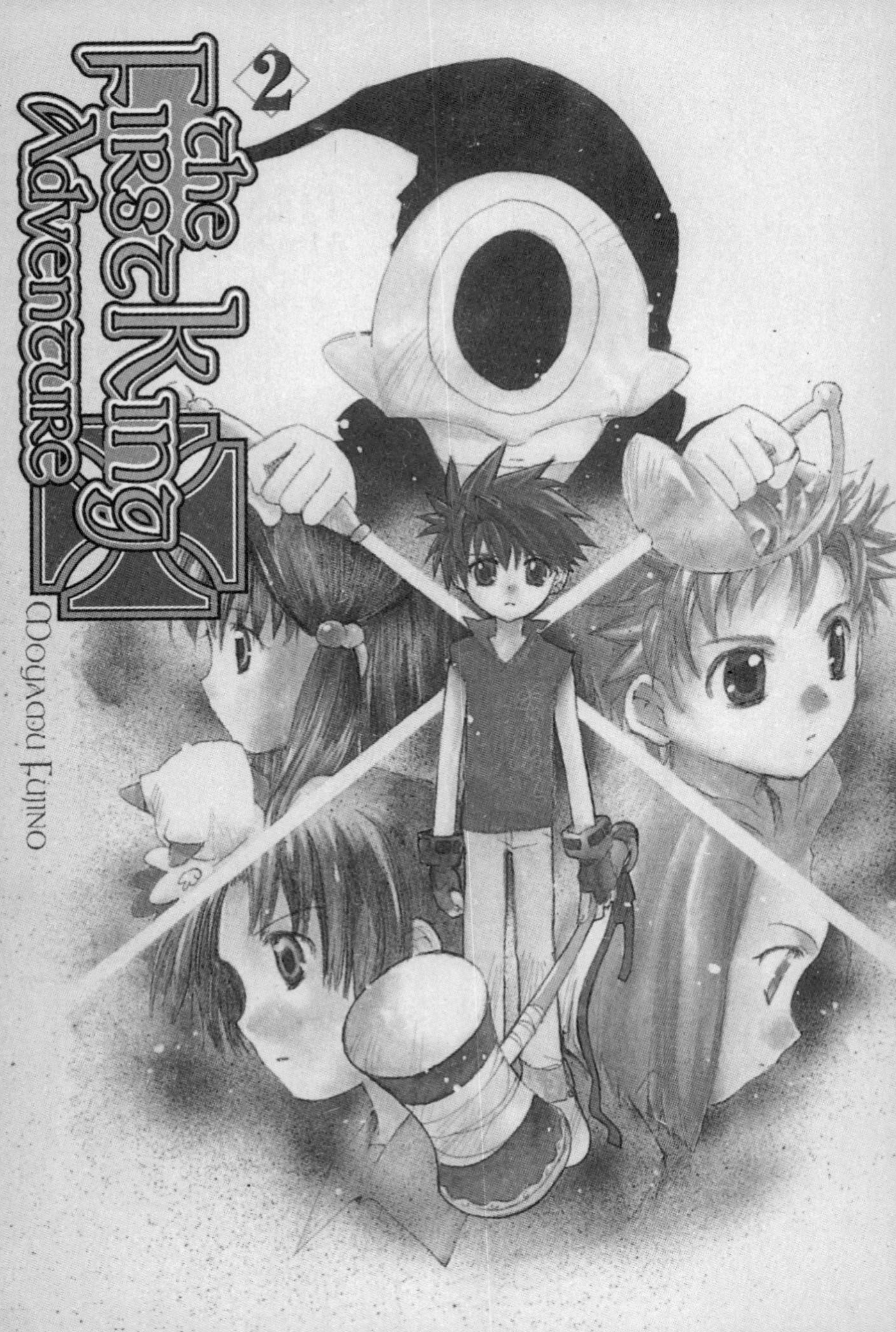
2
the First King Adventure
Moyamu Fujino

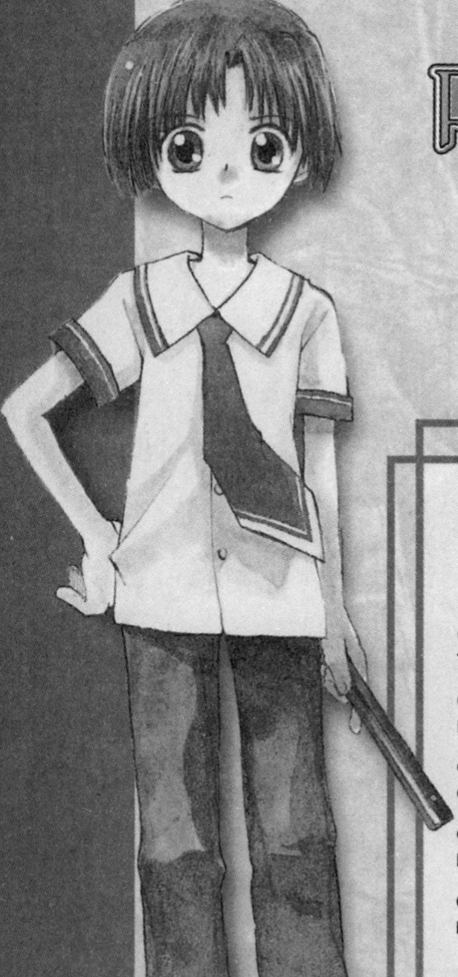

The First King Adventure

2

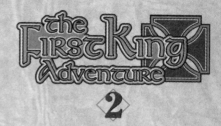

CONTENTS

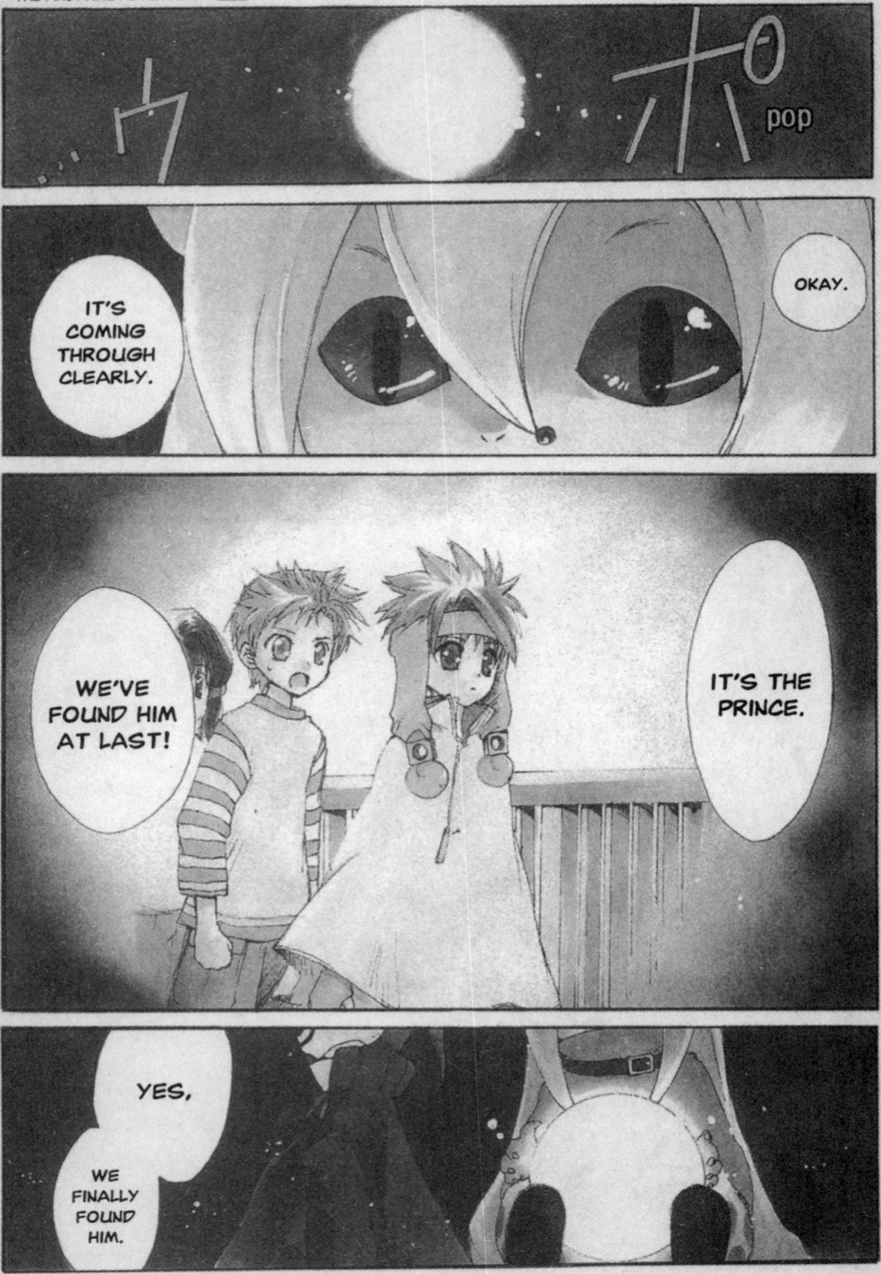
pop
OKAY.
IT'S COMING THROUGH CLEARLY.
IT'S THE PRINCE.
WE'VE FOUND HIM AT LAST!
YES,
WE FINALLY FOUND HIM.

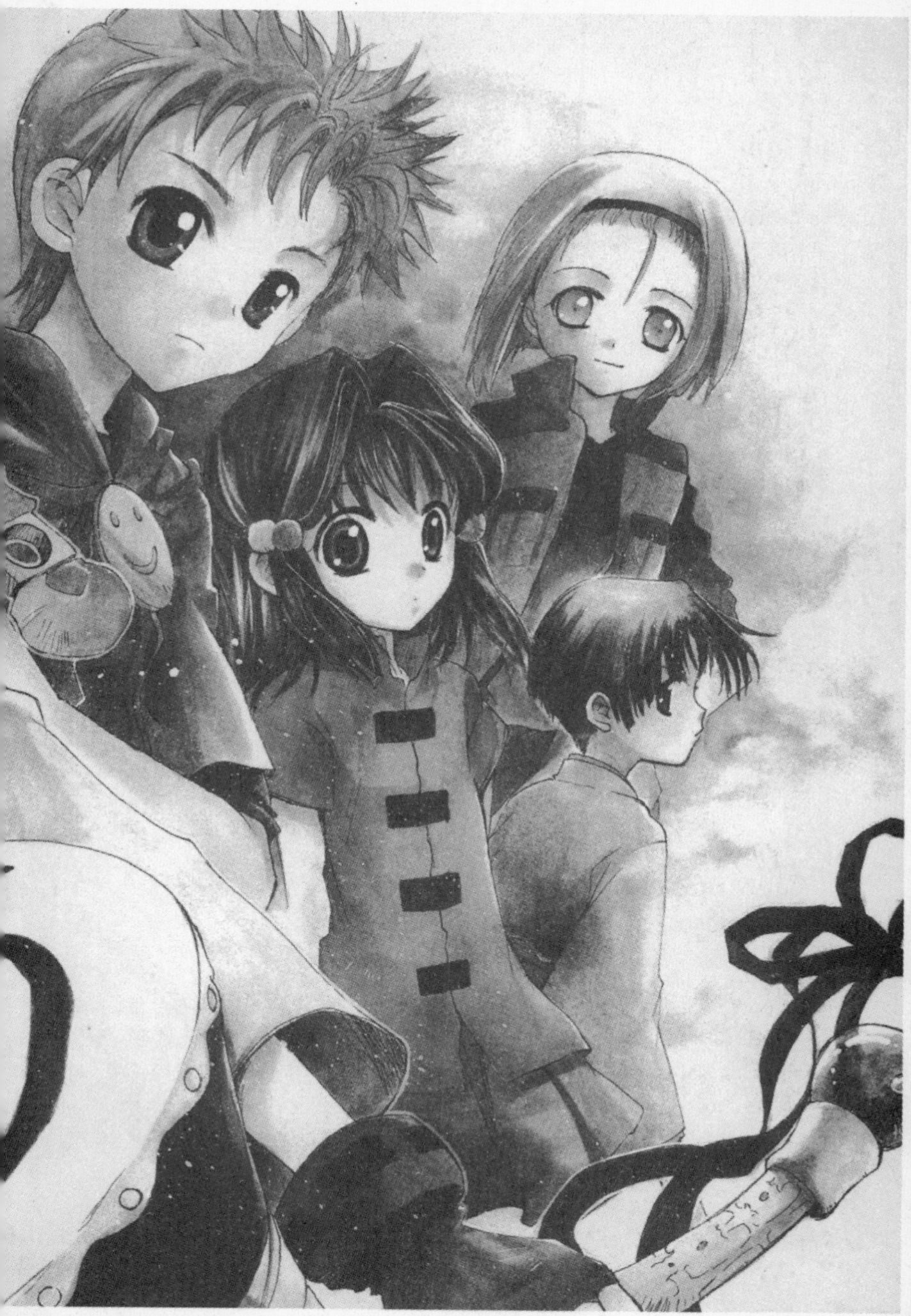

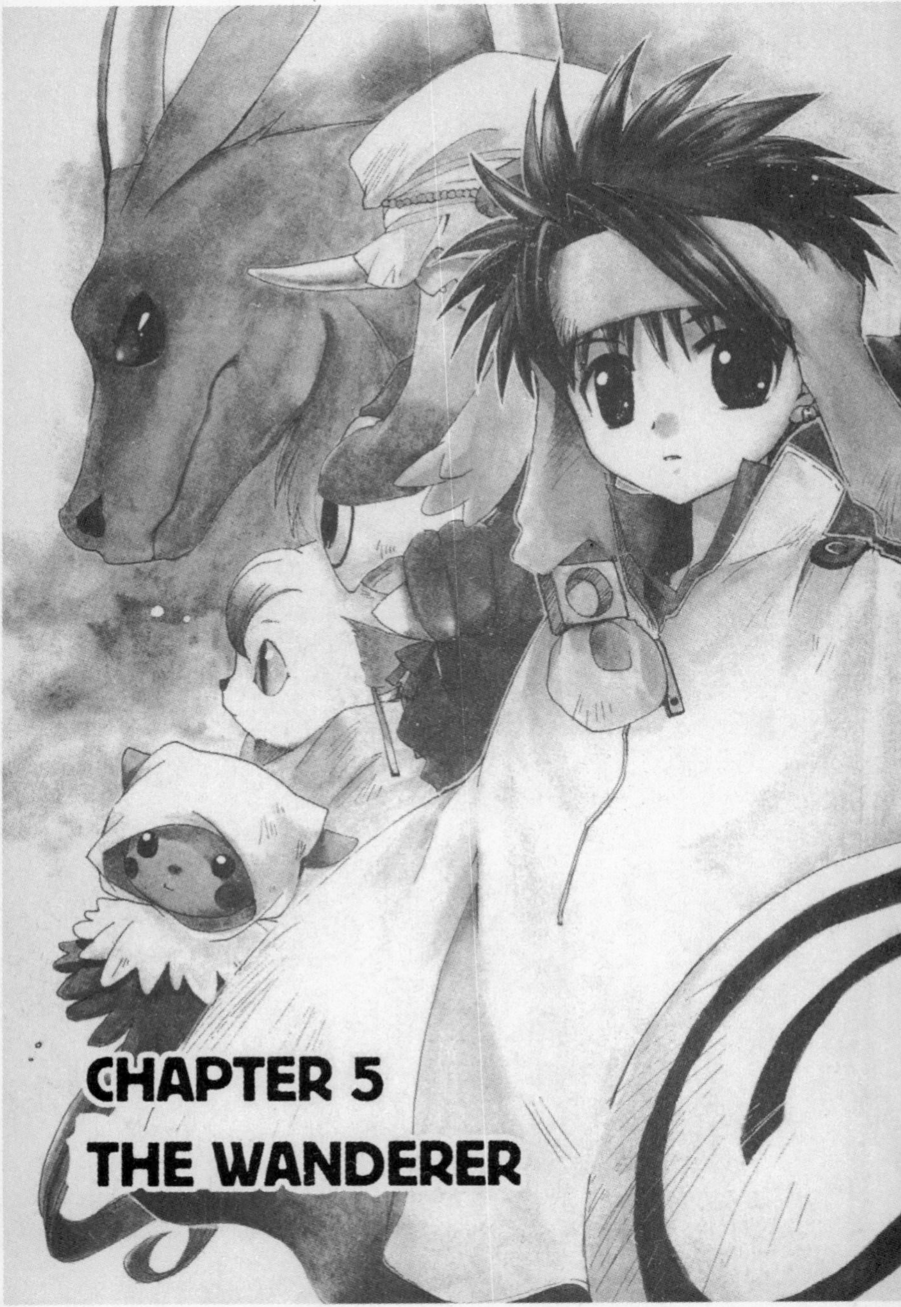
CHAPTER 5
THE WANDERER

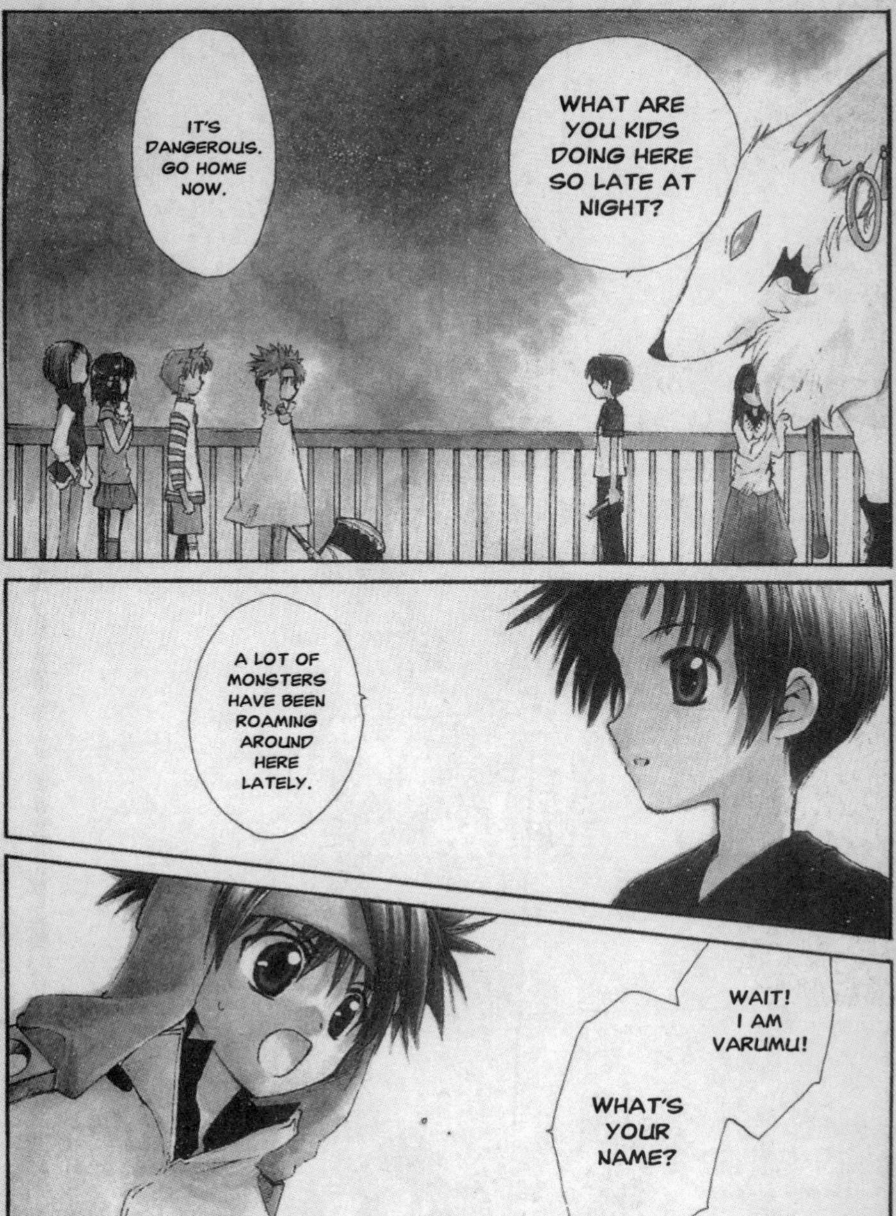
WHAT ARE YOU KIDS DOING HERE SO LATE AT NIGHT?
IT'S DANGEROUS. GO HOME NOW.
A LOT OF MONSTERS HAVE BEEN ROAMING AROUND HERE LATELY.
WAIT! I AM VARUMU!
WHAT'S YOUR NAME?

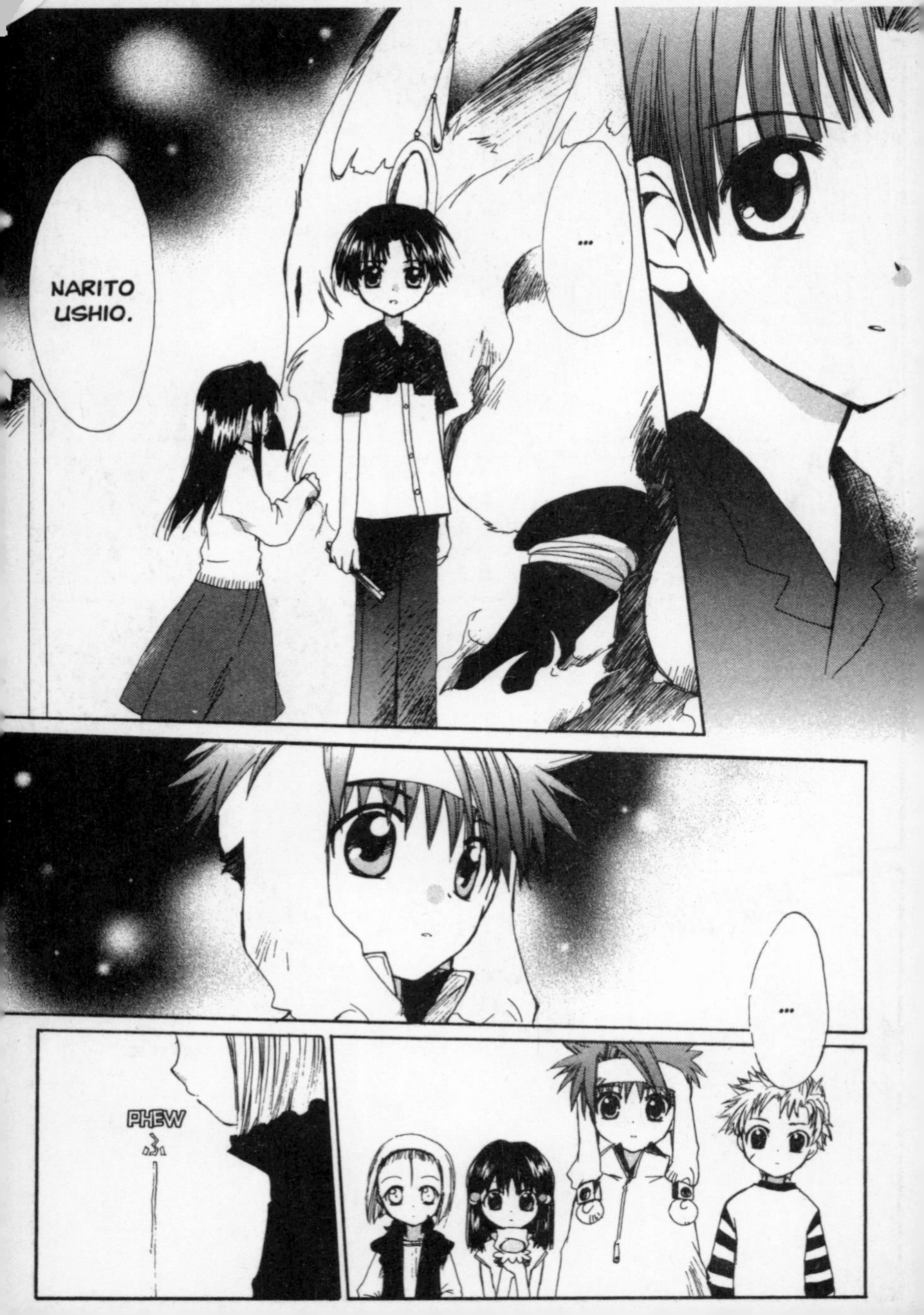
...
NARITO USHIO.
...
PHEW

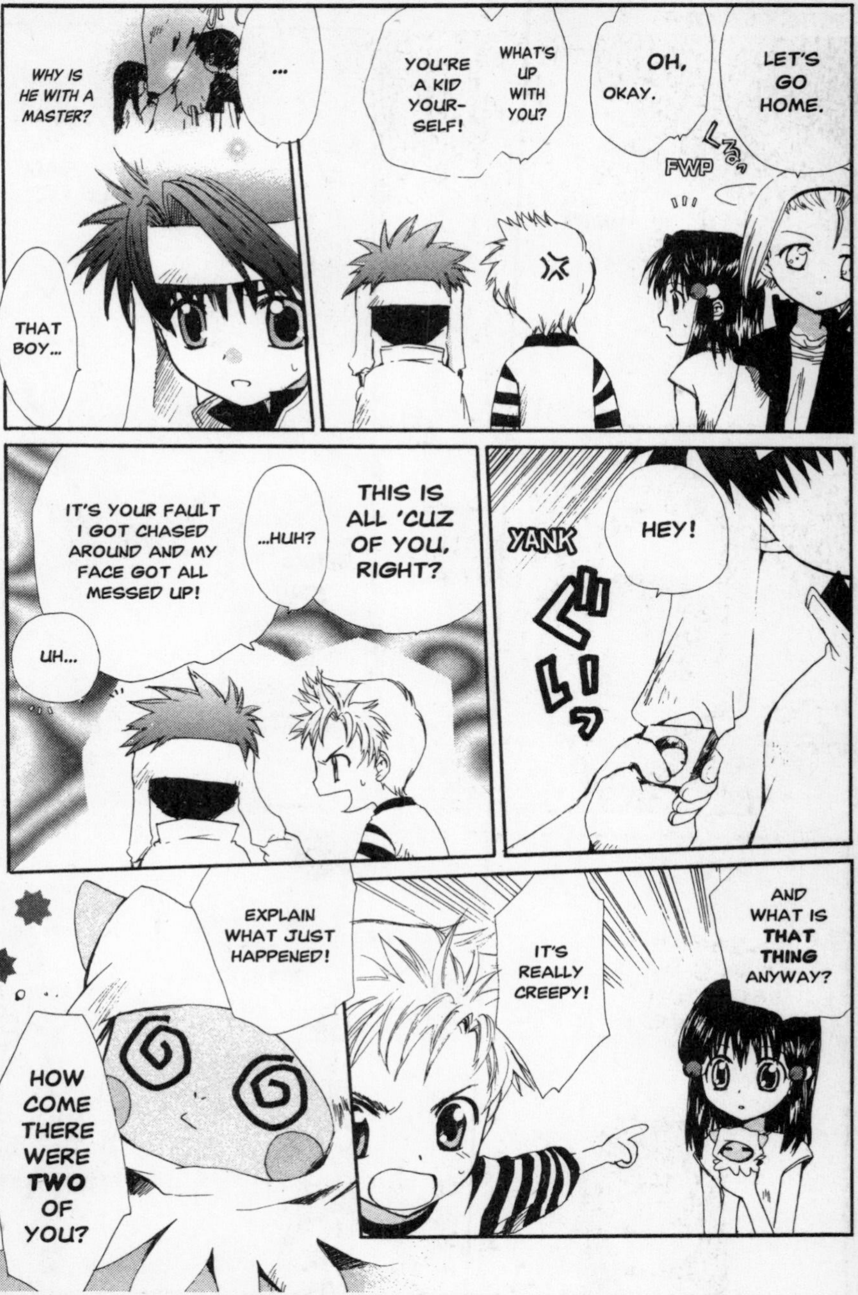
LET'S GO HOME.
OH, OKAY.
FWP
WHAT'S UP WITH YOU?
YOU'RE A KID YOURSELF!
...
WHY IS HE WITH A MASTER?
THAT BOY...
YANK
HEY!
THIS IS ALL 'CUZ OF YOU, RIGHT?
...HUH?
IT'S YOUR FAULT I GOT CHASED AROUND AND MY FACE GOT ALL MESSED UP!
UH...
AND WHAT IS **THAT** THING ANYWAY?
IT'S REALLY CREEPY!
EXPLAIN WHAT JUST HAPPENED!
HOW COME THERE WERE **TWO** OF YOU?

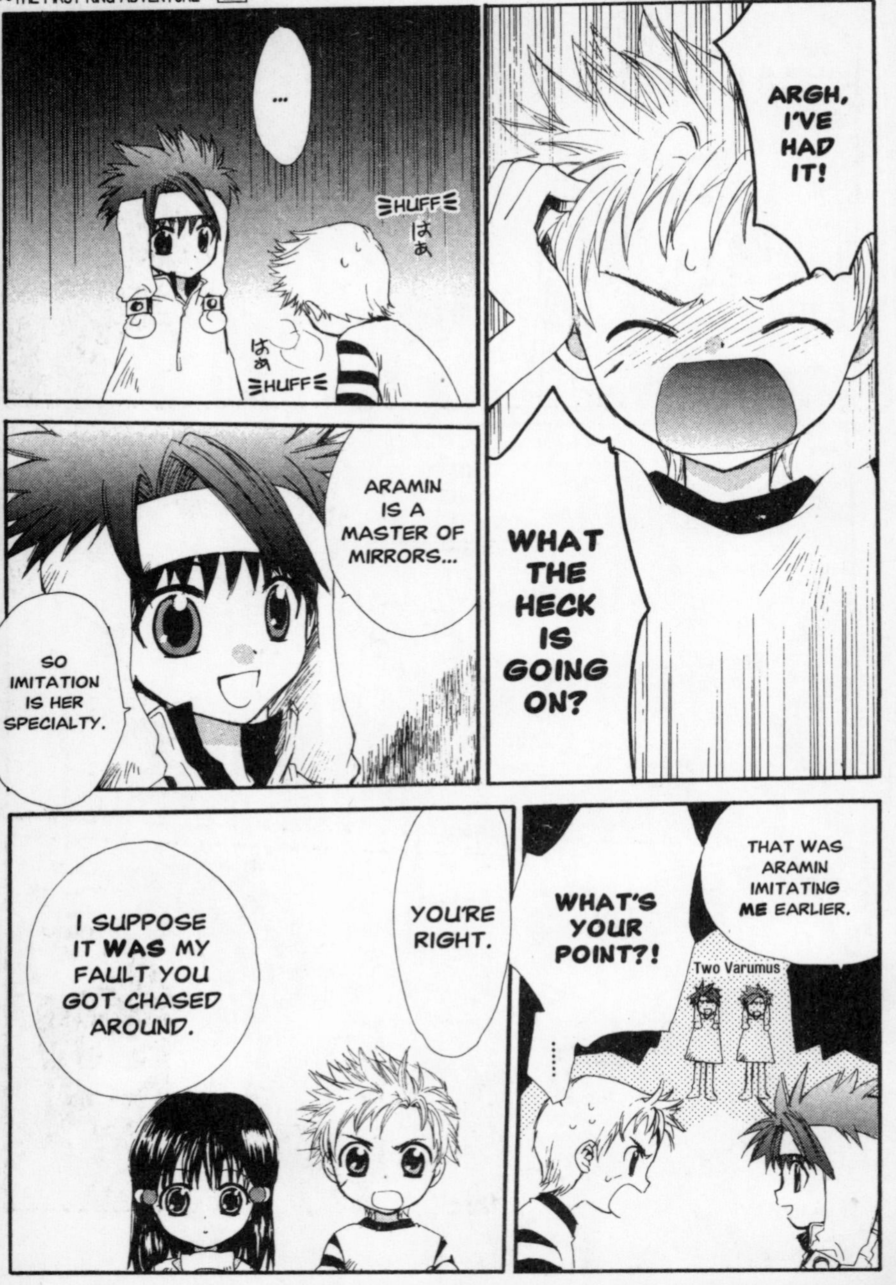
ARGH, I'VE HAD IT!
WHAT THE HECK IS GOING ON?
...
HUFF はあ
はあ HUFF
ARAMIN IS A MASTER OF MIRRORS...
SO IMITATION IS HER SPECIALTY.
THAT WAS ARAMIN IMITATING ME EARLIER.
WHAT'S YOUR POINT?!
Two Varumus
......
YOU'RE RIGHT.
I SUPPOSE IT WAS MY FAULT YOU GOT CHASED AROUND.

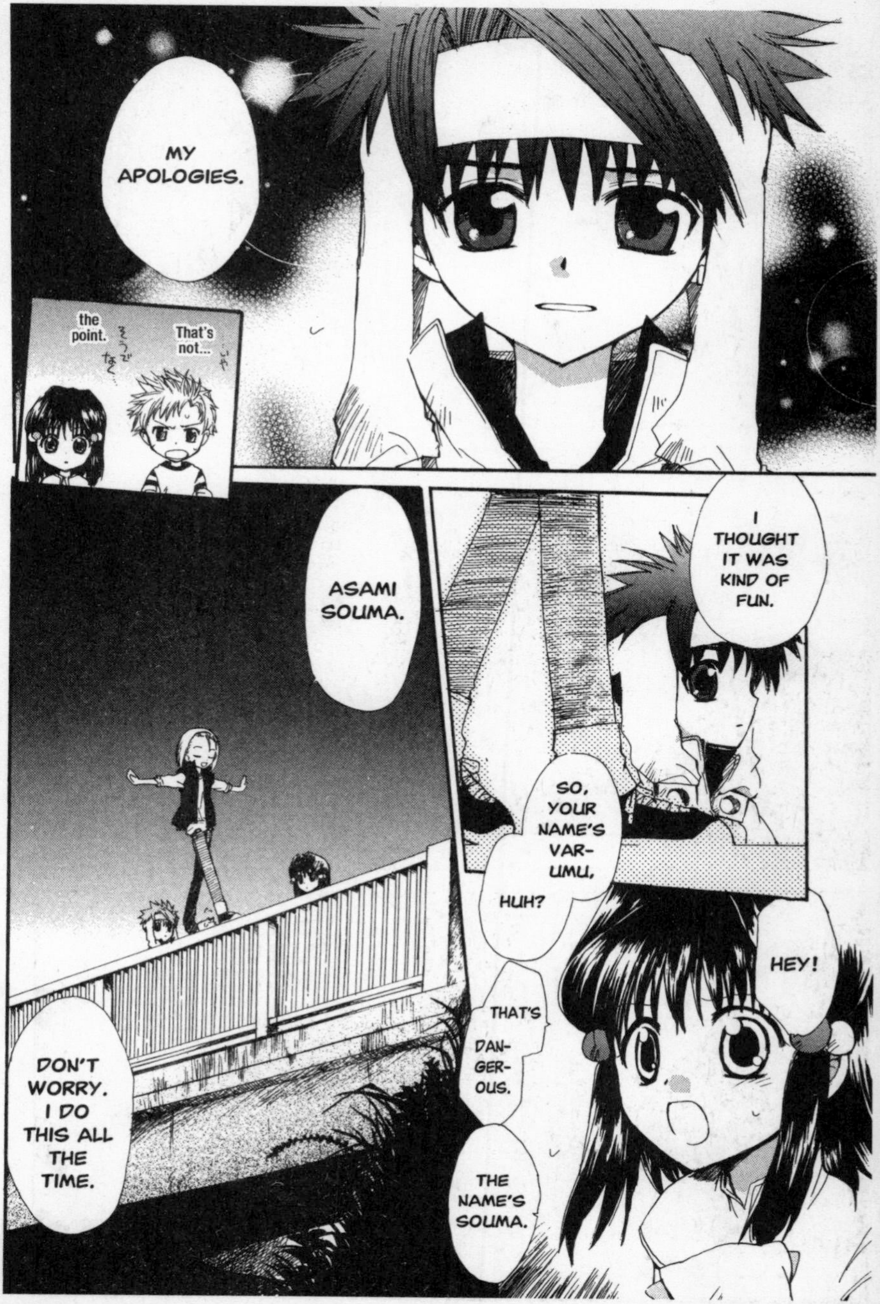
MY APOLOGIES.
That's not...
the point.
I THOUGHT IT WAS KIND OF FUN.
SO, YOUR NAME'S VAR-UMU,
HUH?
ASAMI SOUMA.
HEY!
THAT'S DAN-GER-OUS.
THE NAME'S SOUMA.
DON'T WORRY. I DO THIS ALL THE TIME.

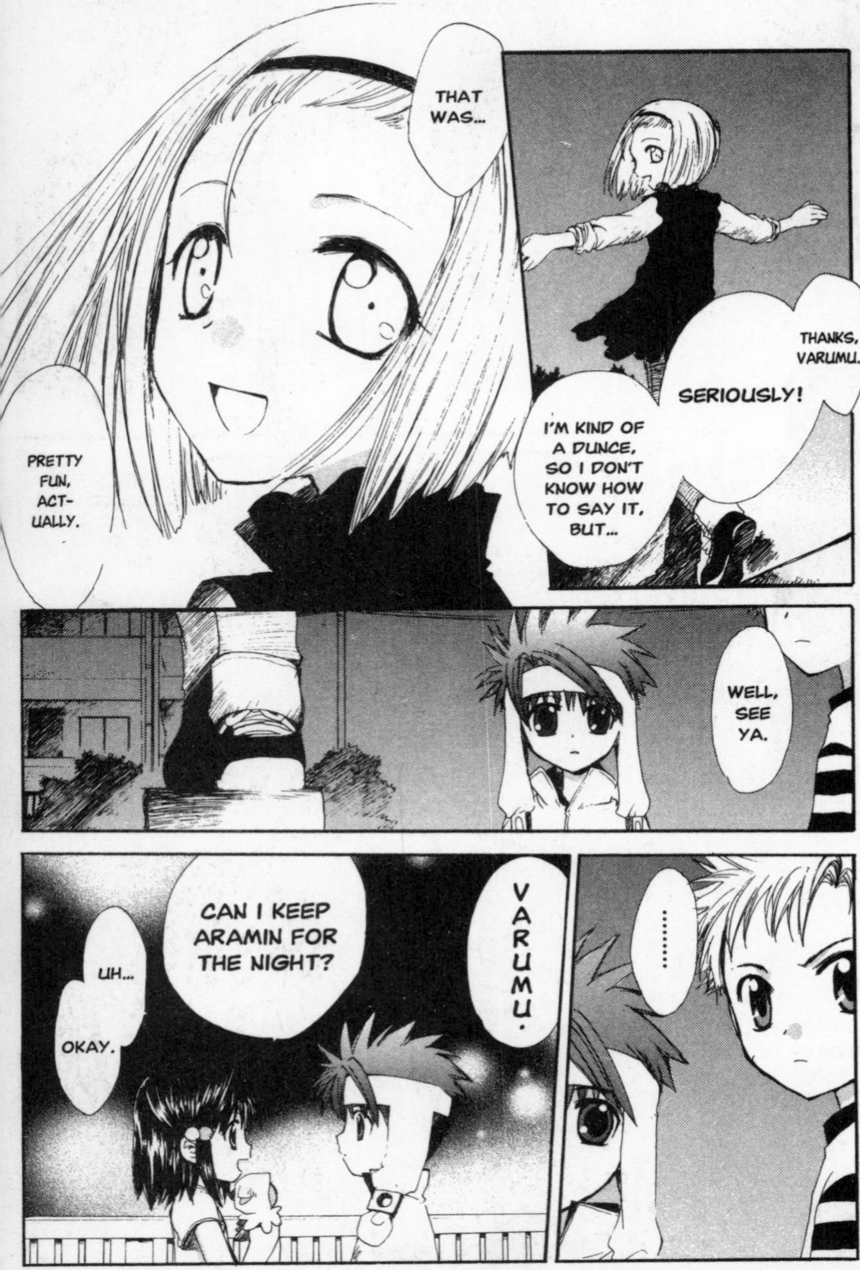
THANKS, VARUMU.
SERIOUSLY!
I'M KIND OF A DUNCE, SO I DON'T KNOW HOW TO SAY IT, BUT...
THAT WAS...
PRETTY FUN, ACT-UALLY.
WELL, SEE YA.
......
VARUMU.
CAN I KEEP ARAMIN FOR THE NIGHT?
UH...
OKAY.

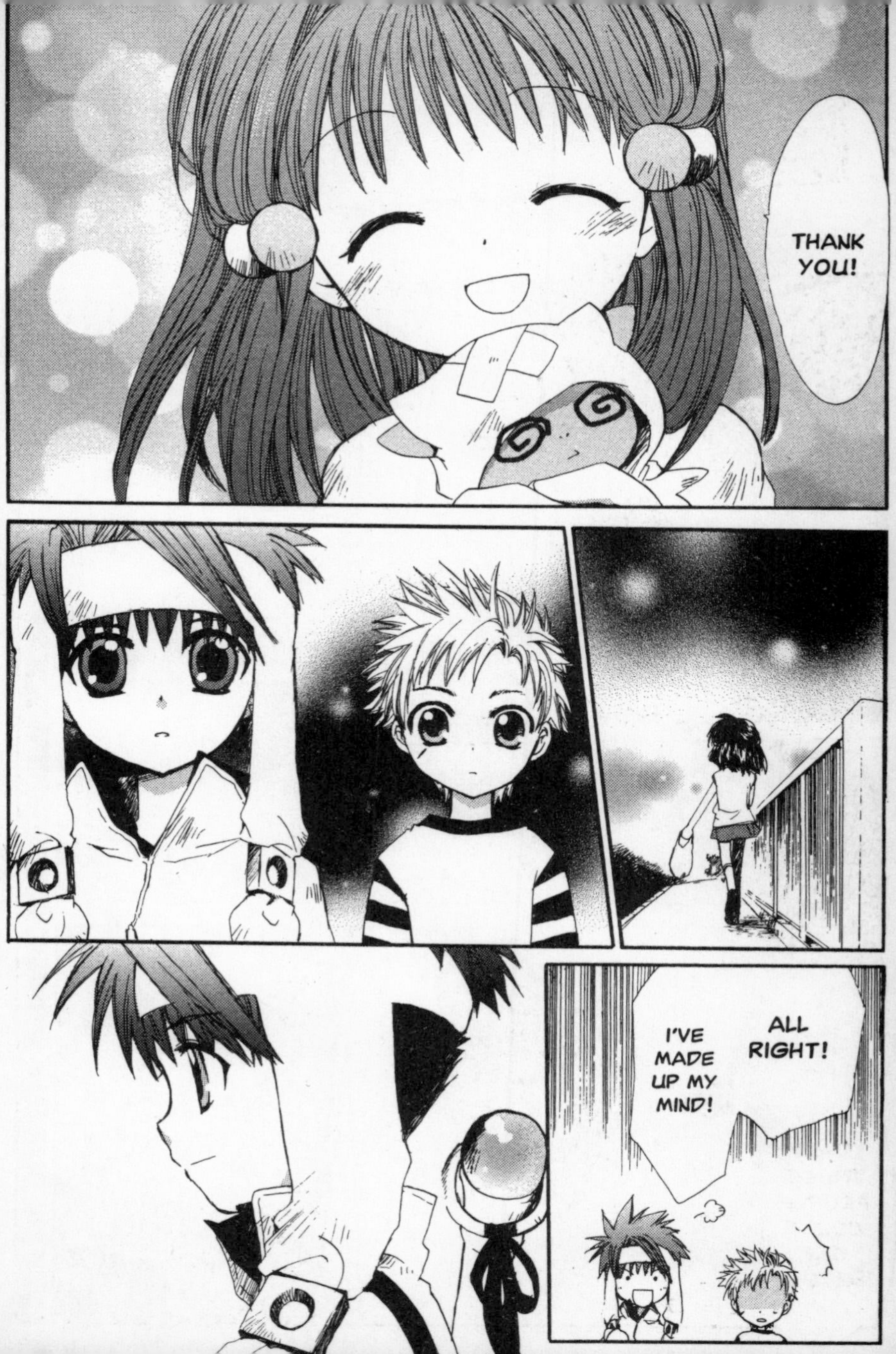
THANK YOU!
ALL RIGHT!
I'VE MADE UP MY MIND!

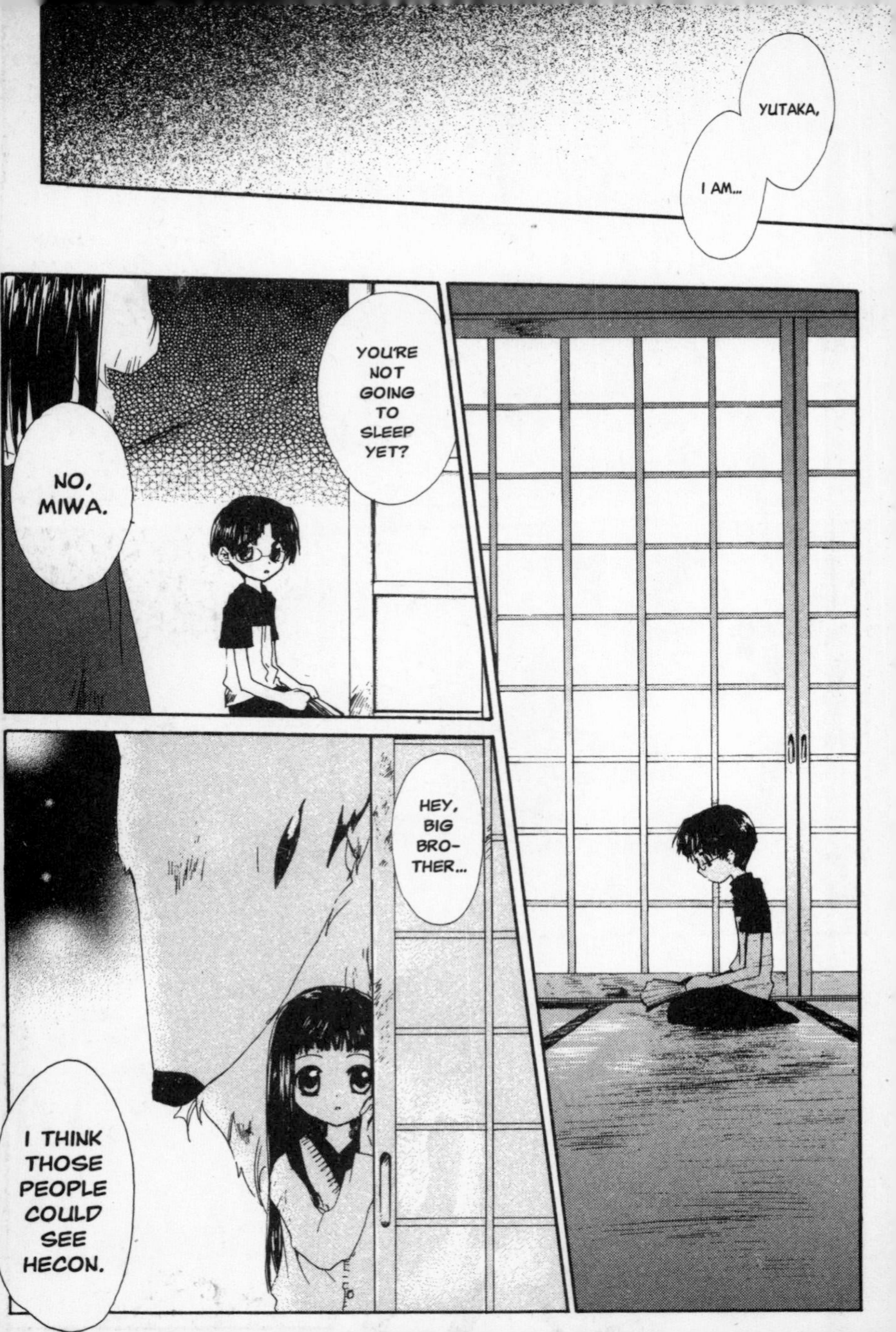
YUTAKA,
I AM...
YOU'RE NOT GOING TO SLEEP YET?
NO, MIWA.
HEY, BIG BRO-THER...
I THINK THOSE PEOPLE COULD SEE HECON.

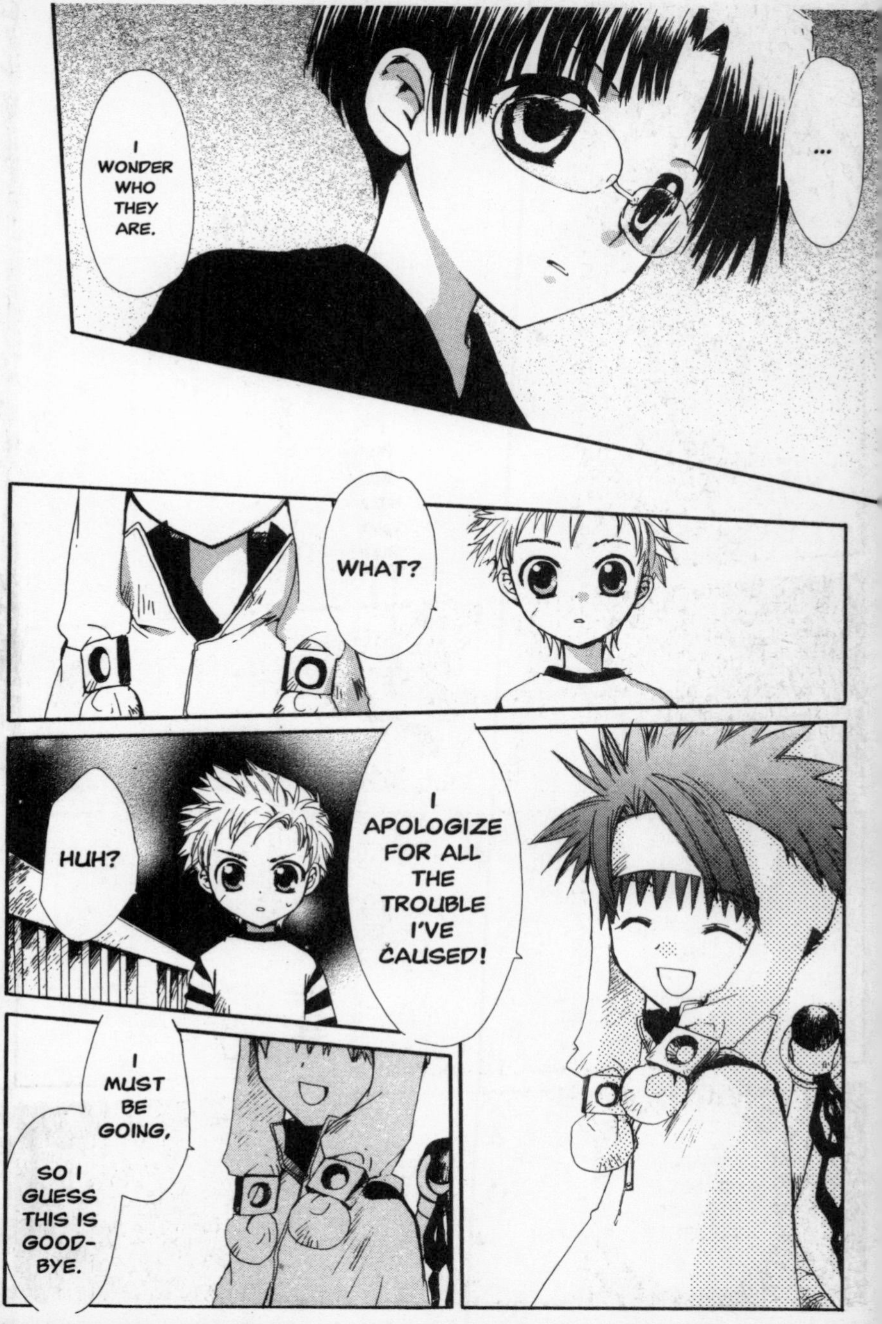
...
I WONDER WHO THEY ARE.
WHAT?
I APOLOGIZE FOR ALL THE TROUBLE I'VE CAUSED!
HUH?
I MUST BE GOING,
SO I GUESS THIS IS GOOD-BYE.

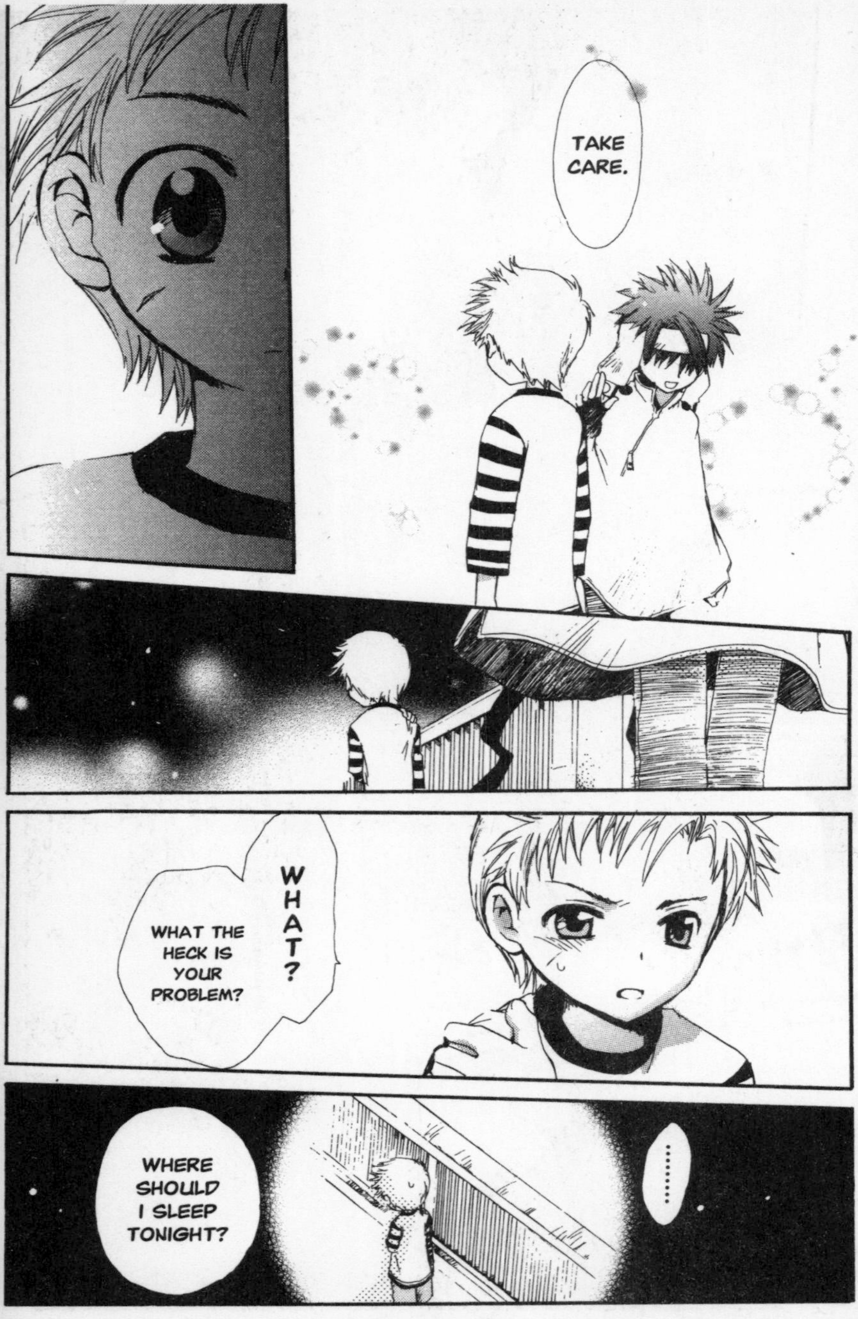
TAKE CARE.
WHAT?
WHAT THE HECK IS YOUR PROBLEM?
......
WHERE SHOULD I SLEEP TONIGHT?

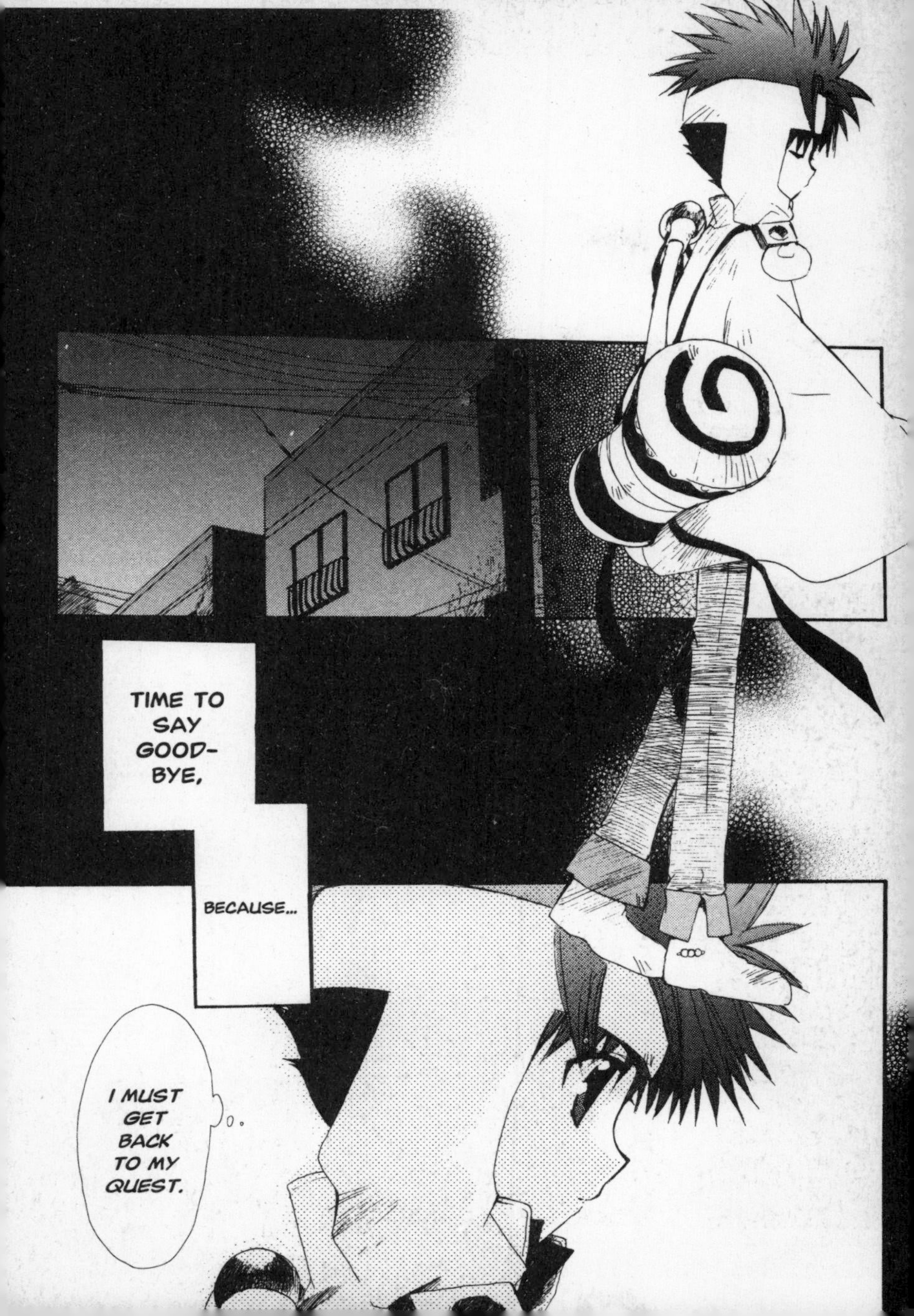

TIME TO SAY GOOD-BYE,
BECAUSE...
I MUST GET BACK TO MY QUEST.

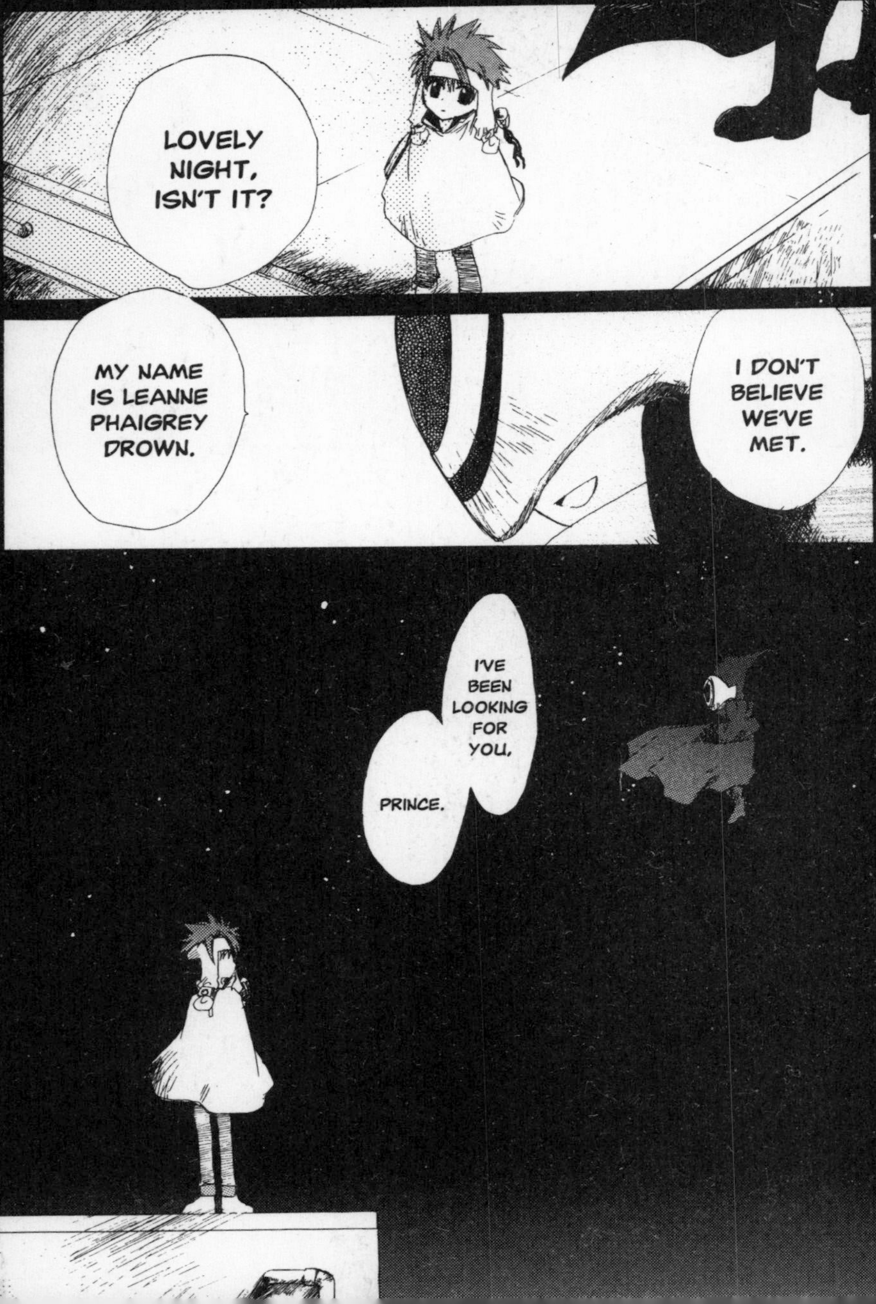
LOVELY NIGHT, ISN'T IT?
I DON'T BELIEVE WE'VE MET.
MY NAME IS LEANNE PHAIGREY DROWN.
I'VE BEEN LOOKING FOR YOU,
PRINCE.

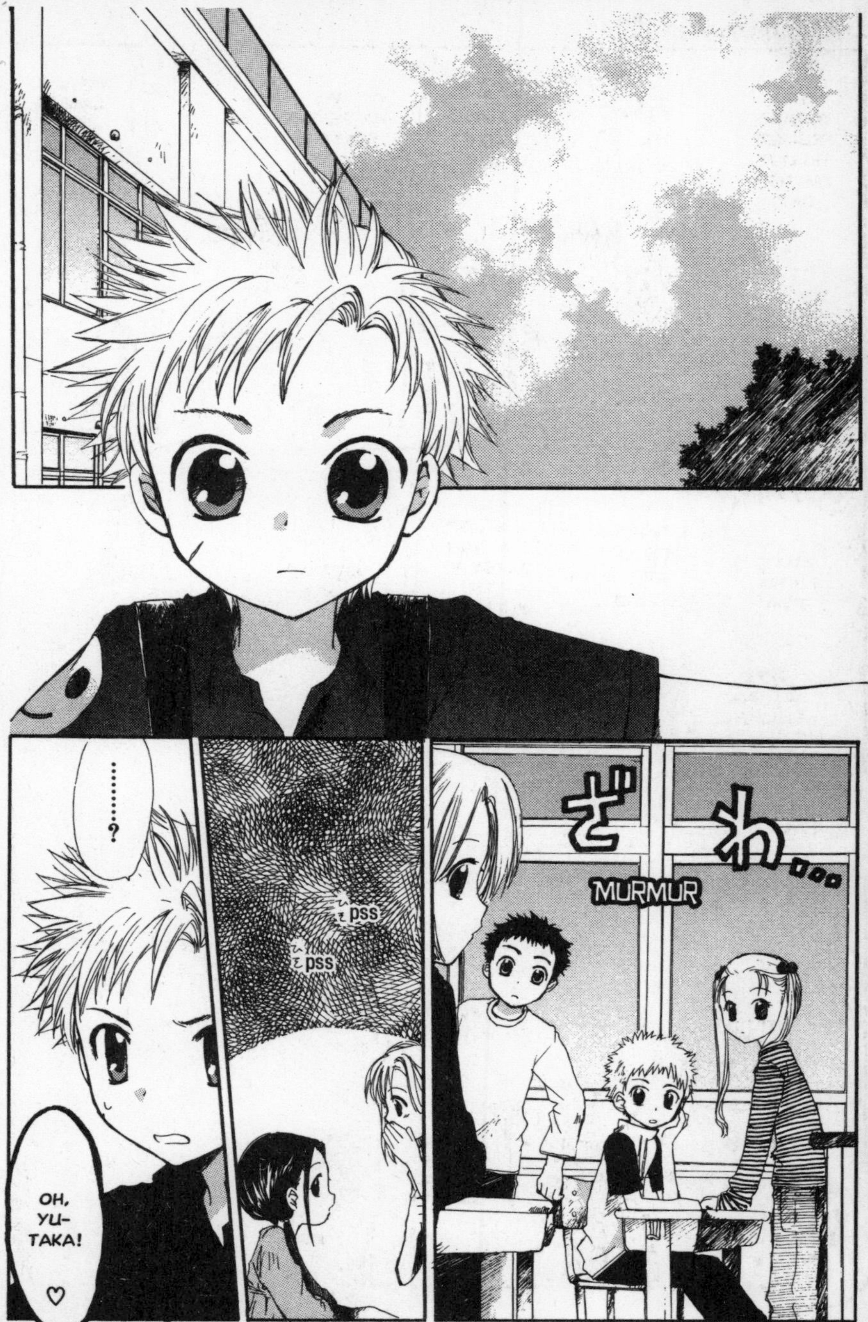

ざわ...
MURMUR
ひそ PSS
ひそ PSS
......?
OH, YU-TAKA! ♡

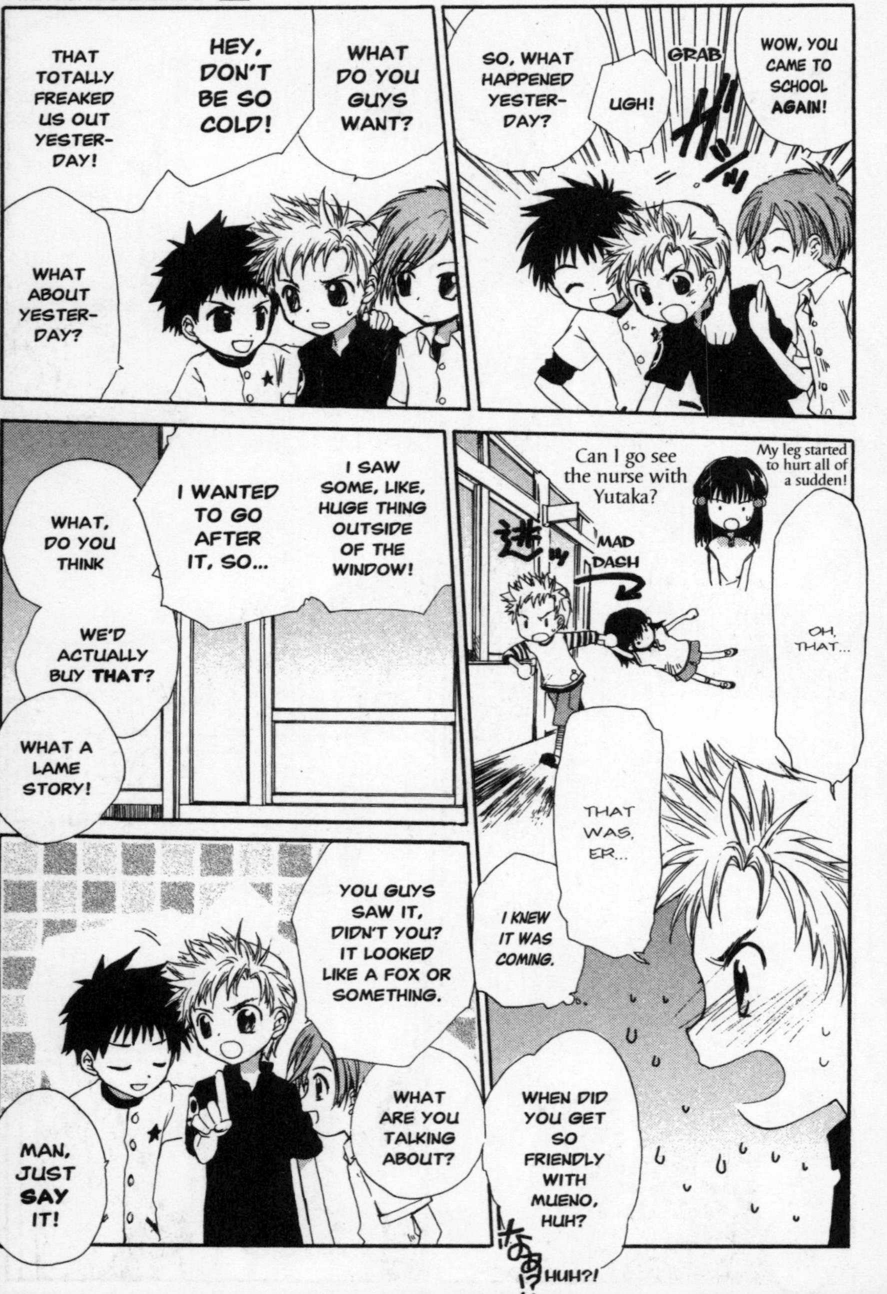
WOW, YOU CAME TO SCHOOL AGAIN!
GRAB
UGH!
SO, WHAT HAPPENED YESTER-DAY?
WHAT DO YOU GUYS WANT?
HEY, DON'T BE SO COLD!
THAT TOTALLY FREAKED US OUT YESTER-DAY!
WHAT ABOUT YESTER-DAY?
My leg started to hurt all of a sudden!
Can I go see the nurse with Yutaka?
MAD DASH
OH, THAT...
THAT WAS, ER...
I KNEW IT WAS COMING.
I SAW SOME, LIKE, HUGE THING OUTSIDE OF THE WINDOW!
I WANTED TO GO AFTER IT, SO...
WHAT, DO YOU THINK
WE'D ACTUALLY BUY THAT?
WHAT A LAME STORY!
YOU GUYS SAW IT, DIDN'T YOU? IT LOOKED LIKE A FOX OR SOMETHING.
WHAT ARE YOU TALKING ABOUT?
MAN, JUST SAY IT!
WHEN DID YOU GET SO FRIENDLY WITH MUENO, HUH?
HUH?!

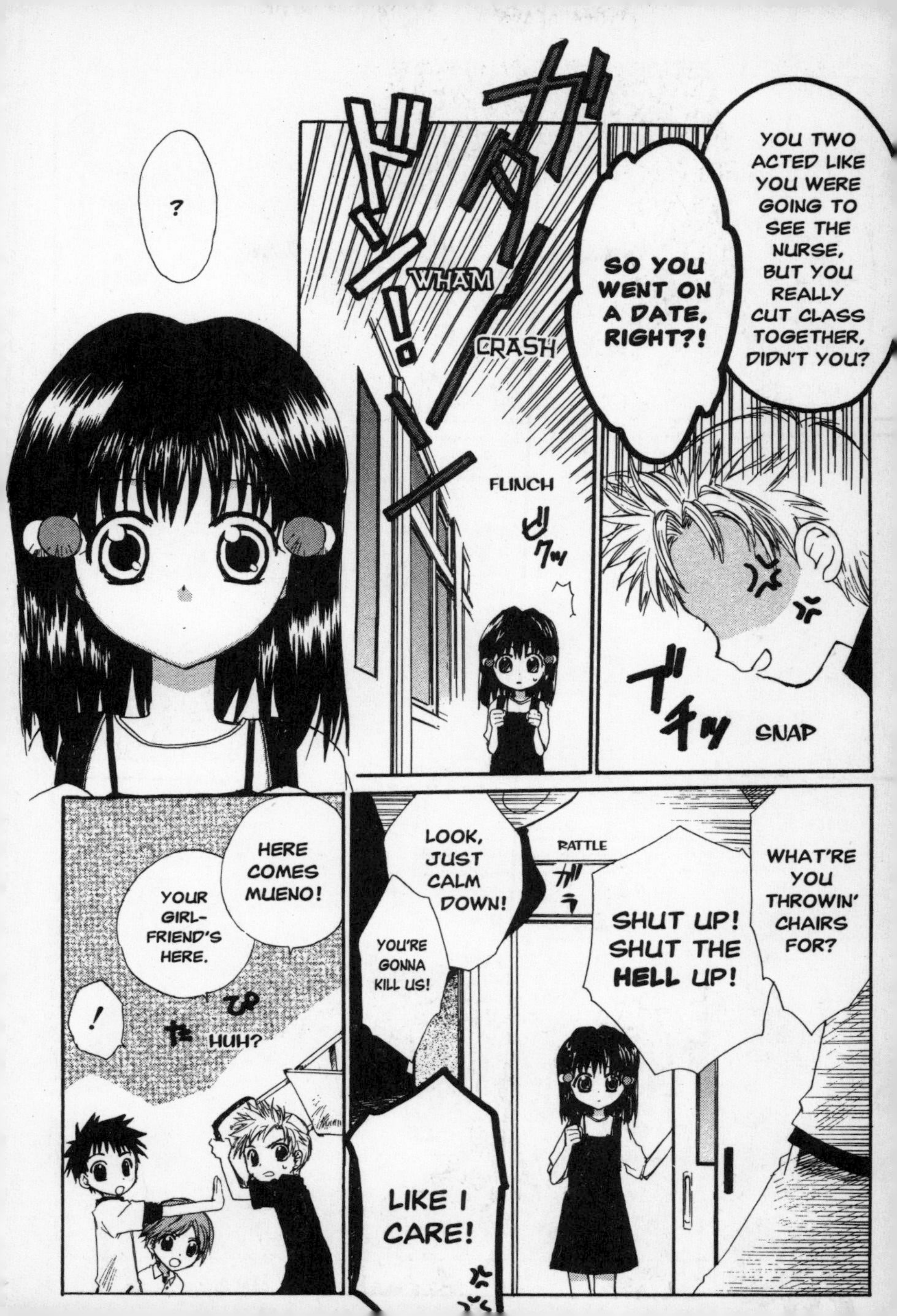
YOU TWO ACTED LIKE YOU WERE GOING TO SEE THE NURSE, BUT YOU REALLY CUT CLASS TOGETHER, DIDN'T YOU?
SO YOU WENT ON A DATE, RIGHT?!
SNAP
WHAM
CRASH
FLINCH
?
WHAT'RE YOU THROWIN' CHAIRS FOR?
SHUT UP! SHUT THE HELL UP!
RATTLE
LOOK, JUST CALM DOWN!
YOU'RE GONNA KILL US!
LIKE I CARE!
HERE COMES MUENO!
YOUR GIRL-FRIEND'S HERE.
!
HUH?

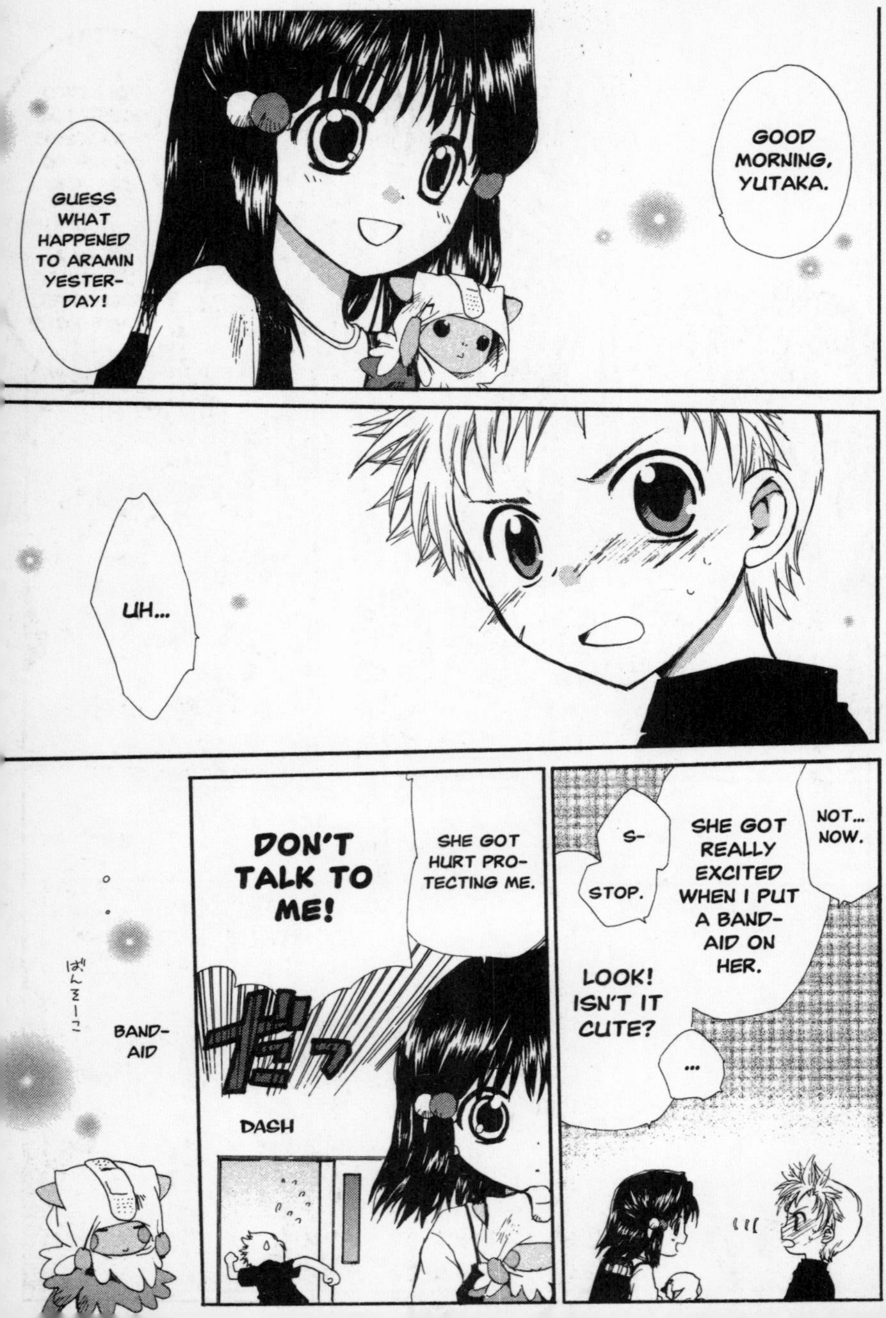
GOOD MORNING, YUTAKA.
GUESS WHAT HAPPENED TO ARAMIN YESTER-DAY!
UH...
NOT... NOW.
SHE GOT REALLY EXCITED WHEN I PUT A BAND-AID ON HER.
S-STOP.
LOOK! ISN'T IT CUTE?
...
SHE GOT HURT PRO-TECTING ME.
DON'T TALK TO ME!
DASH
ばんそーこ
BAND-AID

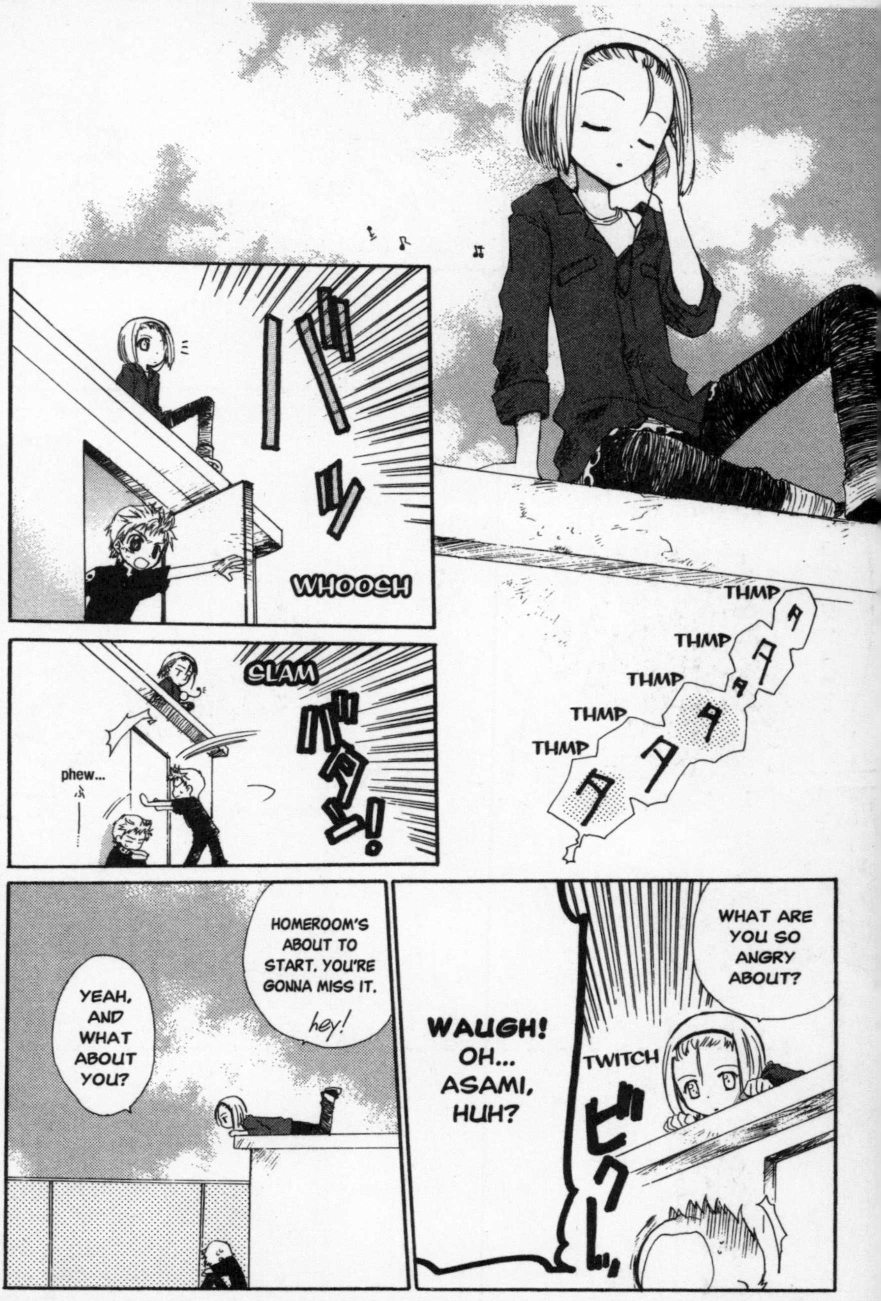
THMP
THMP
THMP
THMP
THMP
WHOOSH
SLAM
phew...
WHAT ARE YOU SO ANGRY ABOUT?
TWITCH
WAUGH! OH... ASAMI, HUH?
HOMEROOM'S ABOUT TO START. YOU'RE GONNA MISS IT.
hey!
YEAH, AND WHAT ABOUT YOU?

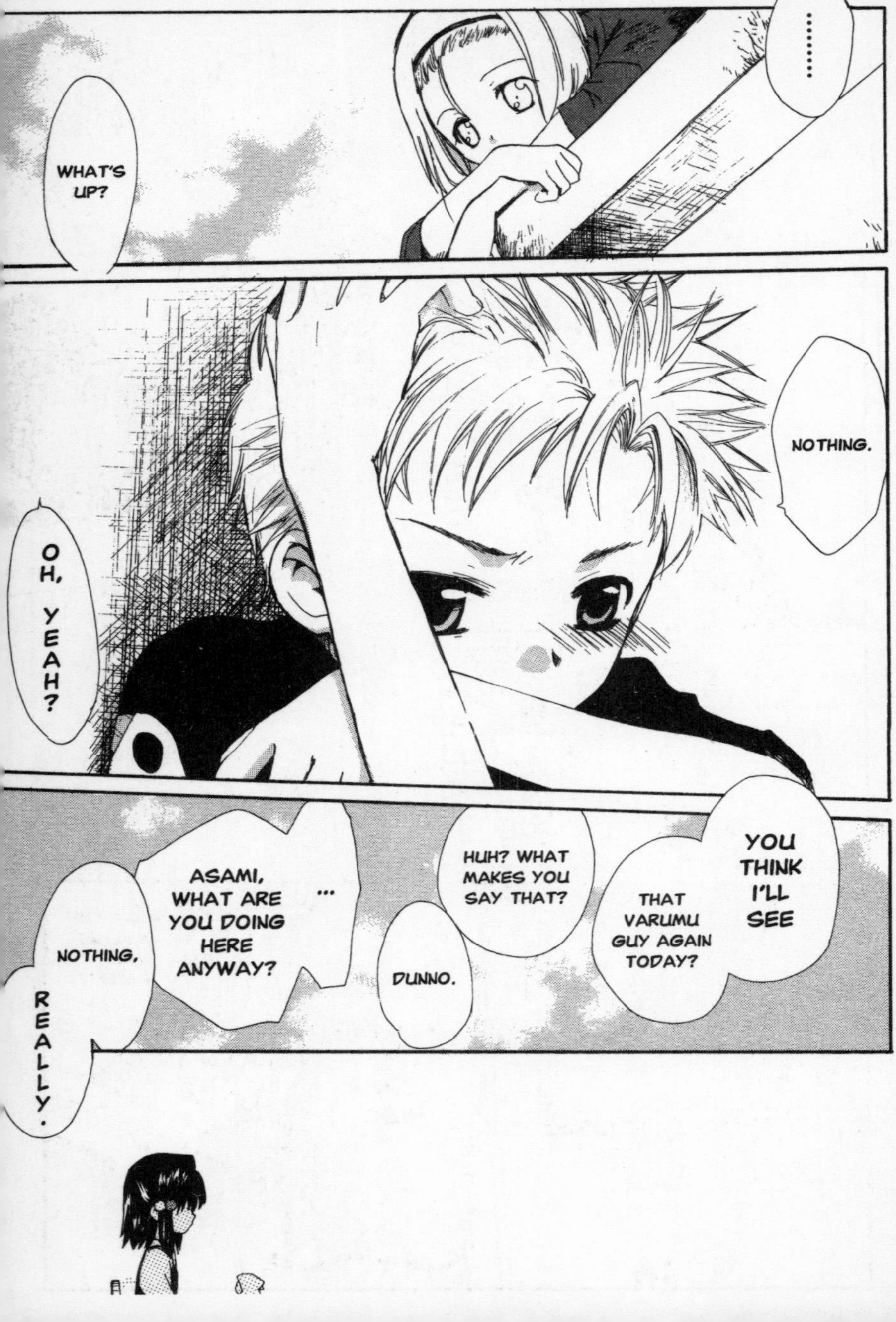
......
WHAT'S UP?
NOTHING.
OH, YEAH?
YOU THINK I'LL SEE THAT VARUMU GUY AGAIN TODAY?
HUH? WHAT MAKES YOU SAY THAT?
DUNNO.
...
ASAMI, WHAT ARE YOU DOING HERE ANYWAY?
NOTHING, REALLY.

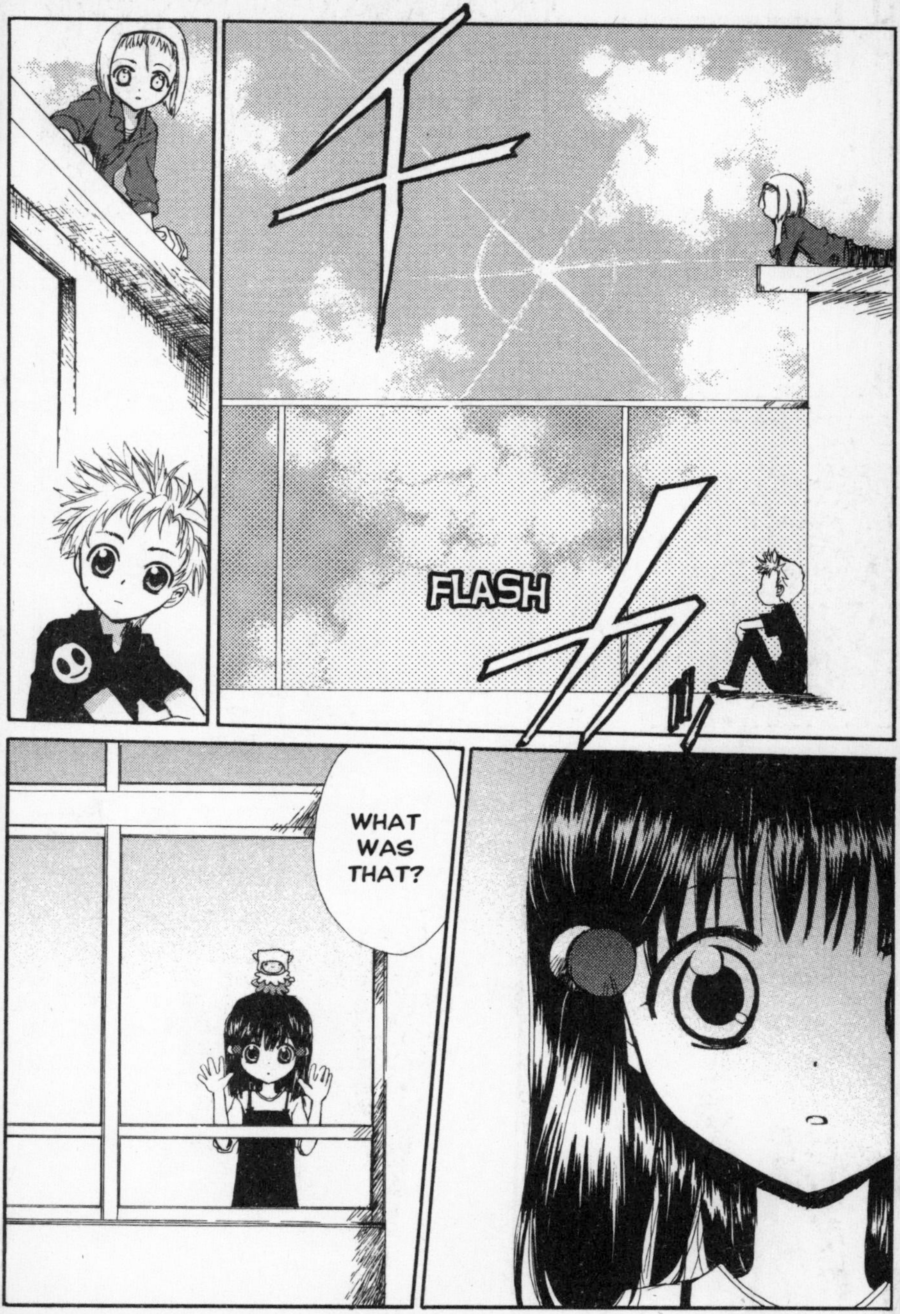
FLASH
WHAT WAS THAT?

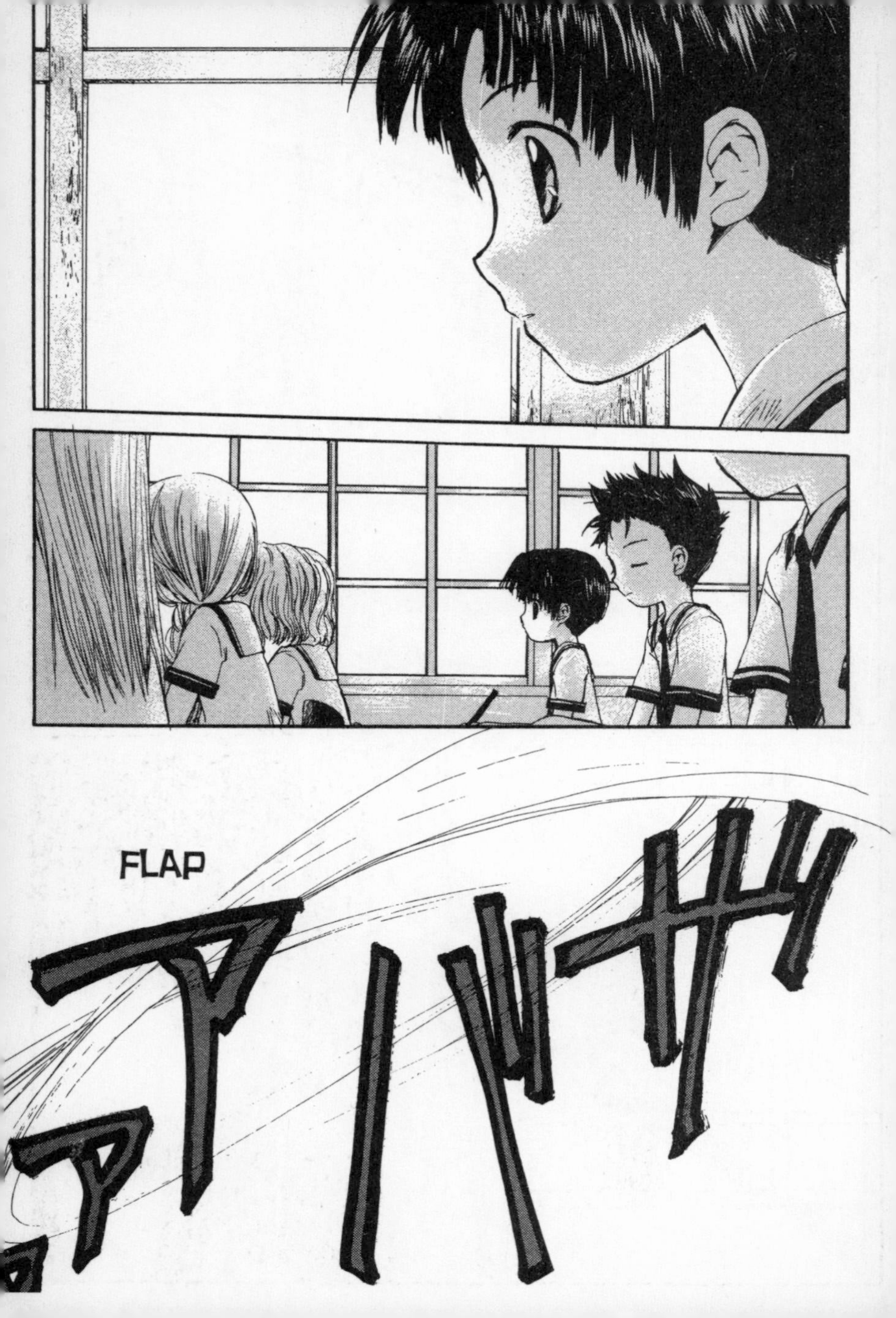
FLAP
ファ
アバサッ

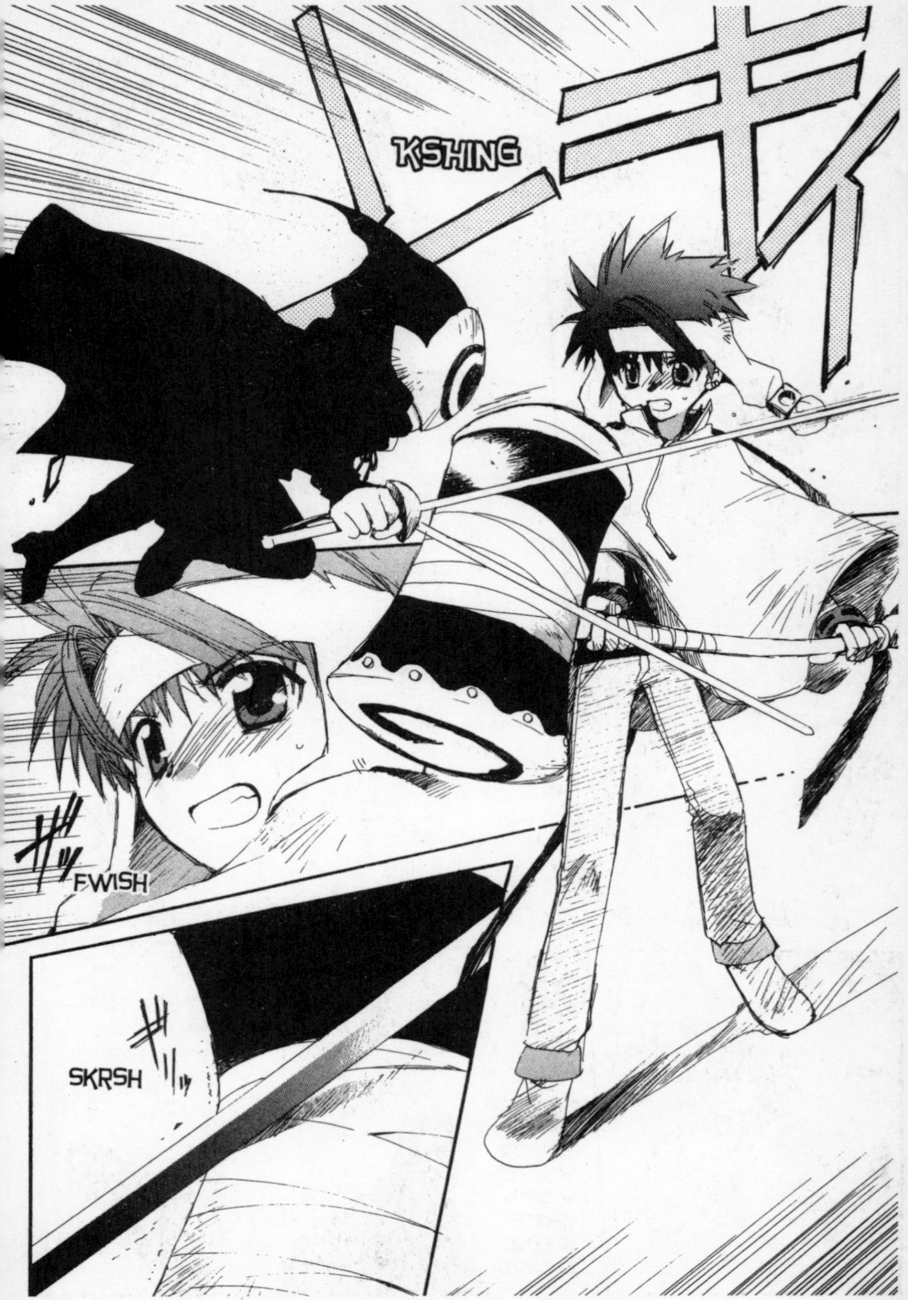
KSHING
FWISH
SKRSH

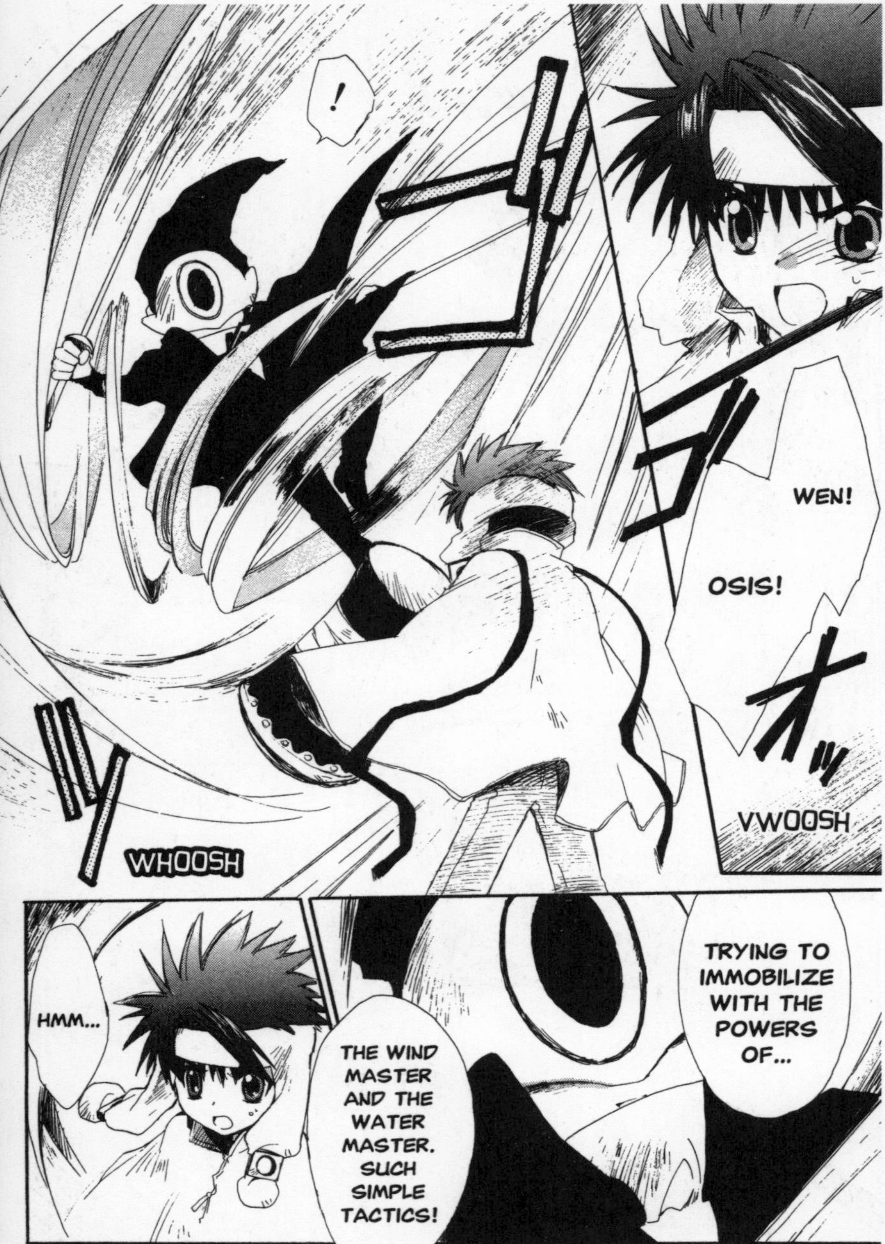
!
WEN!
OSIS!
VWOOSH
WHOOSH
TRYING TO IMMOBILIZE WITH THE POWERS OF...
THE WIND MASTER AND THE WATER MASTER. SUCH SIMPLE TACTICS!
HMM...

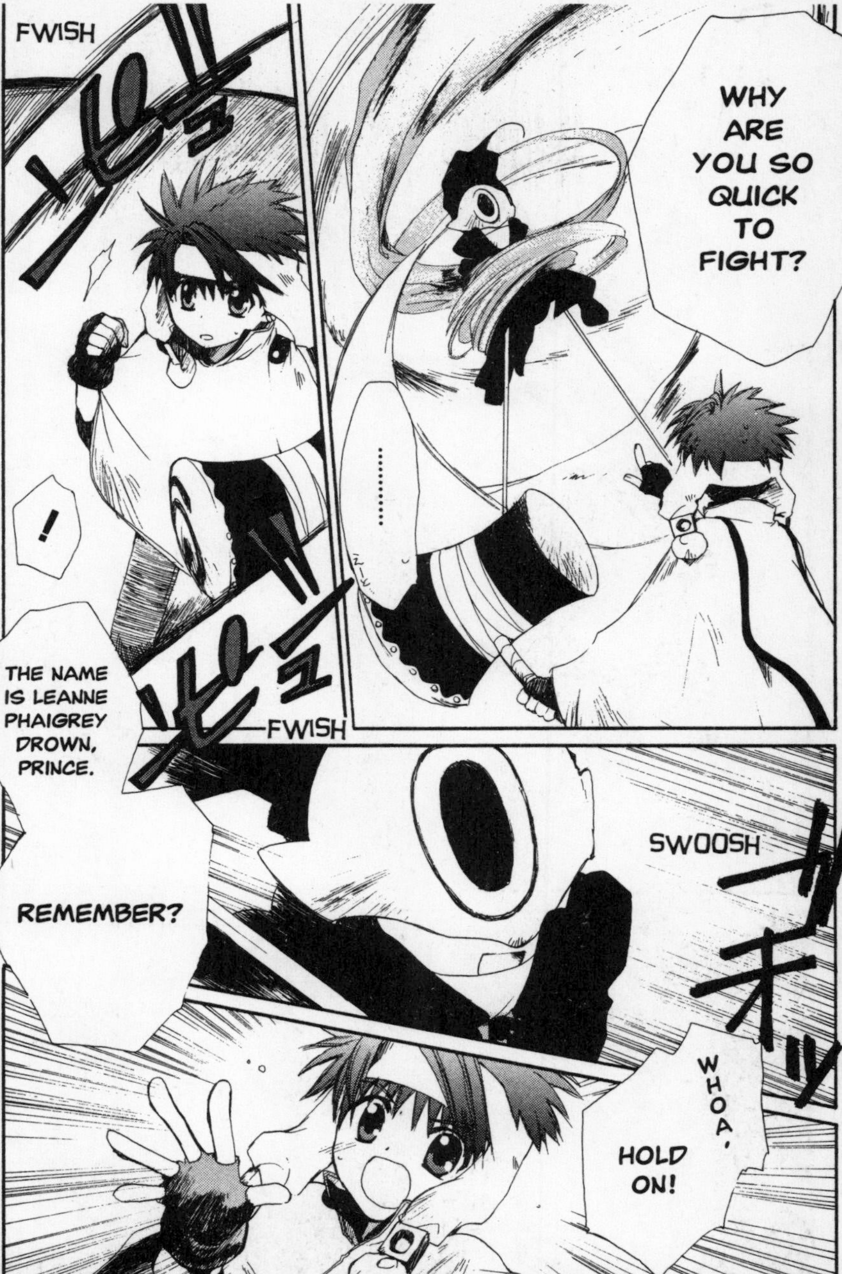
WHY ARE YOU SO QUICK TO FIGHT?
......
FWISH
!
FWISH
THE NAME IS LEANNE PHAIGREY DROWN, PRINCE.
SWOOSH
REMEMBER?
WHOA, HOLD ON!

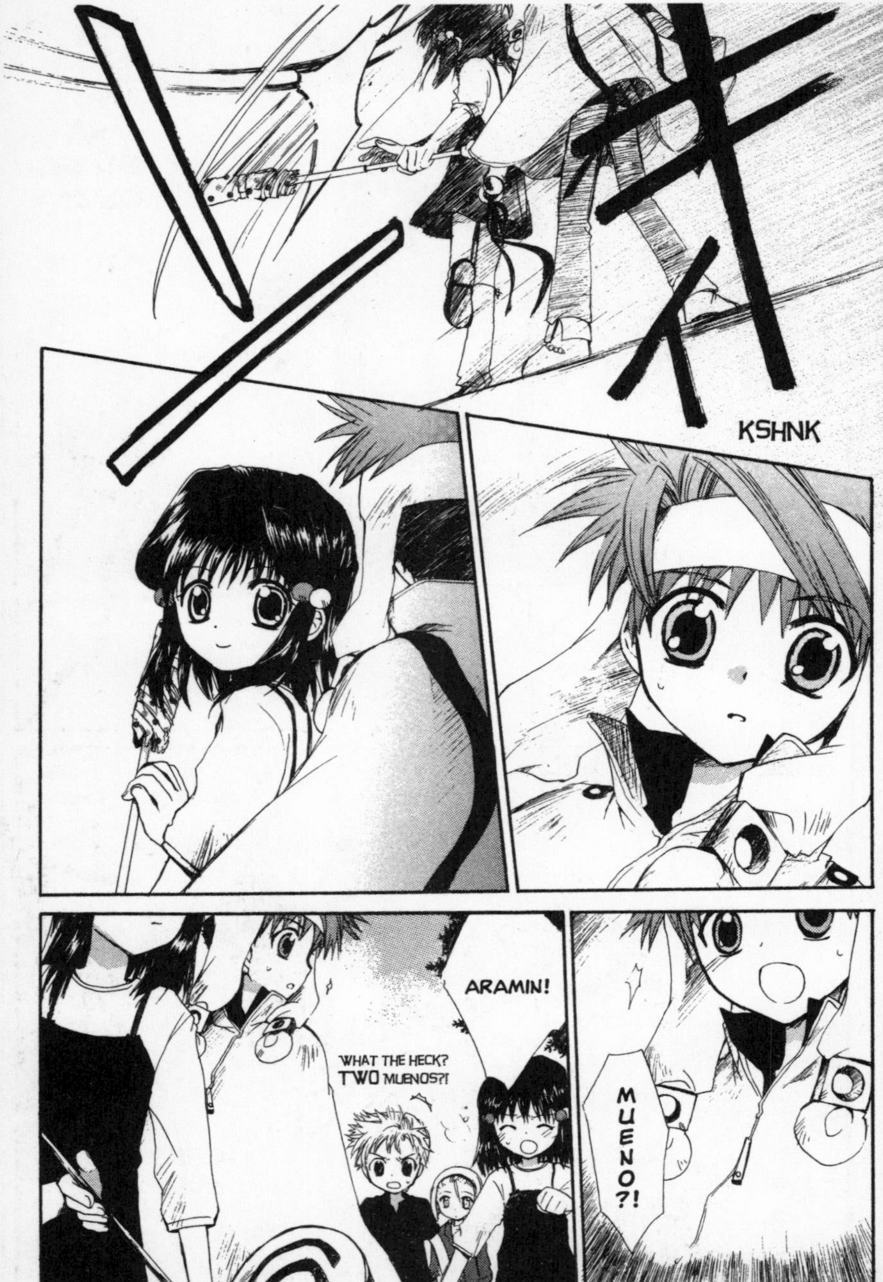
KSHNK
MUENO?!
ARAMIN!
WHAT THE HECK? TWO MUENOS?!

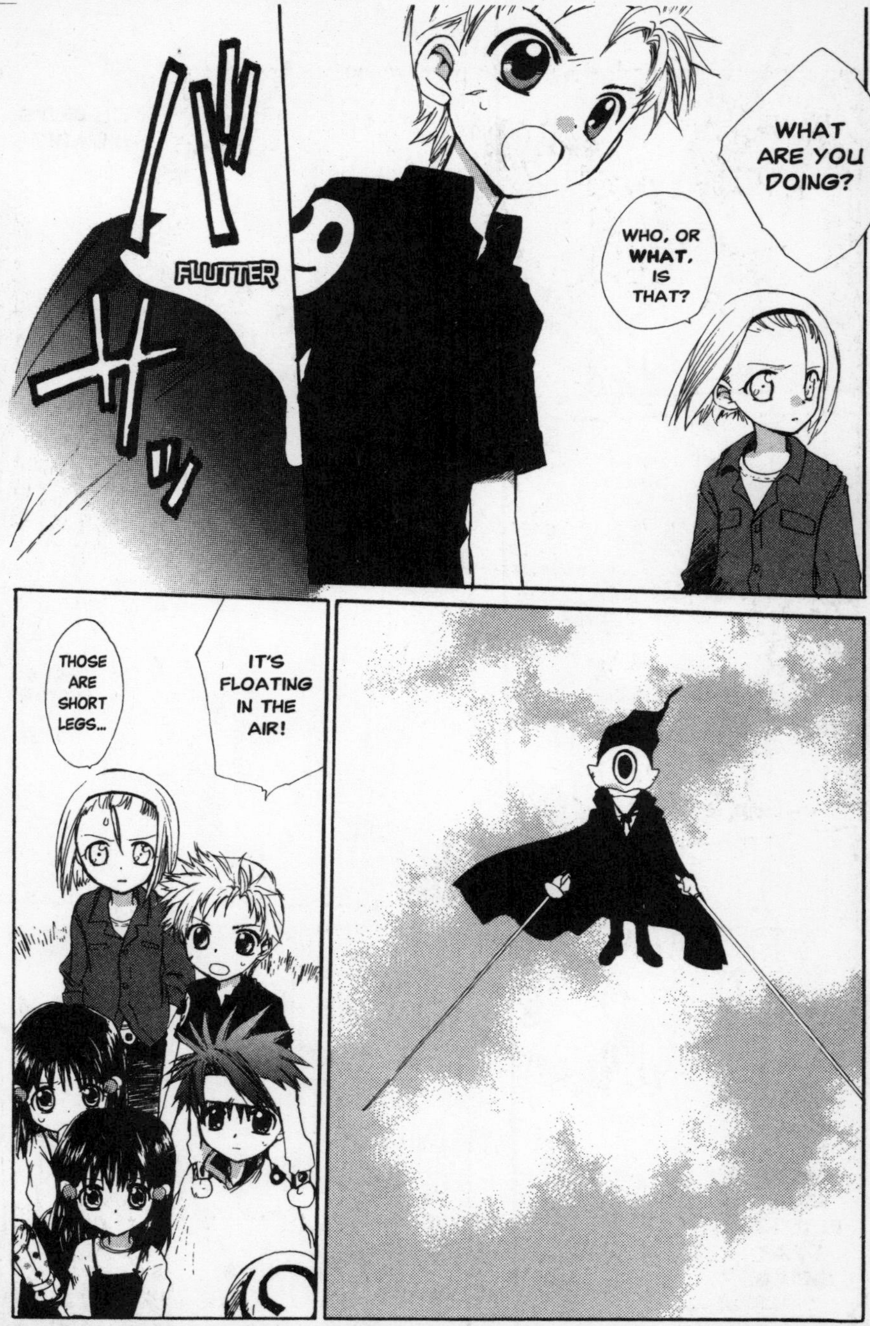
WHAT ARE YOU DOING?
WHO, OR WHAT, IS THAT?
FLUTTER
IT'S FLOATING IN THE AIR!
THOSE ARE SHORT LEGS...

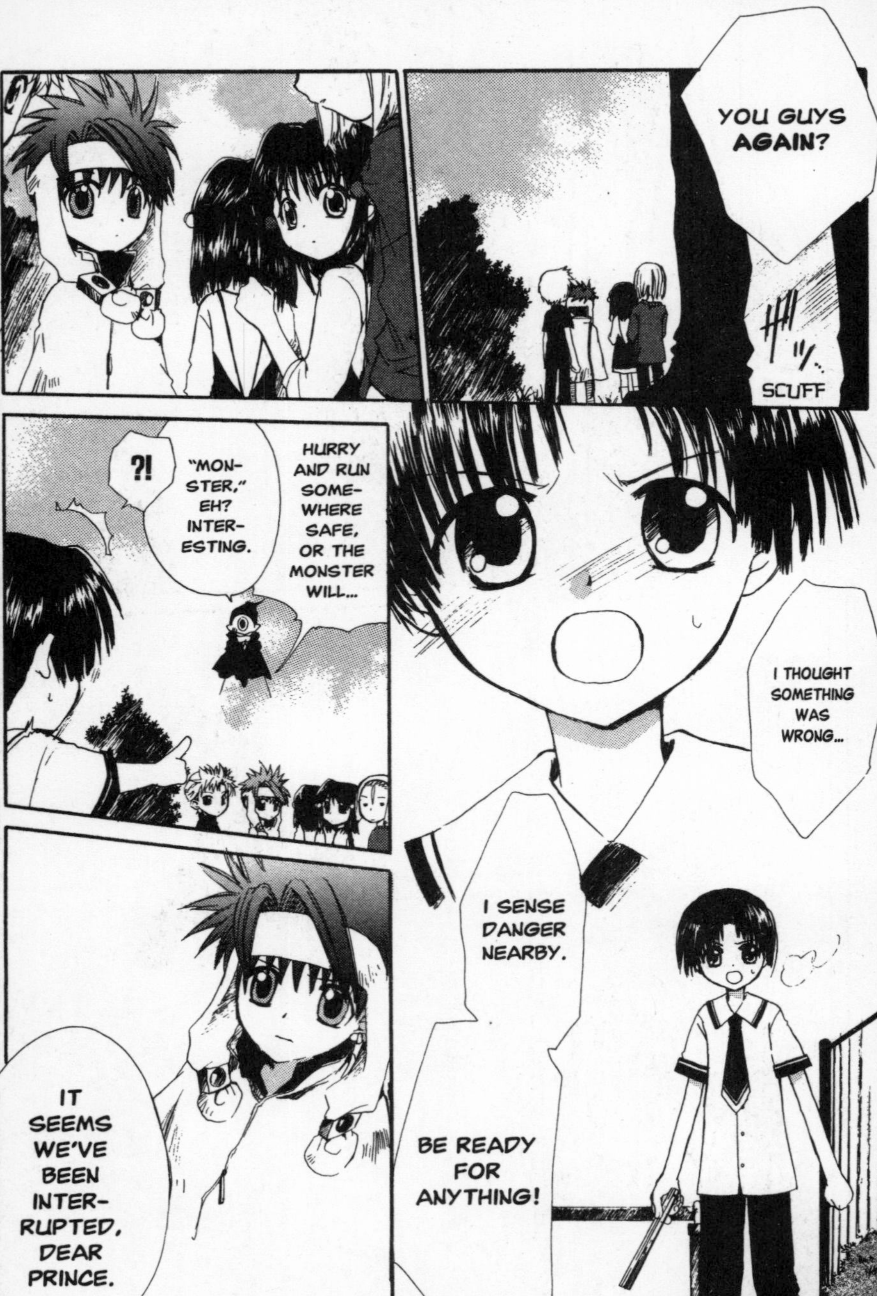
YOU GUYS AGAIN?
SCUFF
I THOUGHT SOMETHING WAS WRONG...
HURRY AND RUN SOME-WHERE SAFE, OR THE MONSTER WILL...
"MON-STER," EH? INTER-ESTING.
?!
I SENSE DANGER NEARBY.
BE READY FOR ANYTHING!
IT SEEMS WE'VE BEEN INTER-RUPTED, DEAR PRINCE.

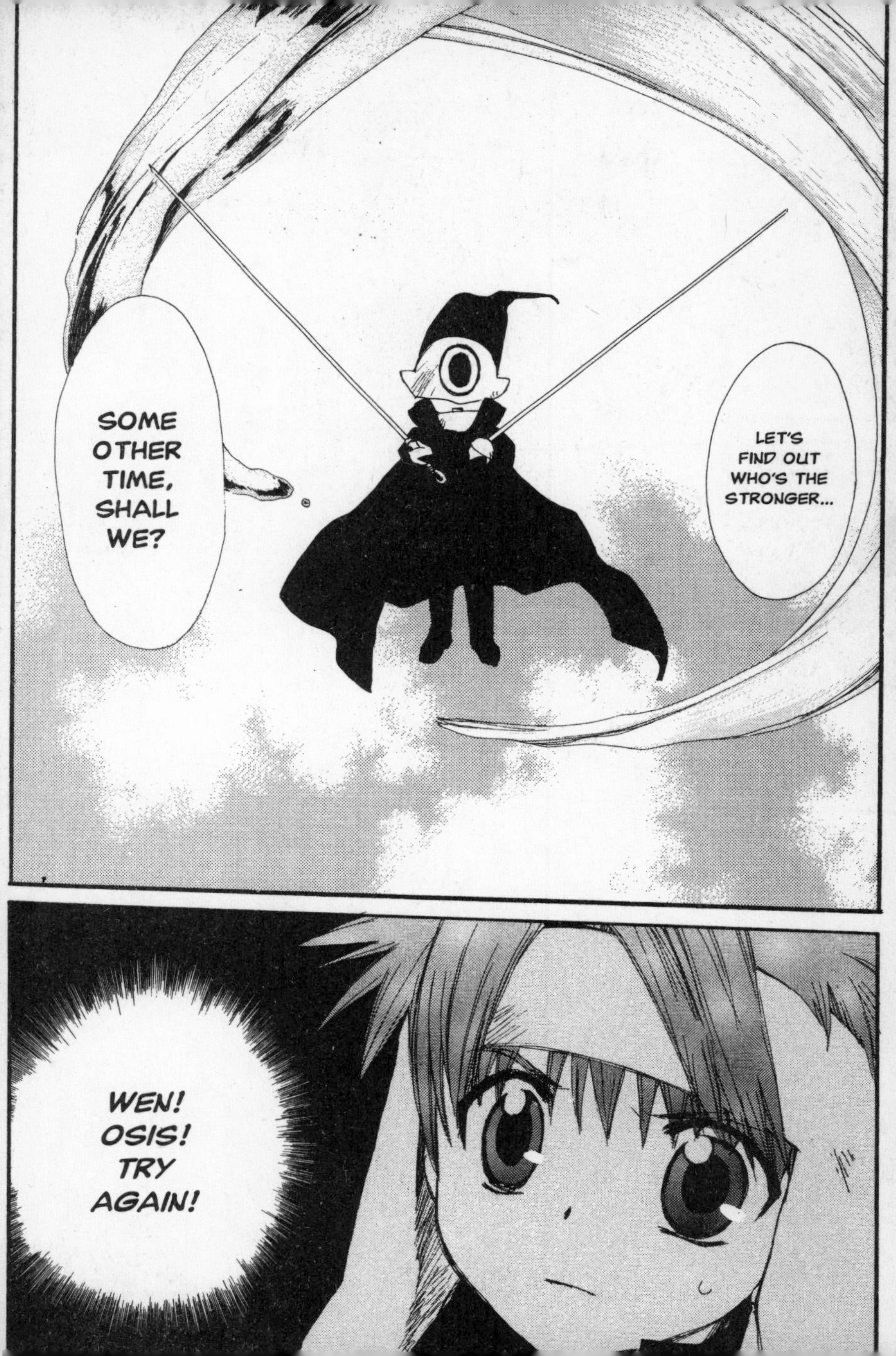
LET'S FIND OUT WHO'S THE STRONGER...
SOME OTHER TIME, SHALL WE?
WEN! OSIS! TRY AGAIN!

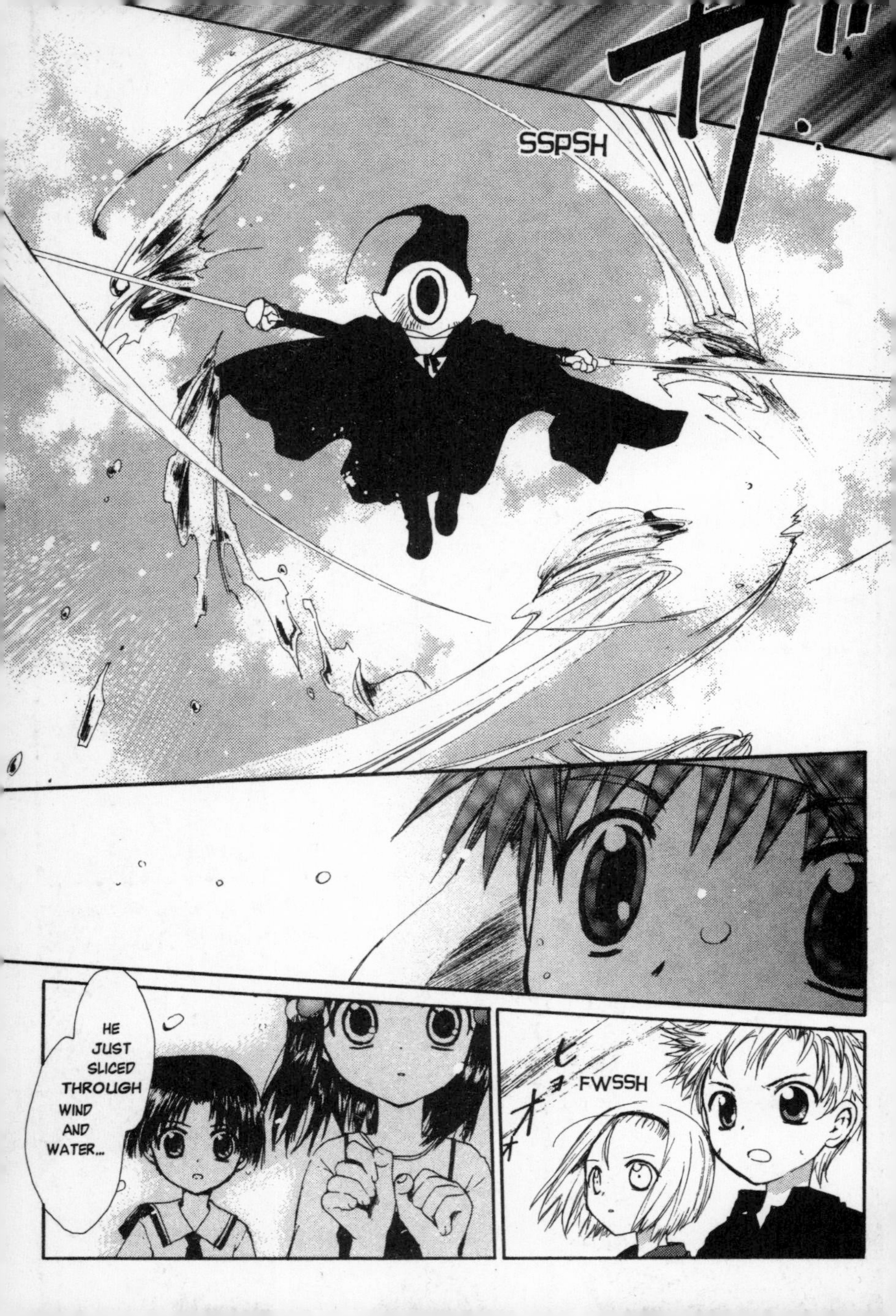
SSPSH
FWSSH
HE JUST SLICED THROUGH WIND AND WATER...

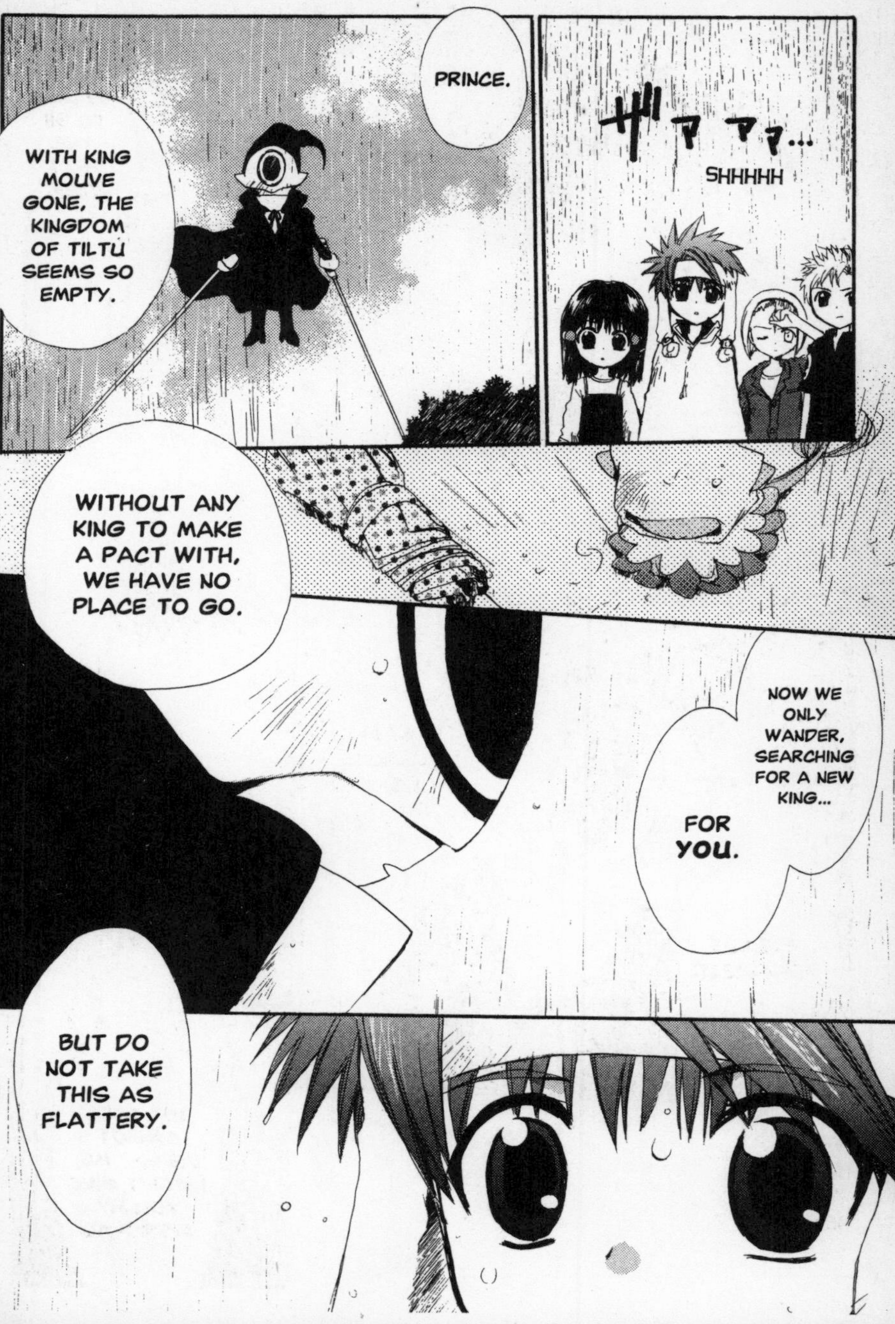
ザァァァ...
SHHHHH
PRINCE.
WITH KING MOUVE GONE, THE KINGDOM OF TILTU SEEMS SO EMPTY.
WITHOUT ANY KING TO MAKE A PACT WITH, WE HAVE NO PLACE TO GO.
NOW WE ONLY WANDER, SEARCHING FOR A NEW KING...
FOR YOU.
BUT DO NOT TAKE THIS AS FLATTERY.

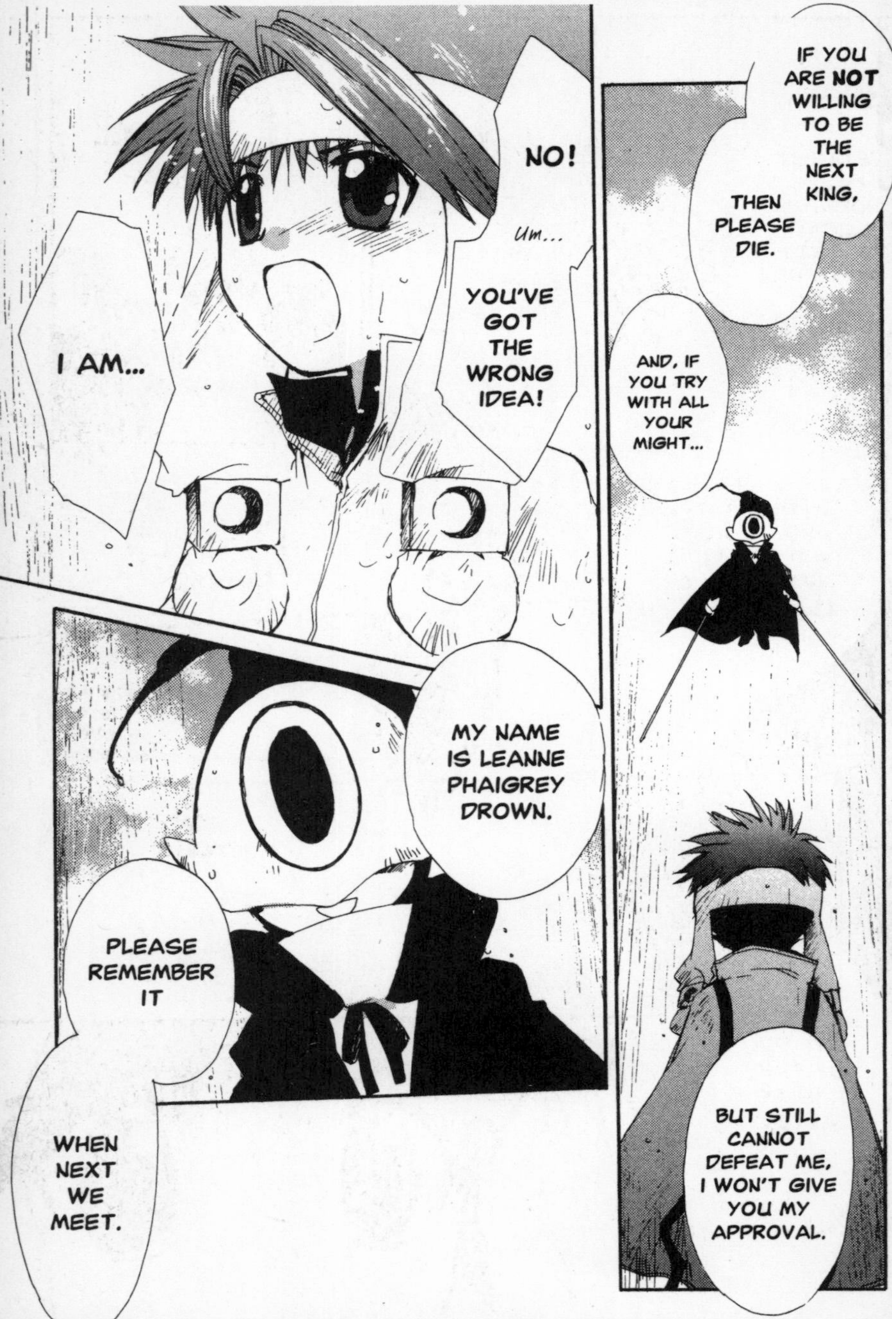
IF YOU ARE **NOT** WILLING TO BE THE NEXT KING,
THEN PLEASE DIE.
AND, IF YOU TRY WITH ALL YOUR MIGHT...
BUT STILL CANNOT DEFEAT ME, I WON'T GIVE YOU MY APPROVAL.
NO!
Um...
YOU'VE GOT THE WRONG IDEA!
I AM...
MY NAME IS LEANNE PHAIGREY DROWN.
PLEASE REMEMBER IT
WHEN NEXT WE MEET.

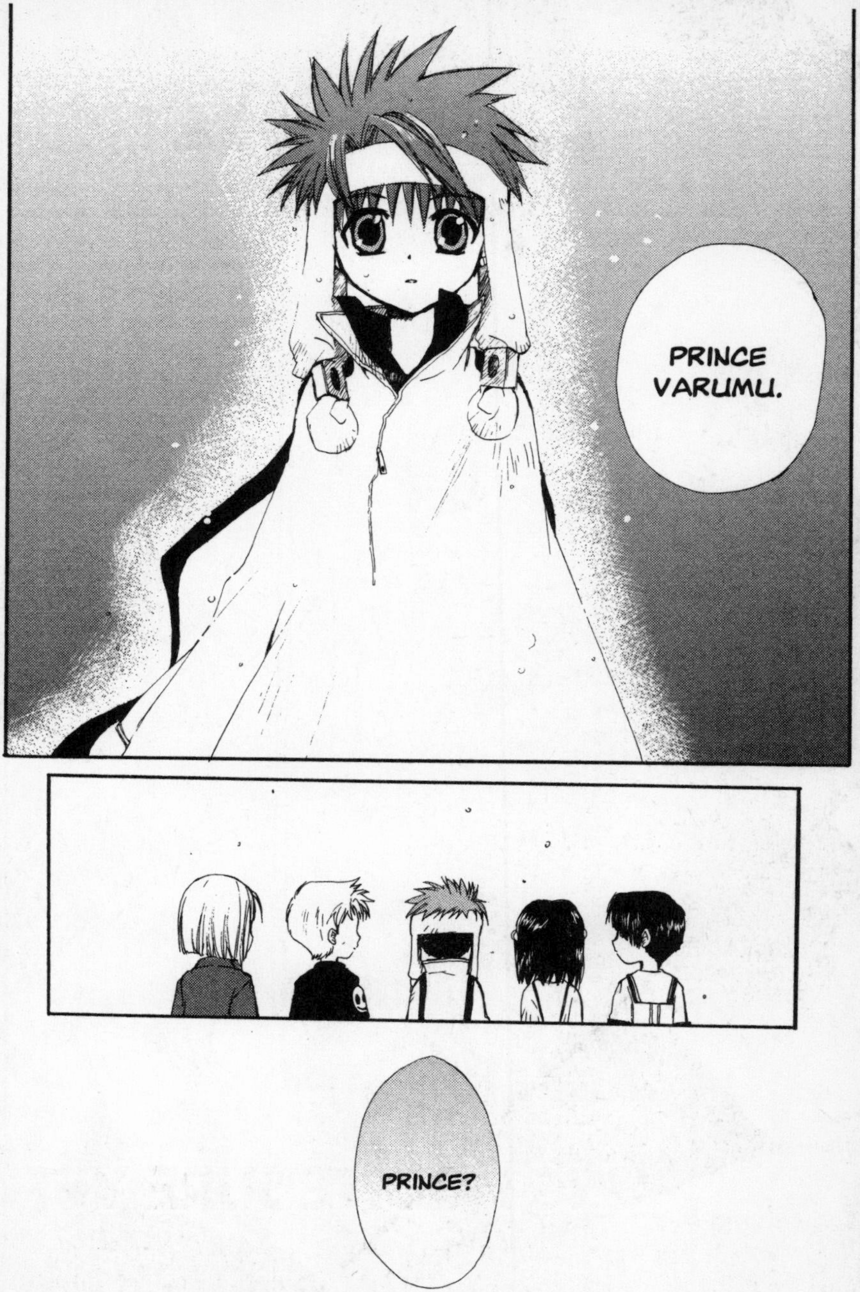
PRINCE VARUMU.
PRINCE?

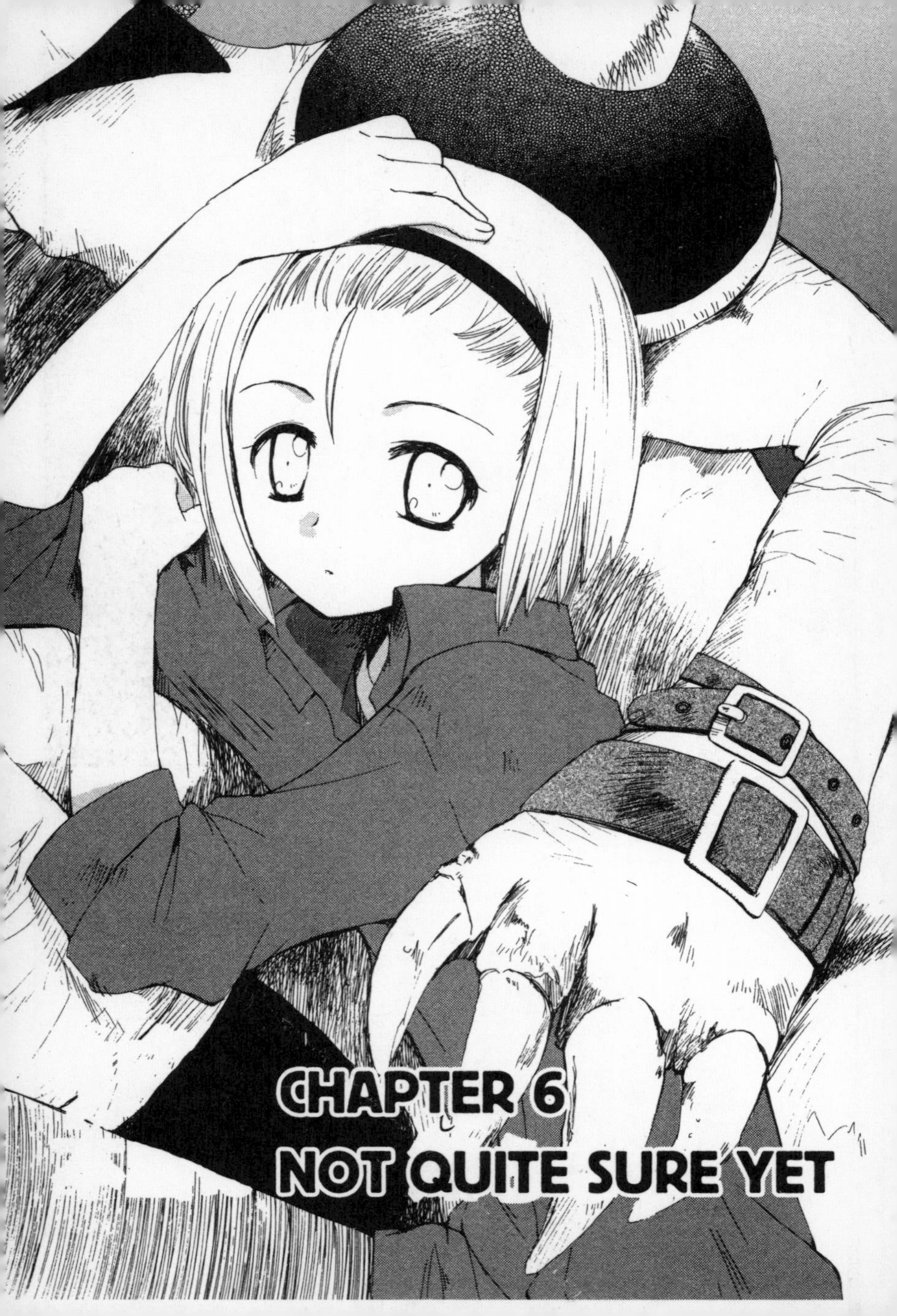
CHAPTER 6
NOT QUITE SURE YET

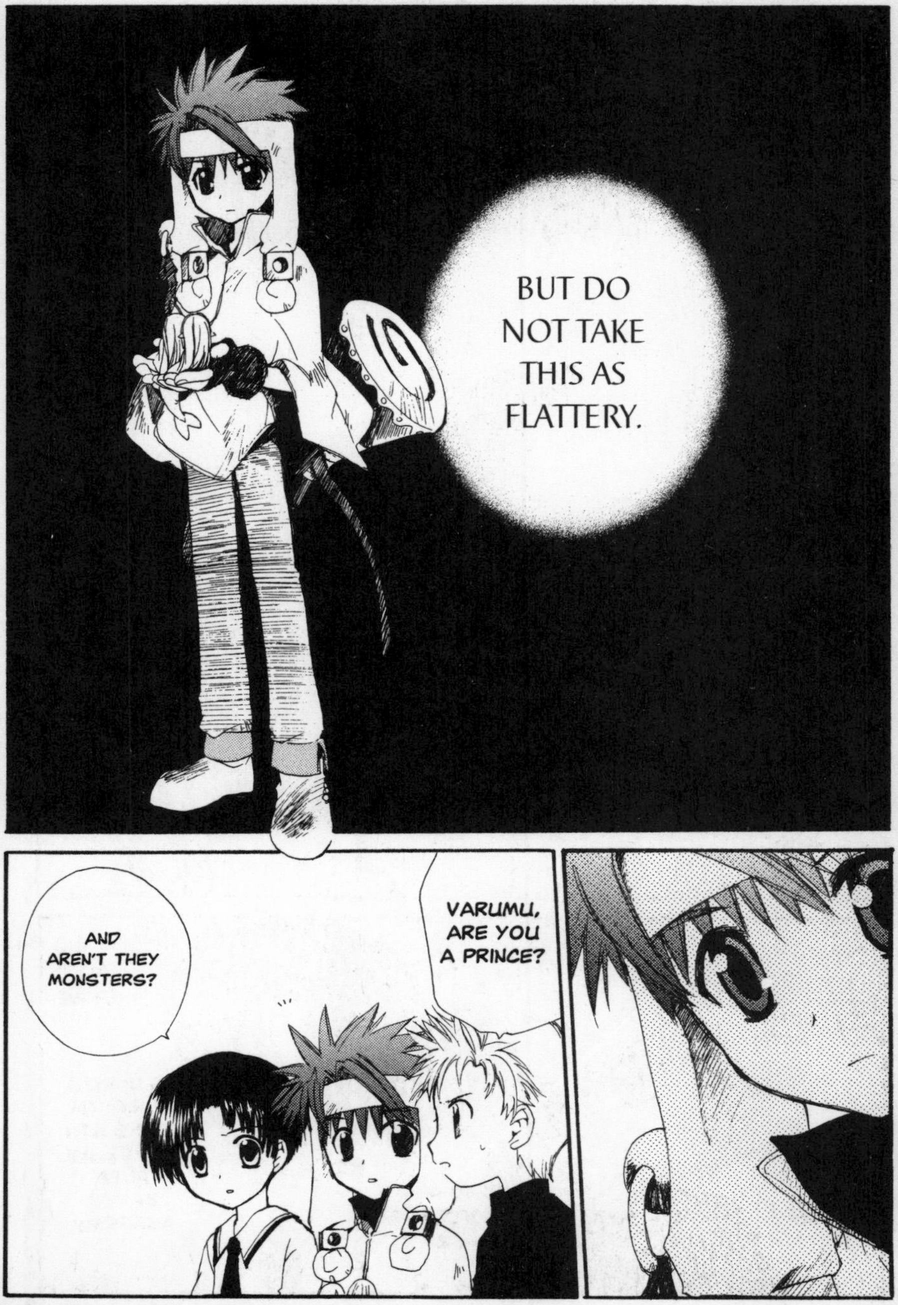
BUT DO NOT TAKE THIS AS FLATTERY.
VARUMU, ARE YOU A PRINCE?
AND AREN'T THEY MONSTERS?

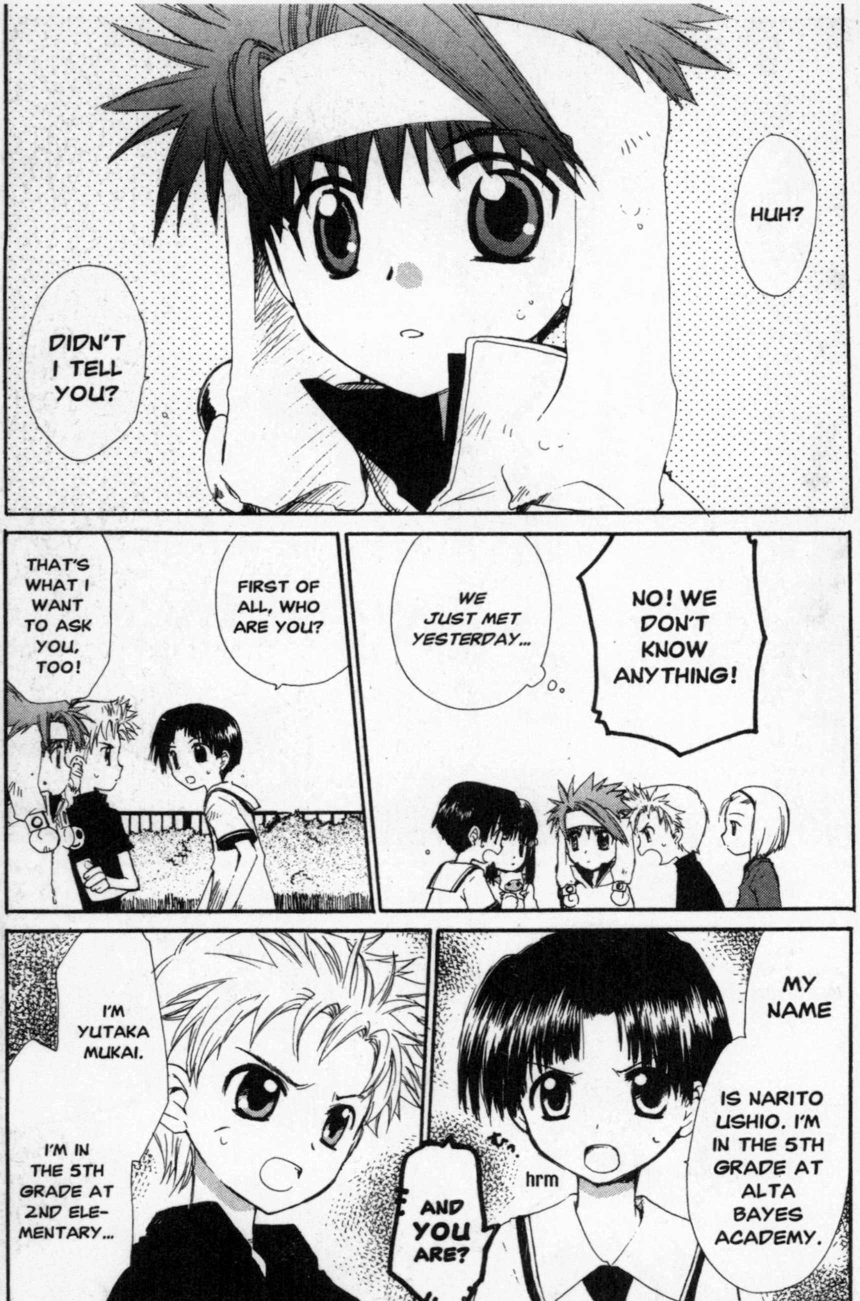
HUH?
DIDN'T I TELL YOU?
NO! WE DON'T KNOW ANYTHING!
WE JUST MET YESTERDAY...
FIRST OF ALL, WHO ARE YOU?
THAT'S WHAT I WANT TO ASK YOU, TOO!
MY NAME
IS NARITO USHIO. I'M IN THE 5TH GRADE AT ALTA BAYES ACADEMY.
hrm
AND YOU ARE?
I'M YUTAKA MUKAI.
I'M IN THE 5TH GRADE AT 2ND ELE-MENTARY...

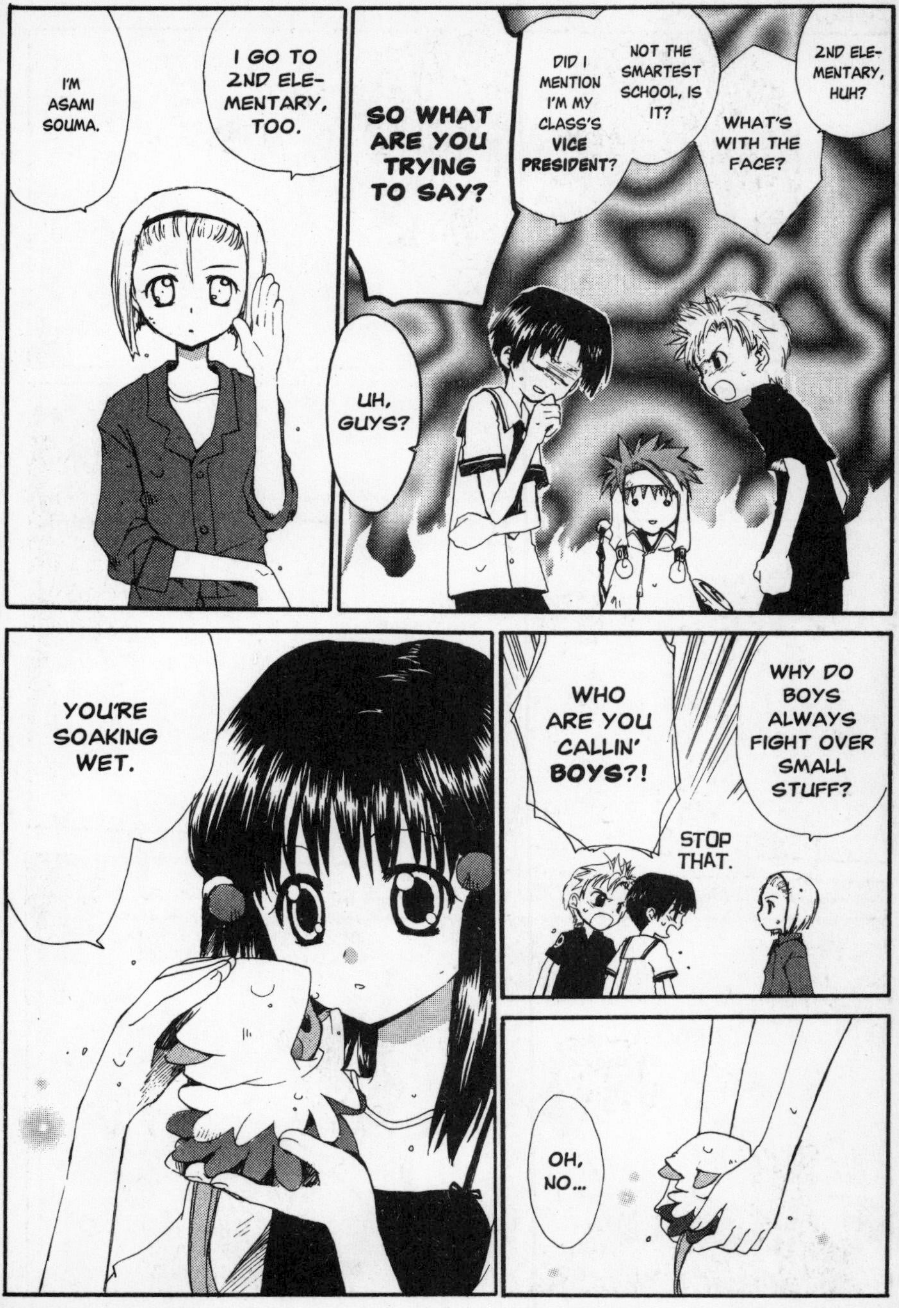
I'M ASAMI SOUMA.
I GO TO 2ND ELE- MENTARY, TOO.
2ND ELE- MENTARY, HUH?
WHAT'S WITH THE FACE?
NOT THE SMARTEST SCHOOL, IS IT?
DID I MENTION I'M MY CLASS'S VICE PRESIDENT?
SO WHAT ARE YOU TRYING TO SAY?
UH, GUYS?
WHY DO BOYS ALWAYS FIGHT OVER SMALL STUFF?
WHO ARE YOU CALLIN' BOYS?!
STOP THAT.
YOU'RE SOAKING WET.
OH, NO...

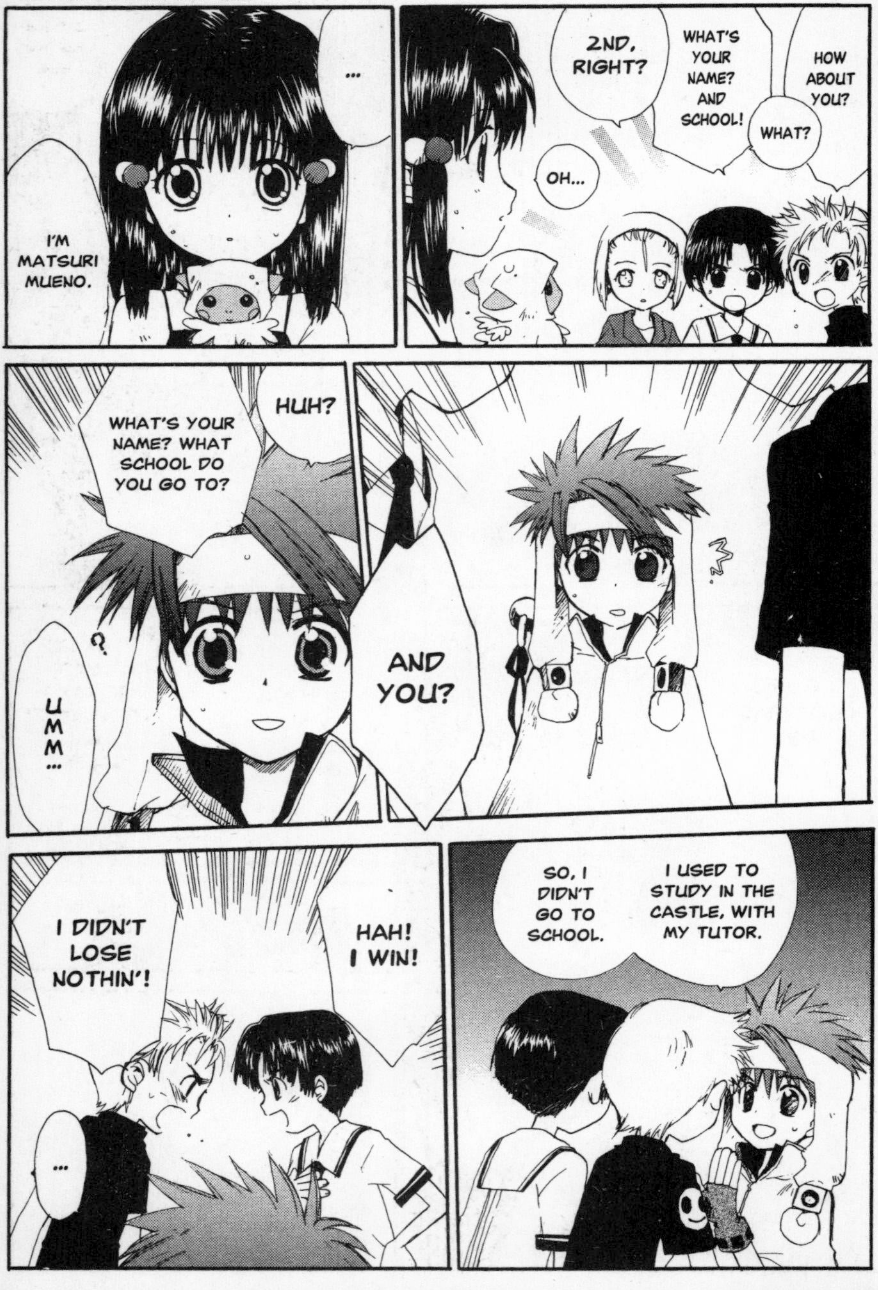
HOW ABOUT YOU?
WHAT?
WHAT'S YOUR NAME? AND SCHOOL!
2ND, RIGHT?
OH...
...
I'M MATSURI MUENO.
AND YOU?
HUH?
WHAT'S YOUR NAME? WHAT SCHOOL DO YOU GO TO?
UMM...
I USED TO STUDY IN THE CASTLE, WITH MY TUTOR.
SO, I DIDN'T GO TO SCHOOL.
HAH! I WIN!
I DIDN'T LOSE NOTHIN'!
...

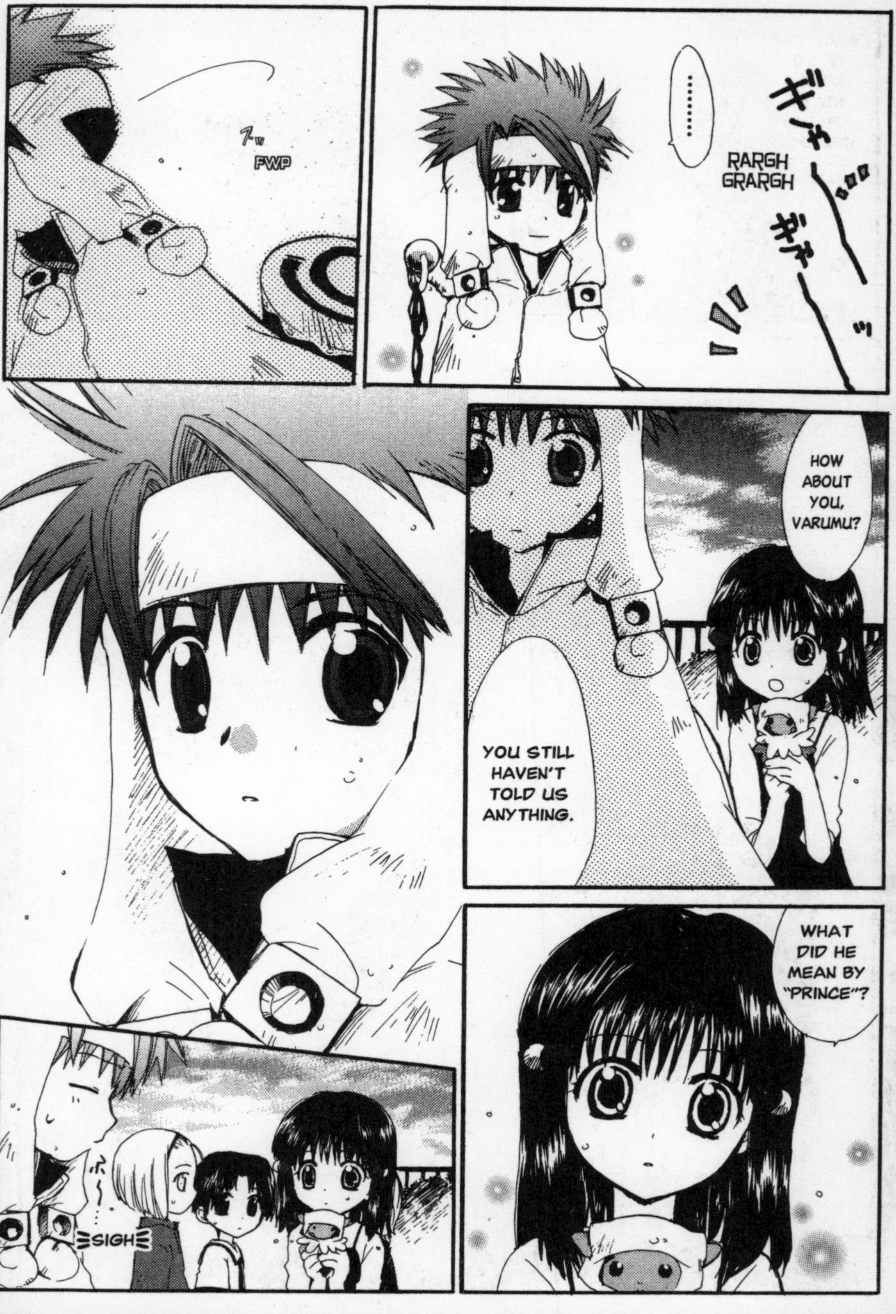

……
ギャーギャー
RARGH GRARGH
フッ
FWP
HOW ABOUT YOU, VARUMU?
YOU STILL HAVEN'T TOLD US ANYTHING.
WHAT DID HE MEAN BY "PRINCE"?
ふ～…
SIGH

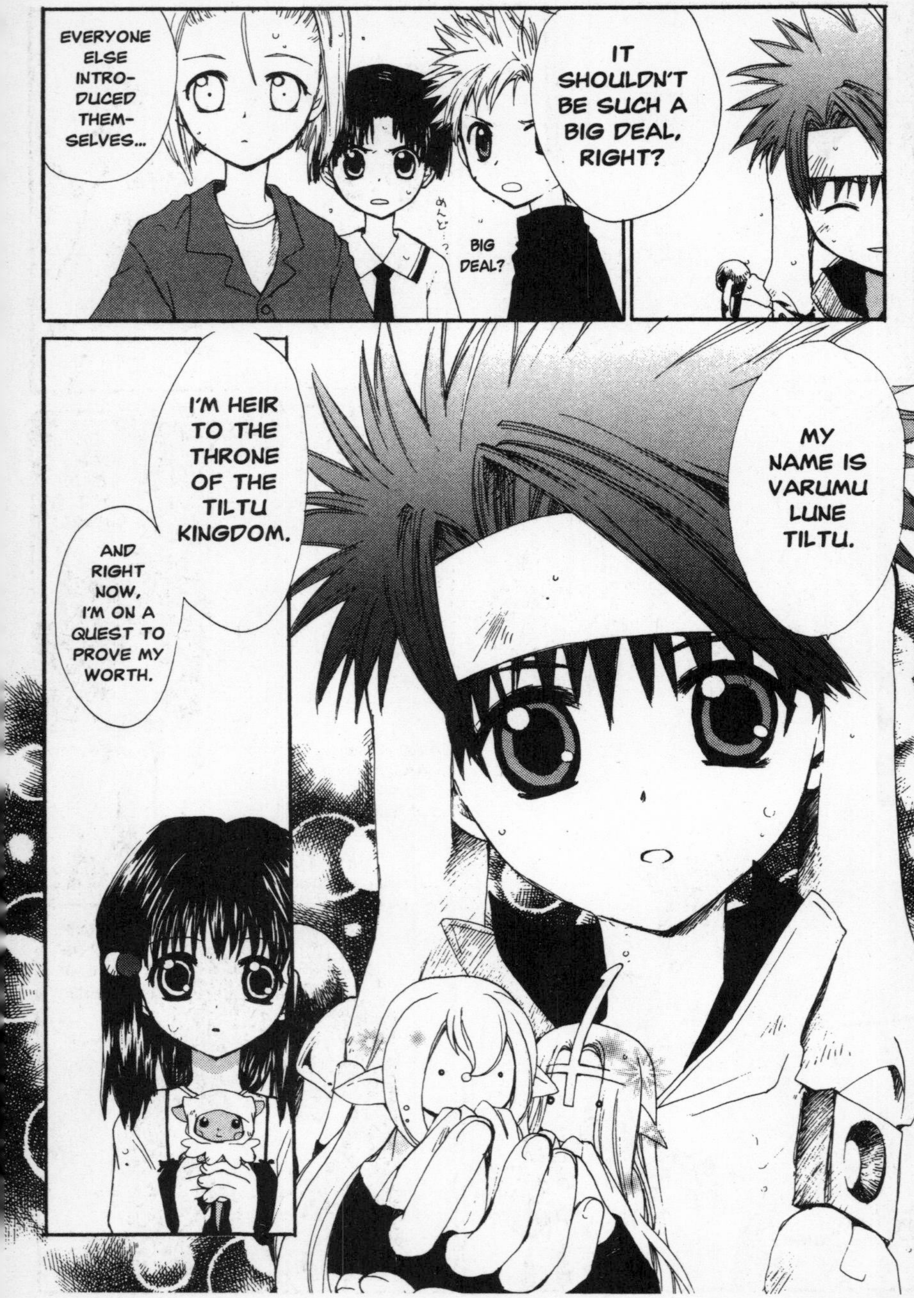

IT SHOULDN'T BE SUCH A BIG DEAL, RIGHT?
BIG DEAL?
EVERYONE ELSE INTRODUCED THEMSELVES...
MY NAME IS VARUMU LUNE TILTU.
I'M HEIR TO THE THRONE OF THE TILTU KINGDOM.
AND RIGHT NOW, I'M ON A QUEST TO PROVE MY WORTH.

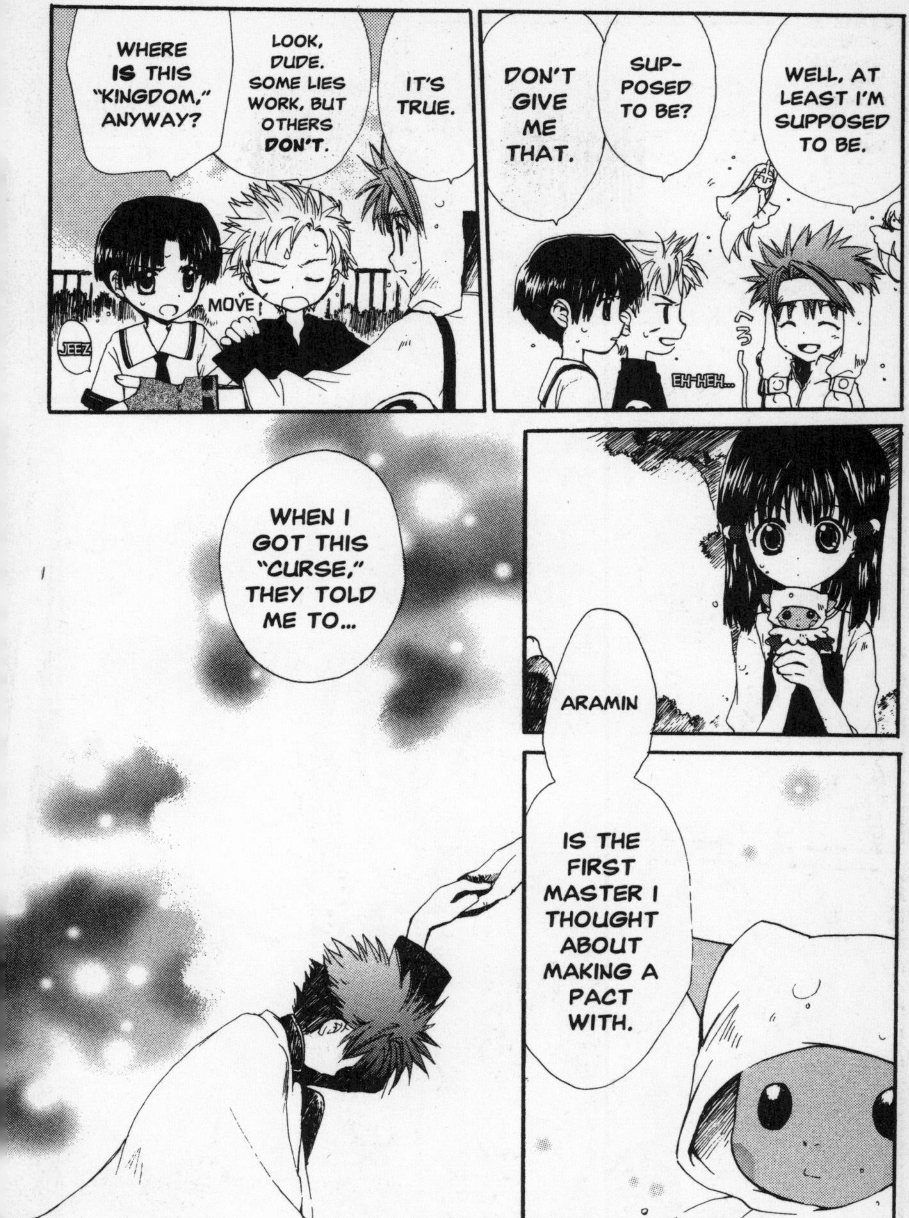
WELL, AT LEAST I'M SUPPOSED TO BE.
EH-HEH...
SUP-POSED TO BE?
DON'T GIVE ME THAT.
IT'S TRUE.
LOOK, DUDE. SOME LIES WORK, BUT OTHERS **DON'T**.
MOVE
WHERE **IS** THIS "KINGDOM," ANYWAY?
JEEZ
WHEN I GOT THIS "CURSE," THEY TOLD ME TO...
ARAMIN
IS THE FIRST MASTER I THOUGHT ABOUT MAKING A PACT WITH.

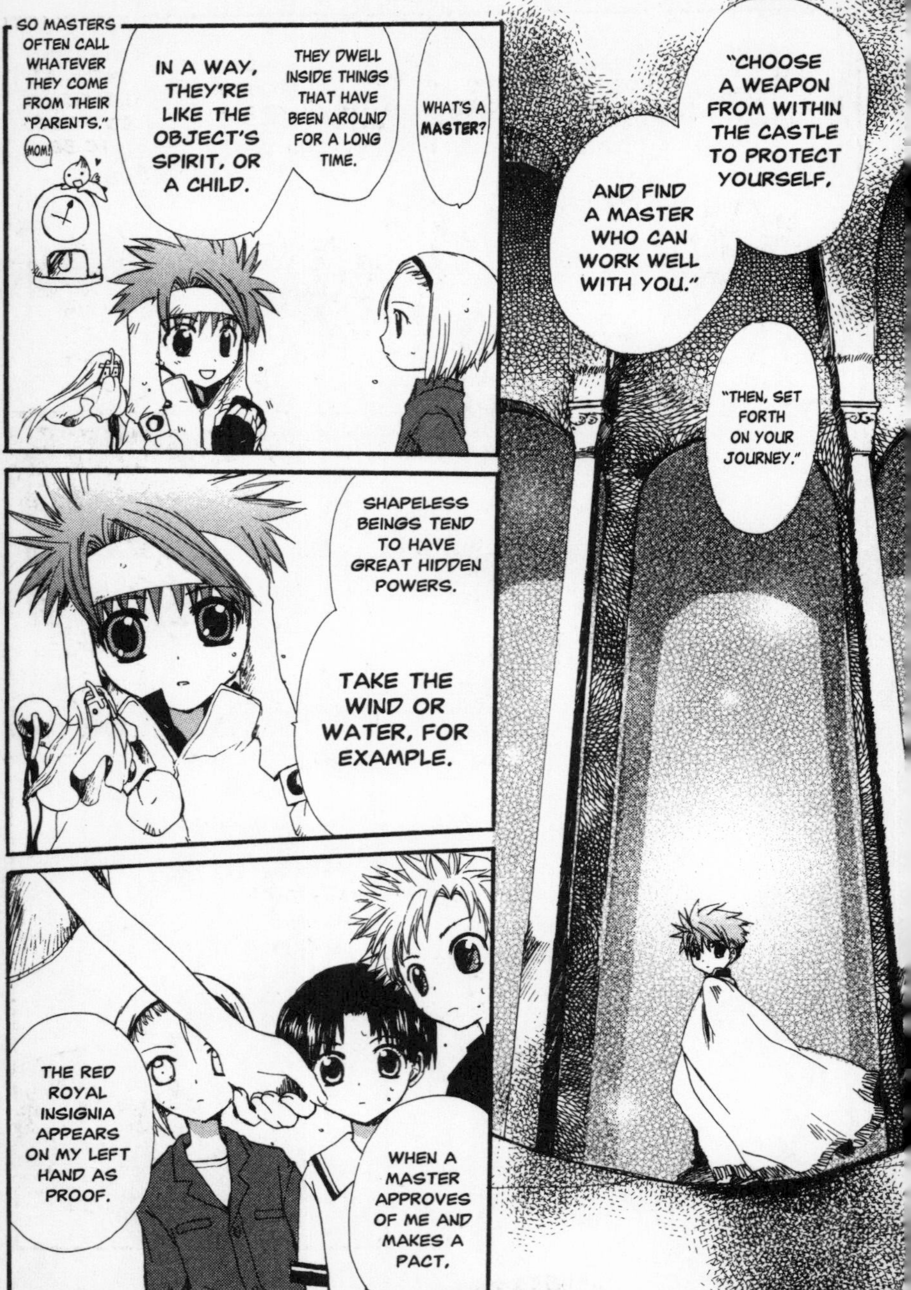
"CHOOSE A WEAPON FROM WITHIN THE CASTLE TO PROTECT YOURSELF,
AND FIND A MASTER WHO CAN WORK WELL WITH YOU."
"THEN, SET FORTH ON YOUR JOURNEY."
WHAT'S A MASTER?
THEY DWELL INSIDE THINGS THAT HAVE BEEN AROUND FOR A LONG TIME.
IN A WAY, THEY'RE LIKE THE OBJECT'S SPIRIT, OR A CHILD.
SO MASTERS OFTEN CALL WHATEVER THEY COME FROM THEIR "PARENTS."
MOM!
SHAPELESS BEINGS TEND TO HAVE GREAT HIDDEN POWERS.
TAKE THE WIND OR WATER, FOR EXAMPLE.
WHEN A MASTER APPROVES OF ME AND MAKES A PACT,
THE RED ROYAL INSIGNIA APPEARS ON MY LEFT HAND AS PROOF.

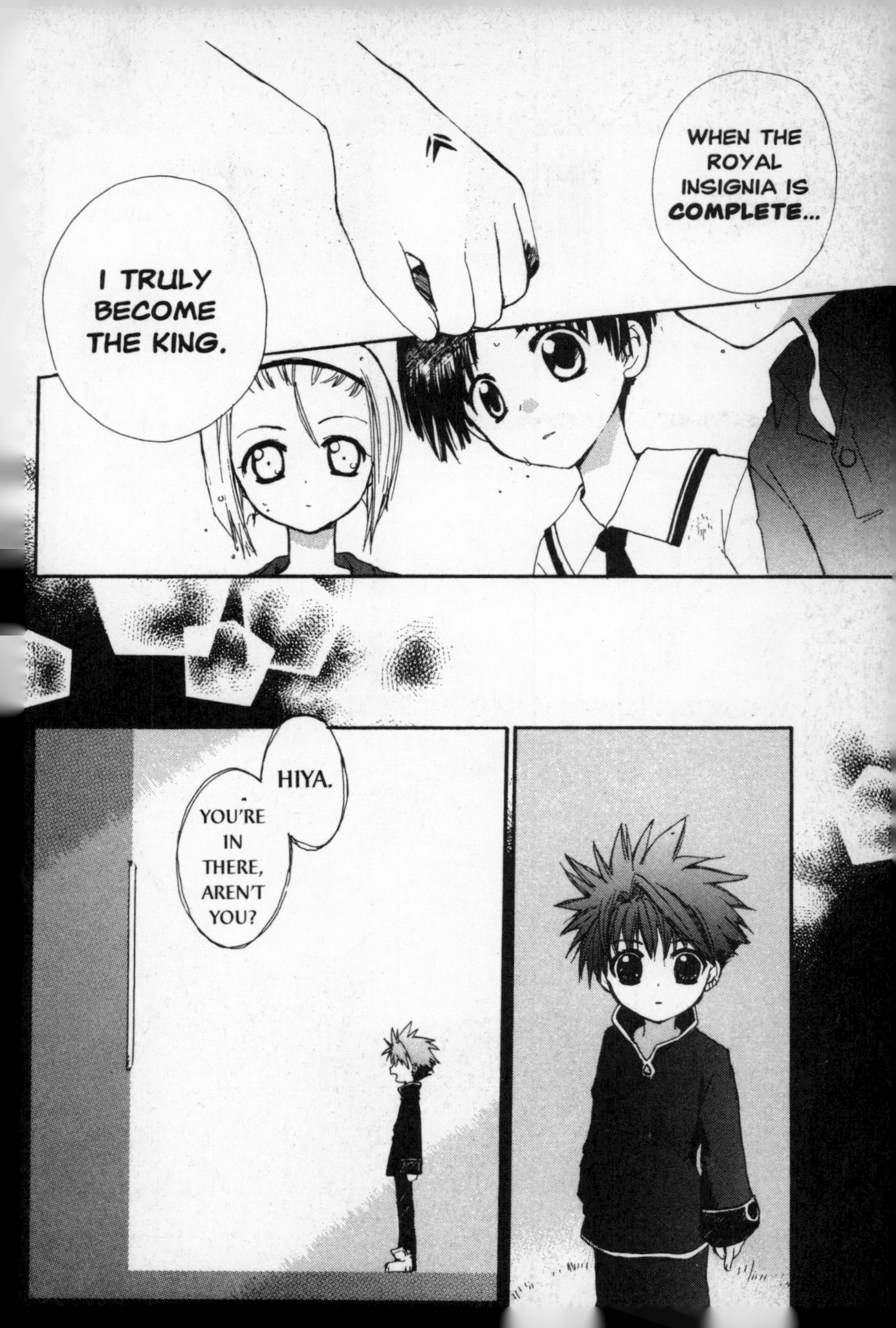
WHEN THE ROYAL INSIGNIA IS COMPLETE...
I TRULY BECOME THE KING.
HIYA.
YOU'RE IN THERE, AREN'T YOU?

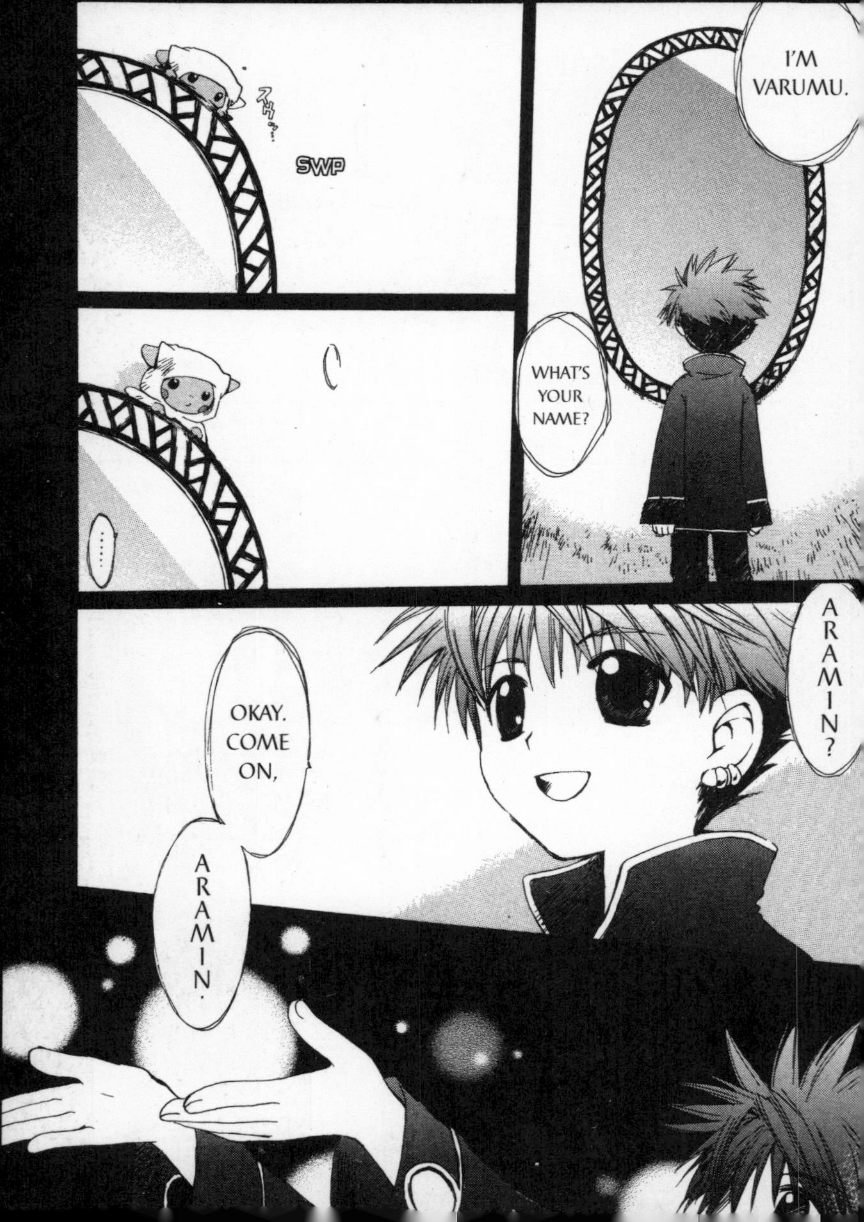
I'M VARUMU.
WHAT'S YOUR NAME?
SWP
......
ARAMIN?
OKAY. COME ON,
ARAMIN.

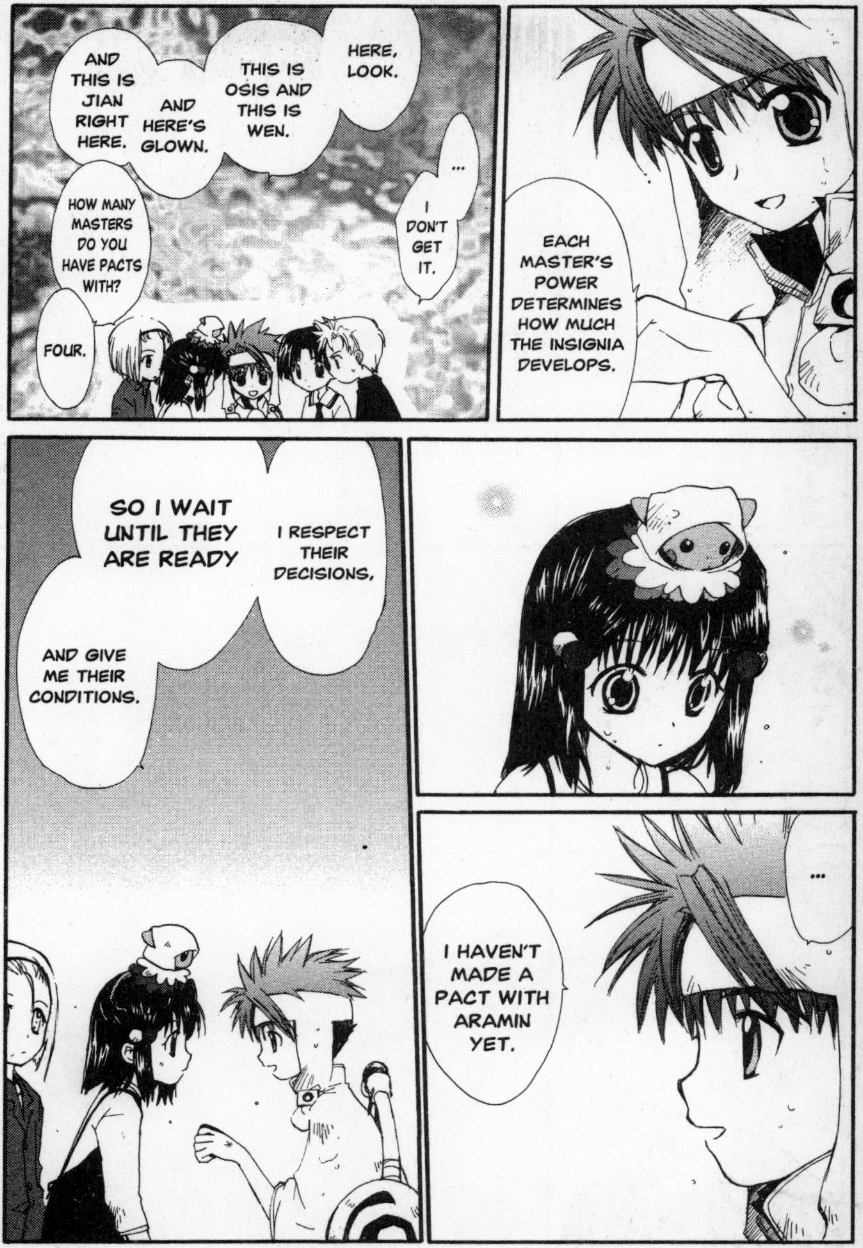
EACH MASTER'S POWER DETERMINES HOW MUCH THE INSIGNIA DEVELOPS.
HERE, LOOK.
THIS IS OSIS AND THIS IS WEN.
AND HERE'S GLOWN.
AND THIS IS JIAN RIGHT HERE.
...
I DON'T GET IT.
HOW MANY MASTERS DO YOU HAVE PACTS WITH?
FOUR.
...
I HAVEN'T MADE A PACT WITH ARAMIN YET.
I RESPECT THEIR DECISIONS,
SO I WAIT UNTIL THEY ARE READY
AND GIVE ME THEIR CONDITIONS.

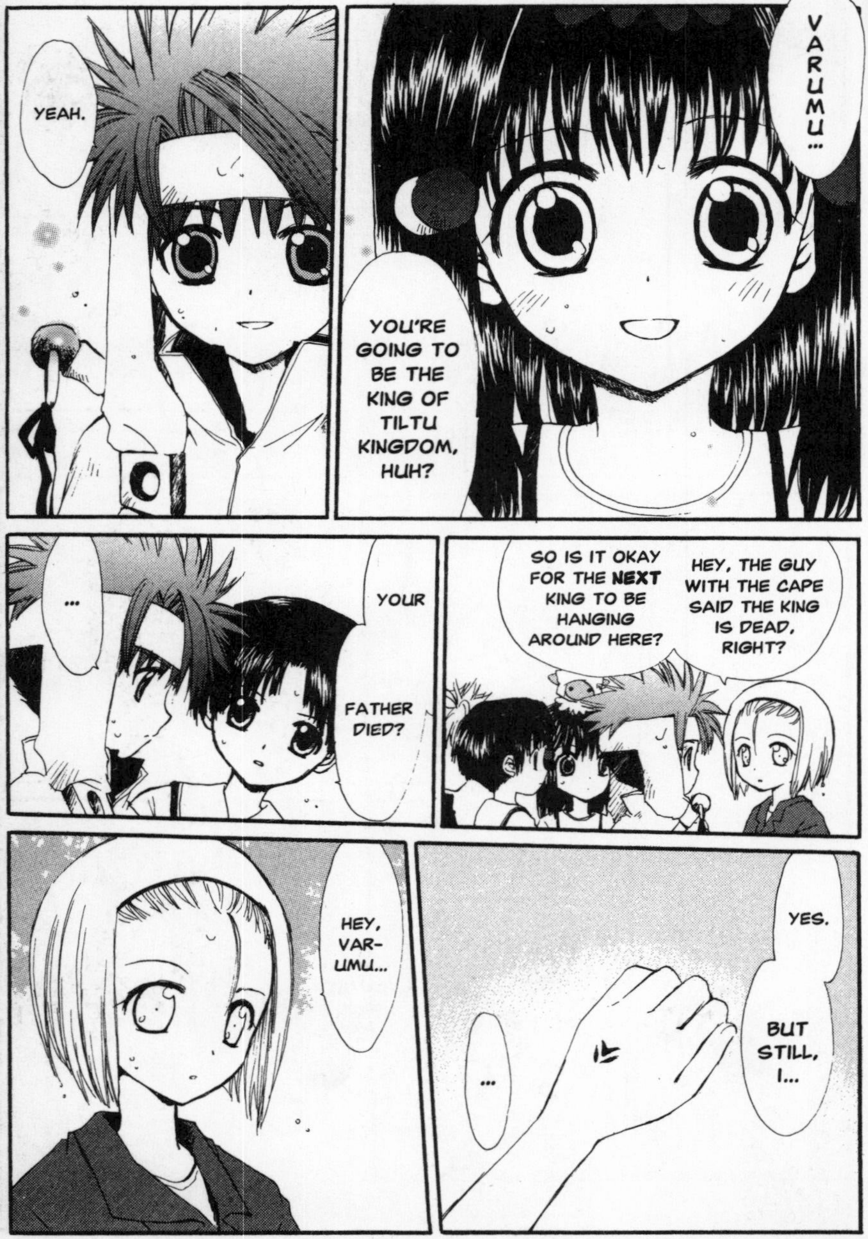
VARUMU...
YOU'RE GOING TO BE THE KING OF TILTU KINGDOM, HUH?
YEAH.
HEY, THE GUY WITH THE CAPE SAID THE KING IS DEAD, RIGHT?
SO IS IT OKAY FOR THE NEXT KING TO BE HANGING AROUND HERE?
YOUR FATHER DIED?
...
YES.
BUT STILL, I...
...
HEY, VAR-UMU...

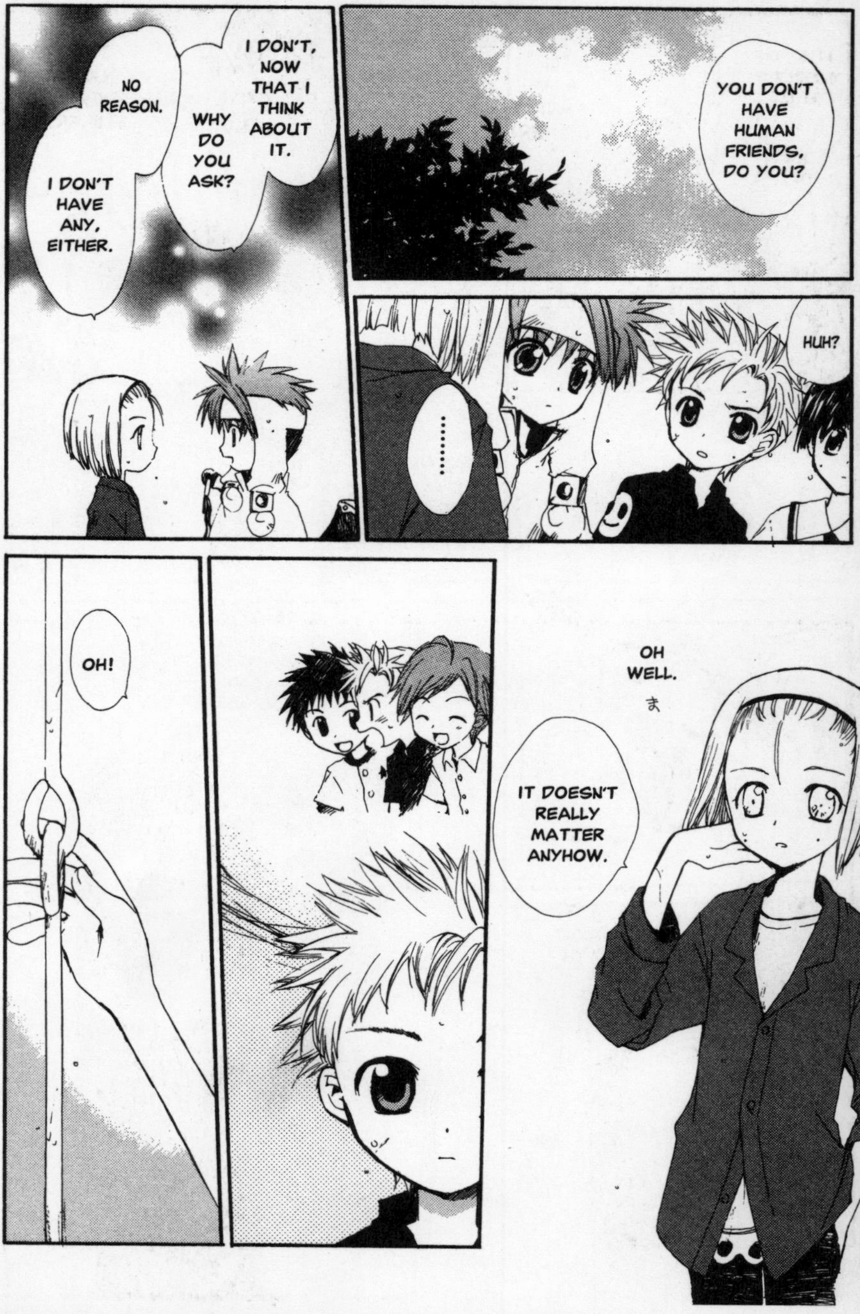
YOU DON'T HAVE HUMAN FRIENDS, DO YOU?
HUH?
....
I DON'T, NOW THAT I THINK ABOUT IT.
WHY DO YOU ASK?
NO REASON.
I DON'T HAVE ANY, EITHER.
OH WELL.
ま
IT DOESN'T REALLY MATTER ANYHOW.
OH!

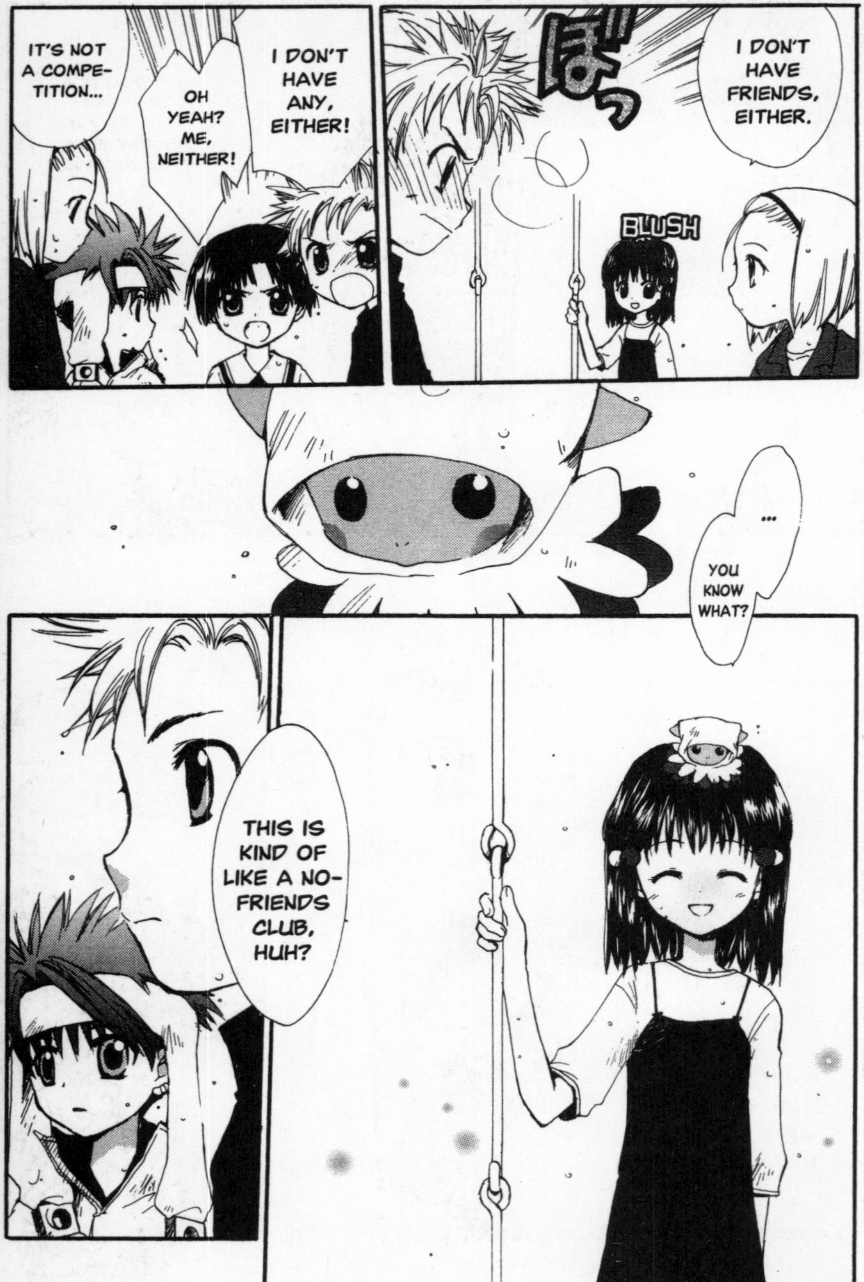
ぼっ
I DON'T HAVE FRIENDS, EITHER.
BLUSH
I DON'T HAVE ANY, EITHER!
OH YEAH? ME, NEITHER!
IT'S NOT A COMPETITION...
...
YOU KNOW WHAT?
THIS IS KIND OF LIKE A NO-FRIENDS CLUB, HUH?

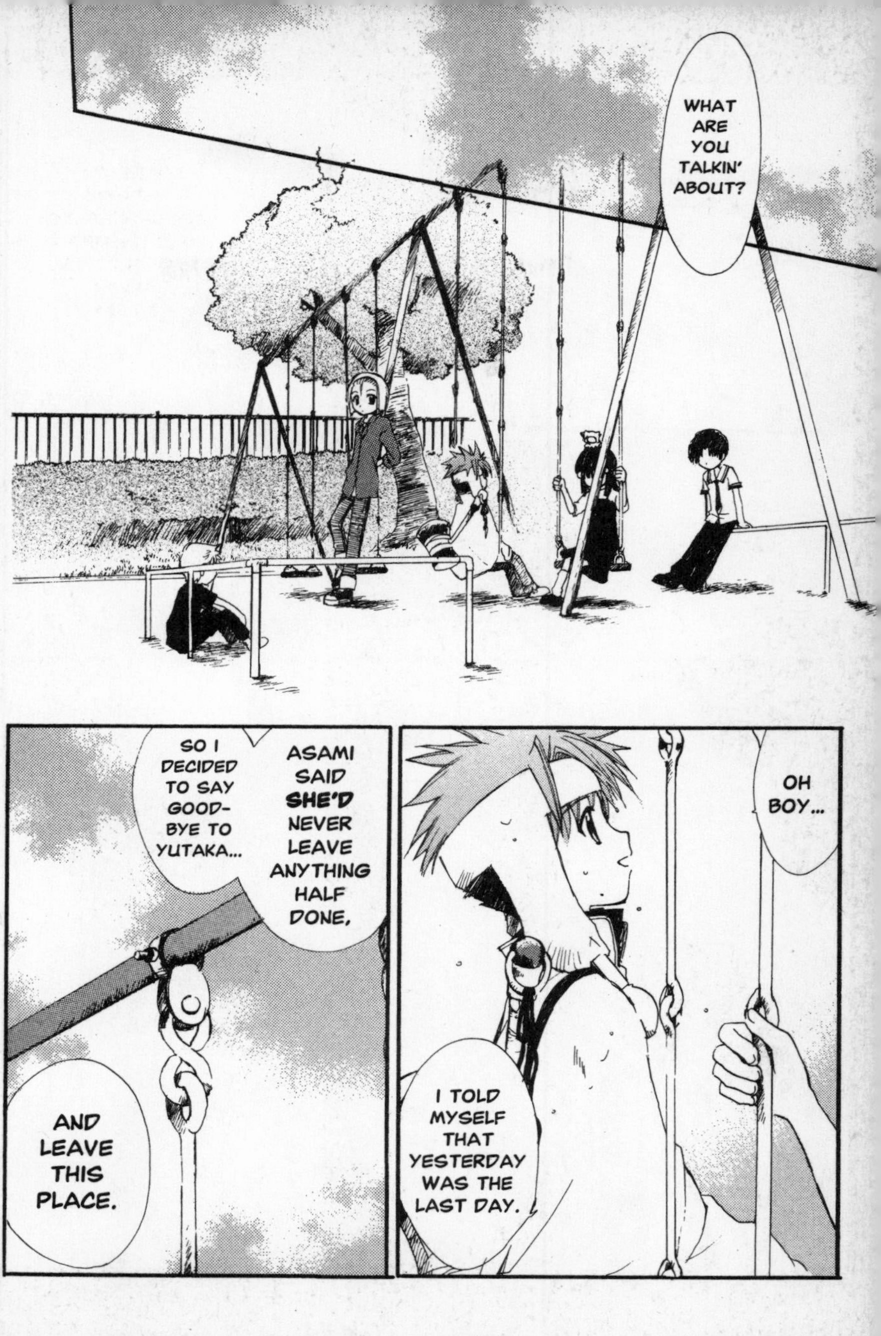
WHAT ARE YOU TALKIN' ABOUT?
OH BOY...
I TOLD MYSELF THAT YESTERDAY WAS THE LAST DAY.
ASAMI SAID **SHE'D** NEVER LEAVE ANYTHING HALF DONE,
SO I DECIDED TO SAY GOOD-BYE TO YUTAKA...
AND LEAVE THIS PLACE.

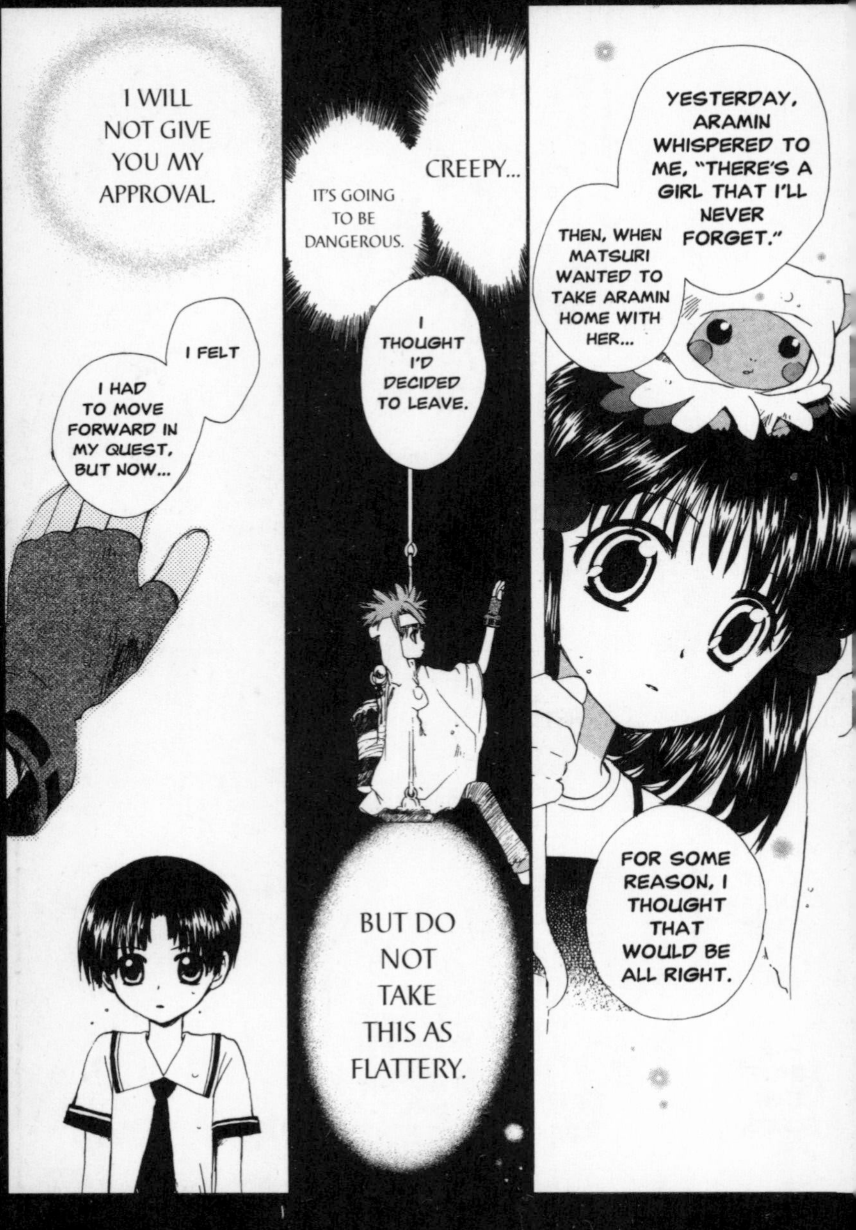
YESTERDAY, ARAMIN WHISPERED TO ME, "THERE'S A GIRL THAT I'LL NEVER FORGET."
THEN, WHEN MATSURI WANTED TO TAKE ARAMIN HOME WITH HER...
FOR SOME REASON, I THOUGHT THAT WOULD BE ALL RIGHT.
CREEPY...
IT'S GOING TO BE DANGEROUS.
I THOUGHT I'D DECIDED TO LEAVE.
BUT DO NOT TAKE THIS AS FLATTERY.
I WILL NOT GIVE YOU MY APPROVAL.
I FELT
I HAD TO MOVE FORWARD IN MY QUEST, BUT NOW...

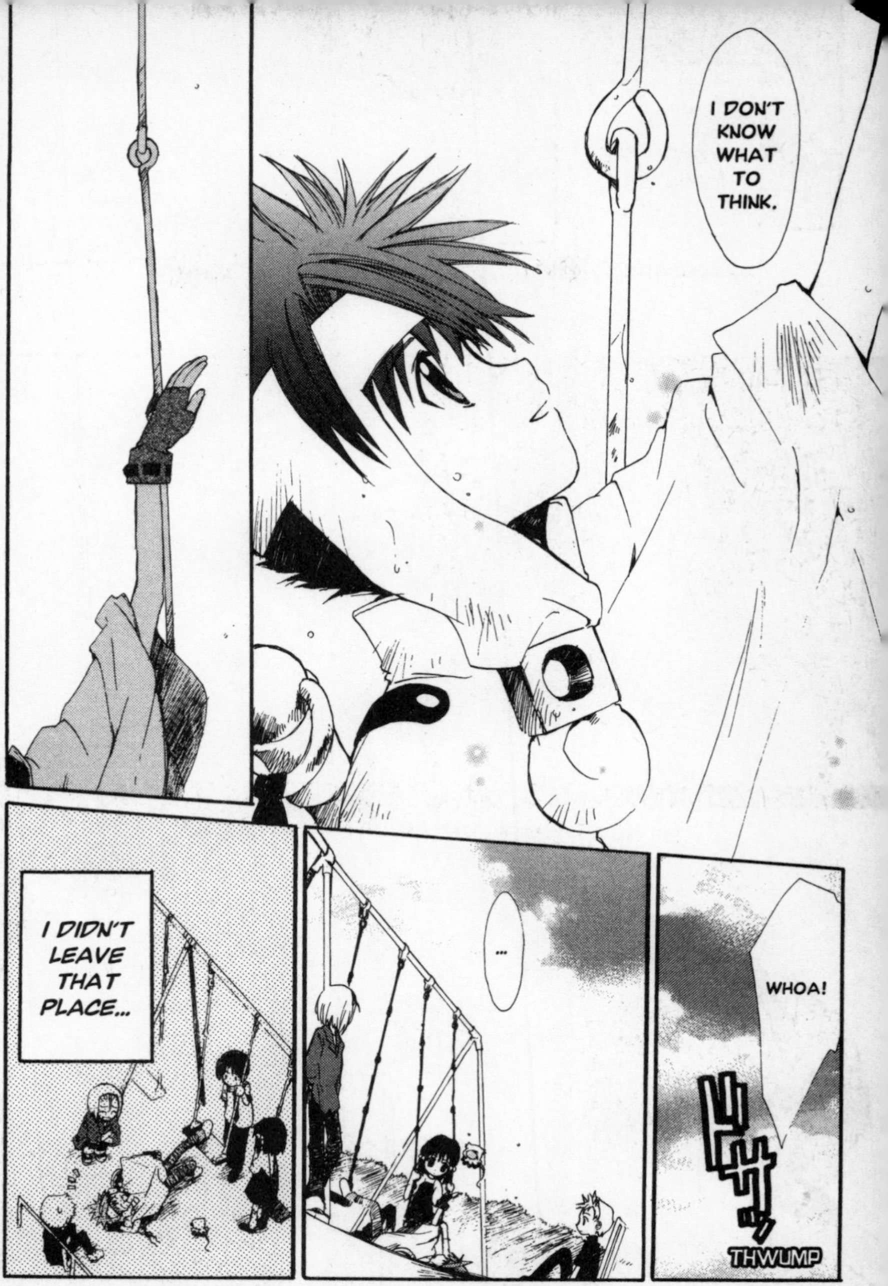
I DON'T KNOW WHAT TO THINK.
WHOA!
THWUMP
...
I DIDN'T LEAVE THAT PLACE...

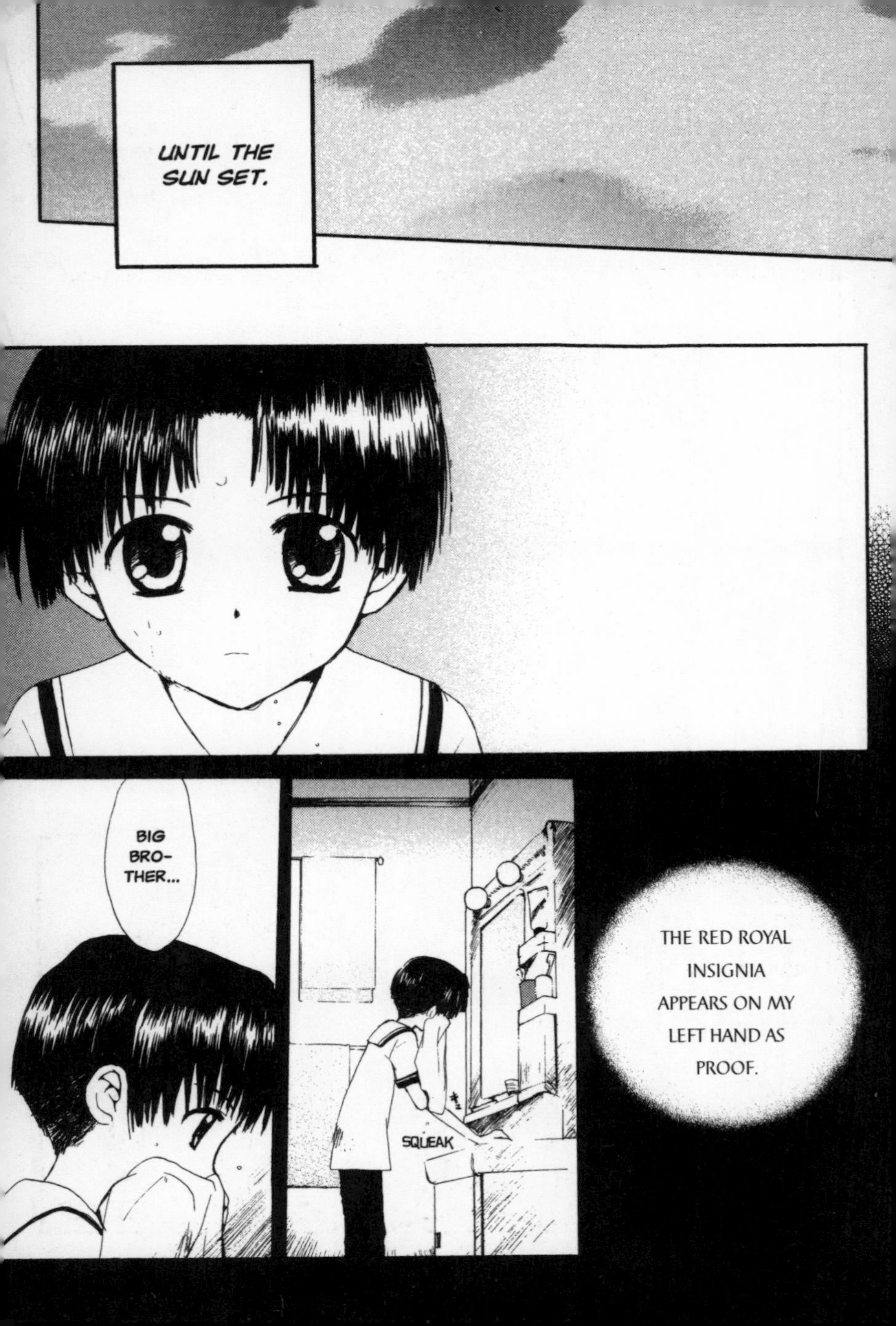

UNTIL THE SUN SET.
BIG BRO- THER...
SQUEAK
THE RED ROYAL INSIGNIA APPEARS ON MY LEFT HAND AS PROOF.

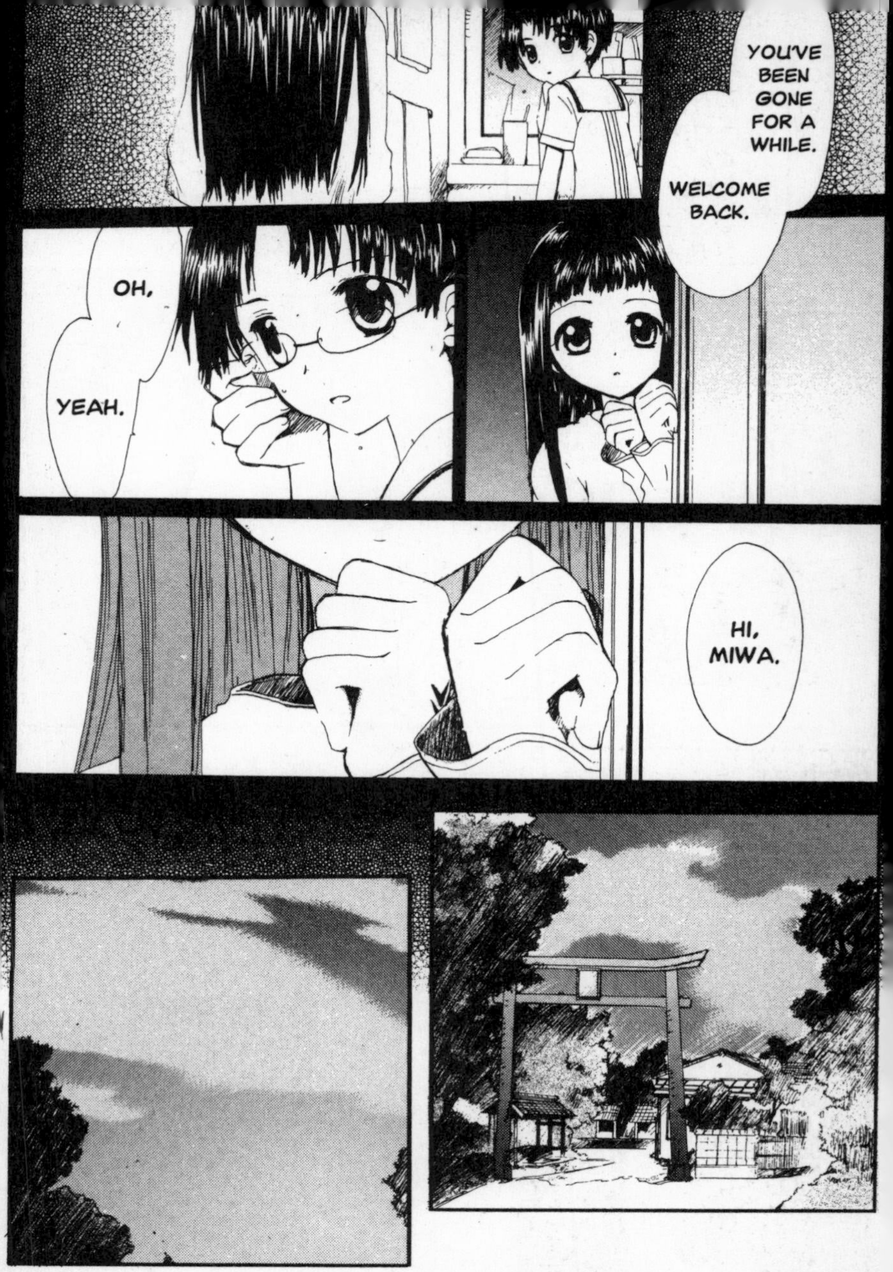
YOU'VE BEEN GONE FOR A WHILE.
WELCOME BACK.
OH,
YEAH.
HI, MIWA.

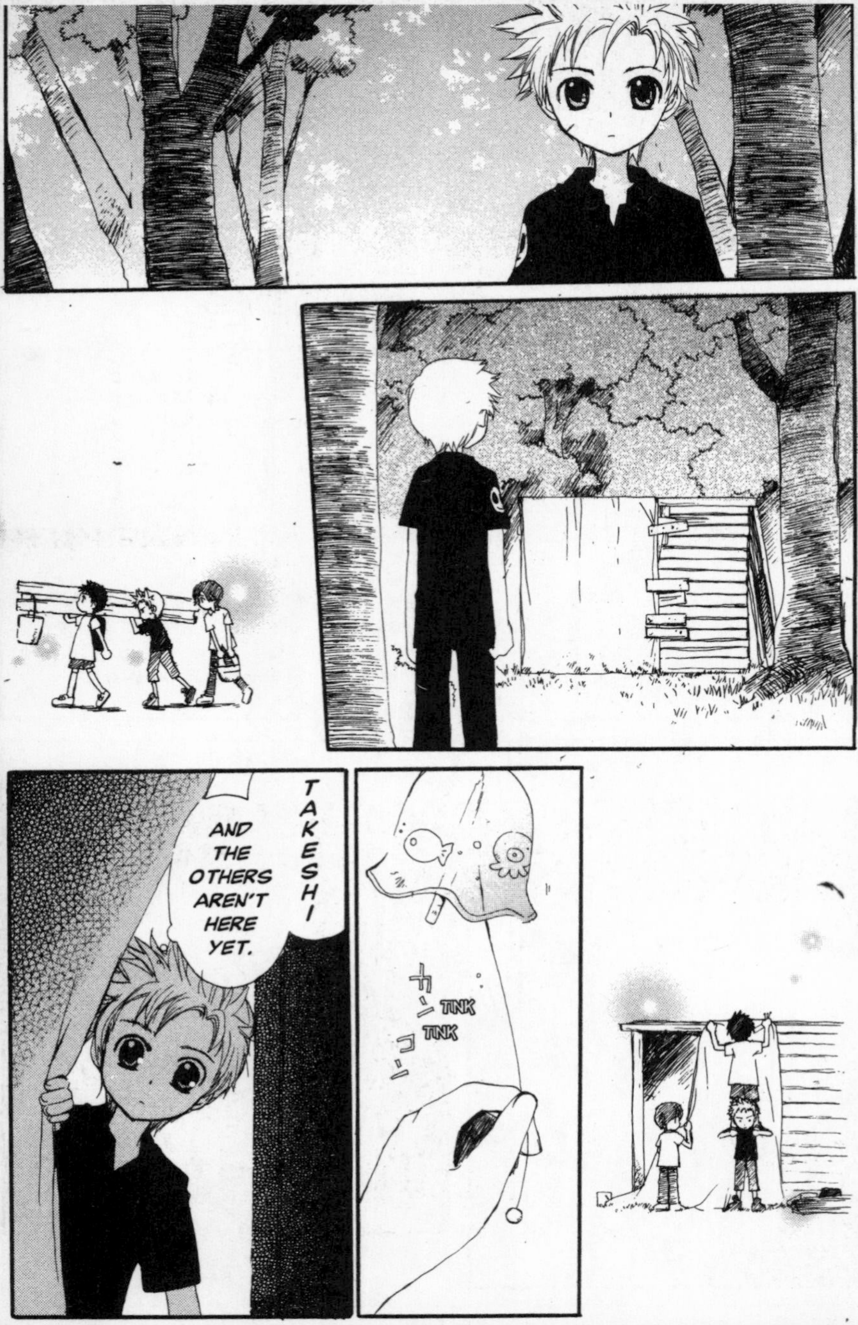
TAKESHI AND THE OTHERS AREN'T HERE YET.
カン TINK
コン TINK

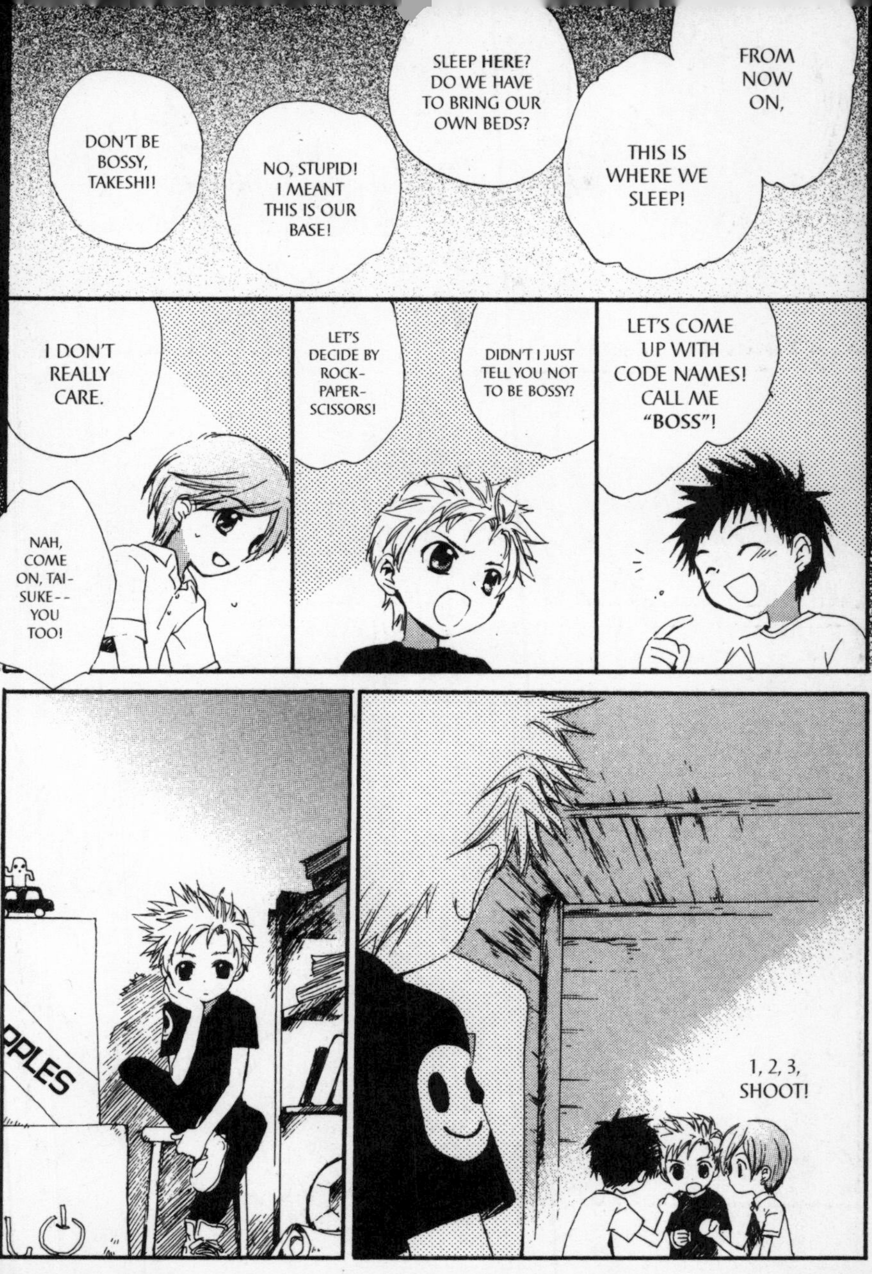
FROM NOW ON,
THIS IS WHERE WE SLEEP!
SLEEP HERE? DO WE HAVE TO BRING OUR OWN BEDS?
NO, STUPID! I MEANT THIS IS OUR BASE!
DON'T BE BOSSY, TAKESHI!
LET'S COME UP WITH CODE NAMES! CALL ME "BOSS"!
DIDN'T I JUST TELL YOU NOT TO BE BOSSY?
LET'S DECIDE BY ROCK-PAPER-SCISSORS!
I DON'T REALLY CARE.
NAH, COME ON, TAI-SUKE-- YOU TOO!
PPLES
1, 2, 3, SHOOT!

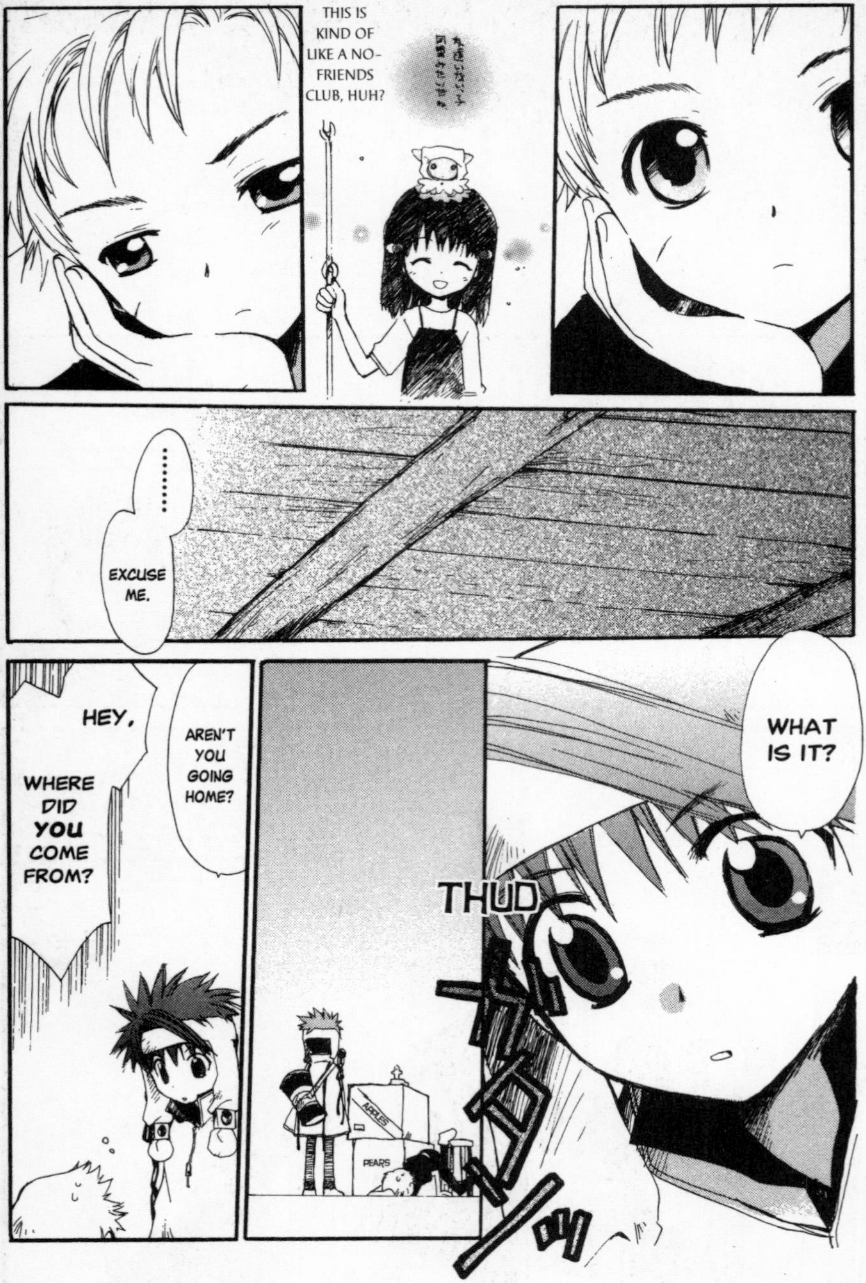
THIS IS KIND OF LIKE A NO-FRIENDS CLUB, HUH?
......
EXCUSE ME.
WHAT IS IT?
THUD
APPLES
PEARS
AREN'T YOU GOING HOME?
HEY,
WHERE DID YOU COME FROM?

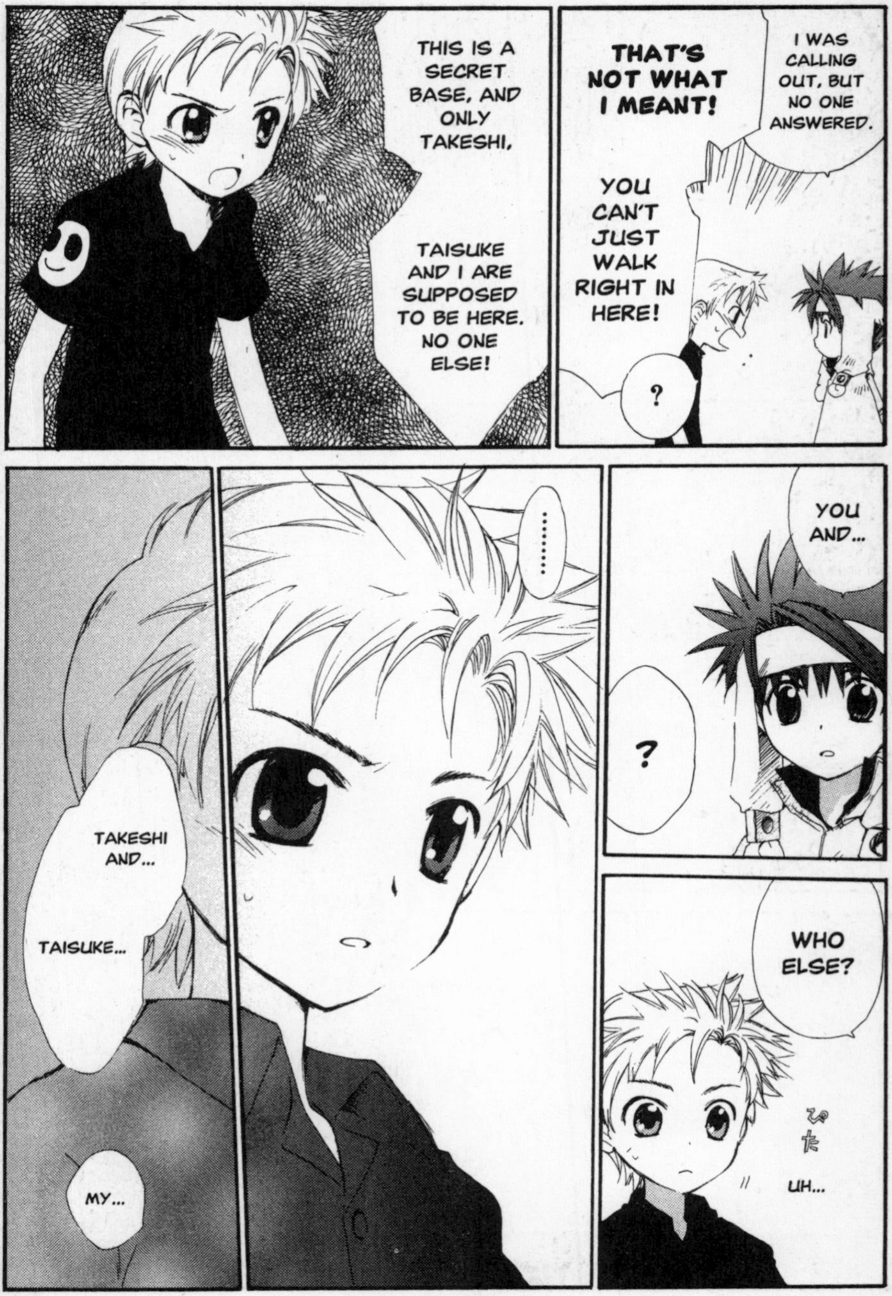
I WAS CALLING OUT, BUT NO ONE ANSWERED.
THAT'S NOT WHAT I MEANT!
YOU CAN'T JUST WALK RIGHT IN HERE!
?
THIS IS A SECRET BASE, AND ONLY TAKESHI,
TAISUKE AND I ARE SUPPOSED TO BE HERE. NO ONE ELSE!
YOU AND...
?
WHO ELSE?
UH...
......
TAKESHI AND...
TAISUKE...
MY...

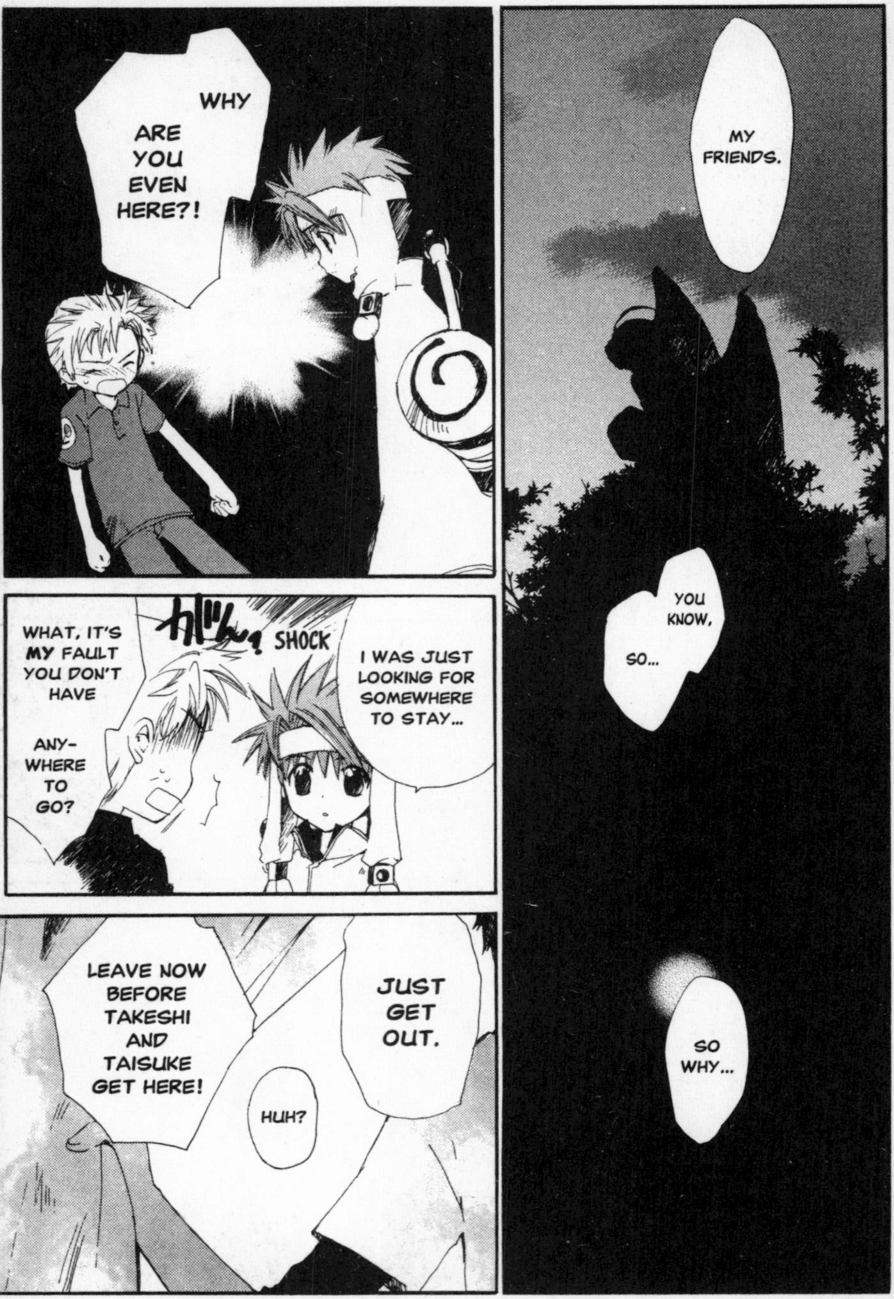
MY FRIENDS.
YOU KNOW, SO...
SO WHY...
WHY ARE YOU EVEN HERE?!
I WAS JUST LOOKING FOR SOMEWHERE TO STAY...
SHOCK
WHAT, IT'S **MY** FAULT YOU DON'T HAVE ANYWHERE TO GO?
JUST GET OUT.
LEAVE NOW BEFORE TAKESHI AND TAISUKE GET HERE!
HUH?

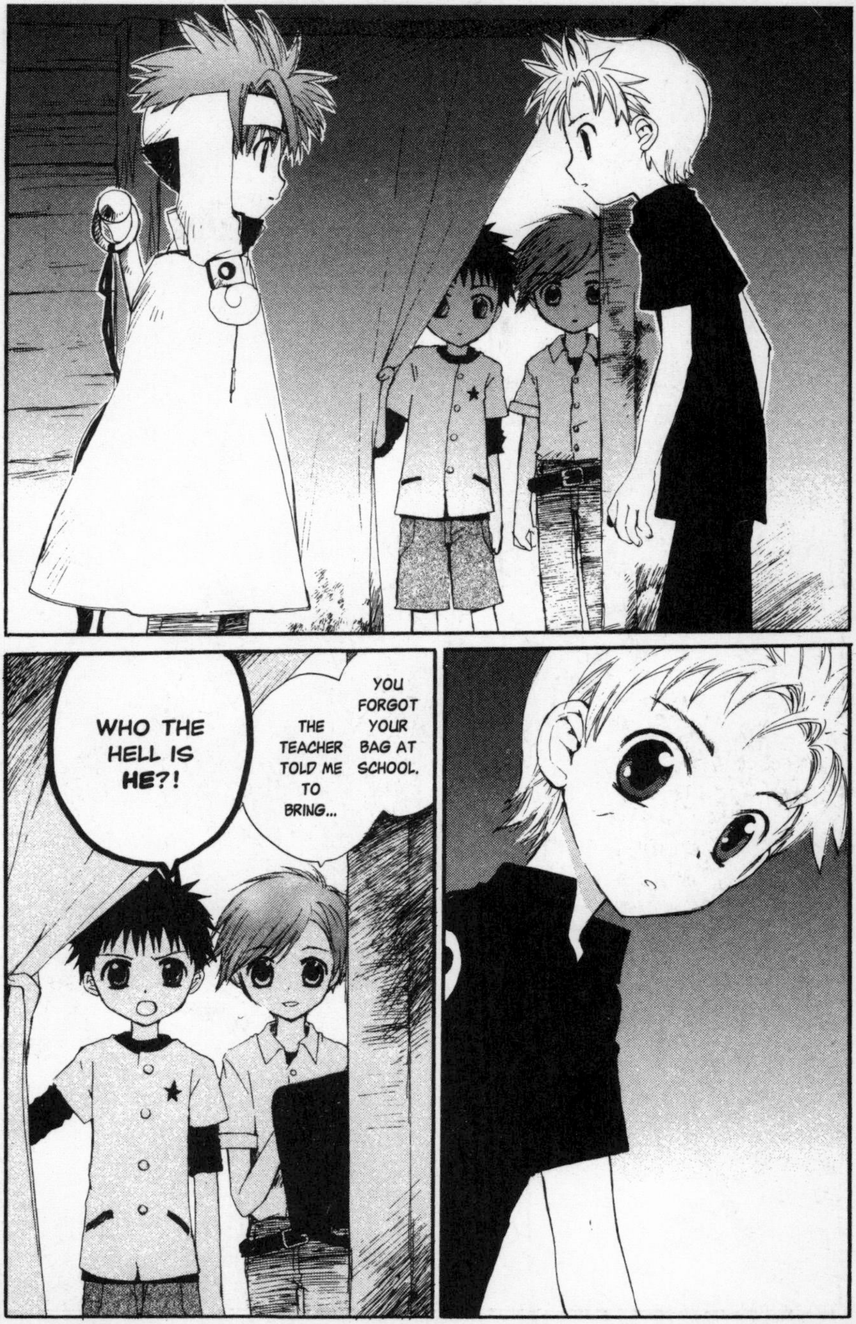
YOU FORGOT YOUR BAG AT SCHOOL.
THE TEACHER TOLD ME TO BRING...
WHO THE HELL IS **HE**?!

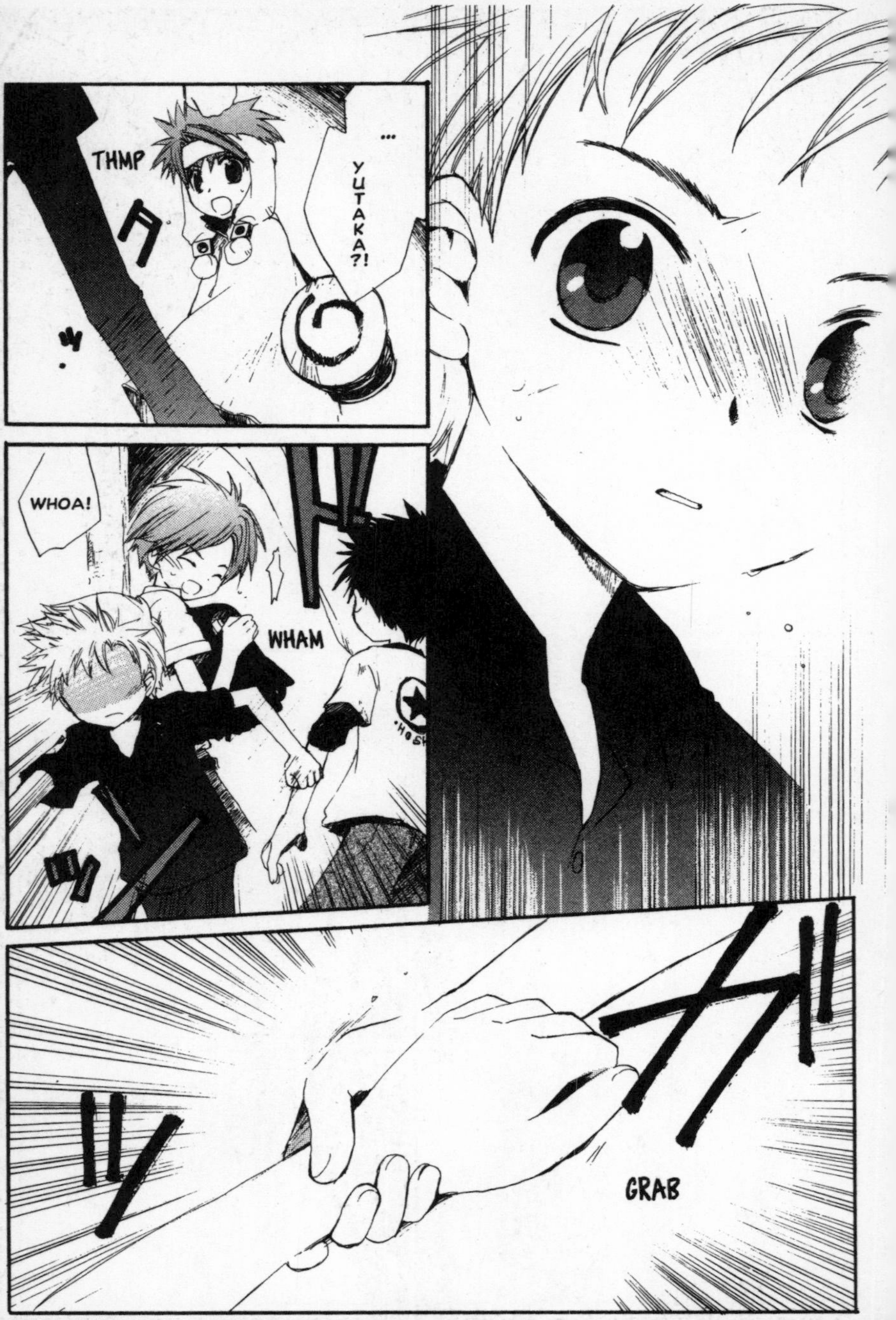

...
YUTAKA?!
THMP
WHOA!
WHAM
GRAB

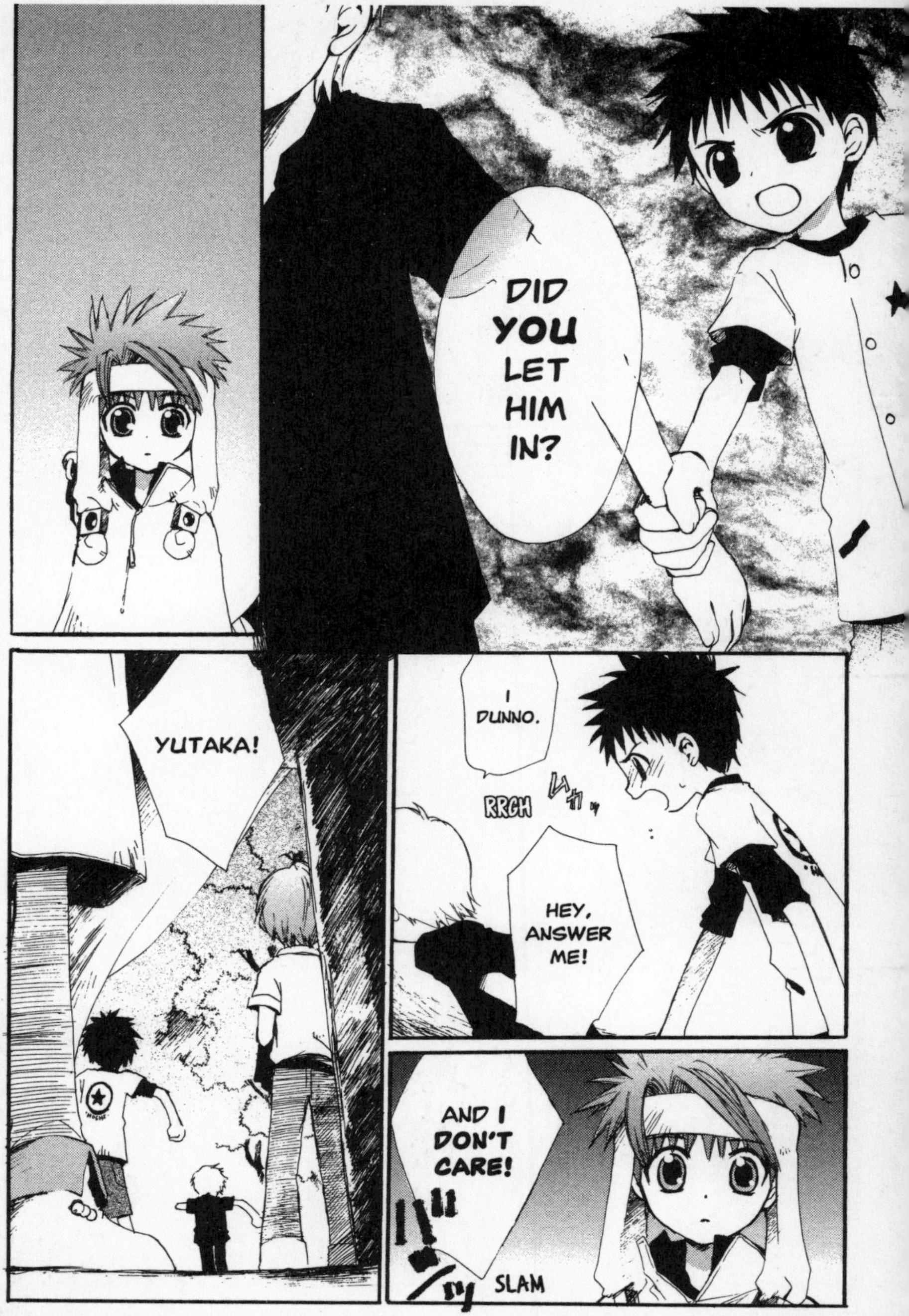
DID YOU LET HIM IN?
I DUNNO.
RRGH
HEY, ANSWER ME!
AND I DON'T CARE!
SLAM
YUTAKA!

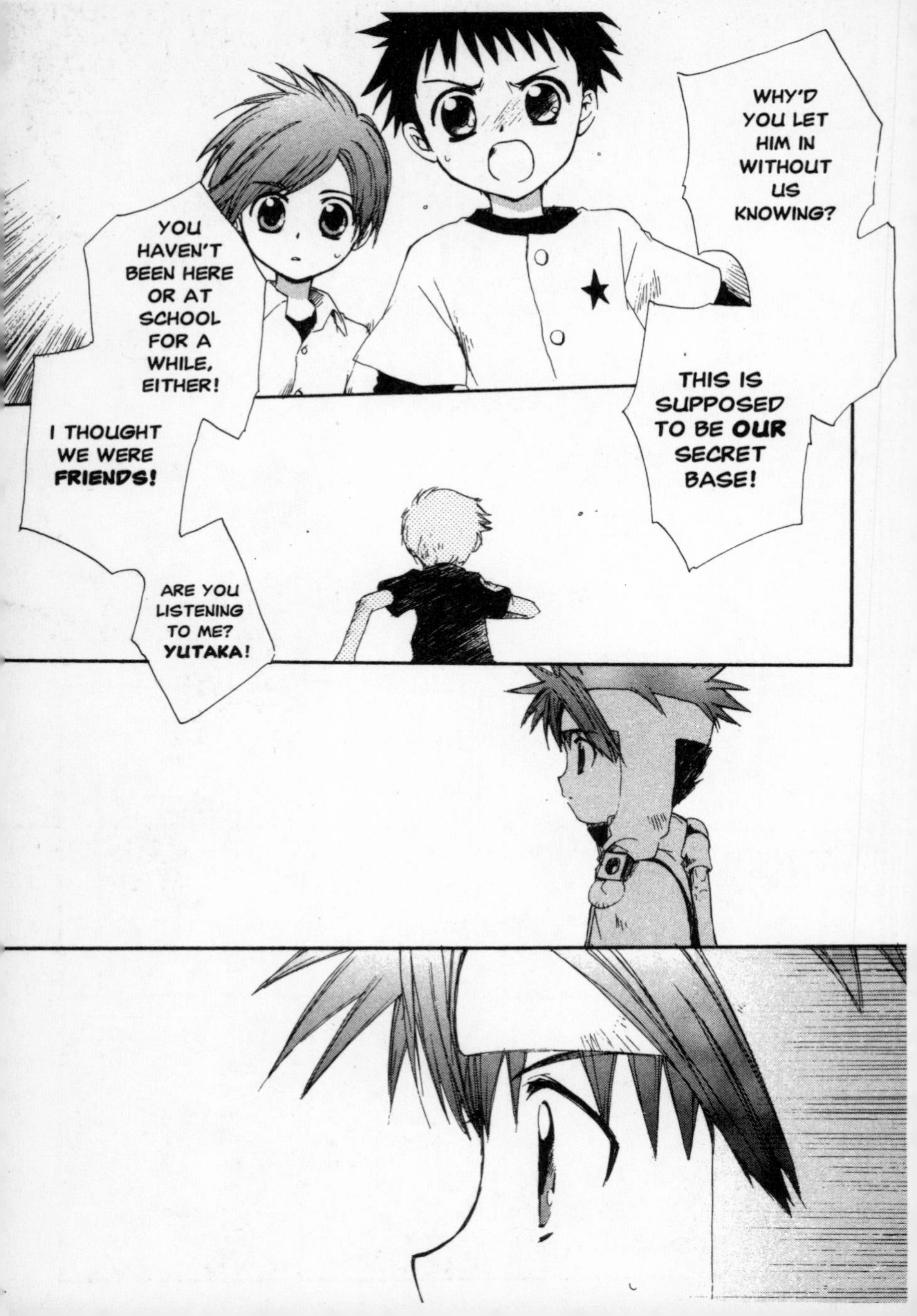
WHY'D YOU LET HIM IN WITHOUT US KNOWING?
YOU HAVEN'T BEEN HERE OR AT SCHOOL FOR A WHILE, EITHER!
THIS IS SUPPOSED TO BE **OUR** SECRET BASE!
I THOUGHT WE WERE **FRIENDS!**
ARE YOU LISTENING TO ME? **YUTAKA!**

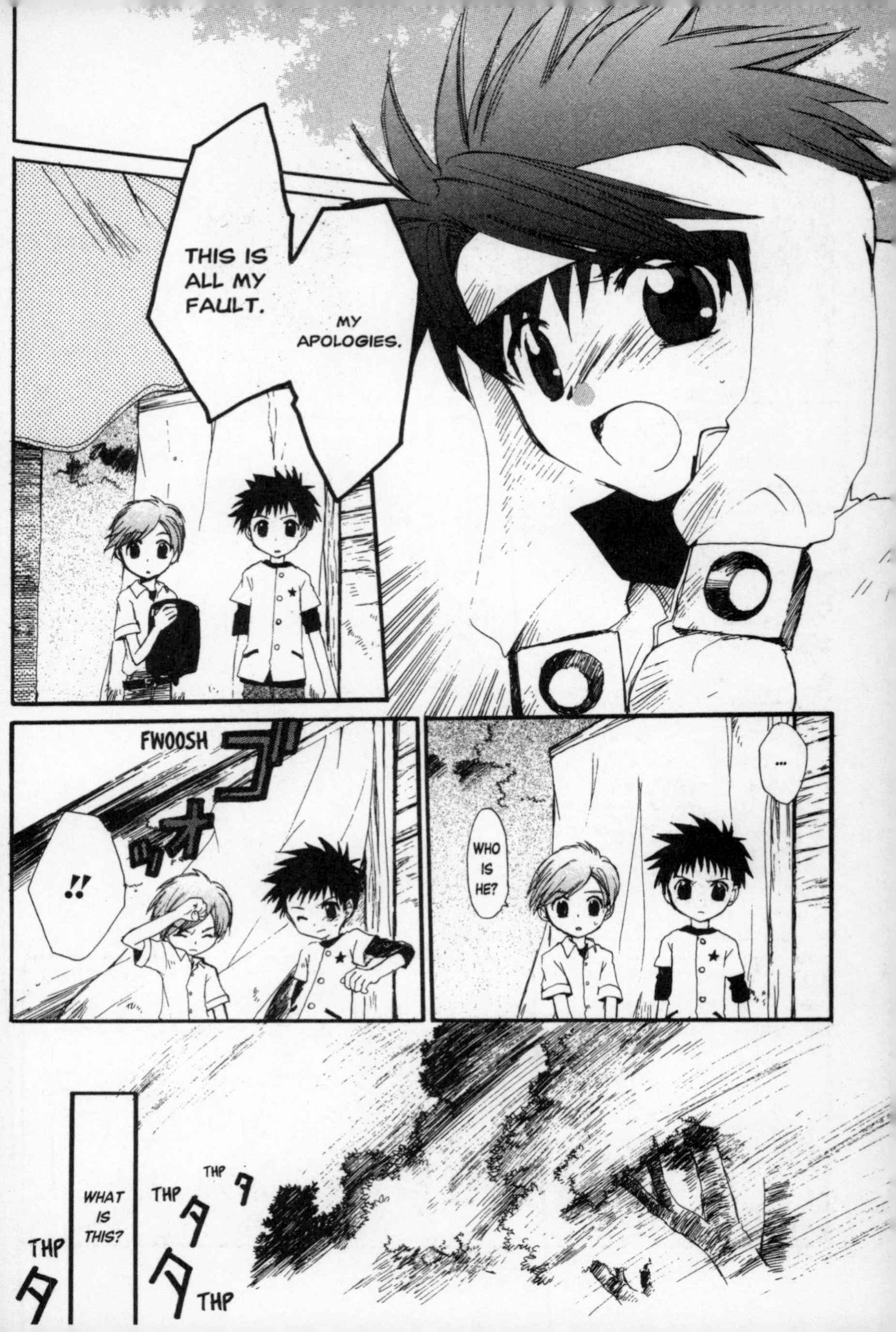

THIS IS ALL MY FAULT.
MY APOLOGIES.
FWOOSH
!!
...
WHO IS HE?
THP
THP
THP
THP
WHAT IS THIS?

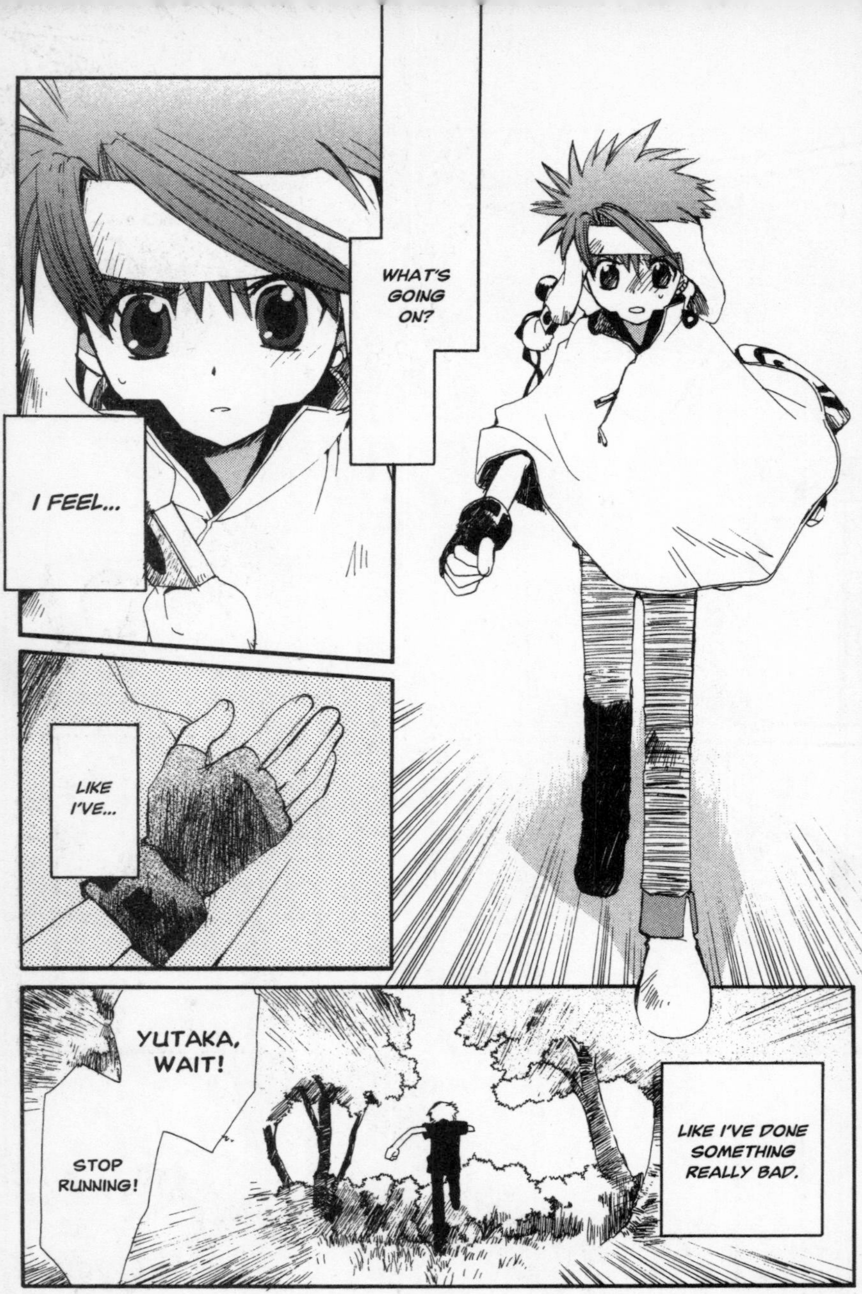
WHAT'S GOING ON?
I FEEL...
LIKE I'VE...
LIKE I'VE DONE SOMETHING REALLY BAD.
YUTAKA, WAIT!
STOP RUNNING!

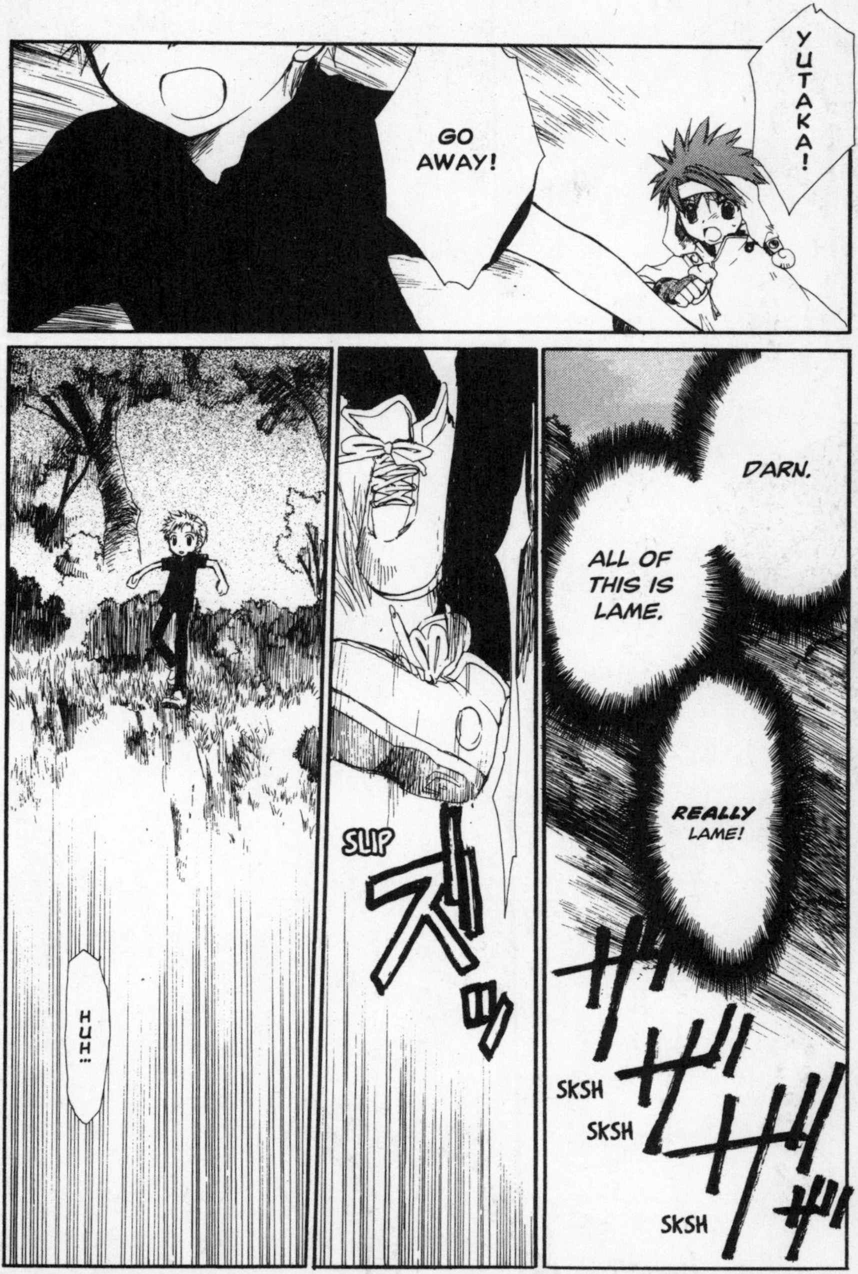
YUTAKA!
GO AWAY!
DARN.
ALL OF THIS IS LAME.
REALLY LAME!
SKSH
SKSH
SKSH
SLIP
HUH!!

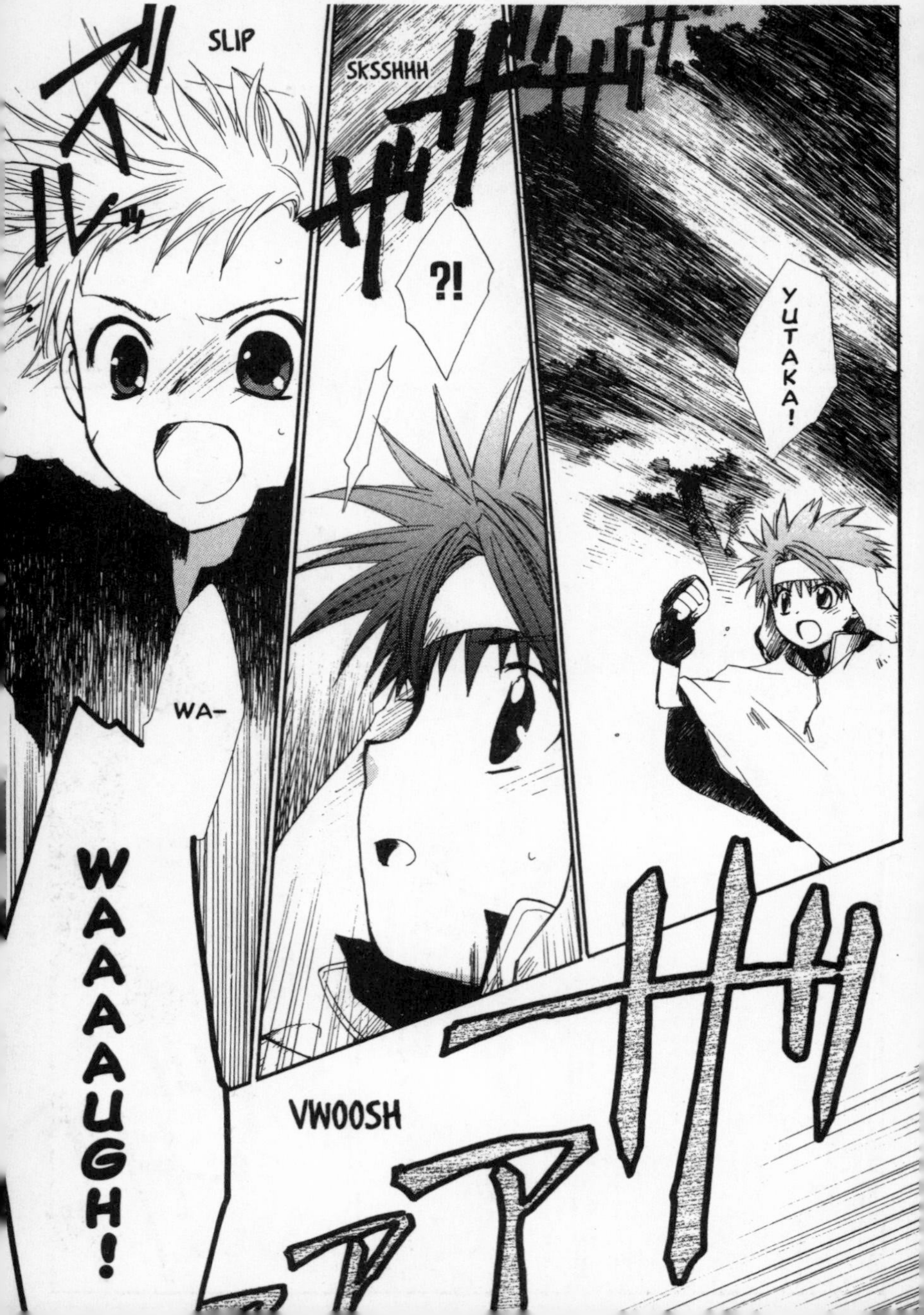
SLIP
SKSSHHH
YUTAKA!
?!
WA-
WAAAAAUGH!
VWOOSH

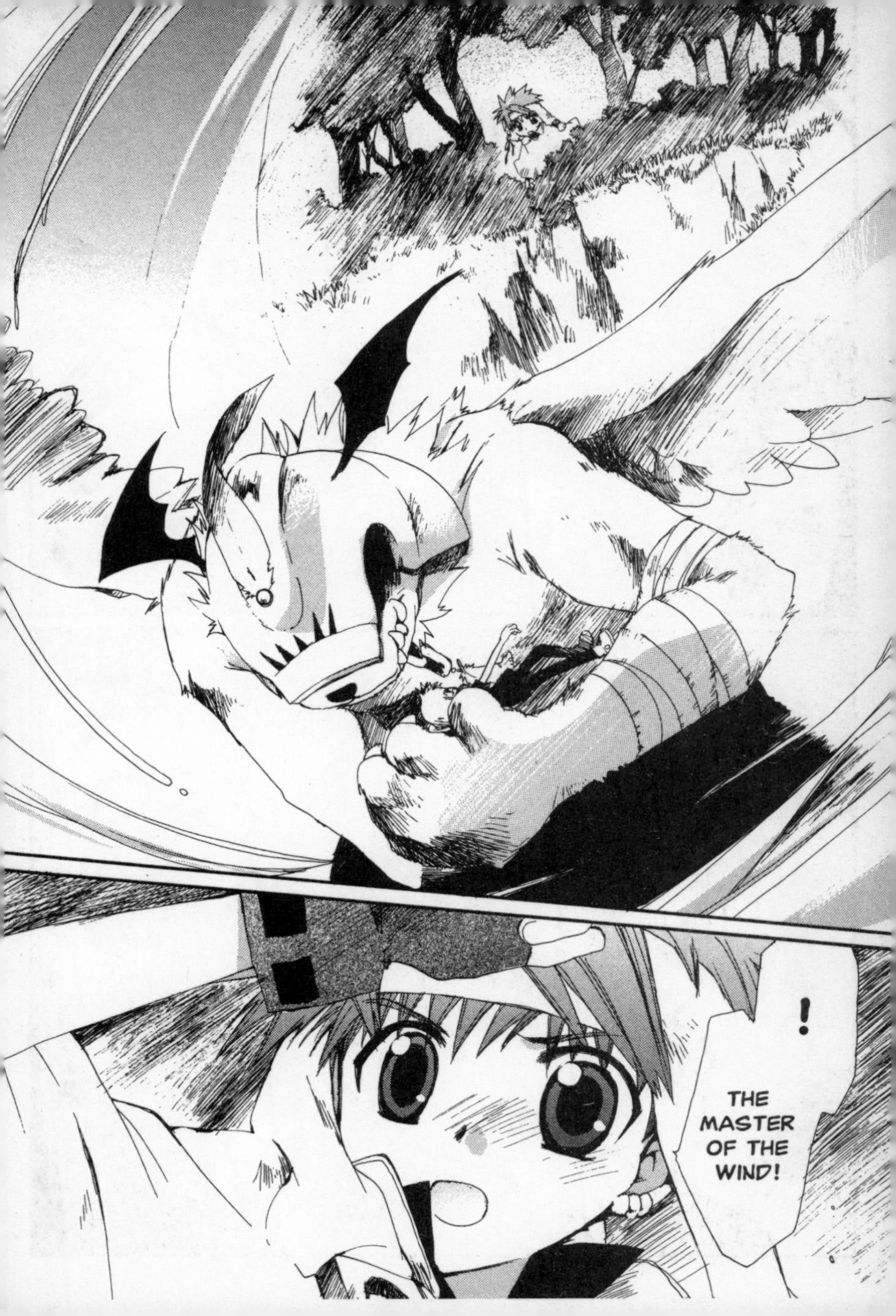
!
THE MASTER OF THE WIND!

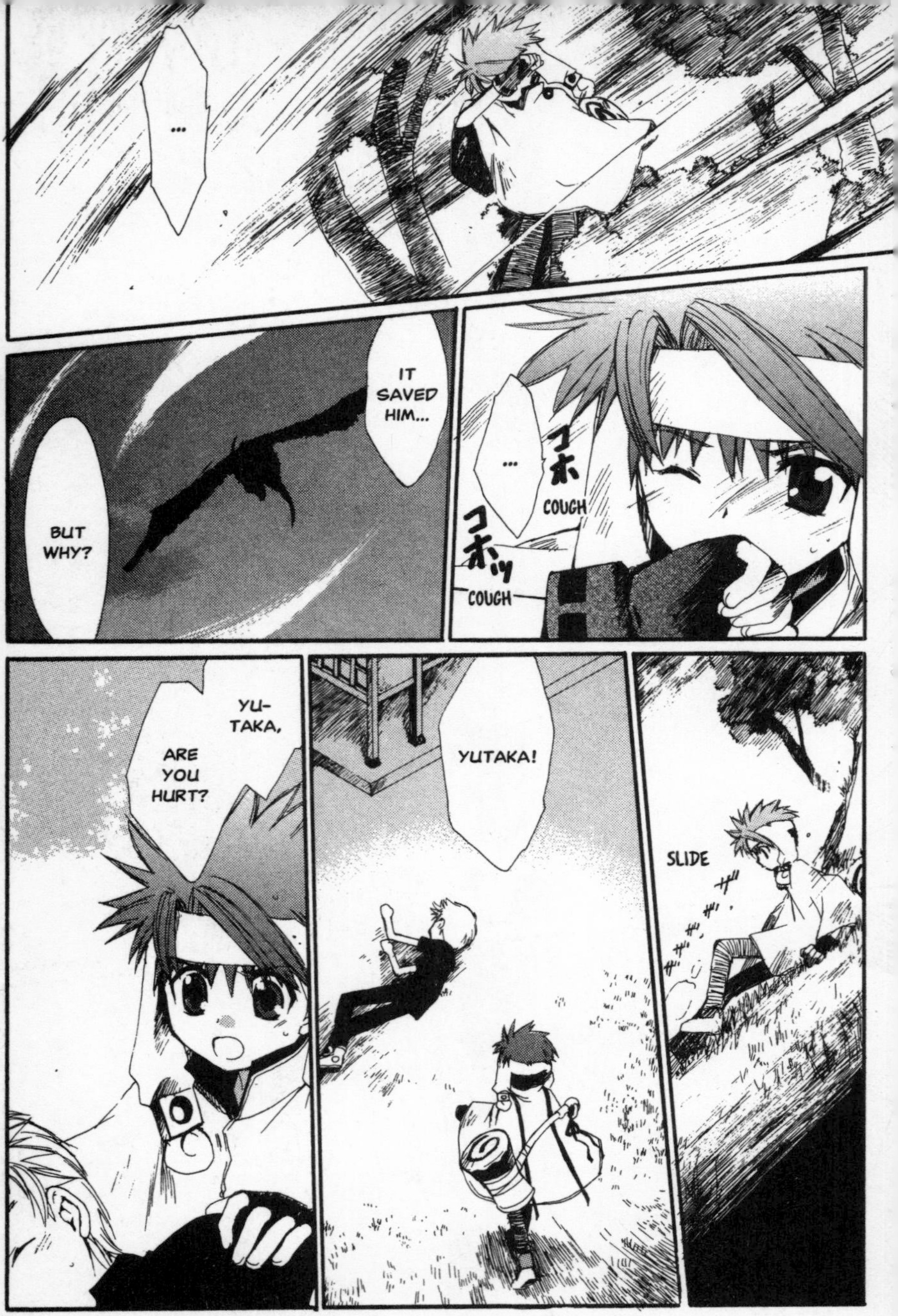
...
...
コホ
COUGH
コホッ
COUGH
IT SAVED HIM...
BUT WHY?
SLIDE
YUTAKA!
YU-TAKA,
ARE YOU HURT?

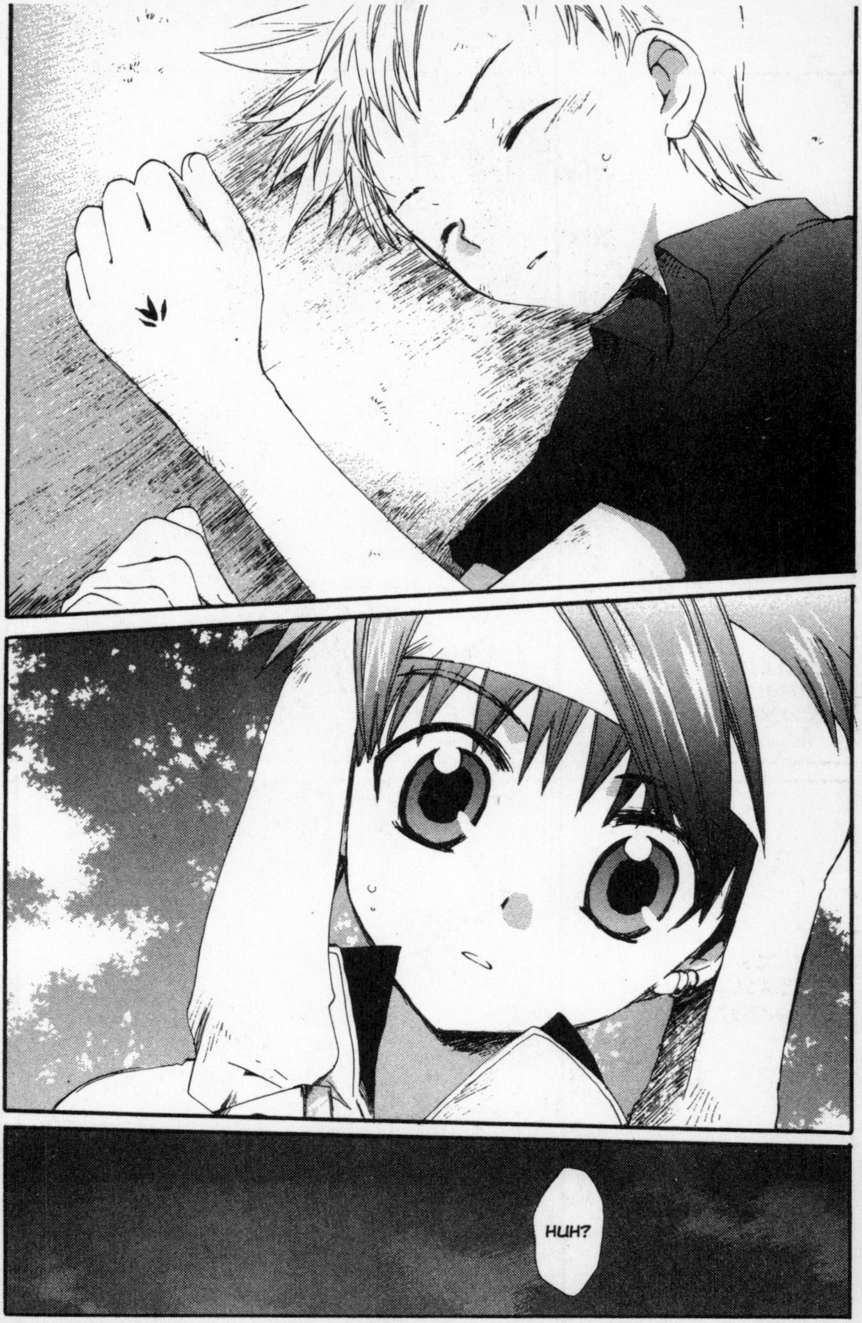
HUH?

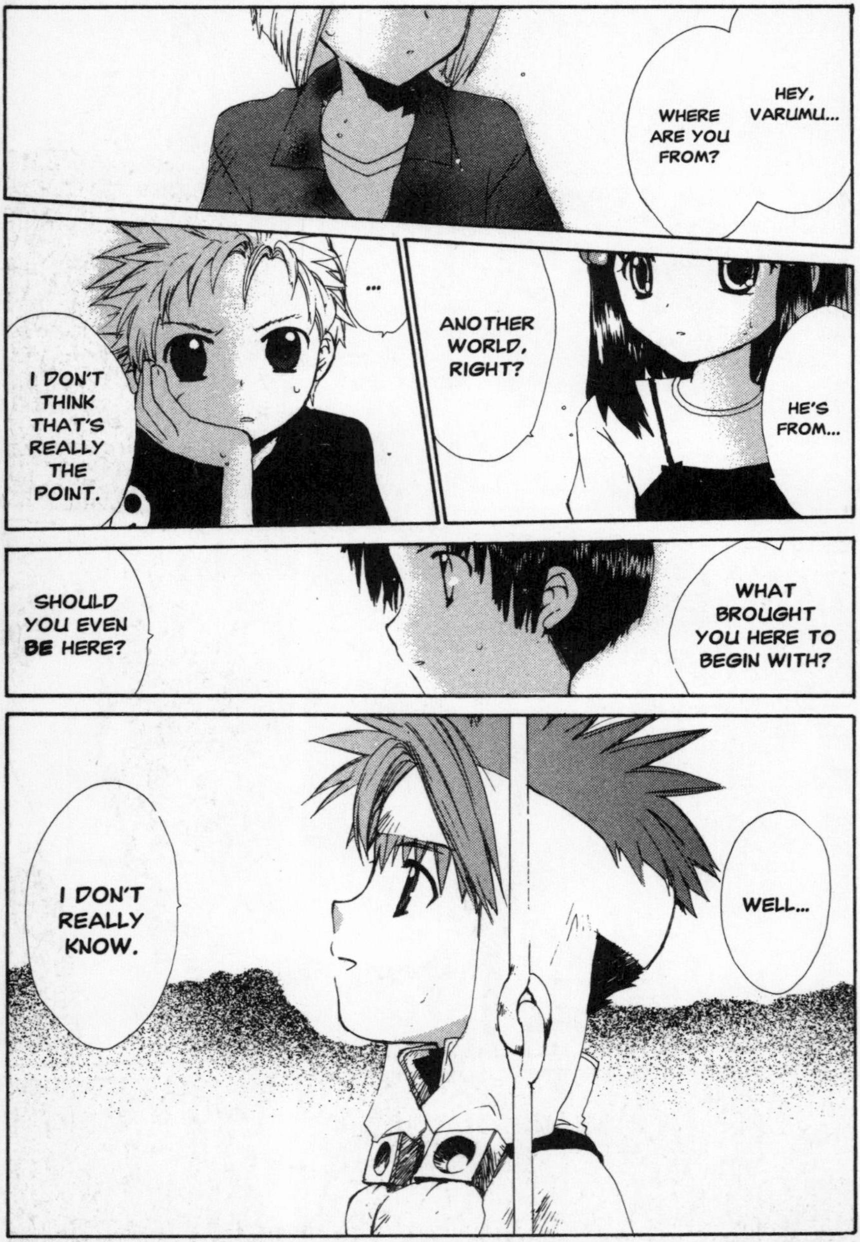
HEY, VARUMU...
WHERE ARE YOU FROM?
HE'S FROM...
ANOTHER WORLD, RIGHT?
...
I DON'T THINK THAT'S REALLY THE POINT.
WHAT BROUGHT YOU HERE TO BEGIN WITH?
SHOULD YOU EVEN **BE** HERE?
WELL...
I DON'T REALLY KNOW.

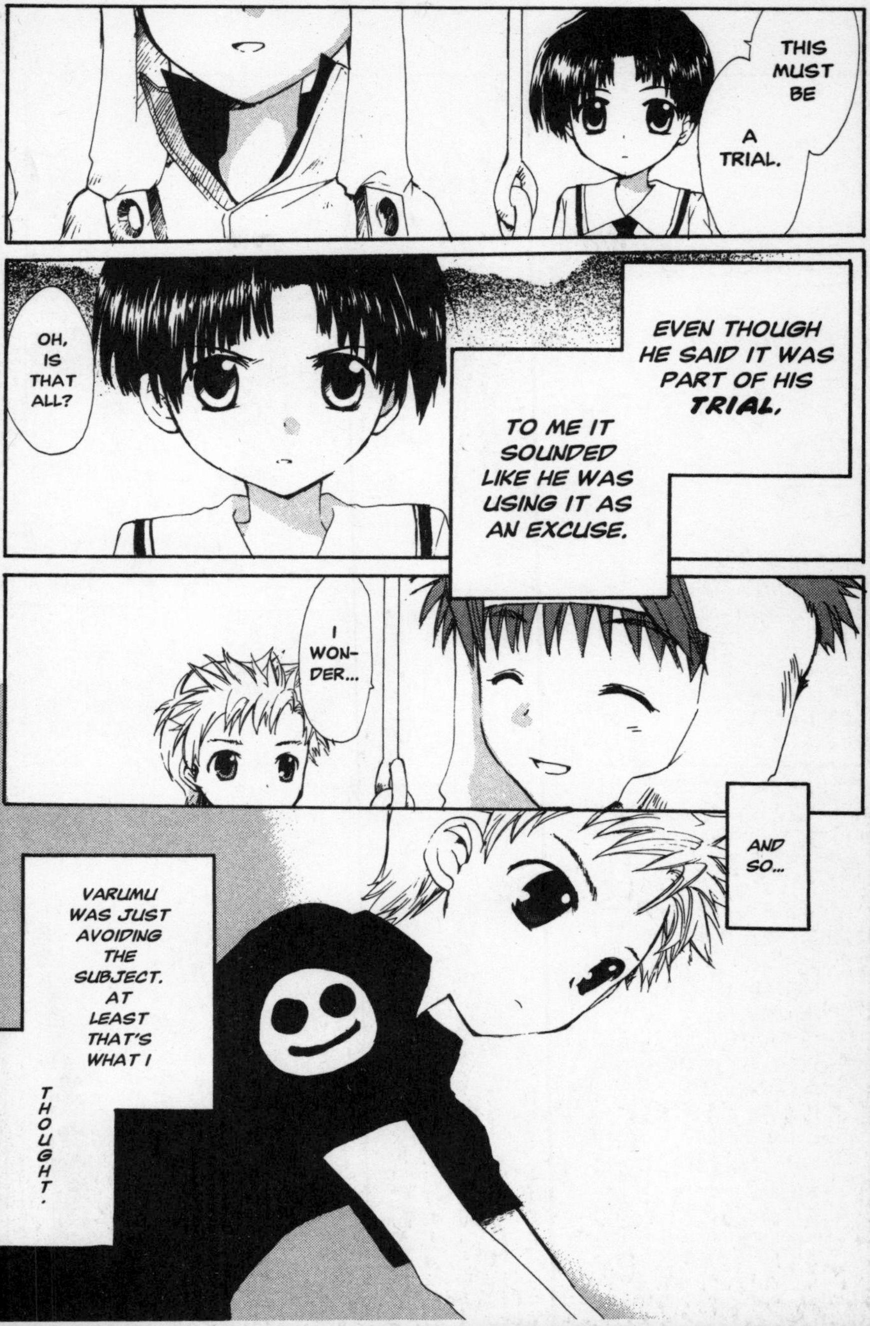
THIS MUST BE A TRIAL.
EVEN THOUGH HE SAID IT WAS PART OF HIS TRIAL,
TO ME IT SOUNDED LIKE HE WAS USING IT AS AN EXCUSE.
OH, IS THAT ALL?
I WONDER...
AND SO...
VARUMU WAS JUST AVOIDING THE SUBJECT. AT LEAST THAT'S WHAT I
THOUGHT.

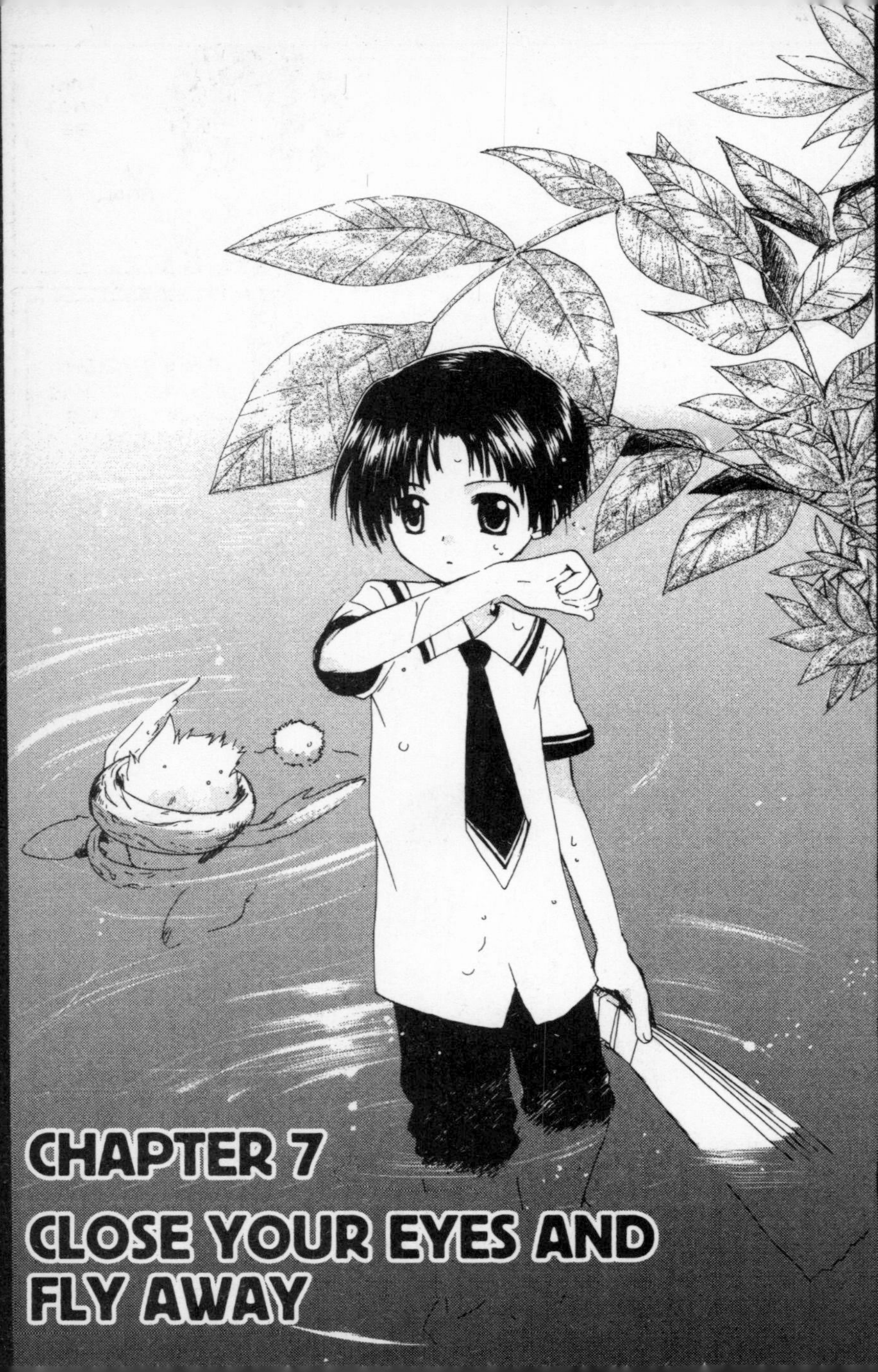
CHAPTER 7
CLOSE YOUR EYES AND FLY AWAY

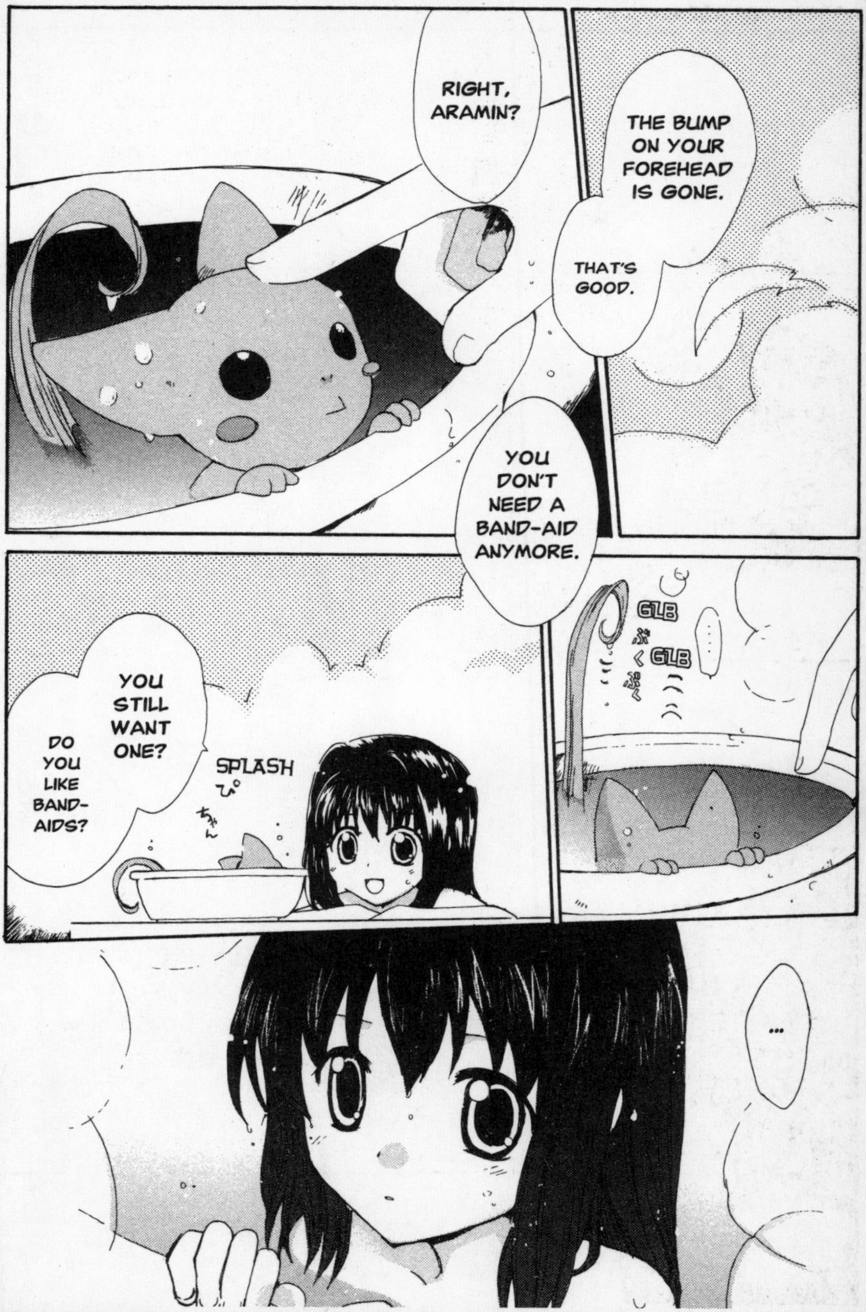
THE BUMP ON YOUR FOREHEAD IS GONE.
THAT'S GOOD.
RIGHT, ARAMIN?
YOU DON'T NEED A BAND-AID ANYMORE.
GLB
ぶく
GLB
ぶく
...
YOU STILL WANT ONE?
DO YOU LIKE BAND-AIDS?
SPLASH
...

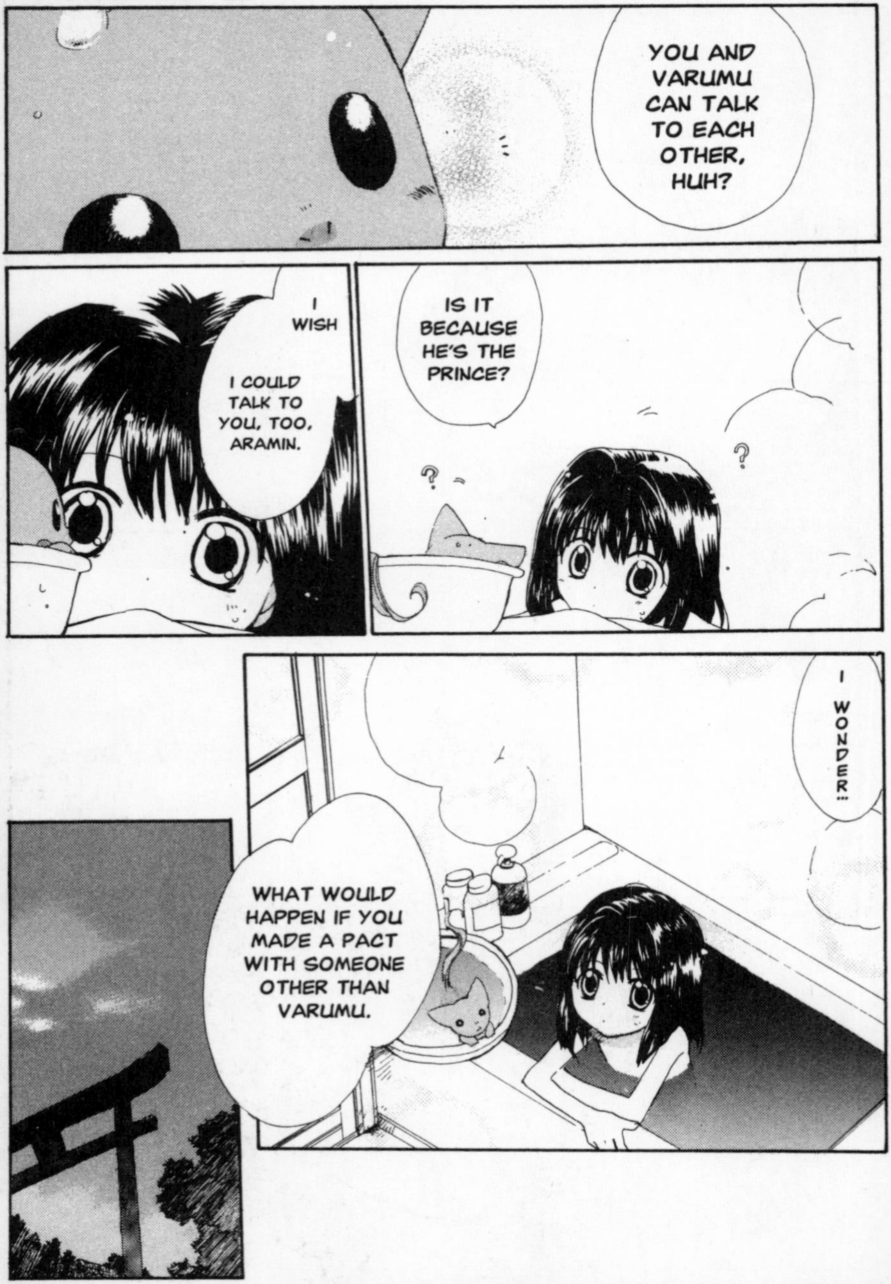
YOU AND VARUMU CAN TALK TO EACH OTHER, HUH?
IS IT BECAUSE HE'S THE PRINCE?
I WISH
I COULD TALK TO YOU, TOO, ARAMIN.
I WONDER...
WHAT WOULD HAPPEN IF YOU MADE A PACT WITH SOMEONE OTHER THAN VARUMU.

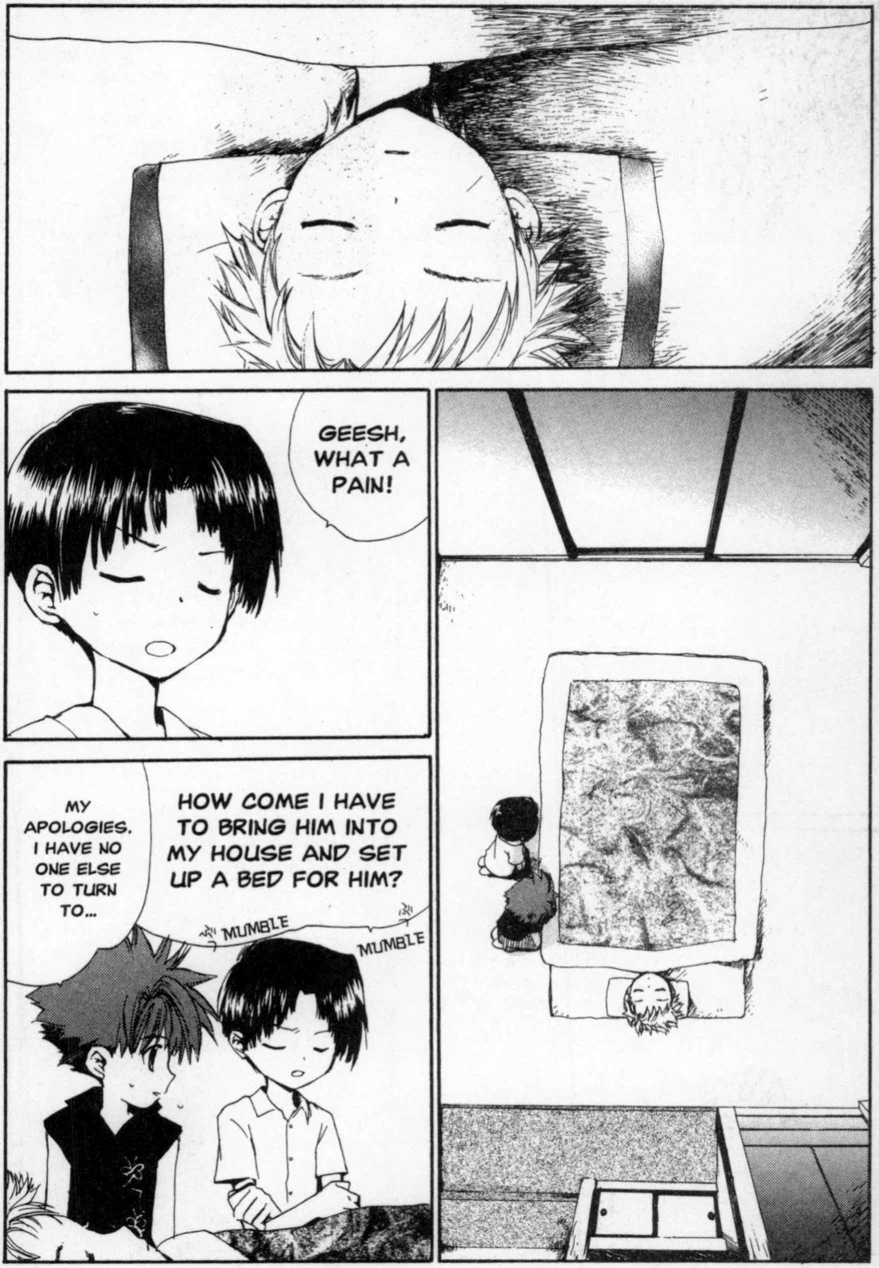
GEESH, WHAT A PAIN!
HOW COME I HAVE TO BRING HIM INTO MY HOUSE AND SET UP A BED FOR HIM?
MUMBLE
MUMBLE
MY APOLOGIES. I HAVE NO ONE ELSE TO TURN TO...

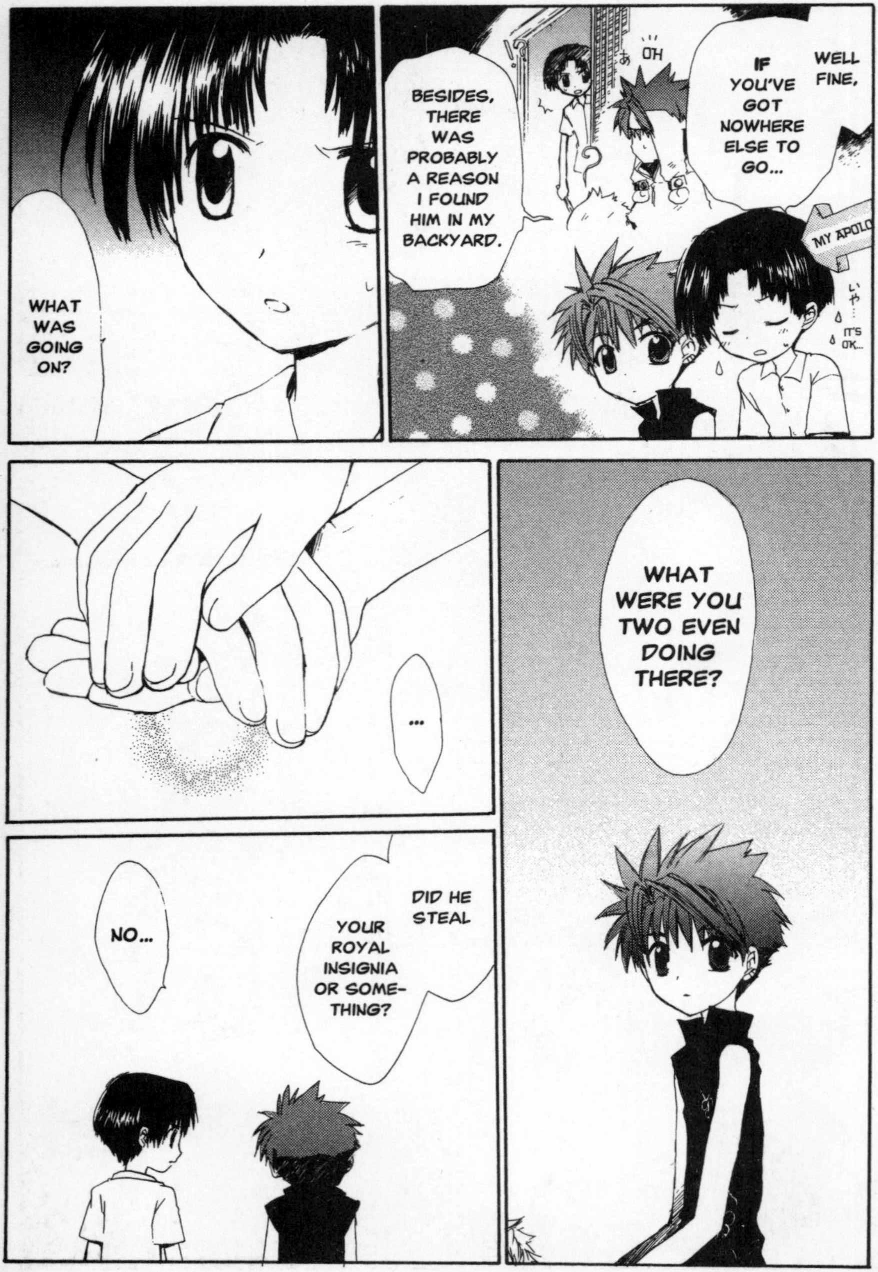
WELL FINE,
IF YOU'VE GOT NOWHERE ELSE TO GO...
あ OH
MY APOLO
いや… IT'S OK...
BESIDES, THERE WAS PROBABLY A REASON I FOUND HIM IN MY BACKYARD.
WHAT WAS GOING ON?
WHAT WERE YOU TWO EVEN DOING THERE?
...
DID HE STEAL YOUR ROYAL INSIGNIA OR SOME-THING?
NO...

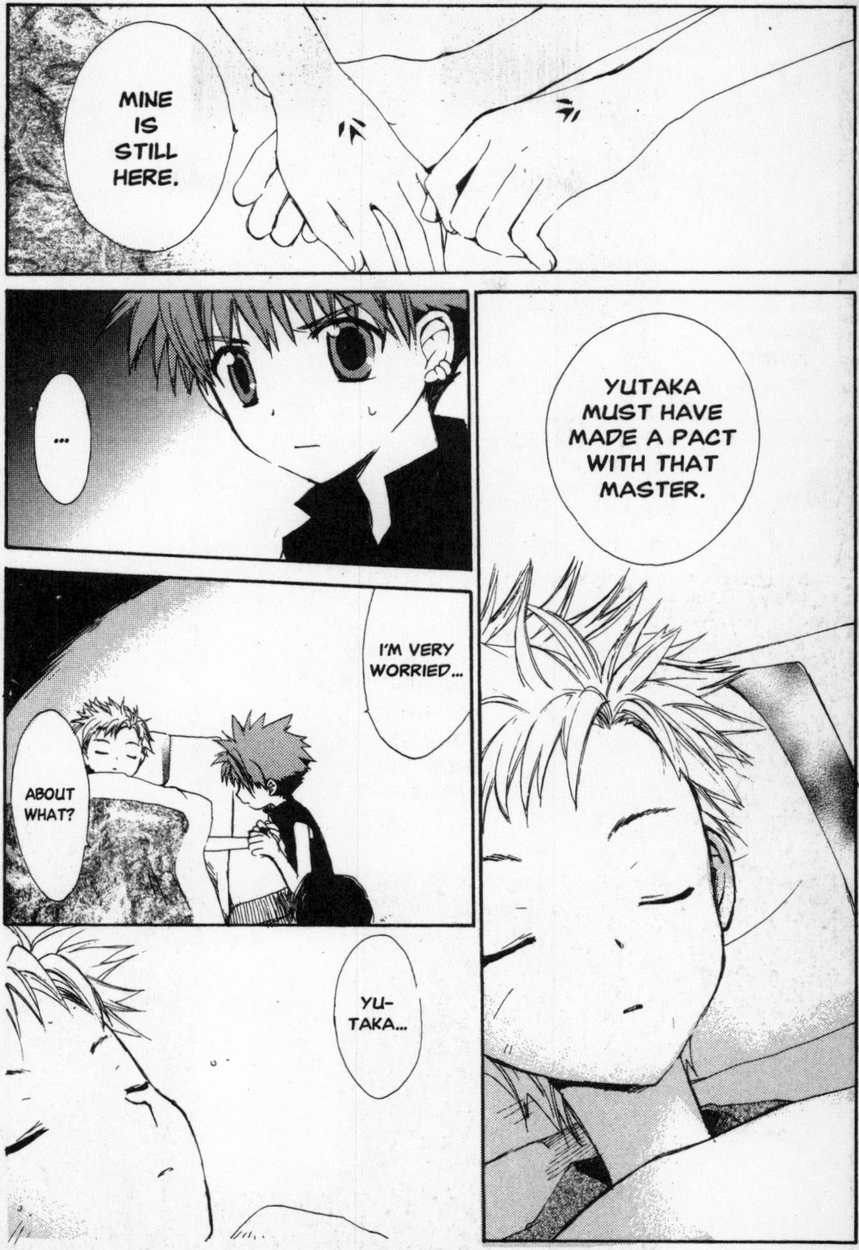
MINE IS STILL HERE.
YUTAKA MUST HAVE MADE A PACT WITH THAT MASTER.
...
I'M VERY WORRIED...
ABOUT WHAT?
YU-TAKA...

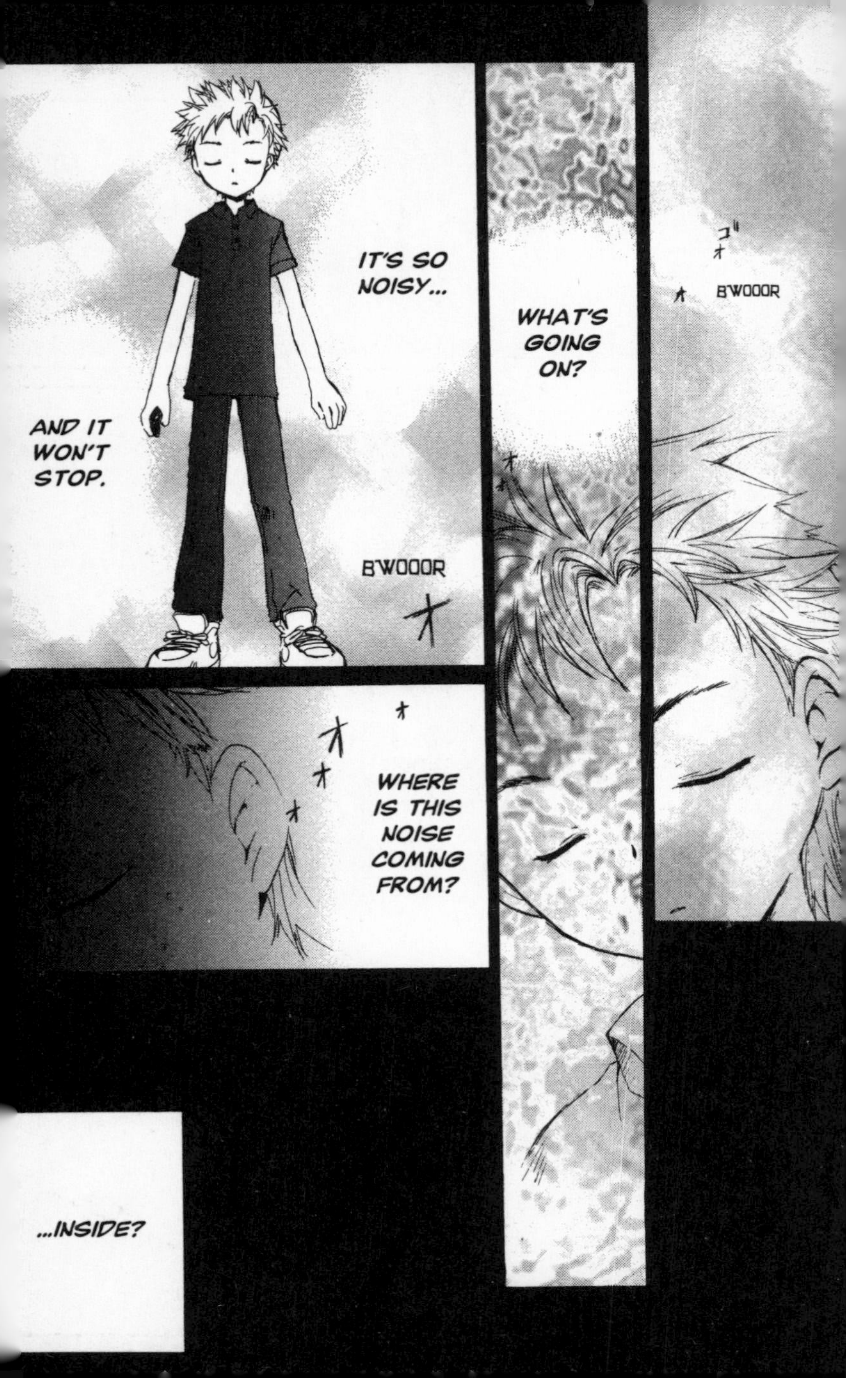
BWOOOR
WHAT'S GOING ON?
IT'S SO NOISY...
AND IT WON'T STOP.
BWOOOR
WHERE IS THIS NOISE COMING FROM?
...INSIDE?

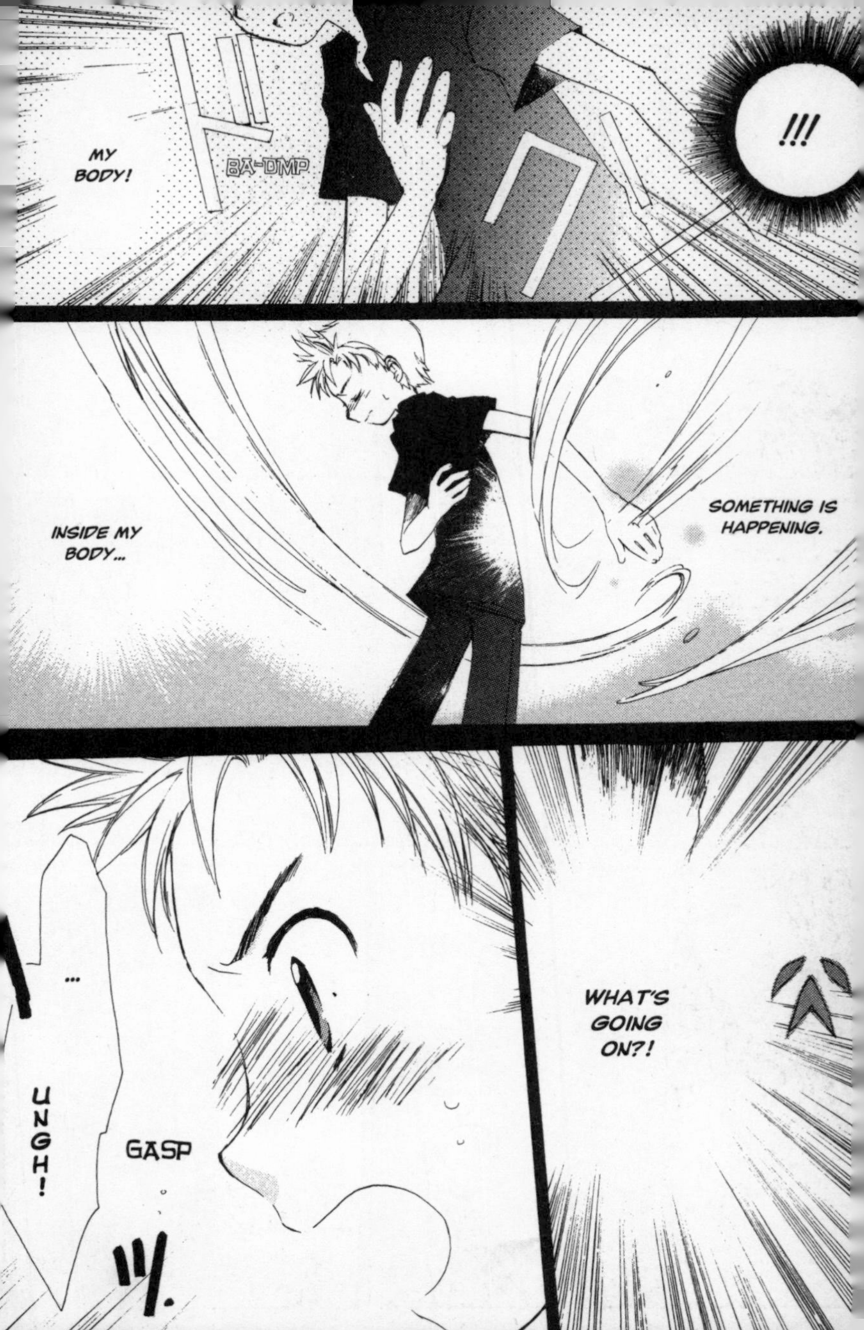
!!!
BA-DMP
MY BODY!
SOMETHING IS HAPPENING.
INSIDE MY BODY...
WHAT'S GOING ON?!
...
GASP
UNGH!

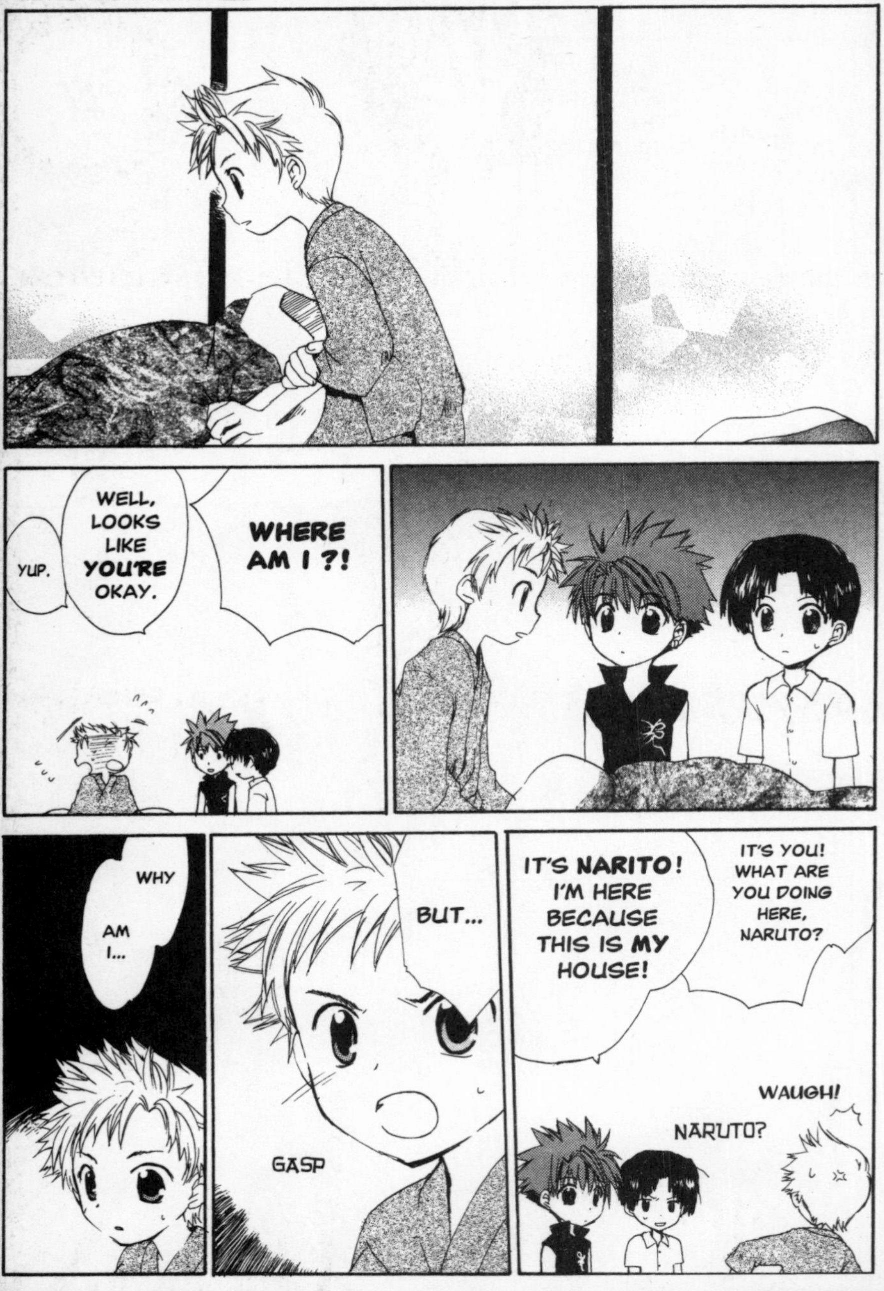
WHERE AM I ?!
WELL, LOOKS LIKE YOU'RE OKAY.
YUP.
IT'S YOU! WHAT ARE YOU DOING HERE, NARUTO?
IT'S NARITO! I'M HERE BECAUSE THIS IS MY HOUSE!
WAUGH!
NARUTO?
BUT...
GASP
WHY
AM I...

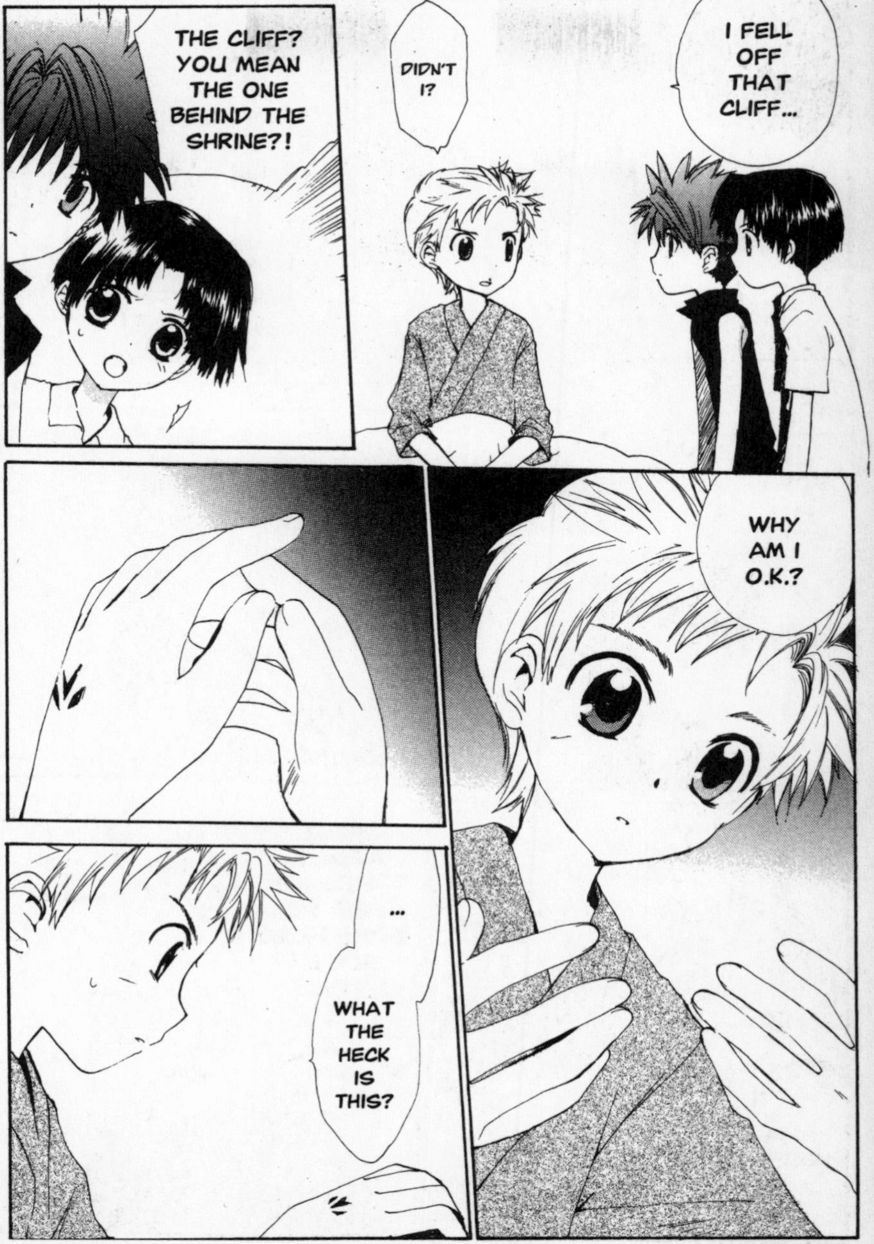
I FELL OFF THAT CLIFF...
DIDN'T I?
THE CLIFF? YOU MEAN THE ONE BEHIND THE SHRINE?!
WHY AM I O.K.?
...
WHAT THE HECK IS THIS?

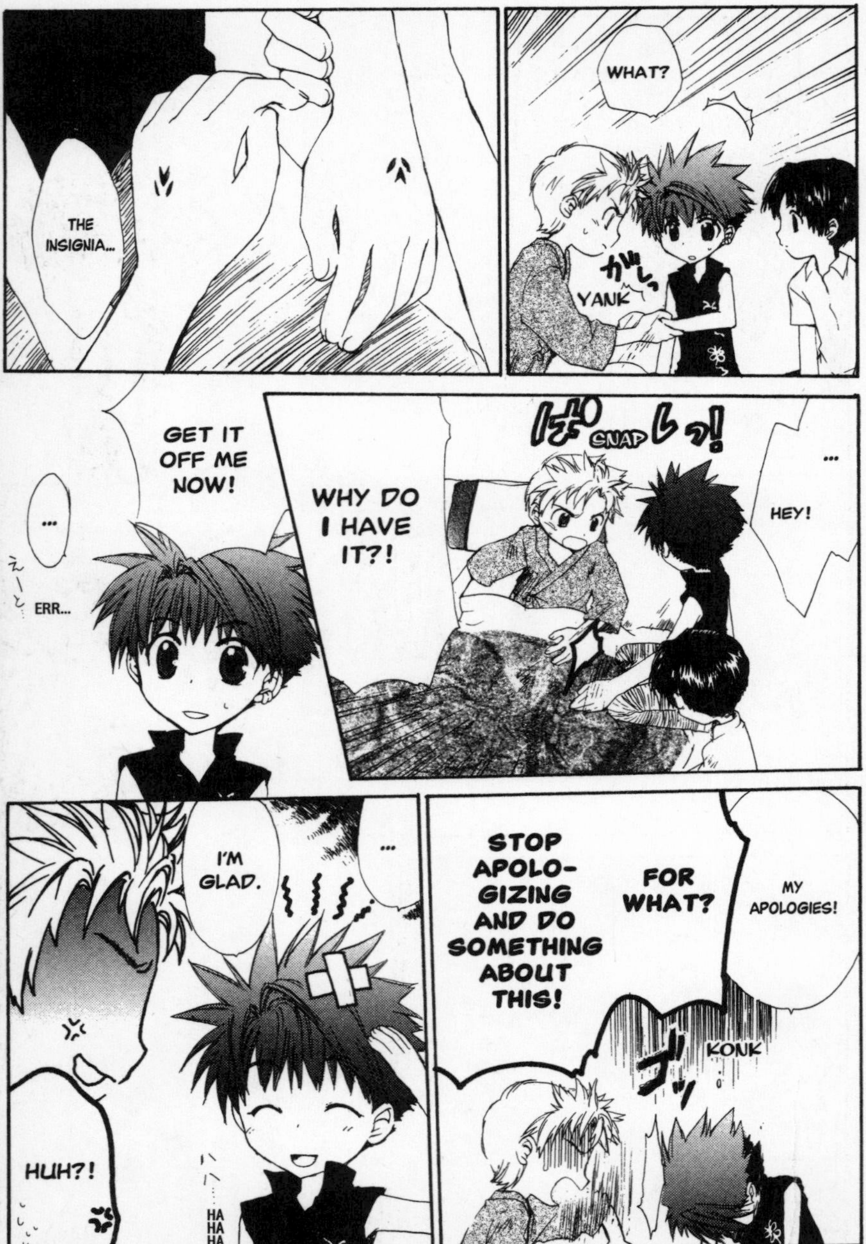
WHAT?
YANK
THE INSIGNIA...
...
HEY!
SNAP
WHY DO I HAVE IT?!
GET IT OFF ME NOW!
...
えーと… ERR...
MY APOLOGIES!
FOR WHAT?
STOP APOLOGIZING AND DO SOMETHING ABOUT THIS!
KONK
...
I'M GLAD.
HUH?!
HA HA HA

PACT?

...

SINCE MAKING PACTS IS A FOREIGN CONCEPT TO YOU,

I THOUGHT IT'D ONLY BE A BURDEN.

A PACT IS...

WHAT I WANT TO KNOW IS WHY THIS IS ON MY HAND!

BURDEN...

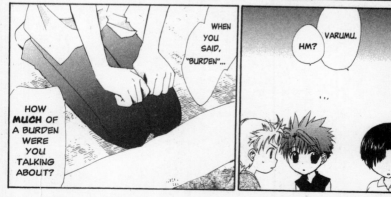

WHEN YOU SAID, "BURDEN"...

HOW MUCH OF A BURDEN WERE YOU TALKING ABOUT?

HM?

VARUMU.

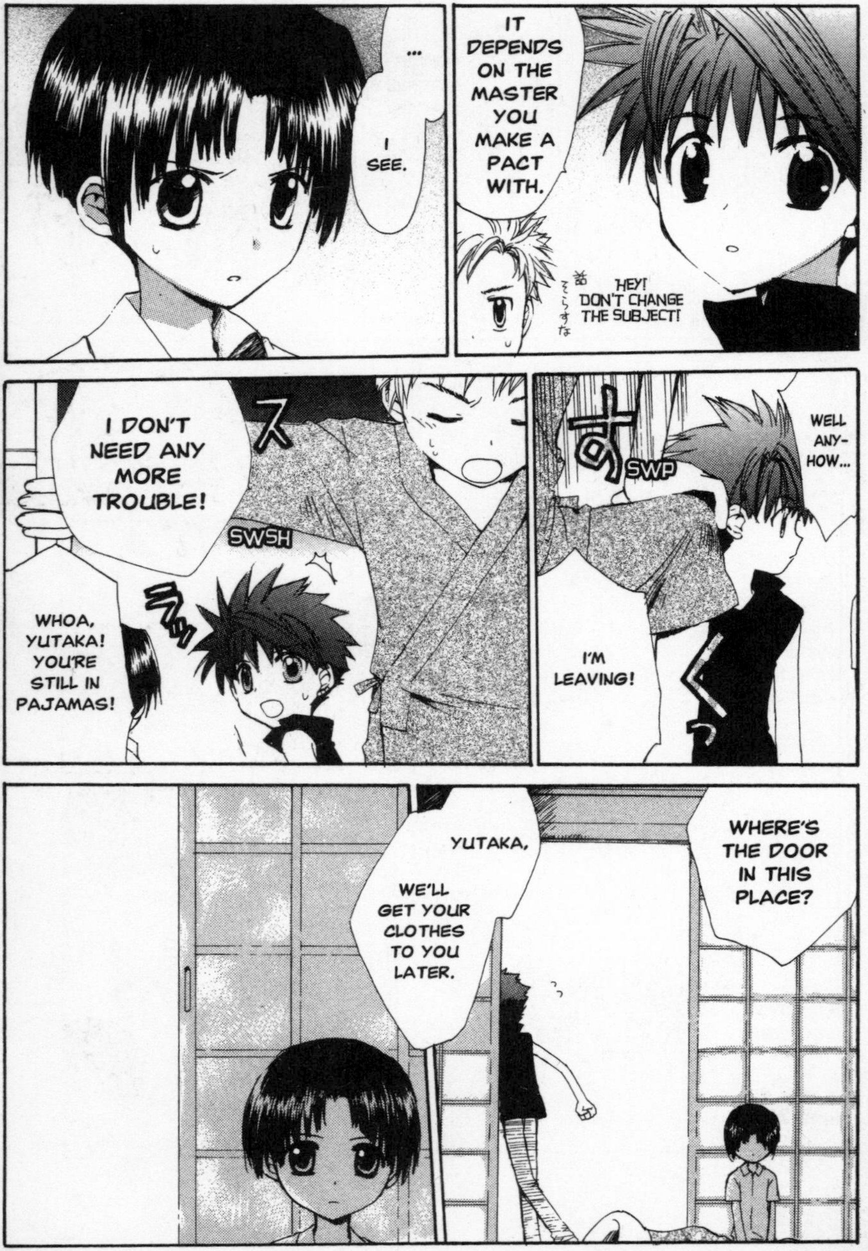
IT DEPENDS ON THE MASTER YOU MAKE A PACT WITH.
HEY! DON'T CHANGE THE SUBJECT!
話そらすな
... I SEE.
WELL ANYHOW...
す
SWP
I'M LEAVING!
I DON'T NEED ANY MORE TROUBLE!
ス
SWSH
WHOA, YUTAKA! YOU'RE STILL IN PAJAMAS!
WHERE'S THE DOOR IN THIS PLACE?
YUTAKA,
WE'LL GET YOUR CLOTHES TO YOU LATER.

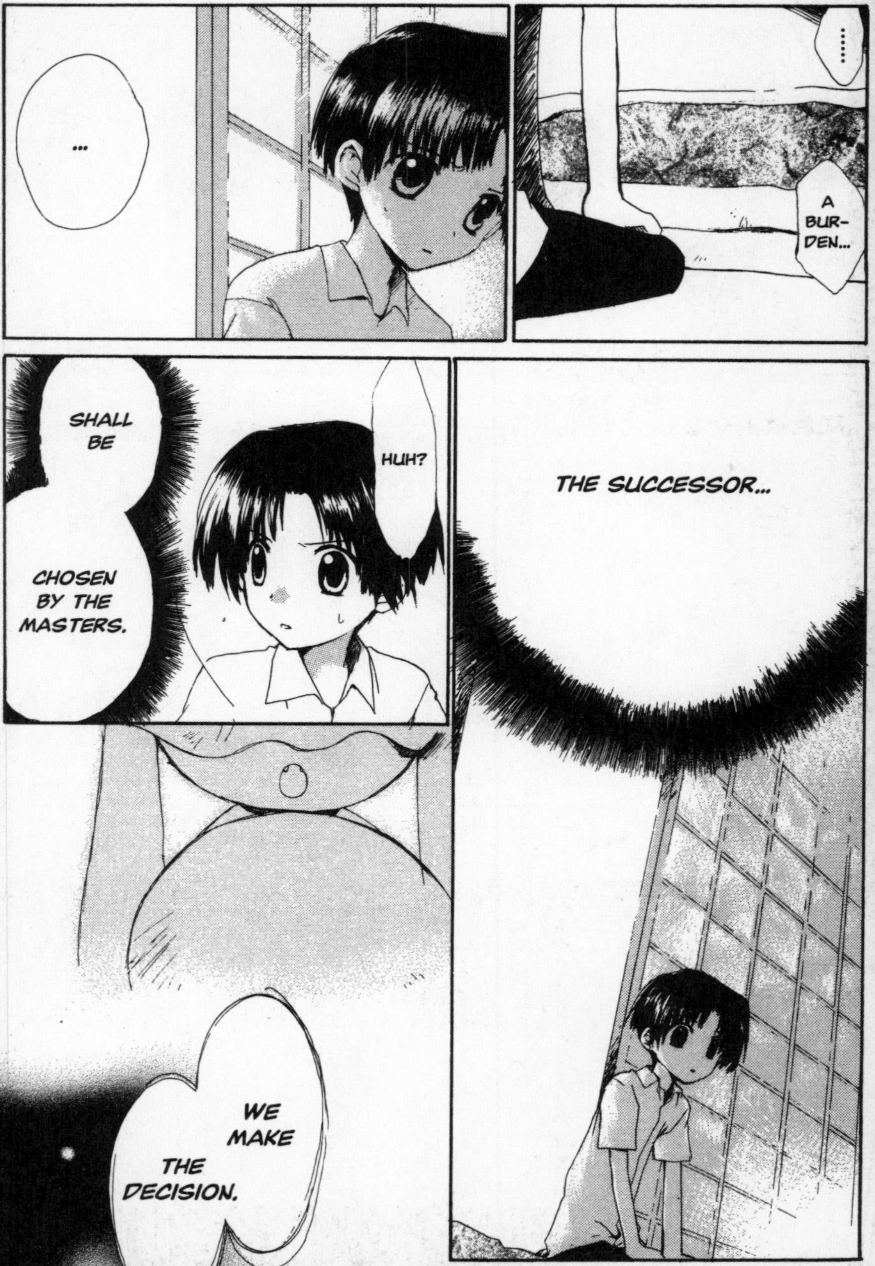
……
A BURDEN...
...
THE SUCCESSOR...
SHALL BE CHOSEN BY THE MASTERS.
HUH?
WE MAKE THE DECISION.

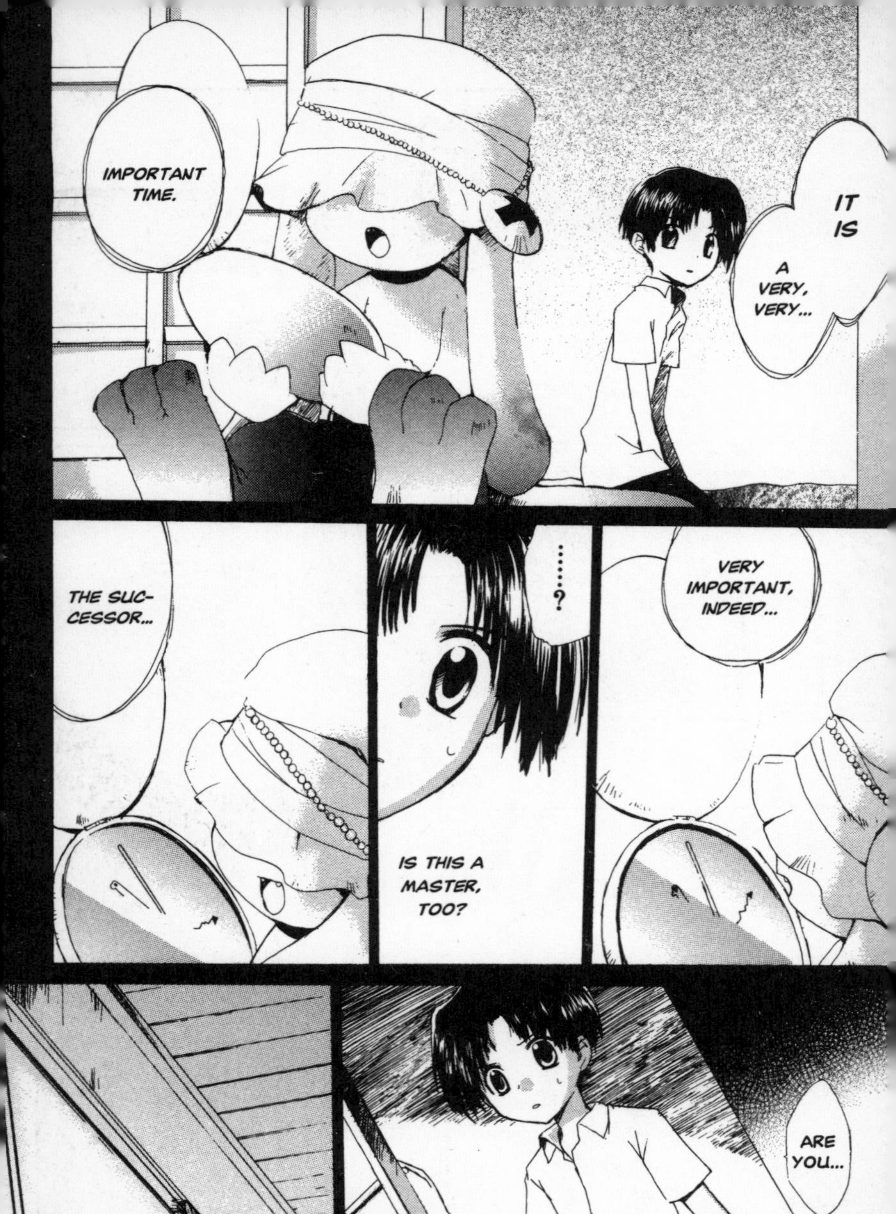
IT IS A VERY, VERY...
IMPORTANT TIME.
VERY IMPORTANT, INDEED...
......?
IS THIS A MASTER, TOO?
THE SUC-CESSOR...
ARE YOU...

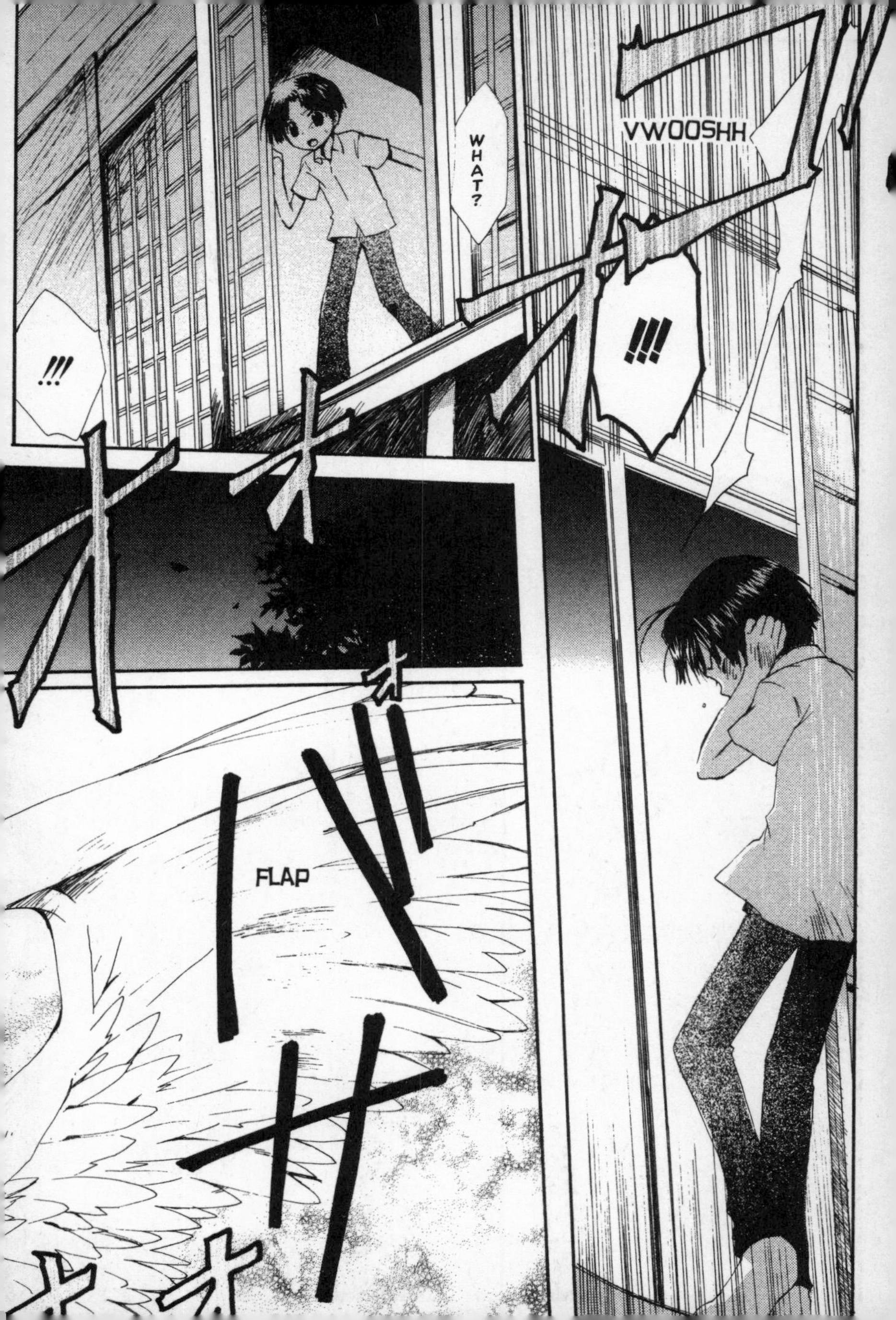
VWOOSHH
!!!!
WHAT?
!!!
FLAP

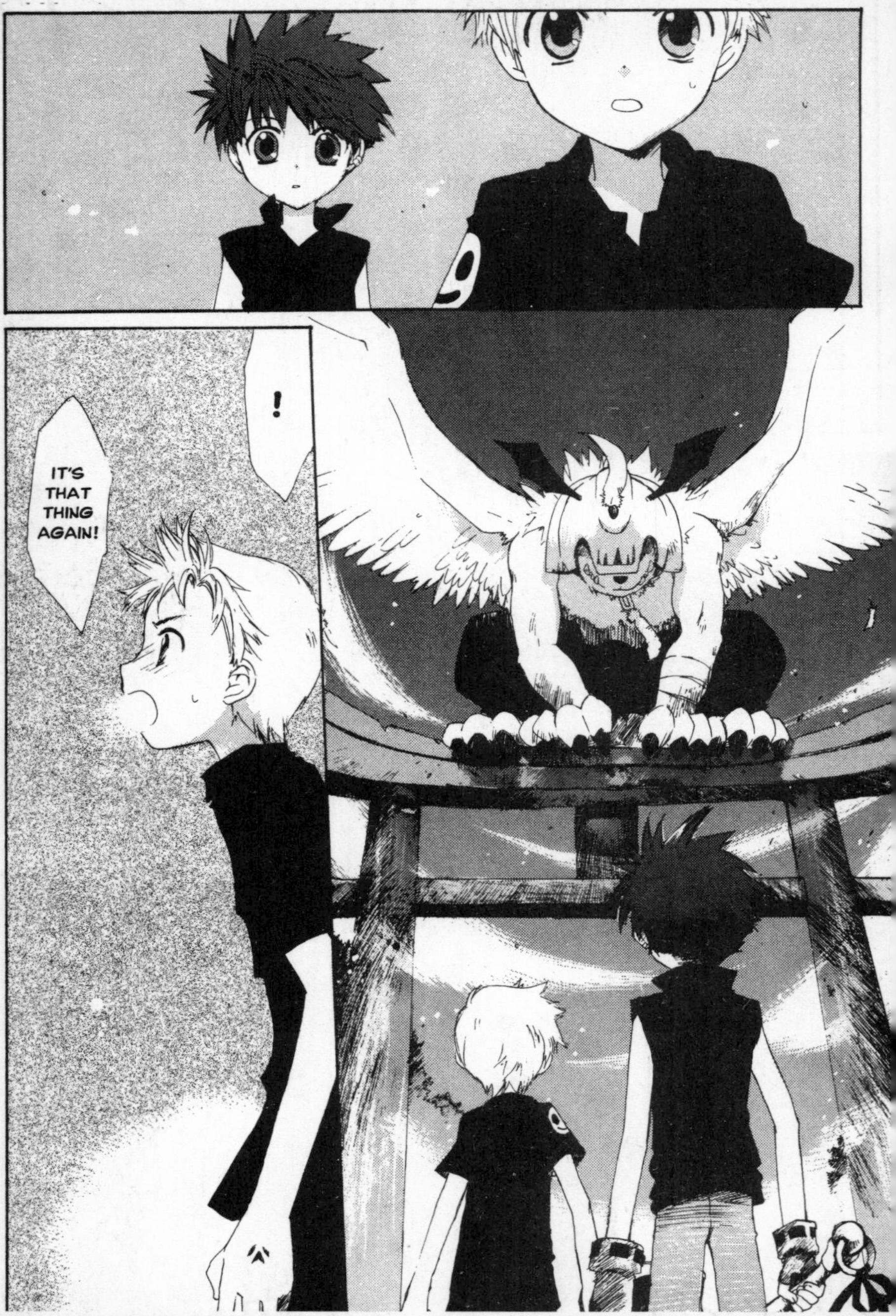
!
IT'S THAT THING AGAIN!

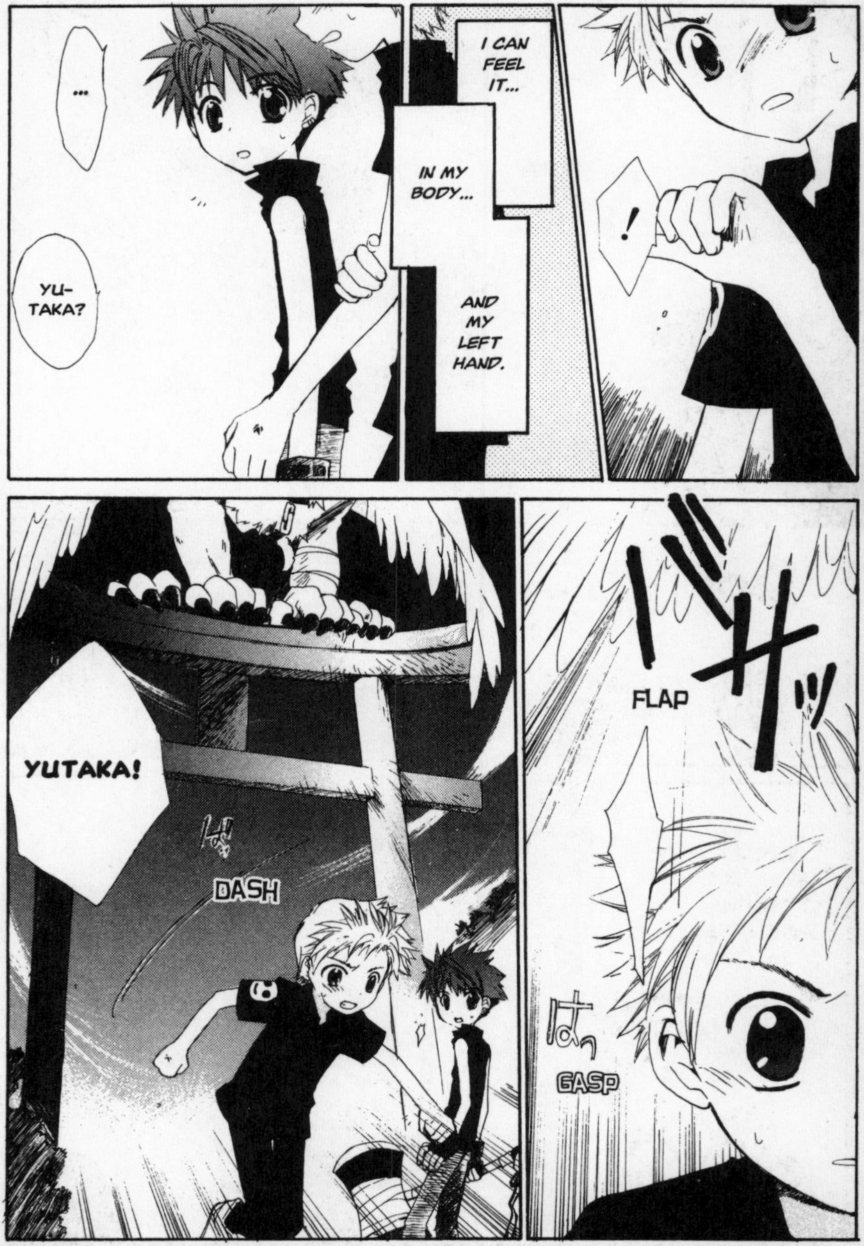
!
I CAN FEEL IT...
IN MY BODY...
AND MY LEFT HAND.
...
YU-TAKA?
バサッ
FLAP
はっ
GASP
YUTAKA!
DASH

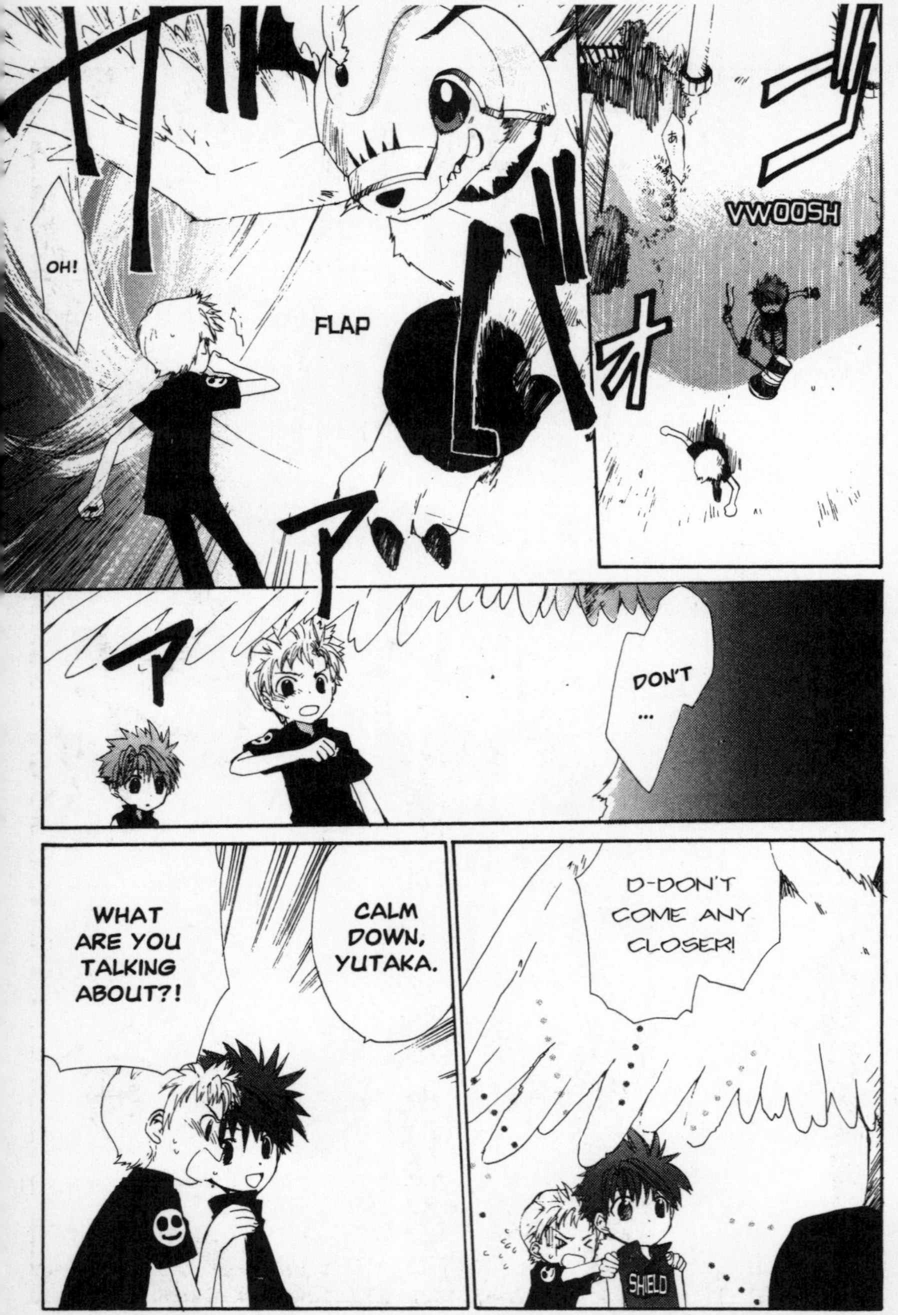
VWOOSH
OH!
FLAP
DON'T ...
D-DON'T COME ANY CLOSER!
SHIELD
CALM DOWN, YUTAKA.
WHAT ARE YOU TALKING ABOUT?!

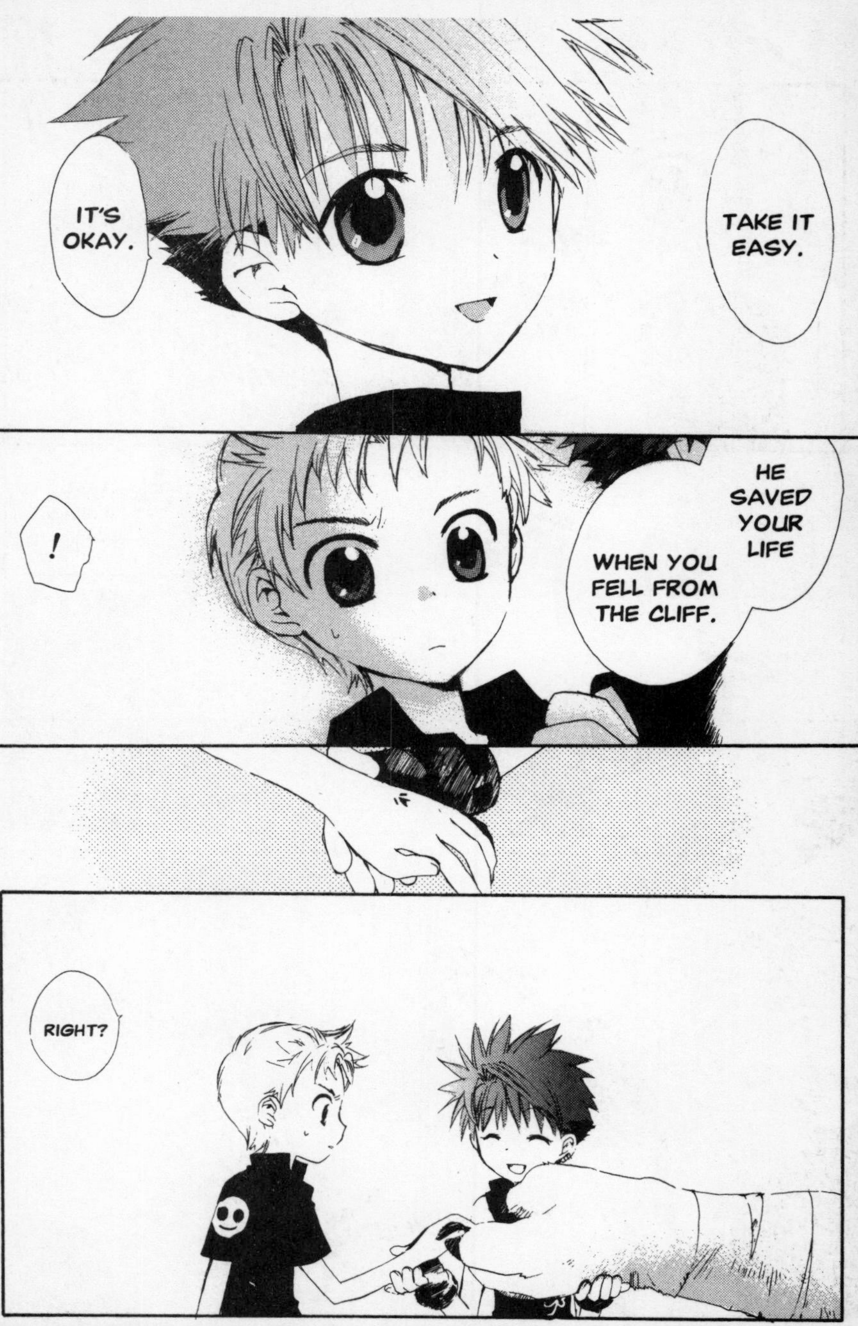
TAKE IT EASY.
IT'S OKAY.
HE SAVED YOUR LIFE
WHEN YOU FELL FROM THE CLIFF.
!
RIGHT?

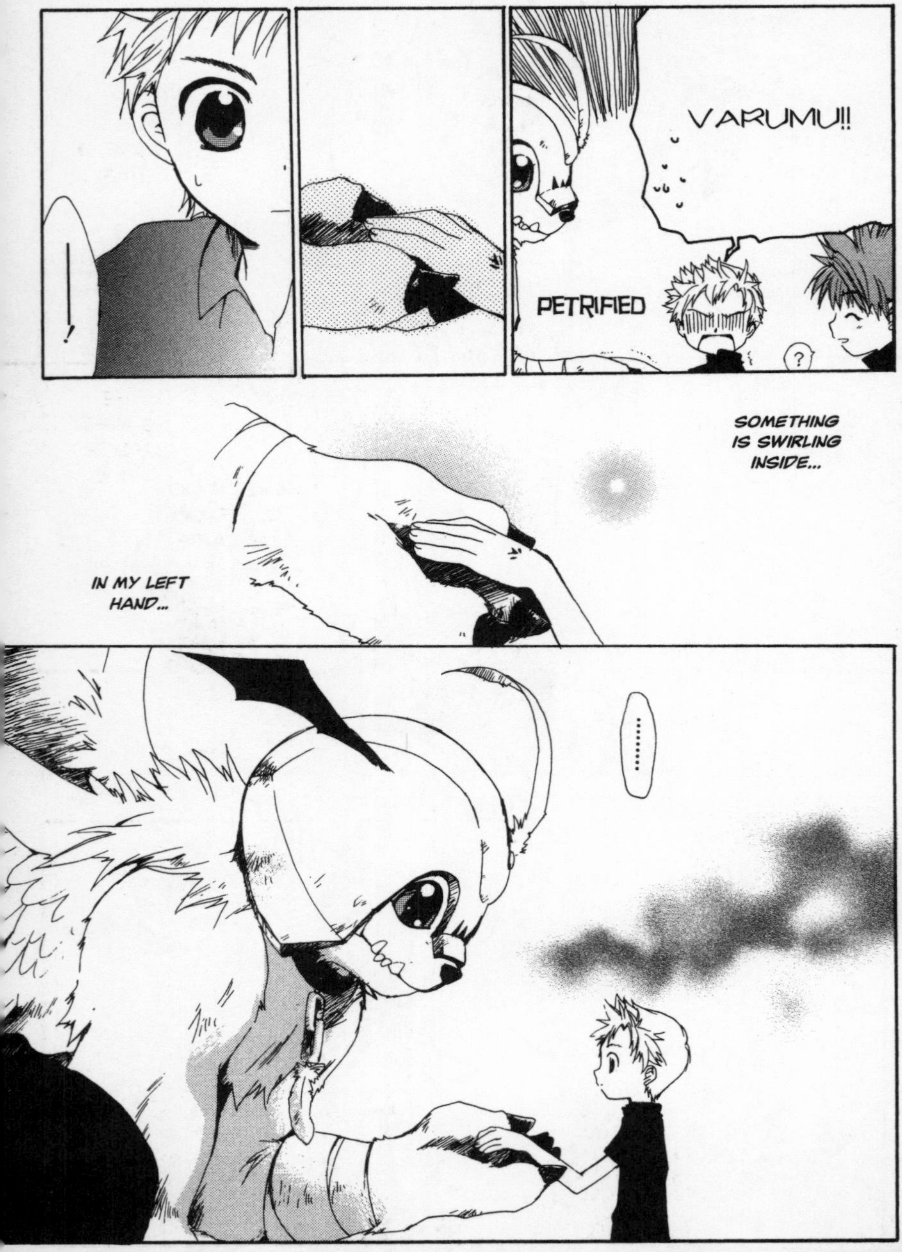

!
VARUMU!!
PETRIFIED
?
SOMETHING IS SWIRLING INSIDE...
IN MY LEFT HAND...
......

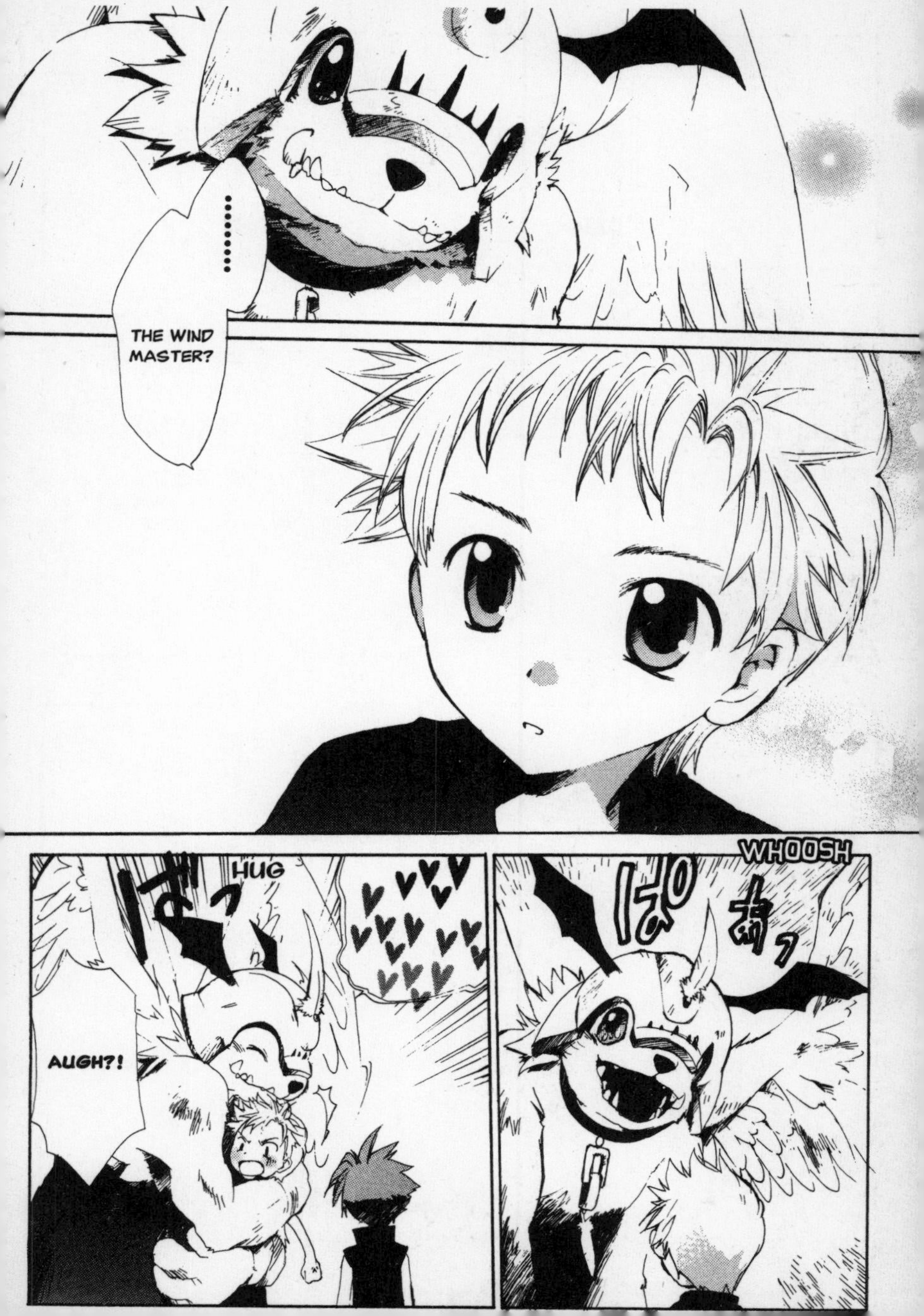
....
THE WIND MASTER?
WHOOSH
HUG
AUGH?!

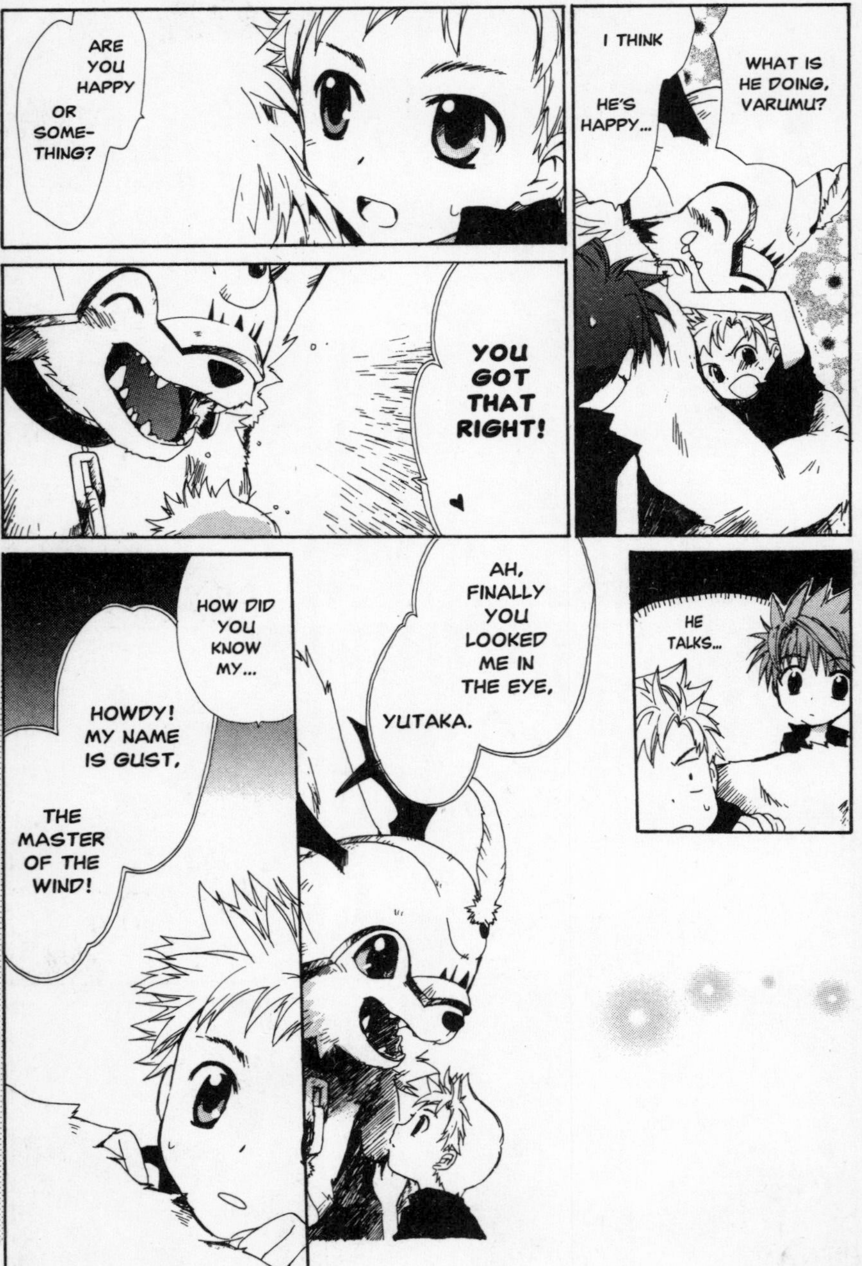
WHAT IS HE DOING, VARUMU?
I THINK HE'S HAPPY...
ARE YOU HAPPY OR SOMETHING?
YOU GOT THAT RIGHT!
HE TALKS...
AH, FINALLY YOU LOOKED ME IN THE EYE, YUTAKA.
HOW DID YOU KNOW MY...
HOWDY! MY NAME IS GUST, THE MASTER OF THE WIND!

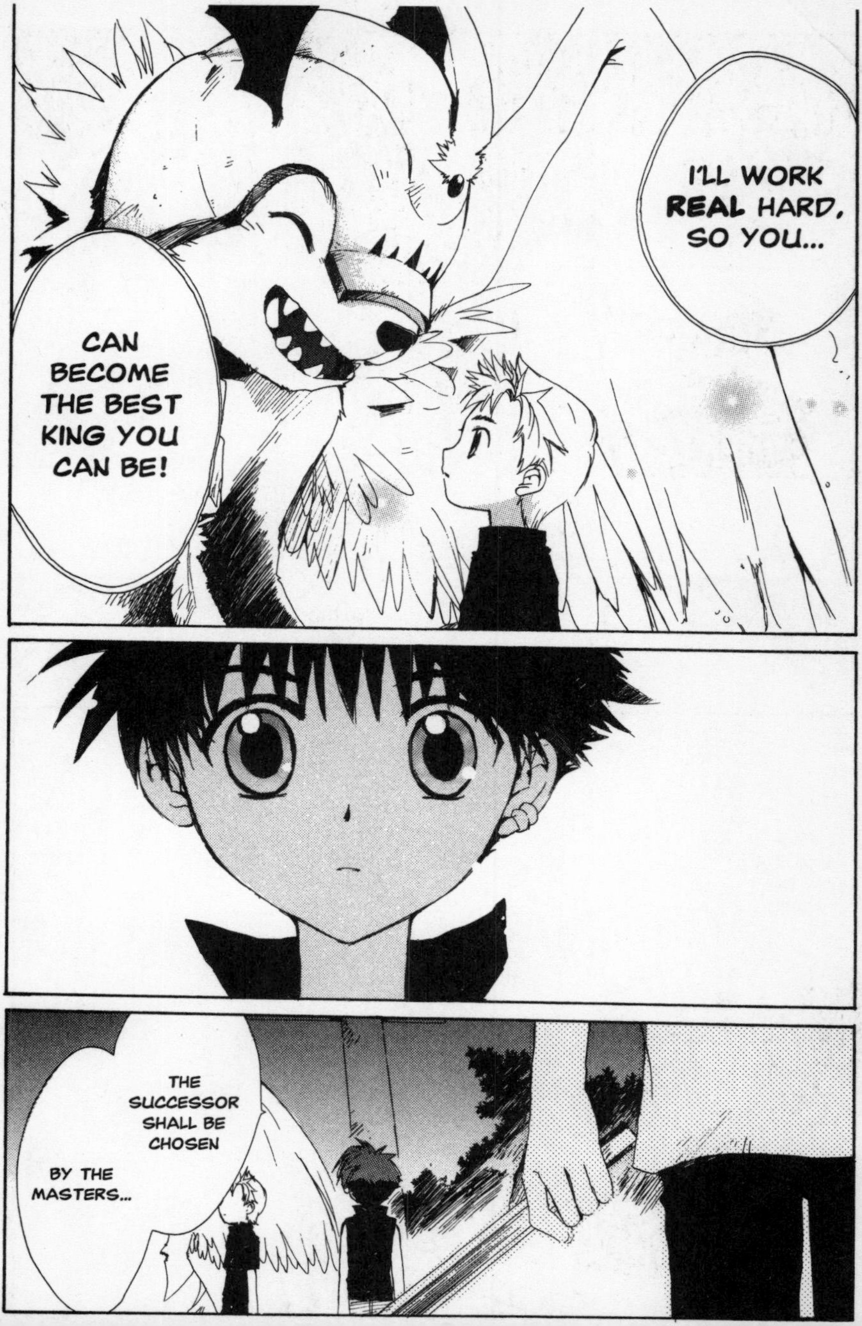
I'LL WORK REAL HARD, SO YOU...
CAN BECOME THE BEST KING YOU CAN BE!
THE SUCCESSOR SHALL BE CHOSEN
BY THE MASTERS...

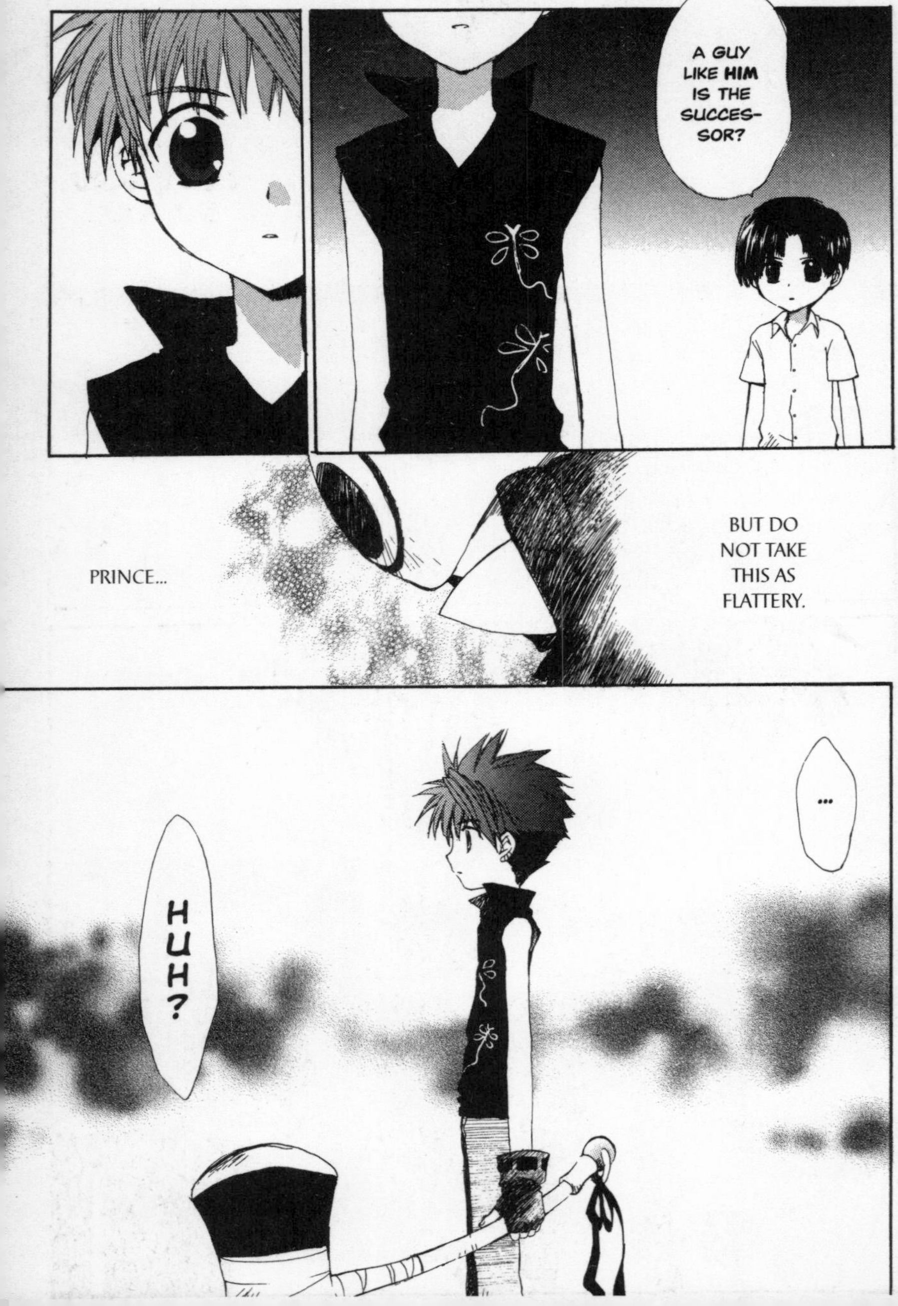
A GUY LIKE HIM IS THE SUCCESSOR?
BUT DO NOT TAKE THIS AS FLATTERY.
PRINCE...
...
HUH?

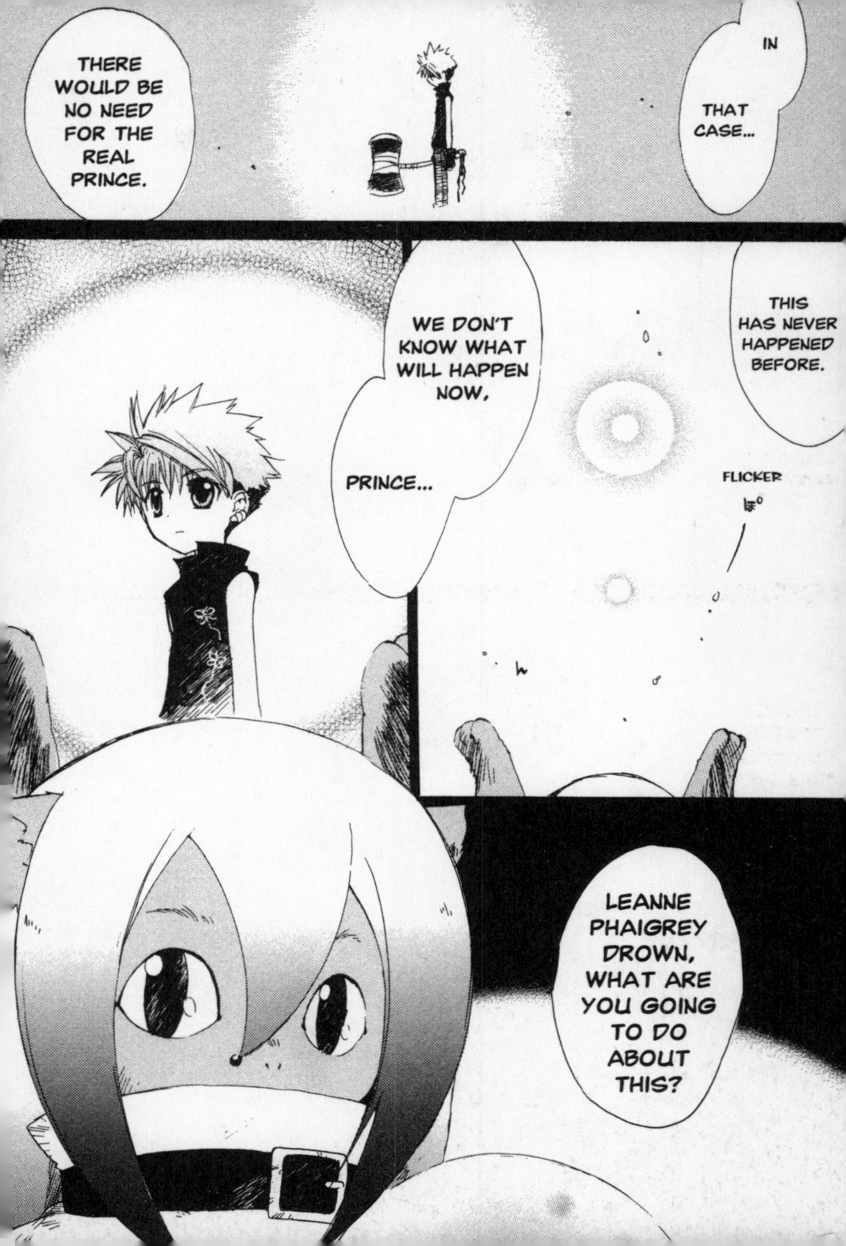

IN THAT CASE...
THERE WOULD BE NO NEED FOR THE REAL PRINCE.
THIS HAS NEVER HAPPENED BEFORE.
FLICKER
ぽ
WE DON'T KNOW WHAT WILL HAPPEN NOW,
PRINCE...
LEANNE PHAIGREY DROWN, WHAT ARE YOU GOING TO DO ABOUT THIS?

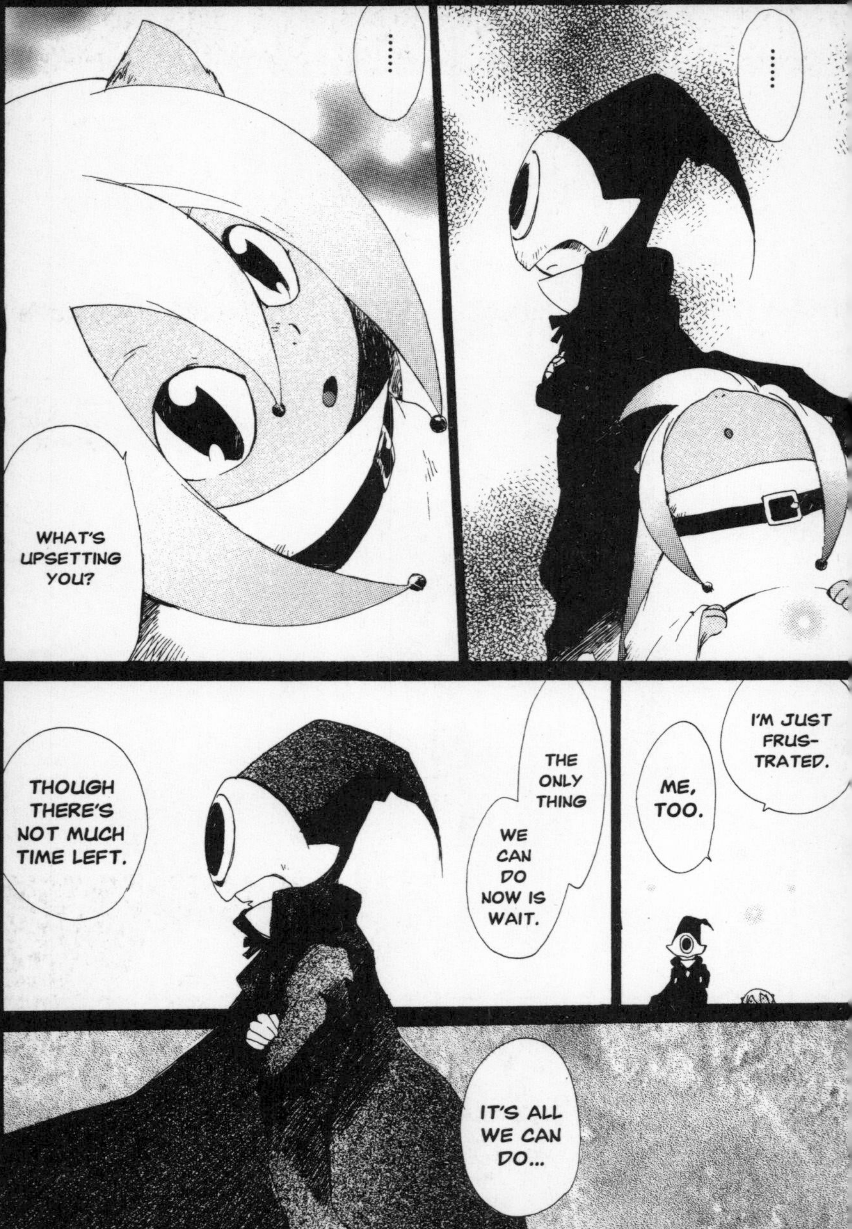
……
……
WHAT'S UPSETTING YOU?
I'M JUST FRUS-TRATED.
ME, TOO.
THE ONLY THING WE CAN DO NOW IS WAIT.
THOUGH THERE'S NOT MUCH TIME LEFT.
IT'S ALL WE CAN DO...

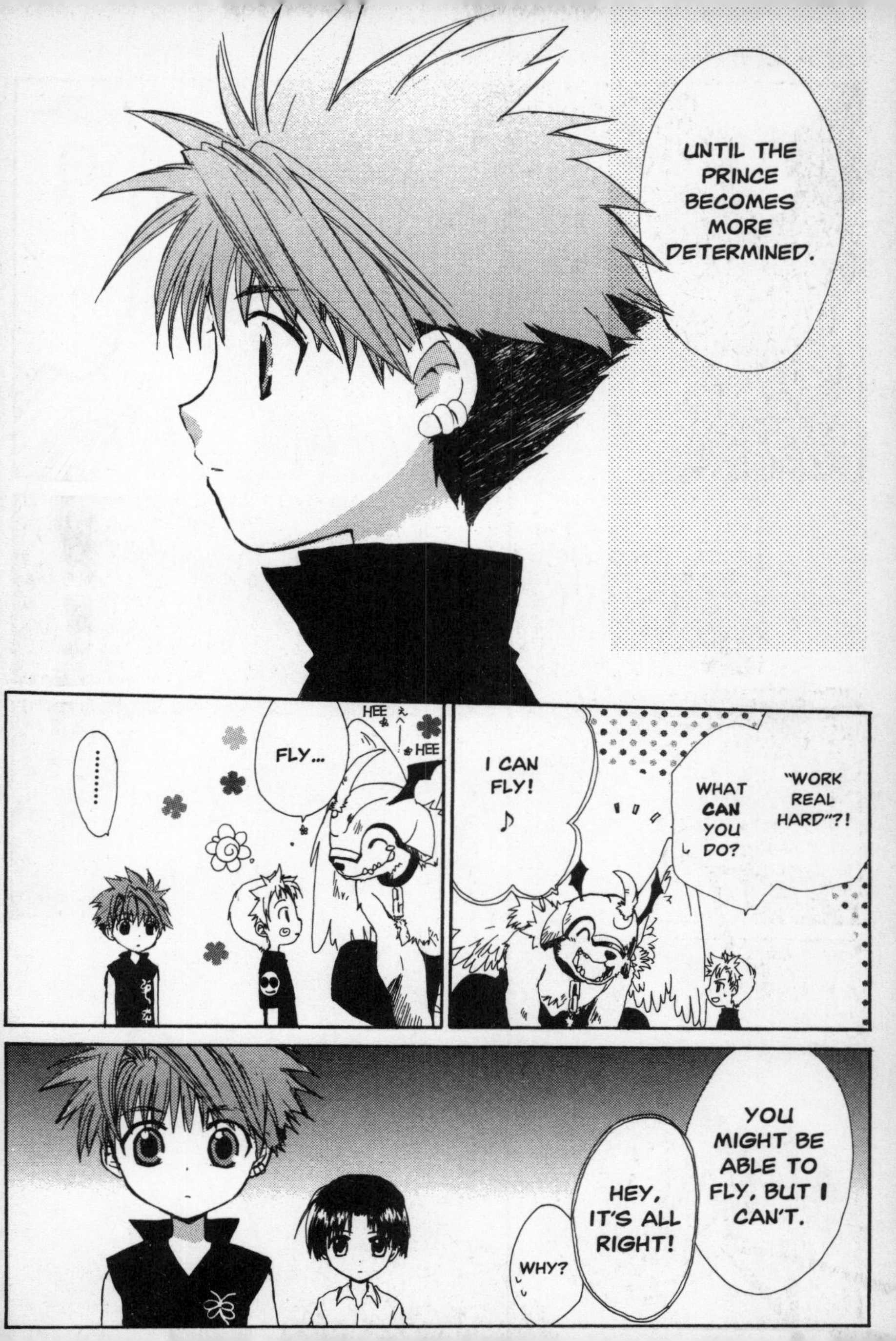
UNTIL THE PRINCE BECOMES MORE DETERMINED.
"WORK REAL HARD"?!
WHAT CAN YOU DO?
I CAN FLY! ♪
HEE えへー HEE
FLY...
......
YOU MIGHT BE ABLE TO FLY, BUT I CAN'T.
HEY, IT'S ALL RIGHT!
WHY?

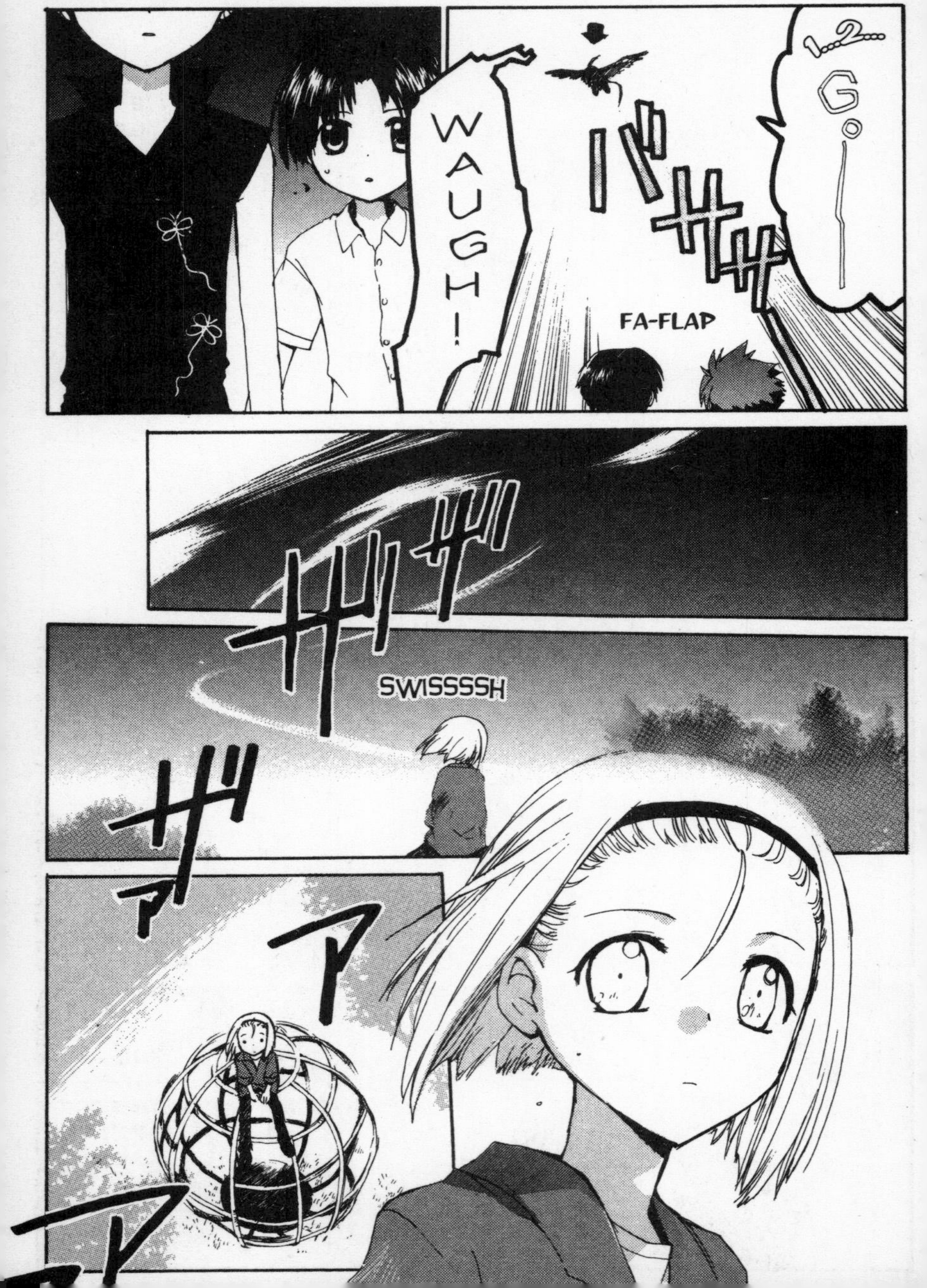
1...2....
GO!
WAUGH!
バサササ
FA-FLAP
ザザ
SWISSSSH
ザァァァ

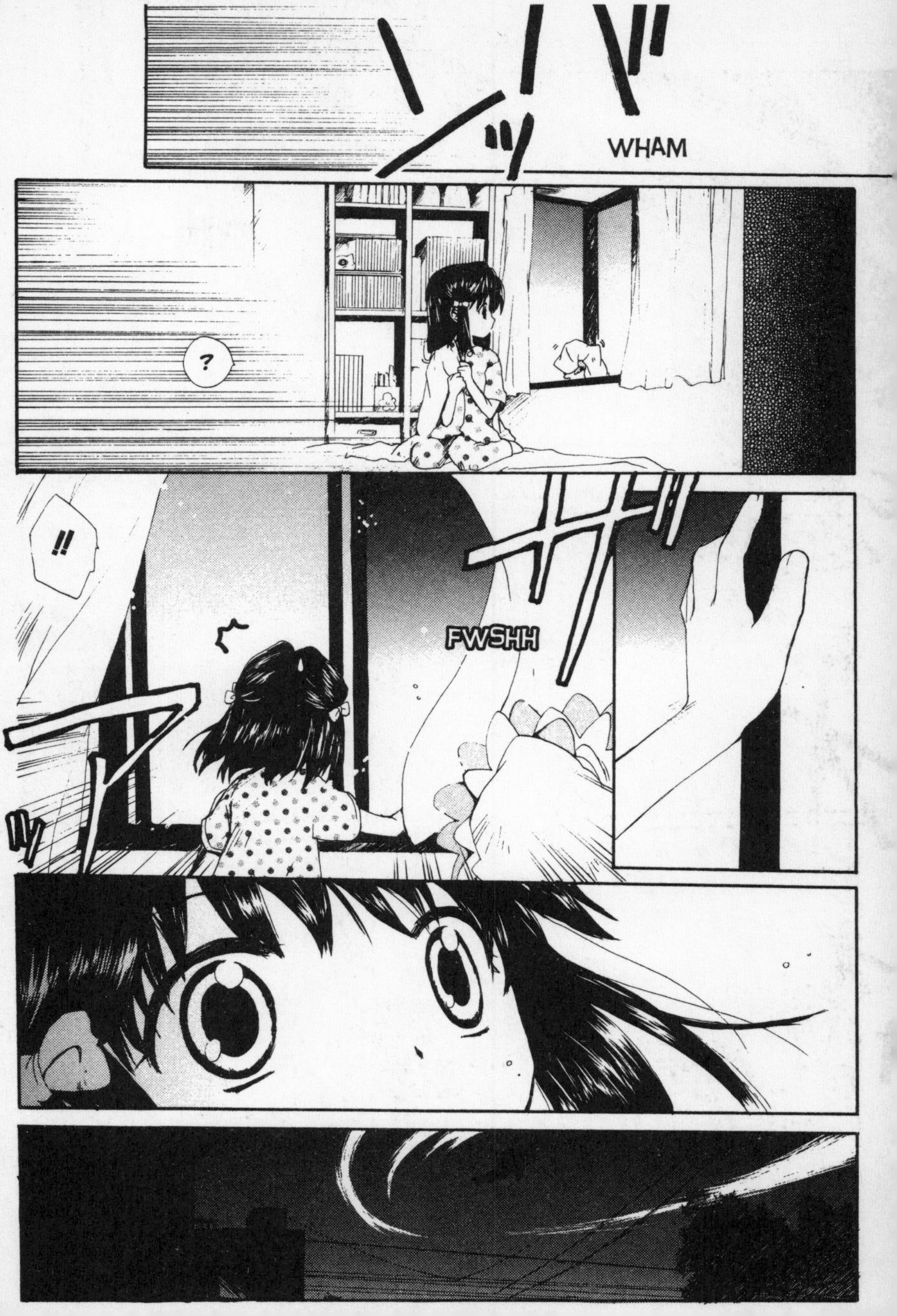
WHAM
?
!!
FWSHH

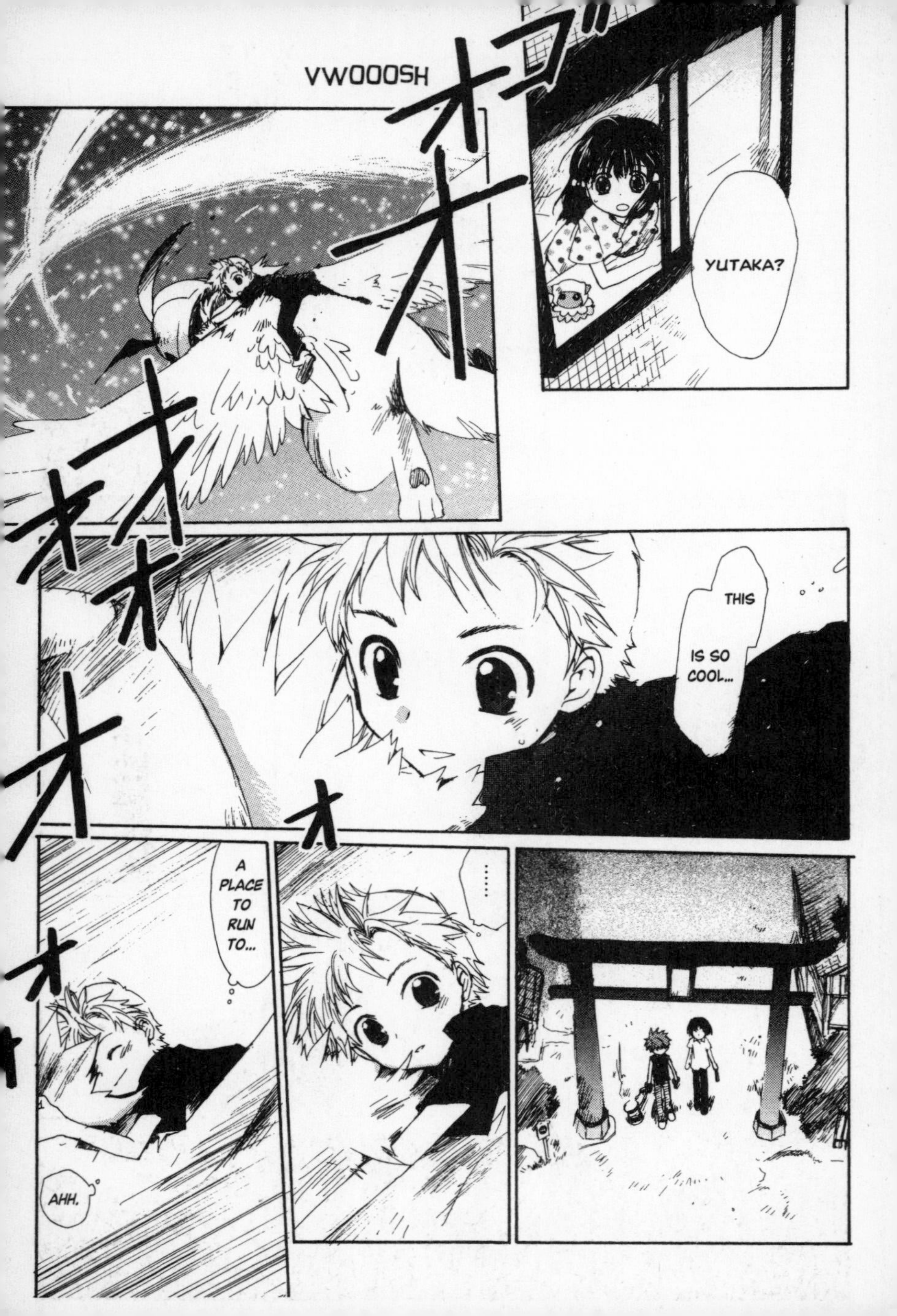

VWOOOSH
YUTAKA?
THIS IS SO COOL...
......
A PLACE TO RUN TO...
AHH.

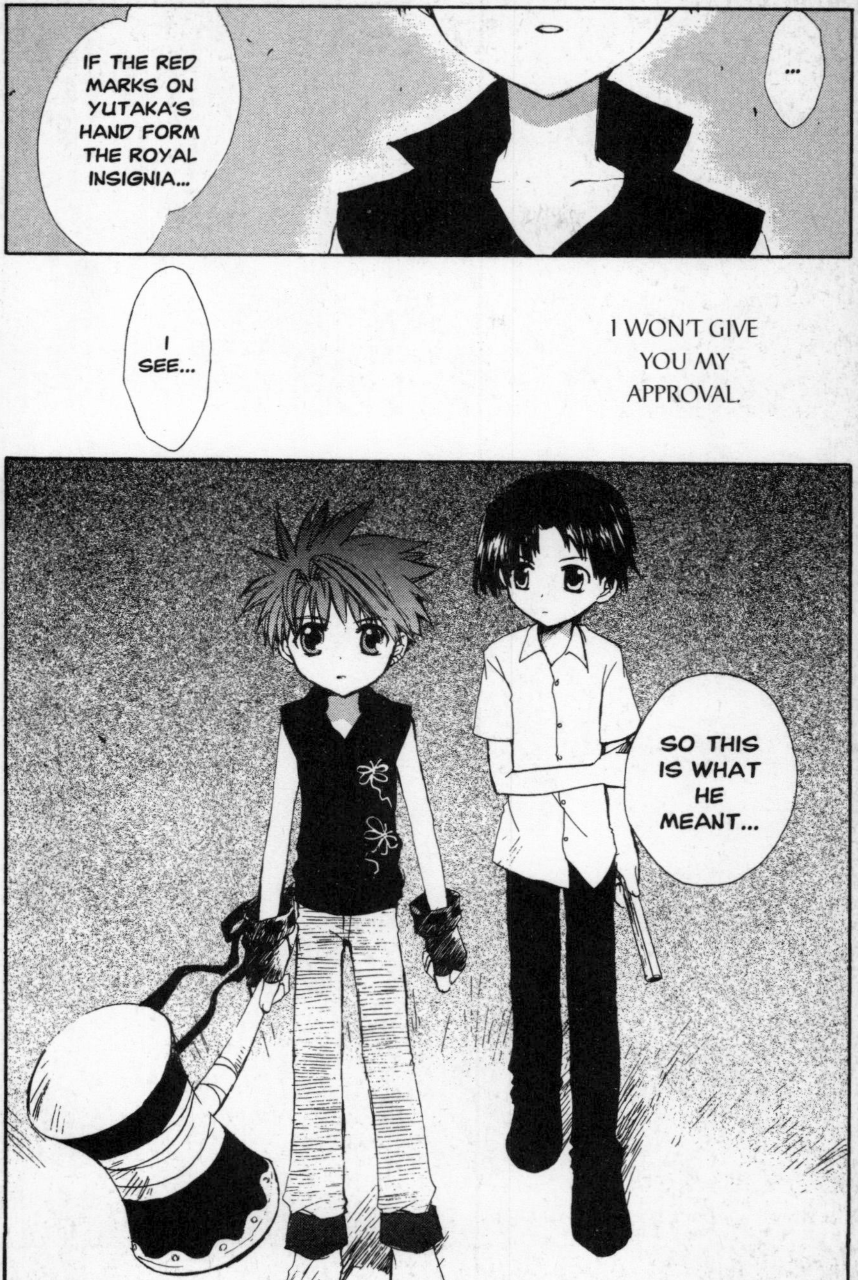
...
IF THE RED MARKS ON YUTAKA'S HAND FORM THE ROYAL INSIGNIA...
I WON'T GIVE YOU MY APPROVAL.
I SEE...
SO THIS IS WHAT HE MEANT...

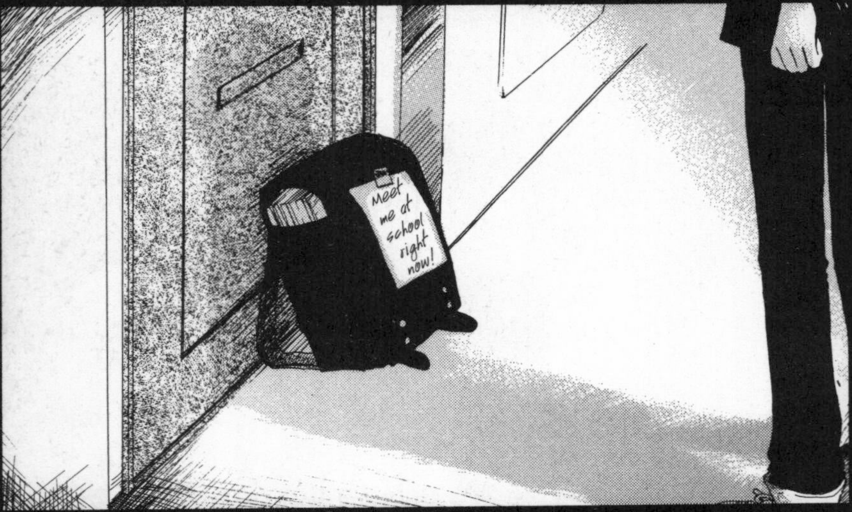
Meet me at school right now!

CHAPTER 8
HOPE FOR ME

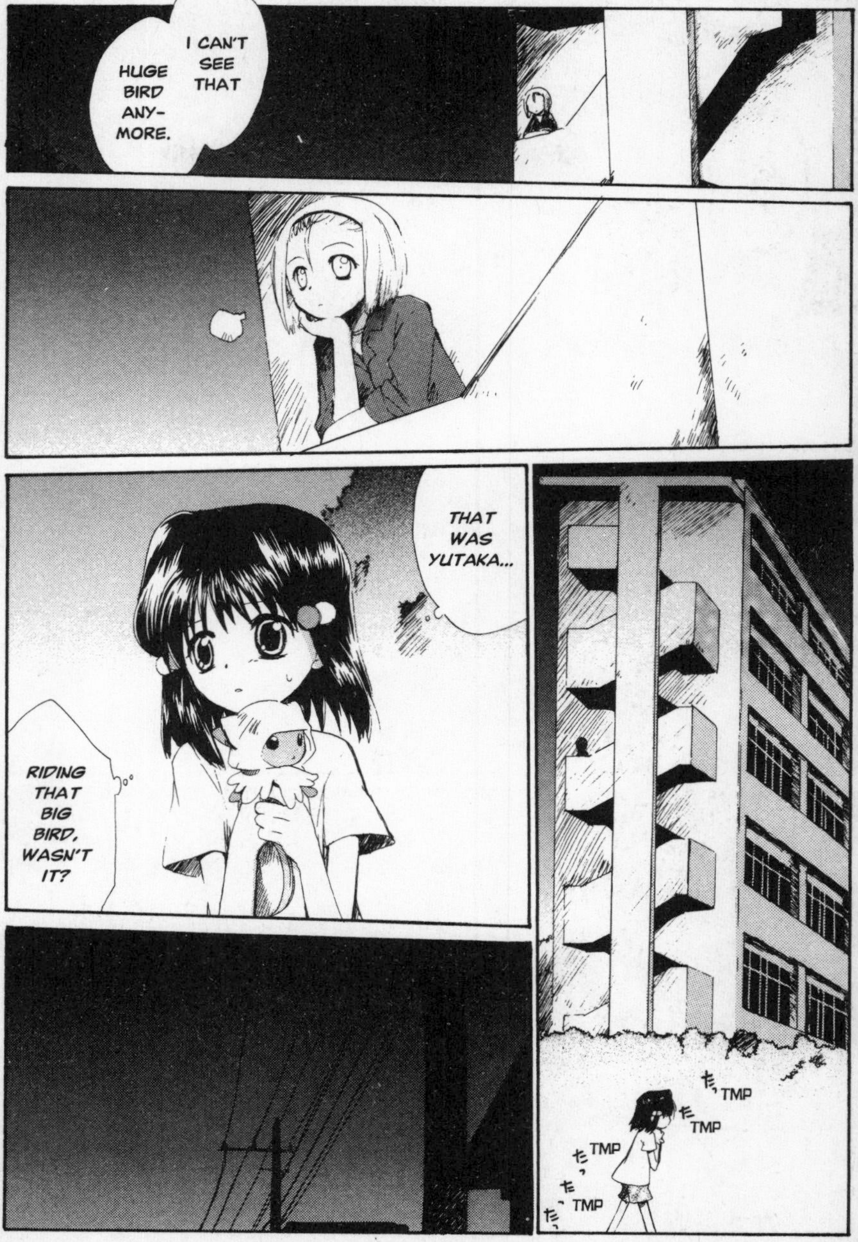
I CAN'T SEE THAT HUGE BIRD ANYMORE.
THAT WAS YUTAKA...
RIDING THAT BIG BIRD, WASN'T IT?
た, TMP
た TMP
た, TMP
た, TMP
た,

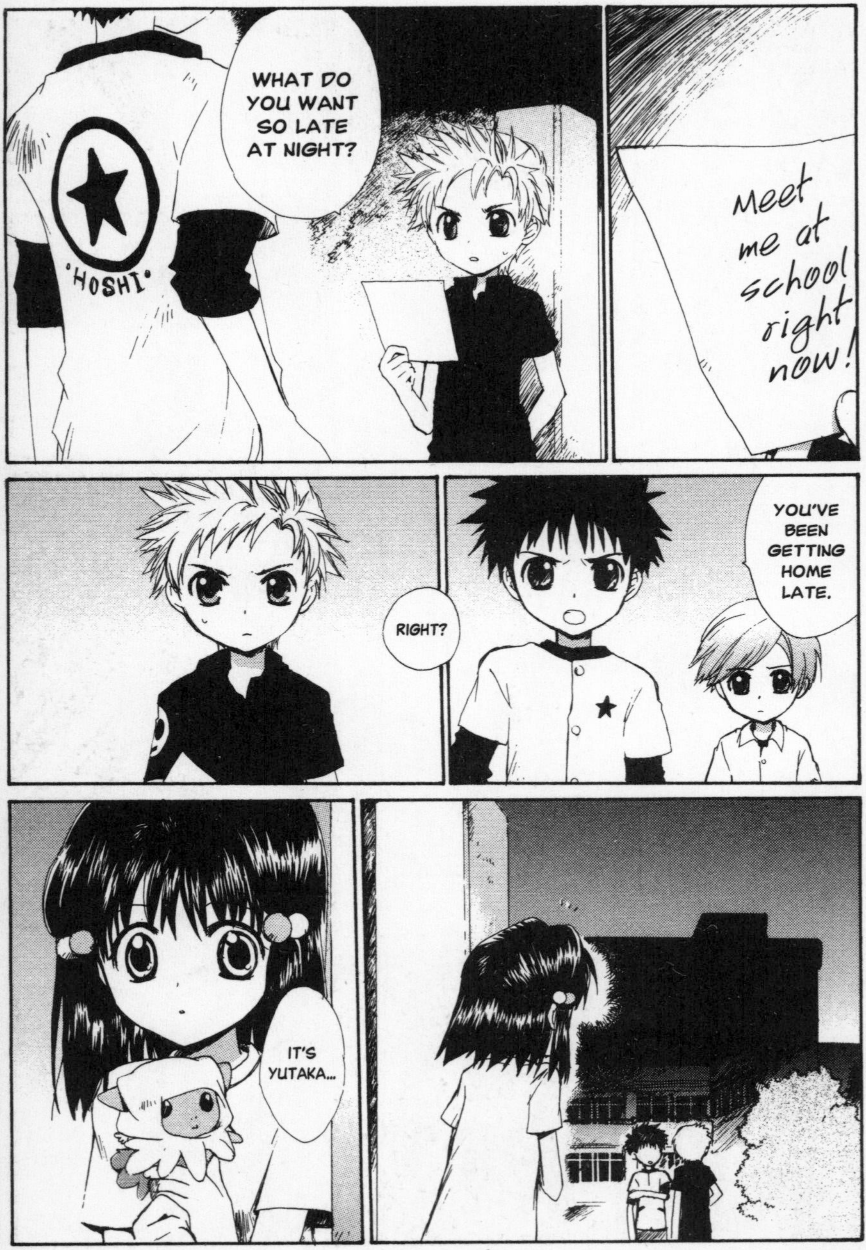
Meet me at school right now!
WHAT DO YOU WANT SO LATE AT NIGHT?
'HOSHI'
YOU'VE BEEN GETTING HOME LATE.
RIGHT?
IT'S YUTAKA...

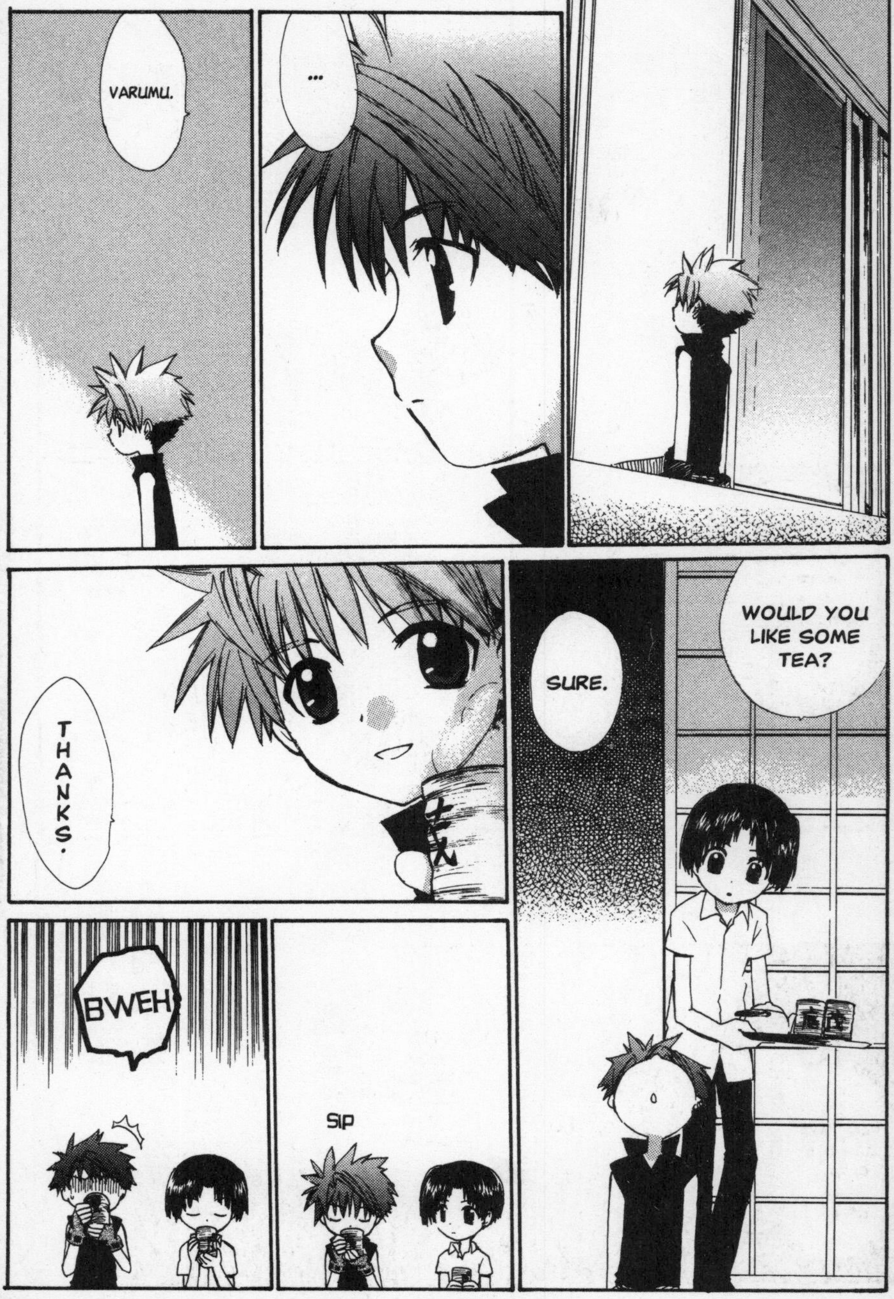

...
VARUMU.
WOULD YOU LIKE SOME TEA?
SURE.
THANKS.
SIP
BWEH

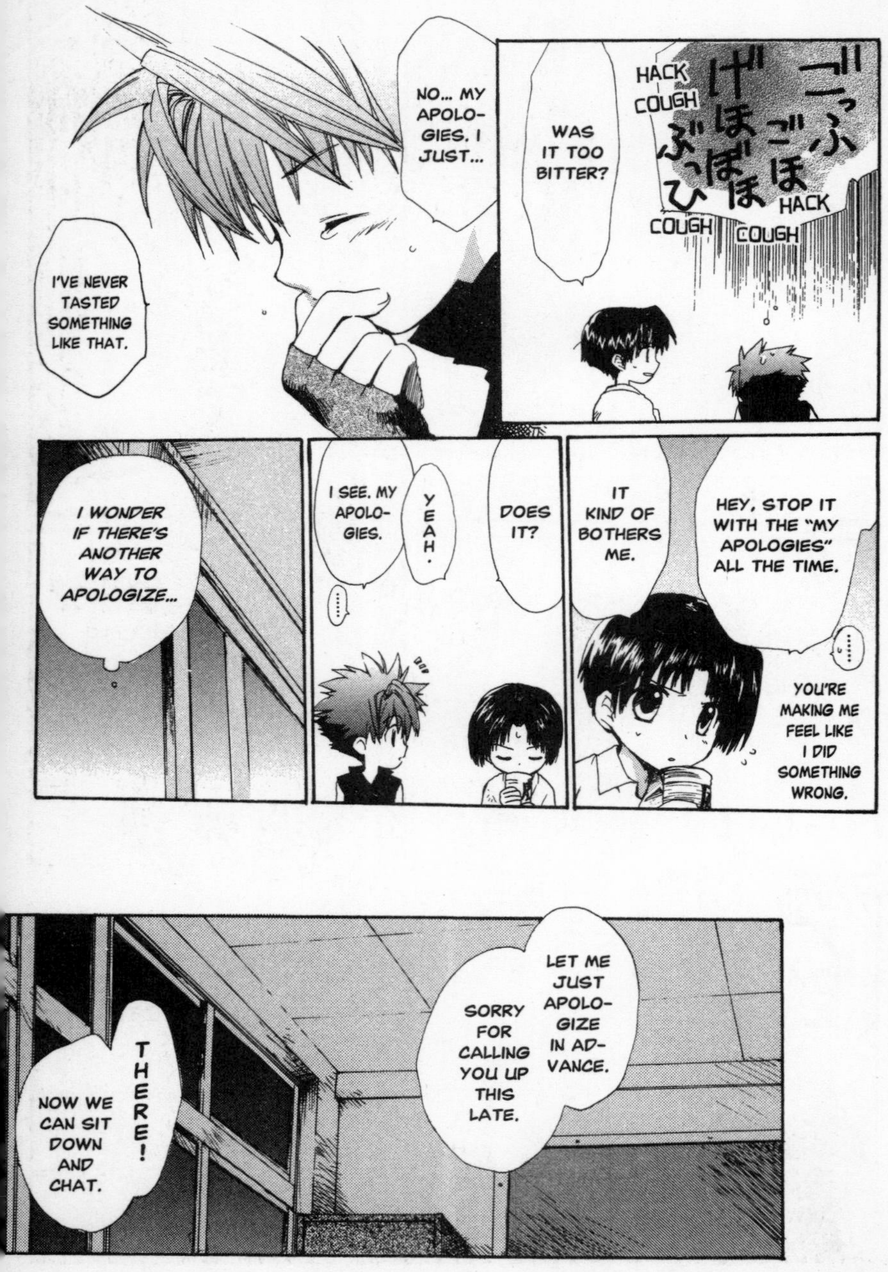

ごふっ
ごほ
げほ
ぼほ
ぶっひ
HACK COUGH
HACK COUGH
COUGH
WAS IT TOO BITTER?
NO... MY APOLOGIES. I JUST...
I'VE NEVER TASTED SOMETHING LIKE THAT.
HEY, STOP IT WITH THE "MY APOLOGIES" ALL THE TIME.
IT KIND OF BOTHERS ME.
......
YOU'RE MAKING ME FEEL LIKE I DID SOMETHING WRONG.
DOES IT?
YEAH.
I SEE. MY APOLOGIES.
......
I WONDER IF THERE'S ANOTHER WAY TO APOLOGIZE...
LET ME JUST APOLOGIZE IN ADVANCE.
SORRY FOR CALLING YOU UP THIS LATE.
THERE!
NOW WE CAN SIT DOWN AND CHAT.

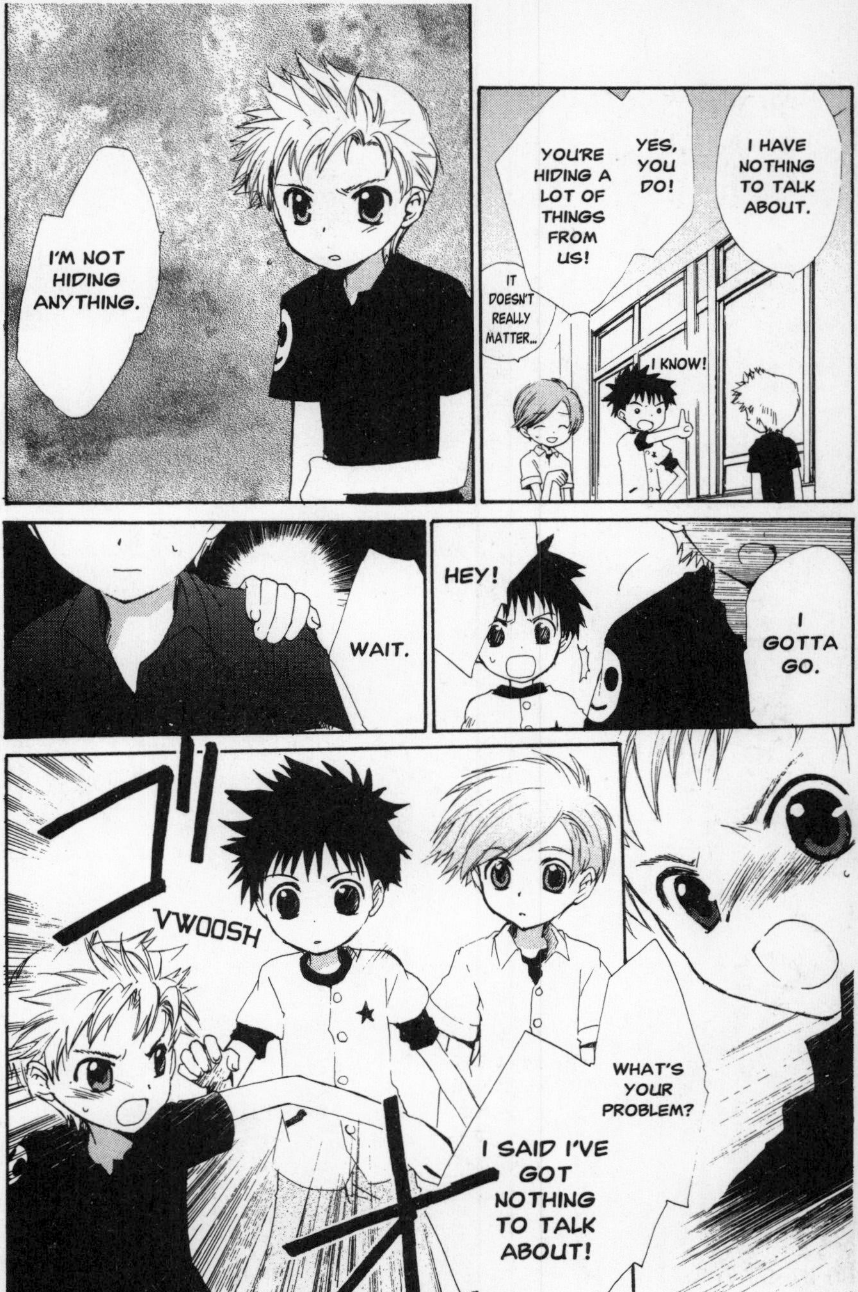
I HAVE NOTHING TO TALK ABOUT.
YES, YOU DO!
YOU'RE HIDING A LOT OF THINGS FROM US!
IT DOESN'T REALLY MATTER...
I KNOW!
I'M NOT HIDING ANYTHING.
I GOTTA GO.
HEY!
WAIT.
WHAT'S YOUR PROBLEM?
I SAID I'VE GOT NOTHING TO TALK ABOUT!
VWOOSH

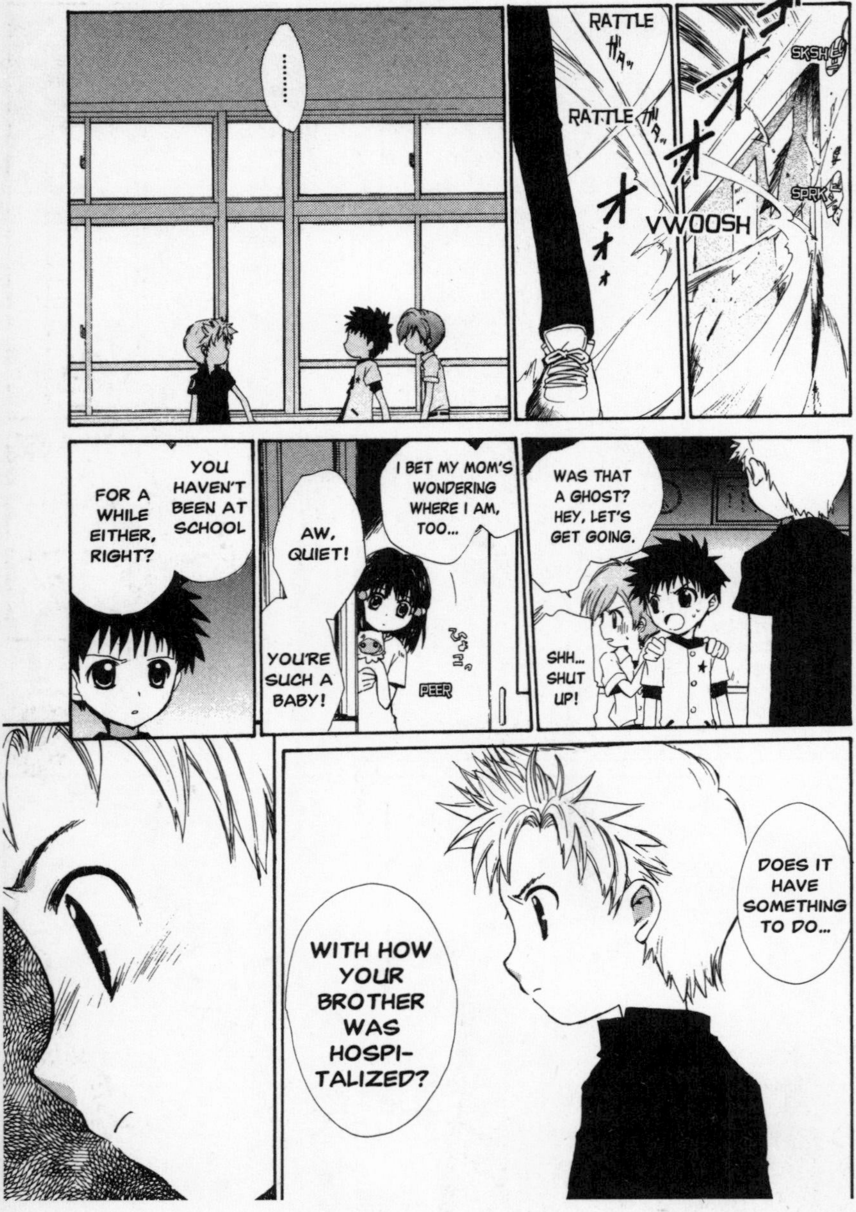
SKSH
VWOOSH
SPRK
RATTLE
RATTLE
......
WAS THAT A GHOST? HEY, LET'S GET GOING.
SHH... SHUT UP!
I BET MY MOM'S WONDERING WHERE I AM, TOO...
AW, QUIET!
YOU'RE SUCH A BABY!
PEER
YOU HAVEN'T BEEN AT SCHOOL
FOR A WHILE EITHER, RIGHT?
DOES IT HAVE SOMETHING TO DO...
WITH HOW YOUR BROTHER WAS HOSPI-TALIZED?

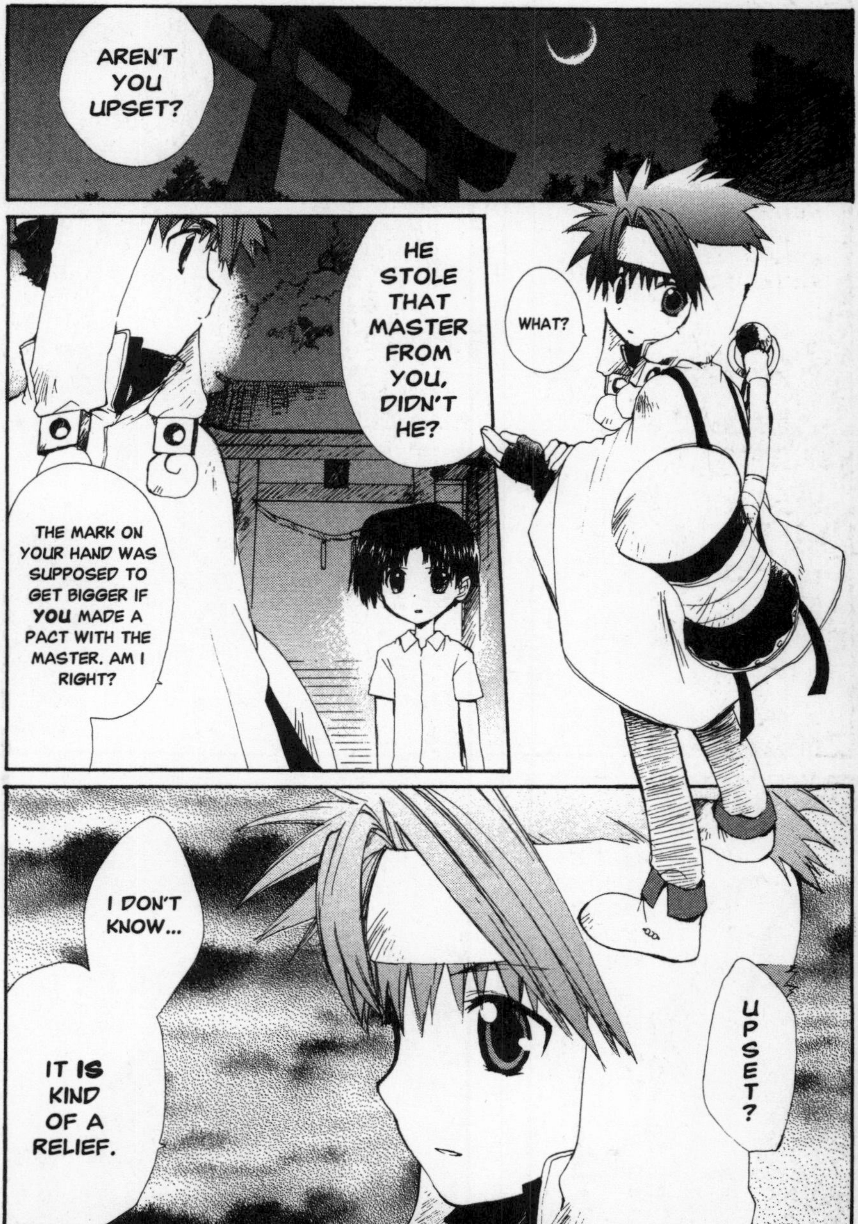
AREN'T YOU UPSET?
WHAT?
HE STOLE THAT MASTER FROM YOU, DIDN'T HE?
THE MARK ON YOUR HAND WAS SUPPOSED TO GET BIGGER IF YOU MADE A PACT WITH THE MASTER. AM I RIGHT?
UPSET?
I DON'T KNOW...
IT IS KIND OF A RELIEF.

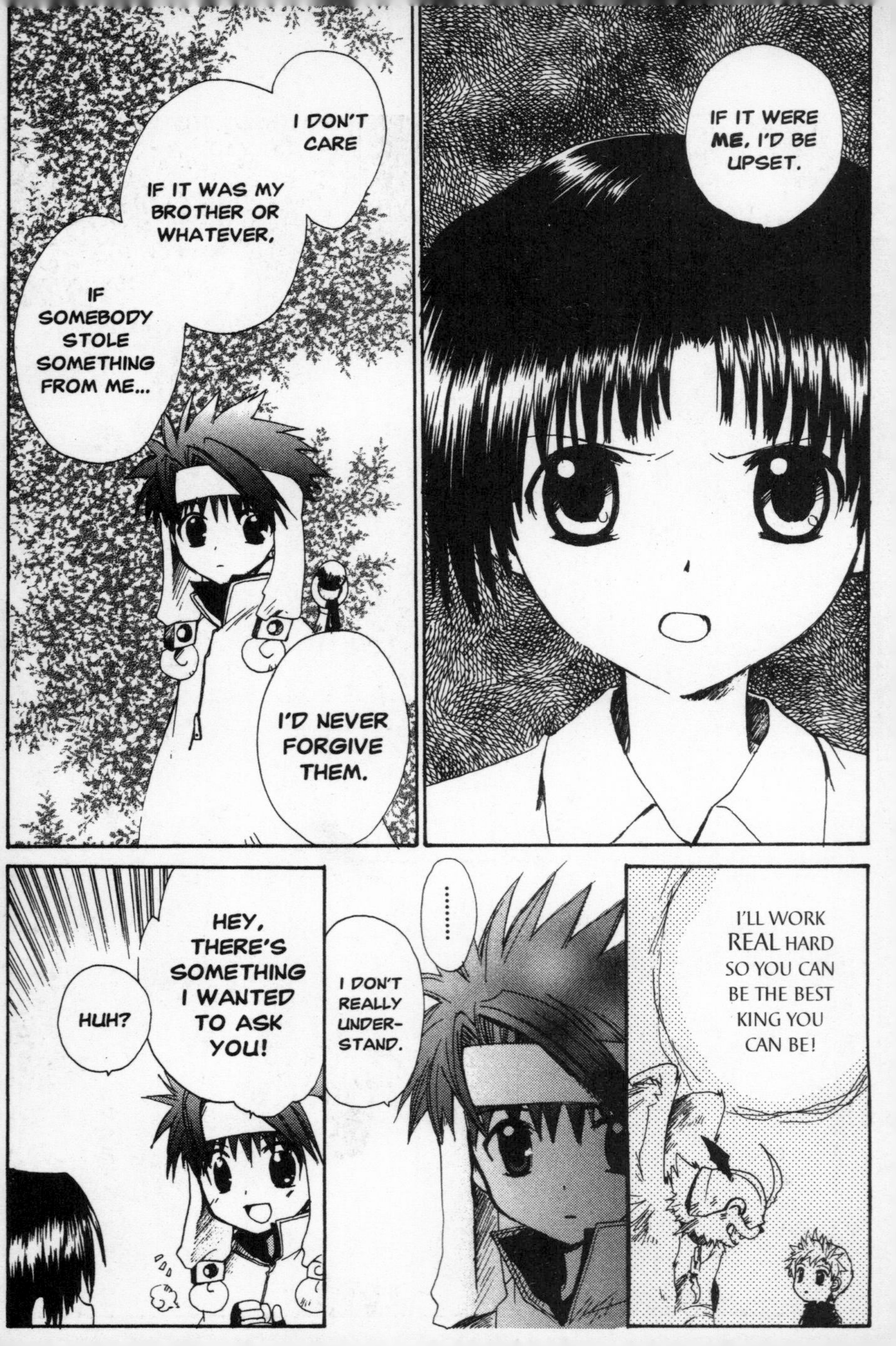
IF IT WERE ME, I'D BE UPSET.
I DON'T CARE
IF IT WAS MY BROTHER OR WHATEVER,
IF SOMEBODY STOLE SOMETHING FROM ME...
I'D NEVER FORGIVE THEM.
I'LL WORK REAL HARD SO YOU CAN BE THE BEST KING YOU CAN BE!
......
I DON'T REALLY UNDER-STAND.
HEY, THERE'S SOMETHING I WANTED TO ASK YOU!
HUH?

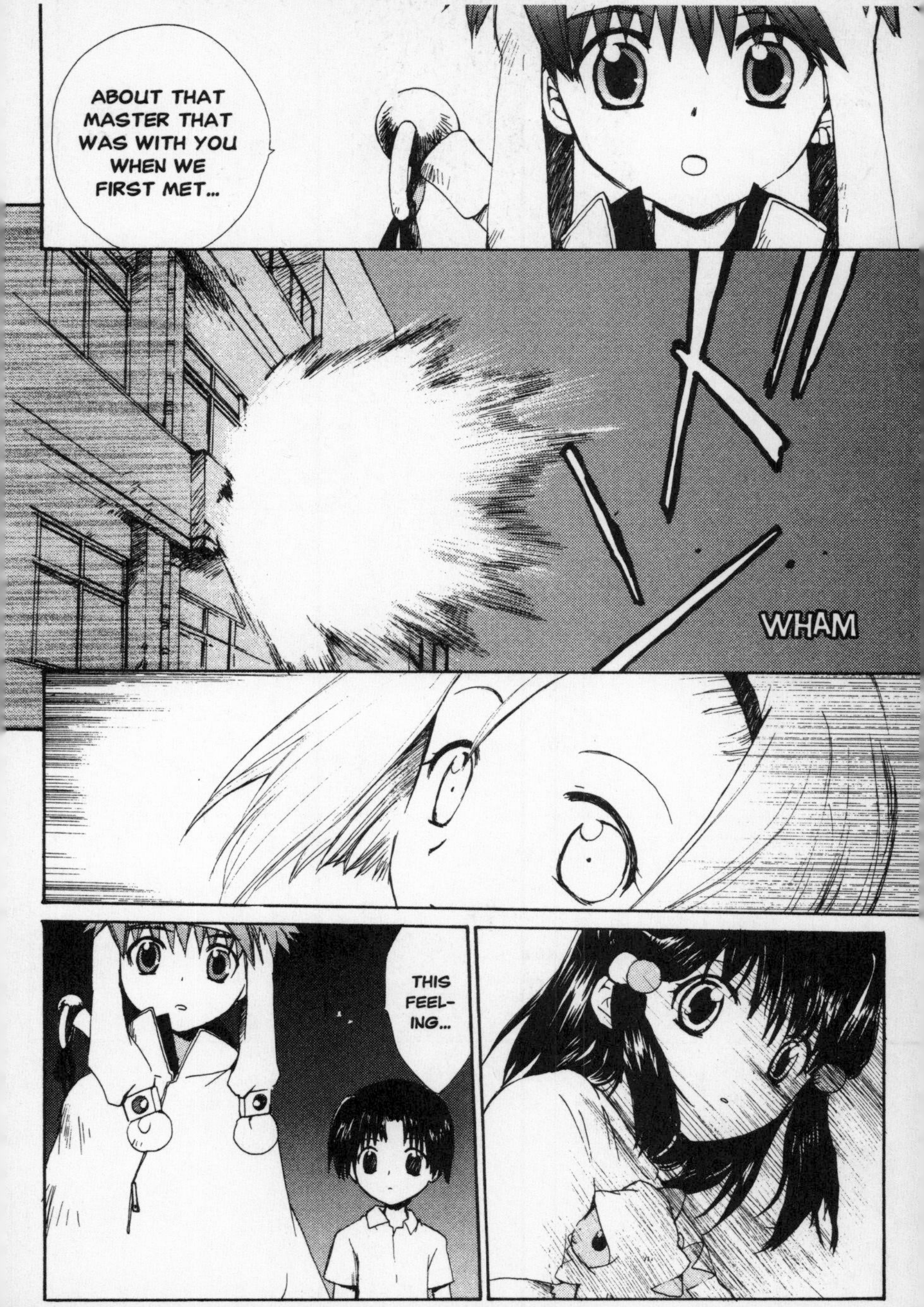
ABOUT THAT MASTER THAT WAS WITH YOU WHEN WE FIRST MET...
WHAM
THIS FEEL-ING...

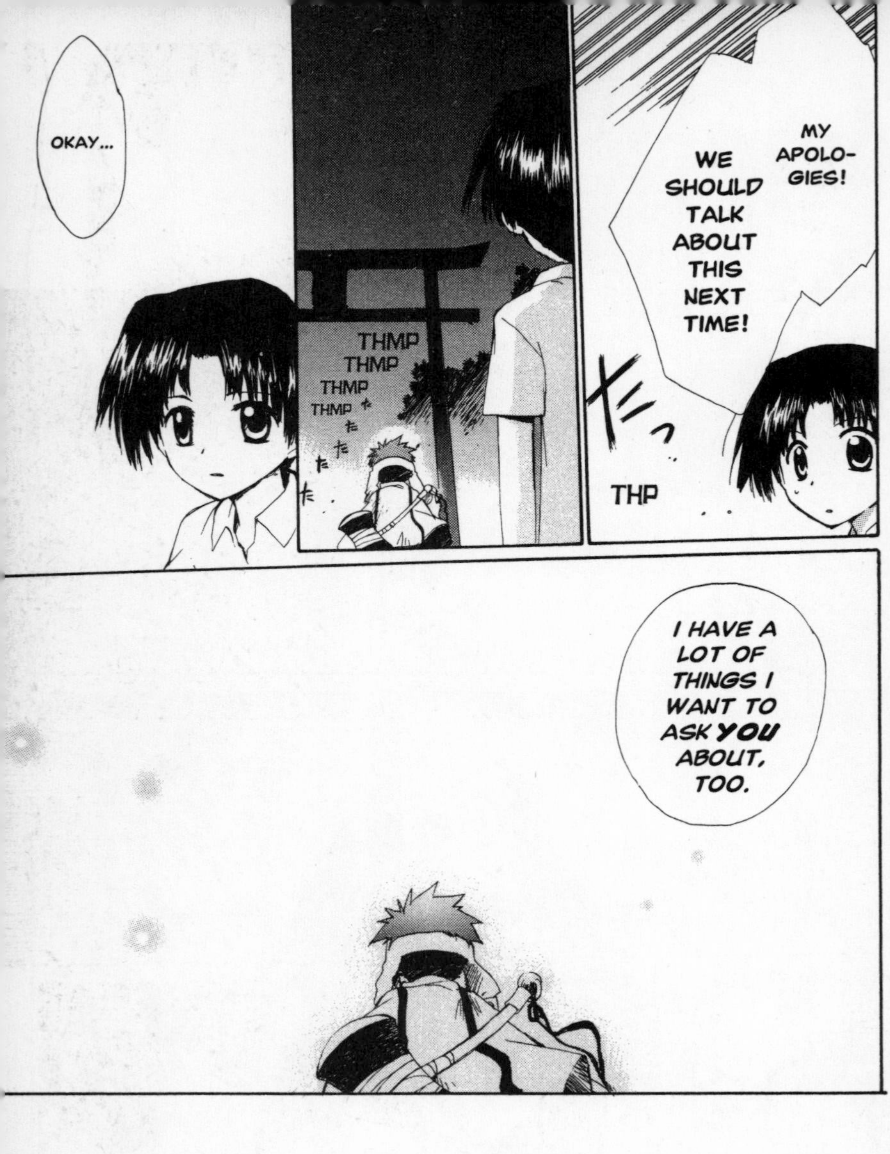
MY APOLO-GIES!
WE SHOULD TALK ABOUT THIS NEXT TIME!
THP
THMP THMP THMP THMP
OKAY...
I HAVE A LOT OF THINGS I WANT TO ASK **YOU** ABOUT, TOO.

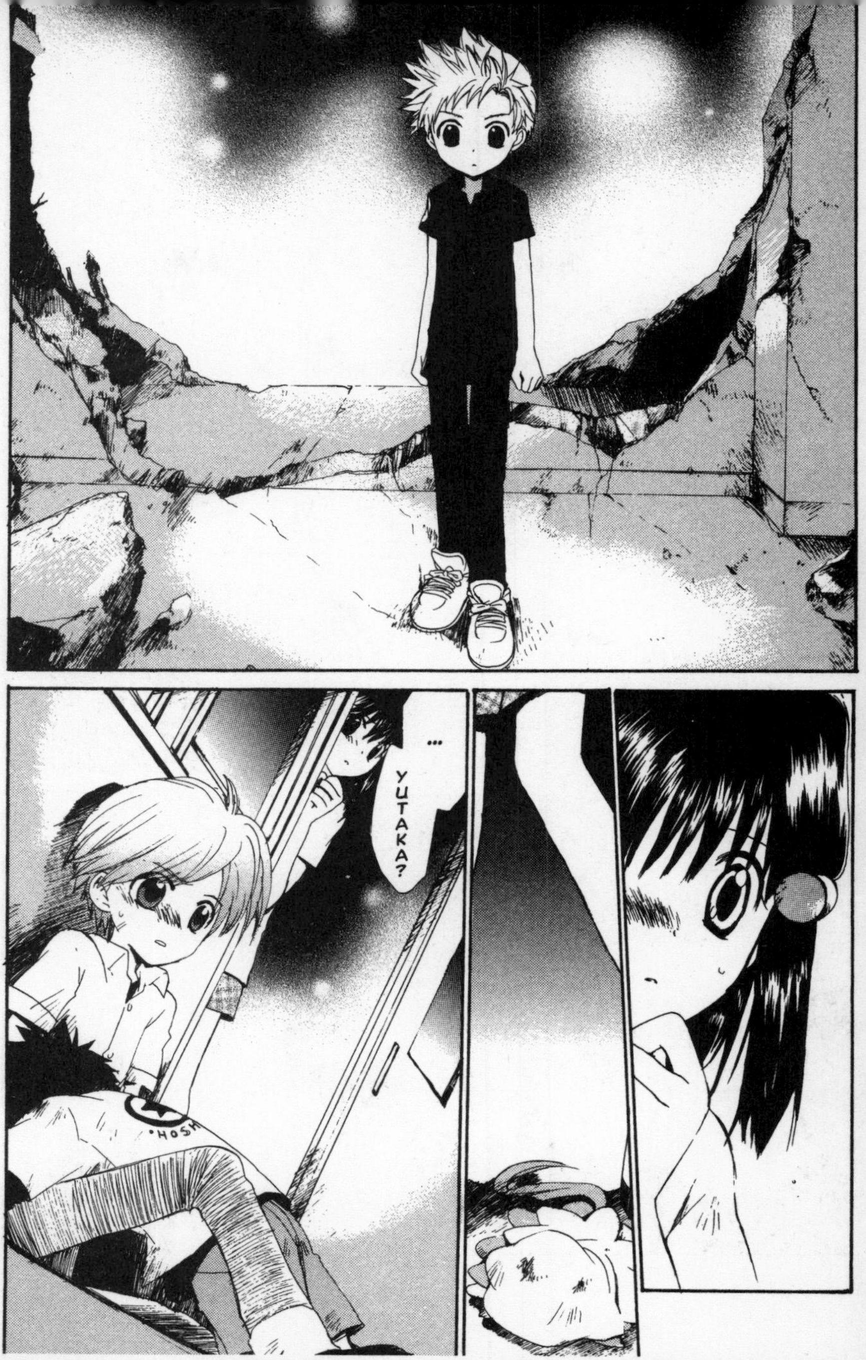

...
...
YUTAKA?

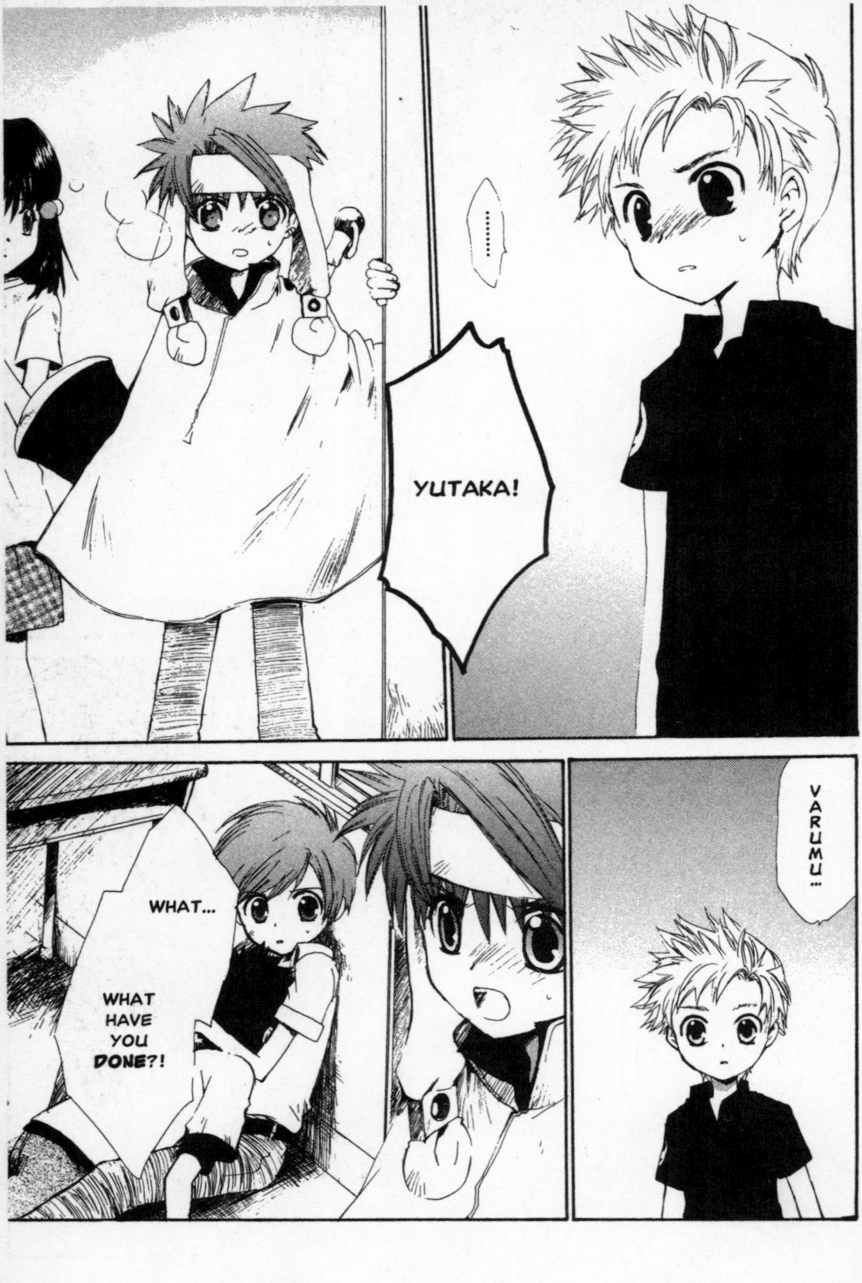
......
YUTAKA!
VARUMU...
WHAT...
WHAT HAVE YOU DONE?!

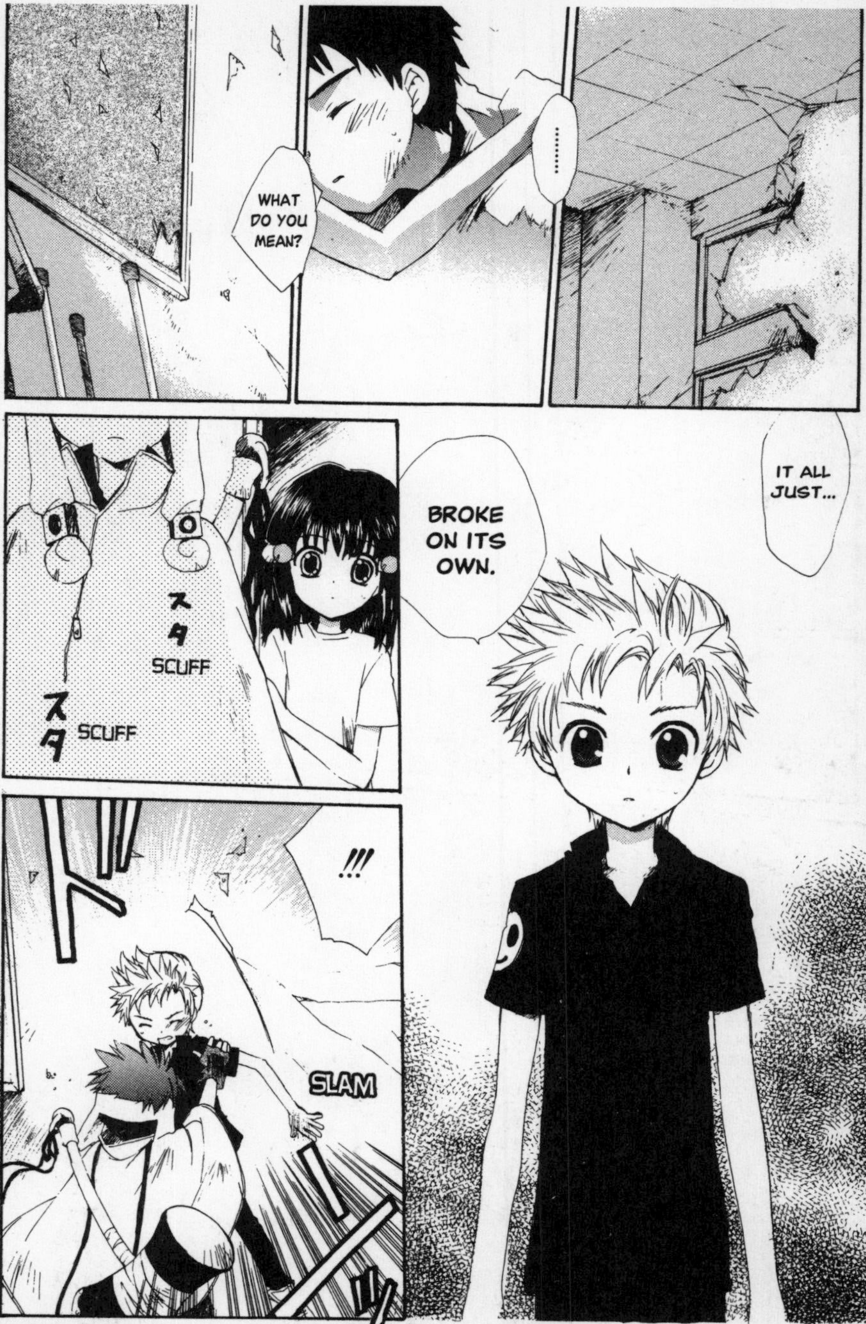
......
WHAT DO YOU MEAN?
IT ALL JUST...
BROKE ON ITS OWN.
スタ SCUFF
スタ SCUFF
!!!
SLAM

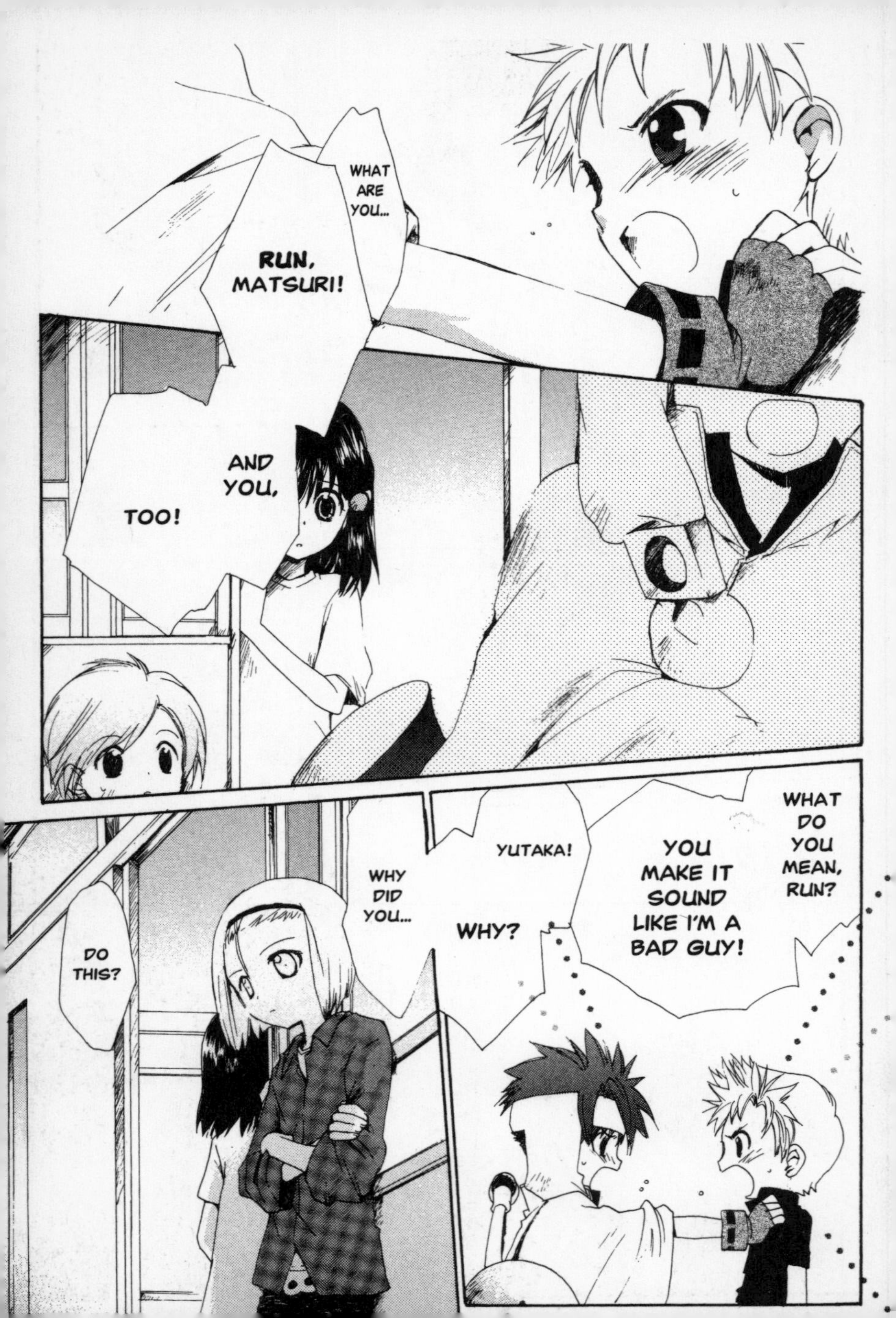
WHAT ARE YOU...
RUN, MATSURI!
AND YOU, TOO!
WHAT DO YOU MEAN, RUN?
YOU MAKE IT SOUND LIKE I'M A BAD GUY!
YUTAKA!
WHY?
WHY DID YOU...
DO THIS?

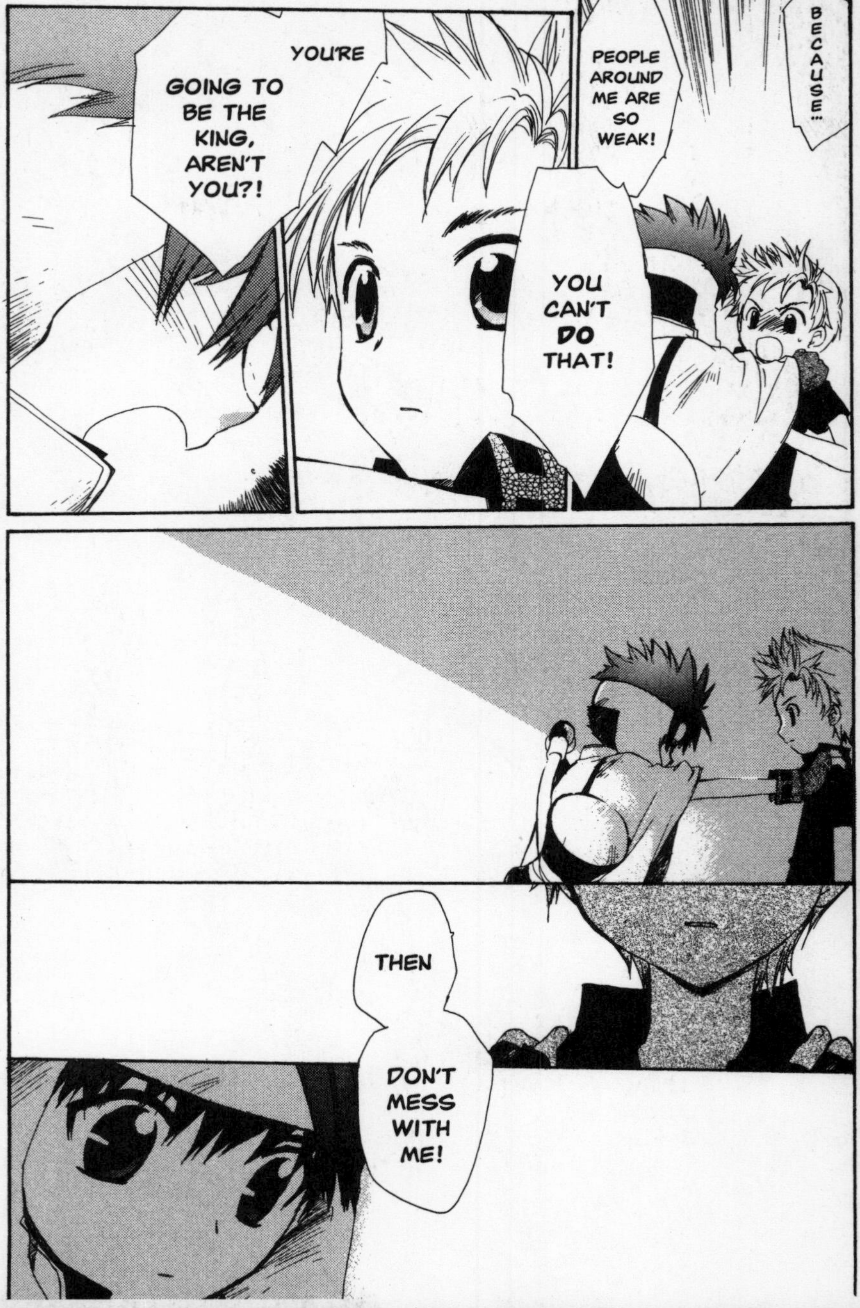
BECAUSE...
PEOPLE AROUND ME ARE SO WEAK!
YOU CAN'T DO THAT!
YOU'RE GOING TO BE THE KING, AREN'T YOU?!
THEN DON'T MESS WITH ME!

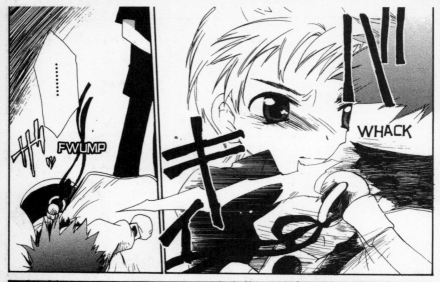

· · · · ·

FWUMP

WHACK

WHO DO YOU THINK YOU ARE, GRABBING ME LIKE THAT?

PRETTY **DANGEROUS** BEING AROUND ME, HUH?

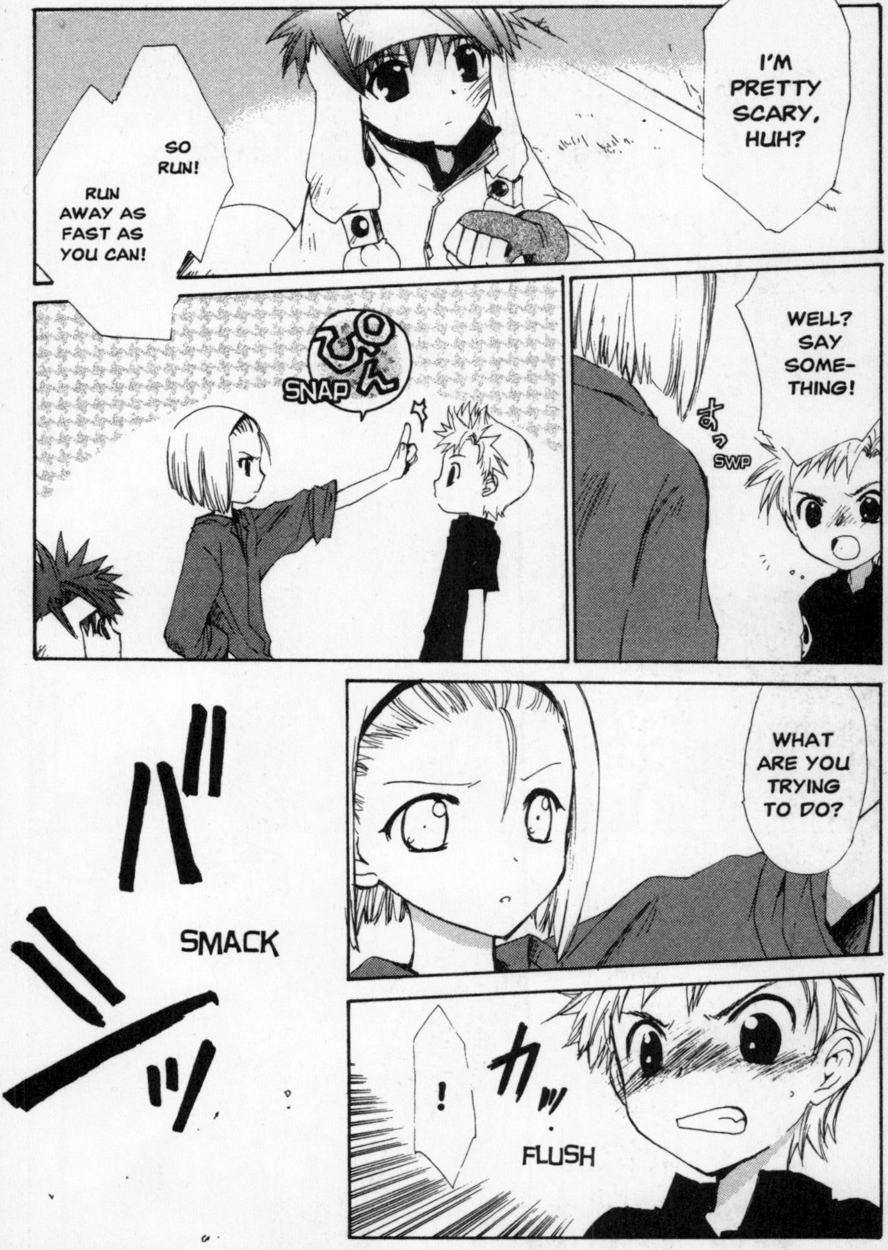
I'M PRETTY SCARY, HUH?
SO RUN!
RUN AWAY AS FAST AS YOU CAN!
WELL? SAY SOME-THING!
すっ
SWP
ぴん
SNAP
WHAT ARE YOU TRYING TO DO?
バシッ
SMACK
!
カッ
FLUSH

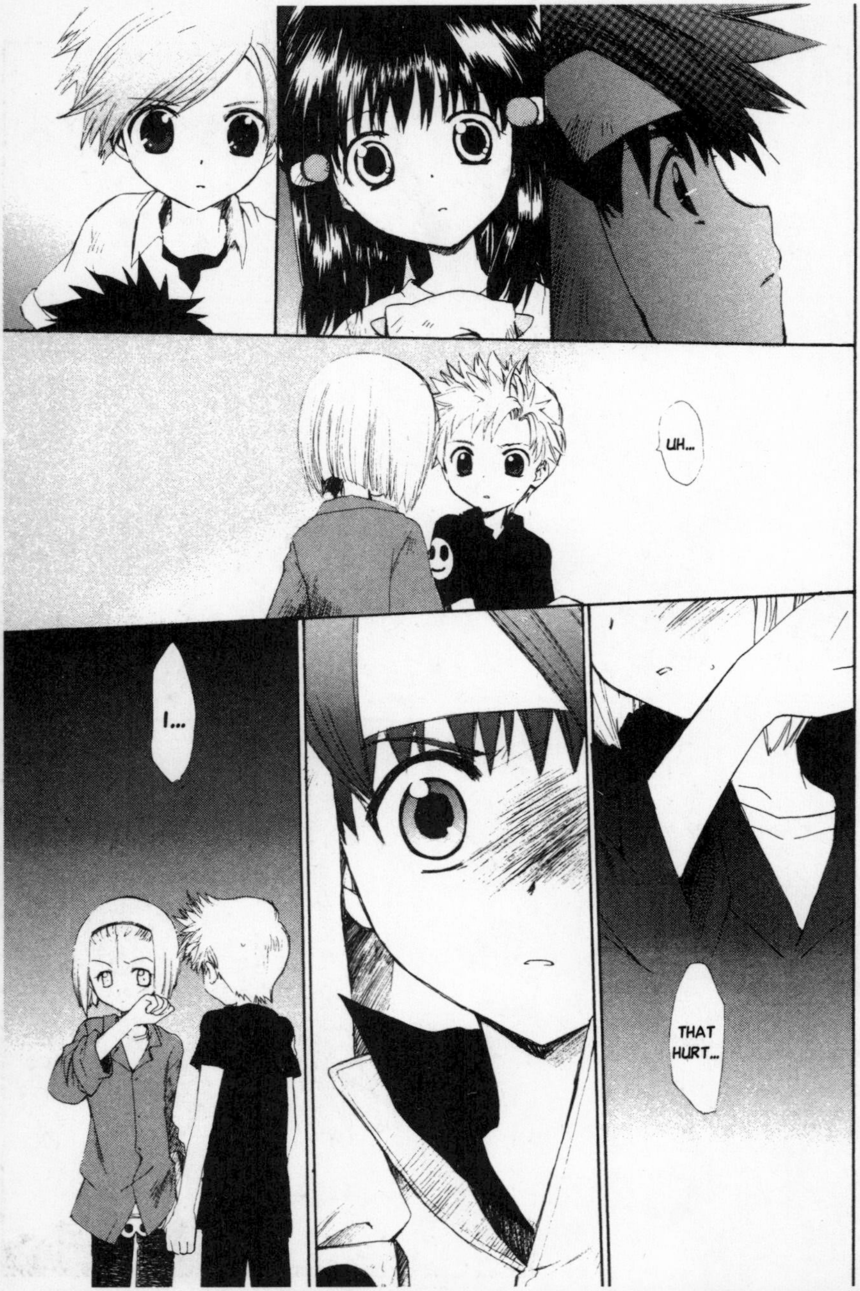
UH...
THAT HURT...
I...

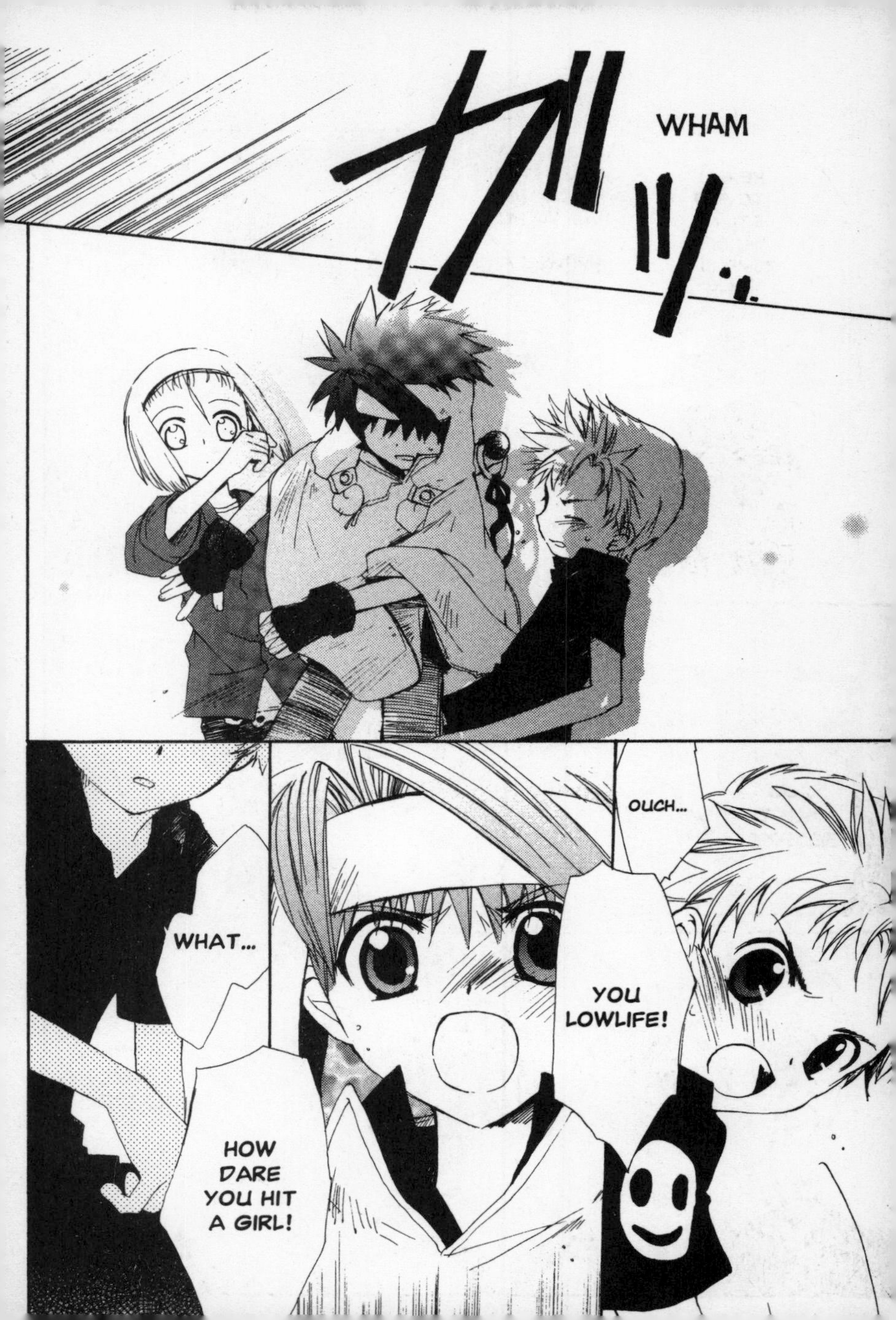
WHAM
OUCH...
YOU LOWLIFE!
HOW DARE YOU HIT A GIRL!
WHAT...

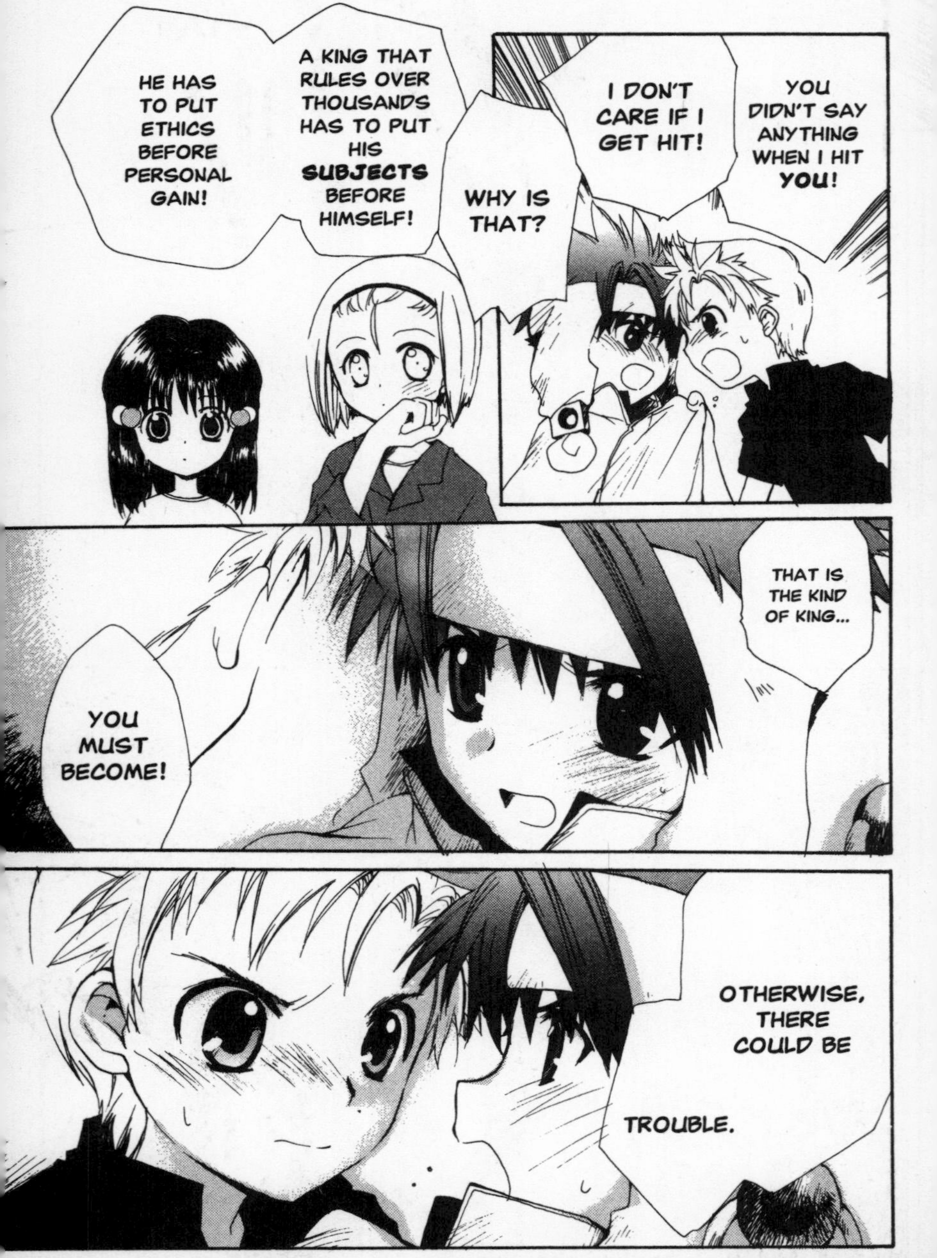
YOU DIDN'T SAY ANYTHING WHEN I HIT **YOU**!
I DON'T CARE IF I GET HIT!
WHY IS THAT?
A KING THAT RULES OVER THOUSANDS HAS TO PUT HIS **SUBJECTS** BEFORE HIMSELF!
HE HAS TO PUT ETHICS BEFORE PERSONAL GAIN!
THAT IS THE KIND OF KING...
YOU MUST BECOME!
OTHERWISE, THERE COULD BE
TROUBLE.

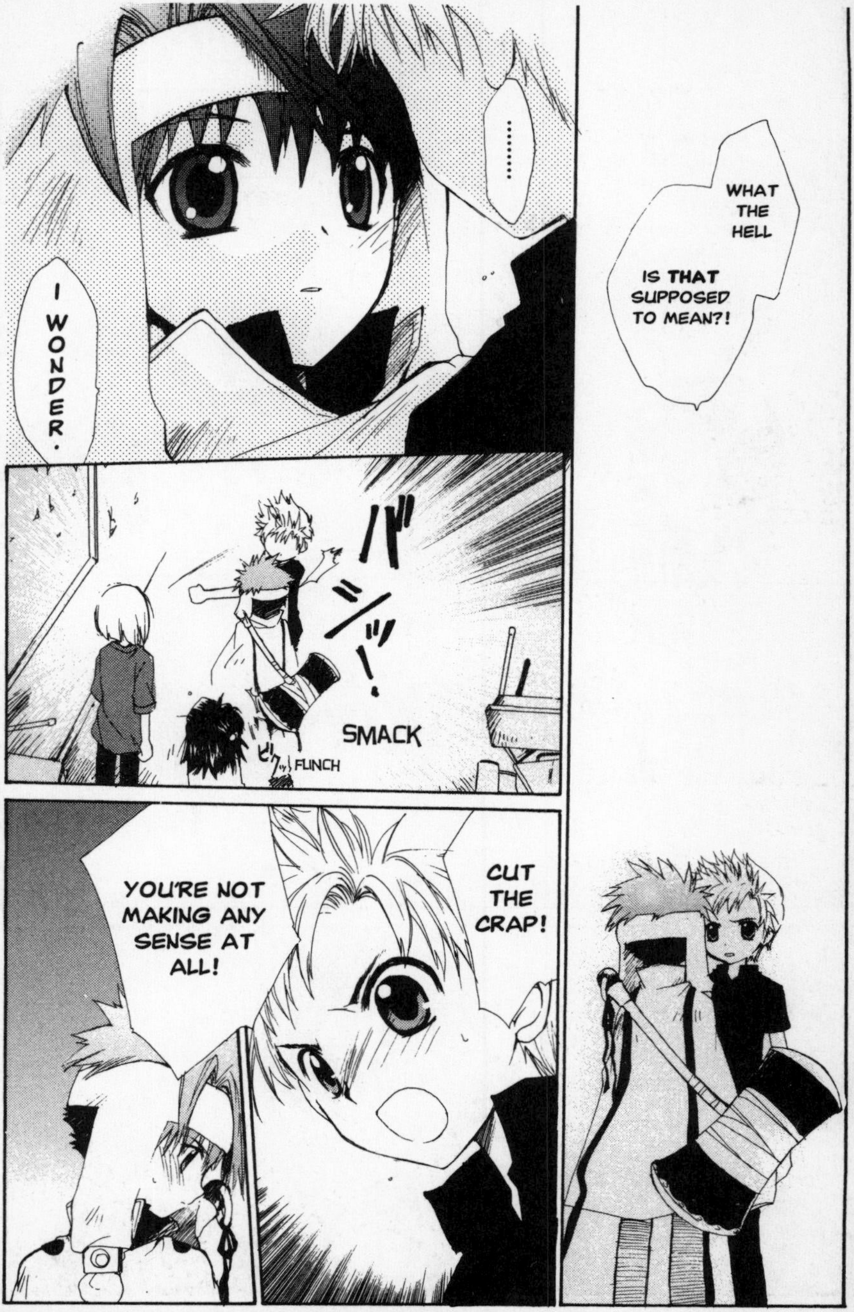
WHAT THE HELL IS THAT SUPPOSED TO MEAN?!
......
I WONDER.
バ=ンッ!
SMACK
ビクッ
FLINCH
CUT THE CRAP!
YOU'RE NOT MAKING ANY SENSE AT ALL!

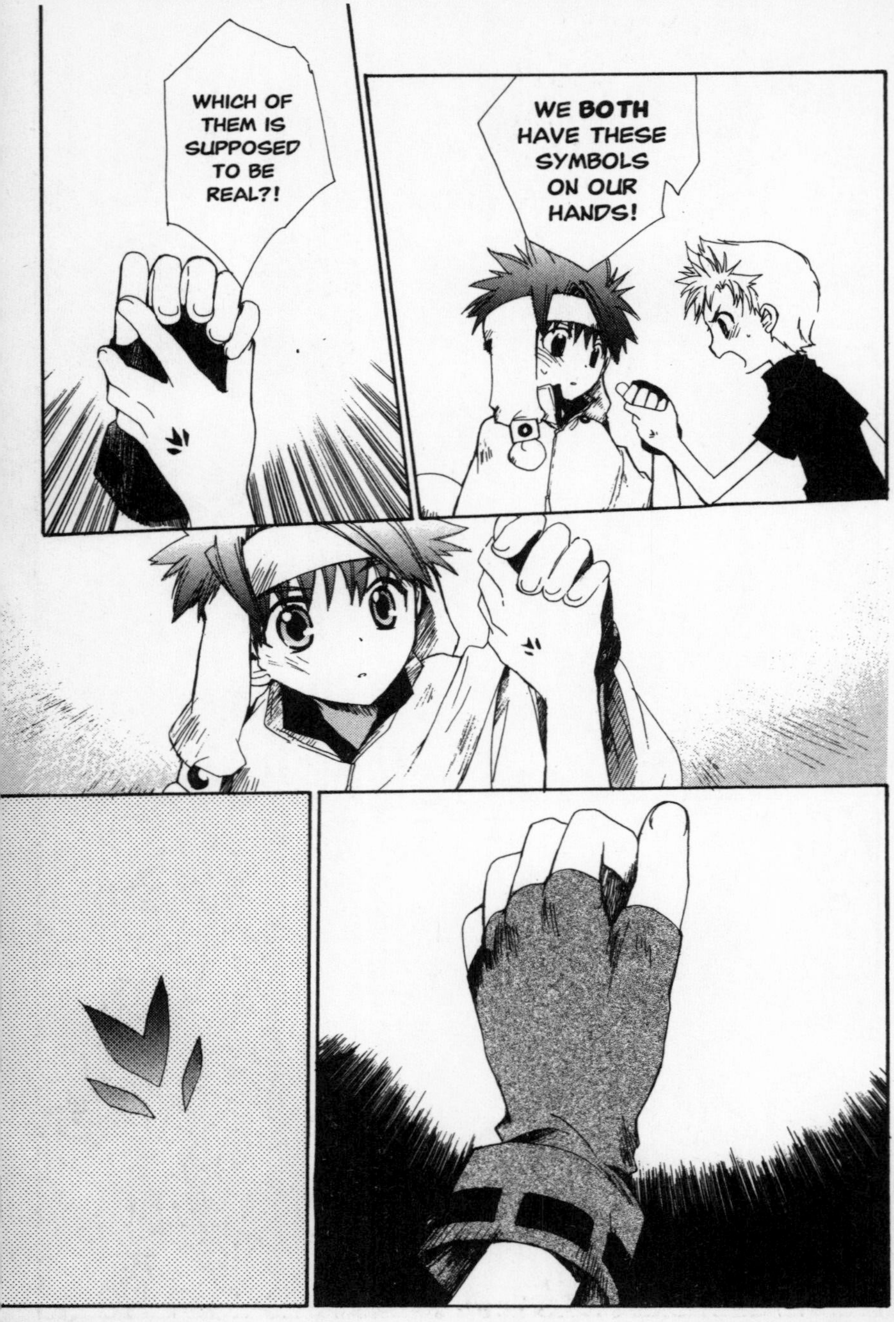
WE **BOTH** HAVE THESE SYMBOLS ON OUR HANDS!
WHICH OF THEM IS SUPPOSED TO BE REAL?!

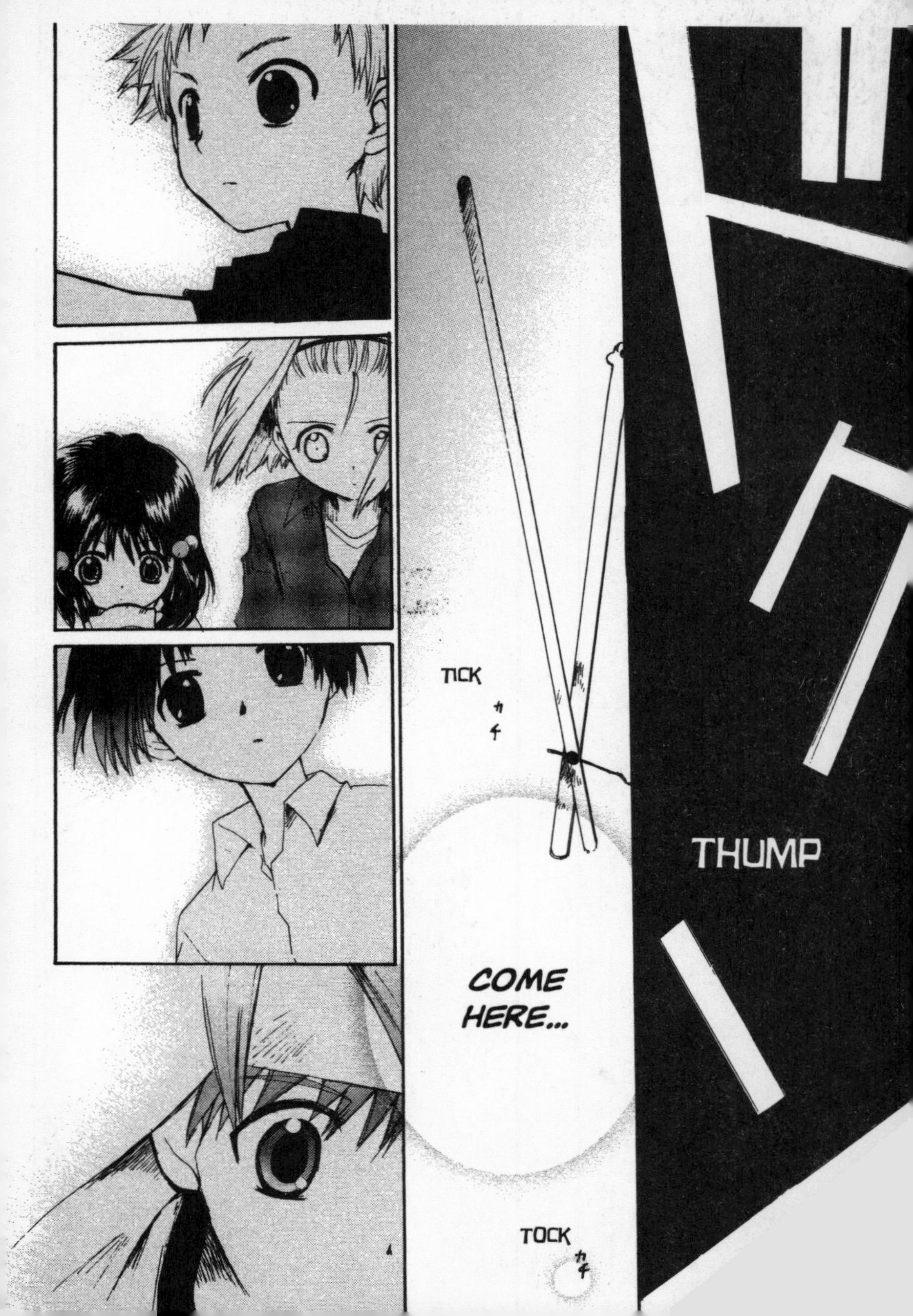
THUMP
TICK
カチ
COME HERE...
TOCK
カチ

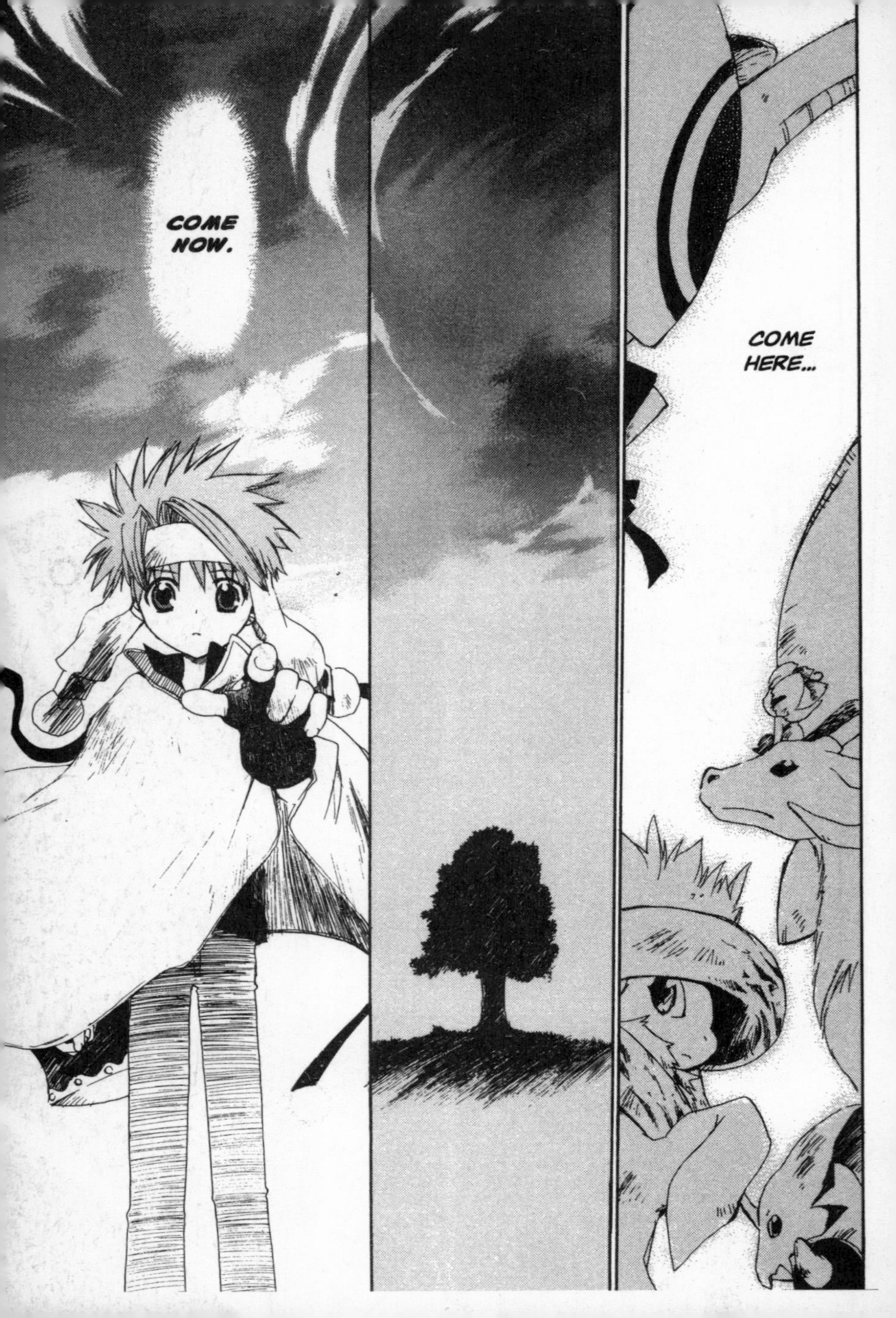
COME HERE...
COME NOW.

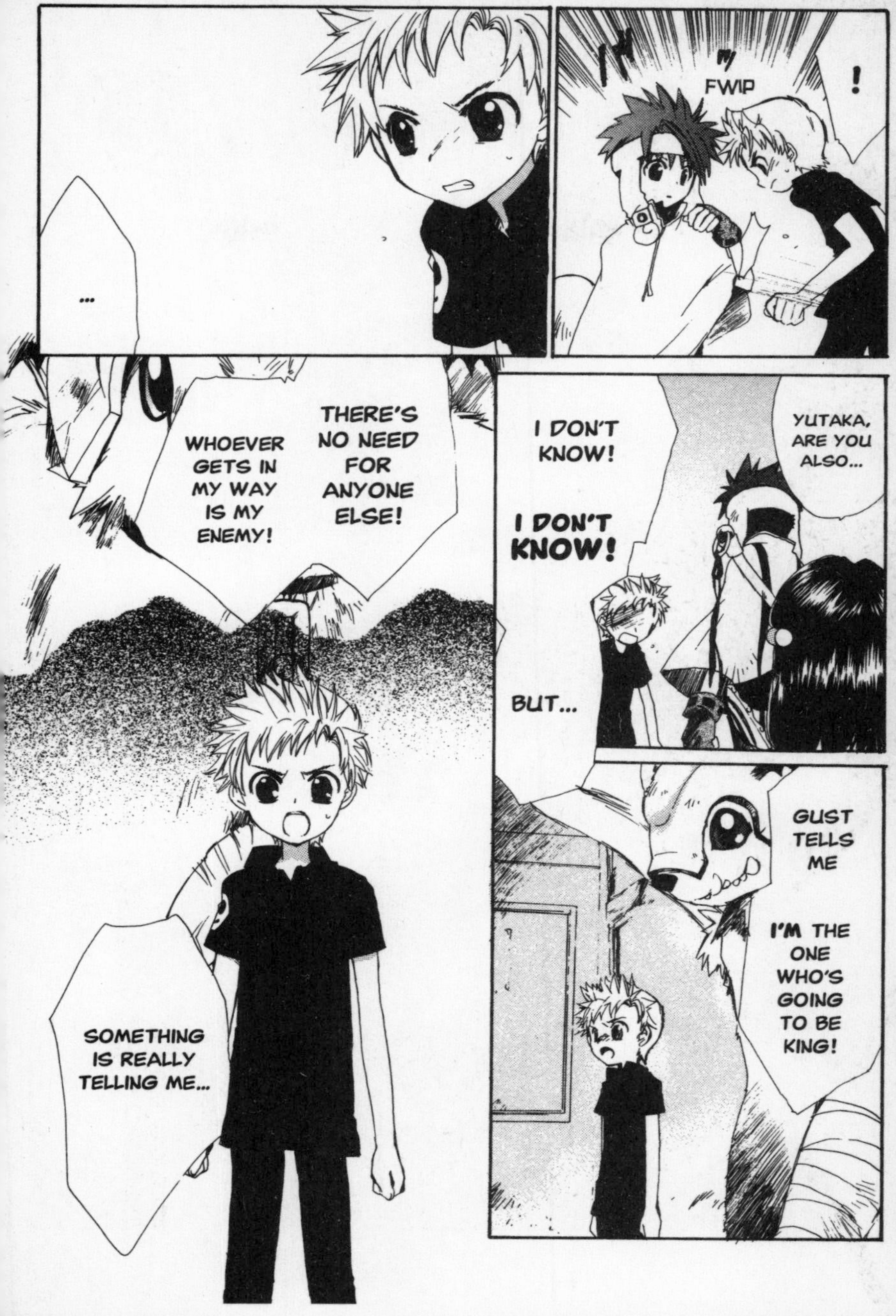
FWIP
!
...
YUTAKA, ARE YOU ALSO...
I DON'T KNOW!
I DON'T KNOW!
BUT...
THERE'S NO NEED FOR ANYONE ELSE!
WHOEVER GETS IN MY WAY IS MY ENEMY!
GUST TELLS ME
I'M THE ONE WHO'S GOING TO BE KING!
SOMETHING IS REALLY TELLING ME...

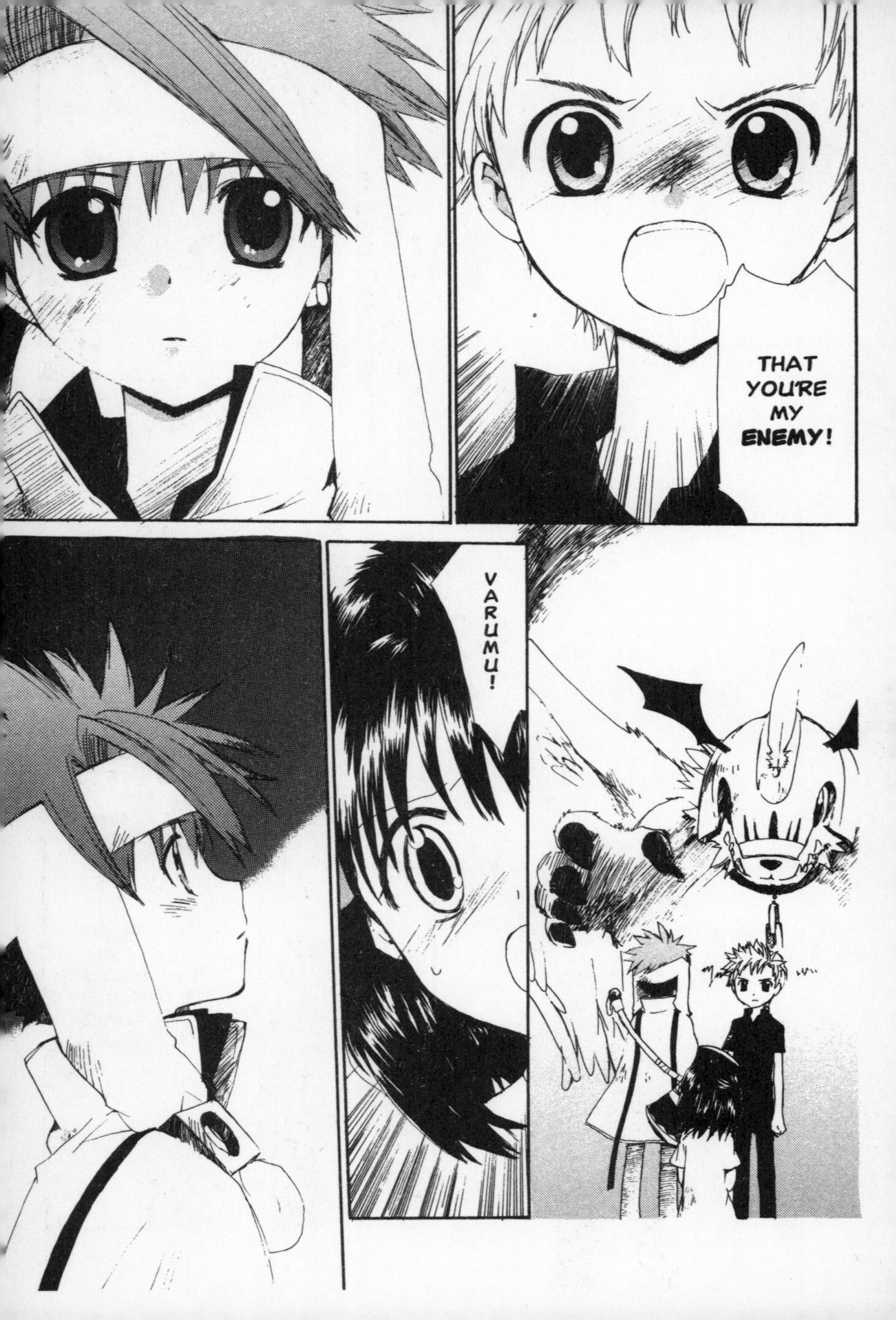

THAT YOU'RE MY ENEMY!
VARUMU!

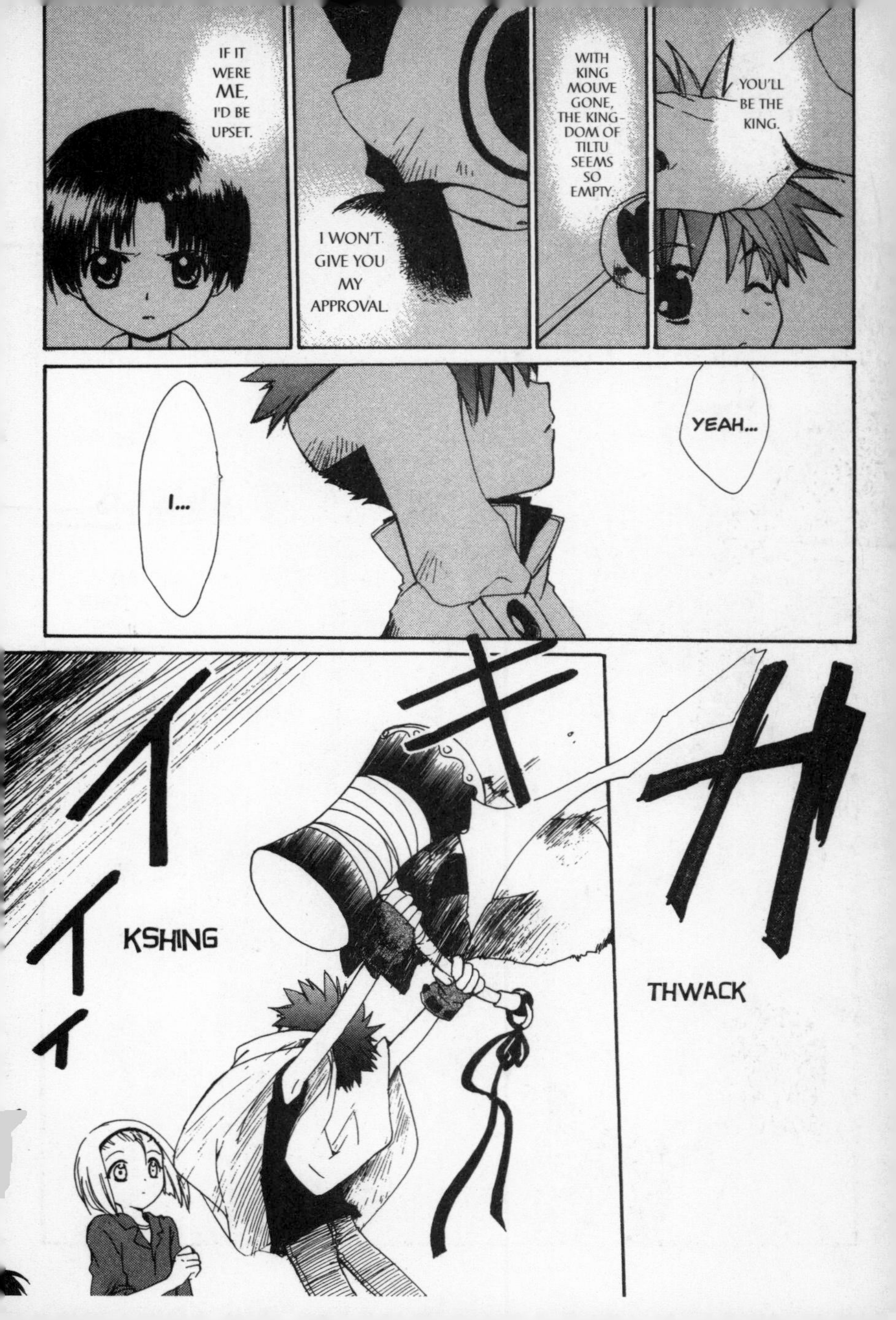
YOU'LL BE THE KING.
WITH KING MOUVE GONE, THE KING-DOM OF TILTU SEEMS SO EMPTY.
I WON'T GIVE YOU MY APPROVAL.
IF IT WERE ME, I'D BE UPSET.
YEAH...
I...
カ
THWACK
キイイイ
KSHING

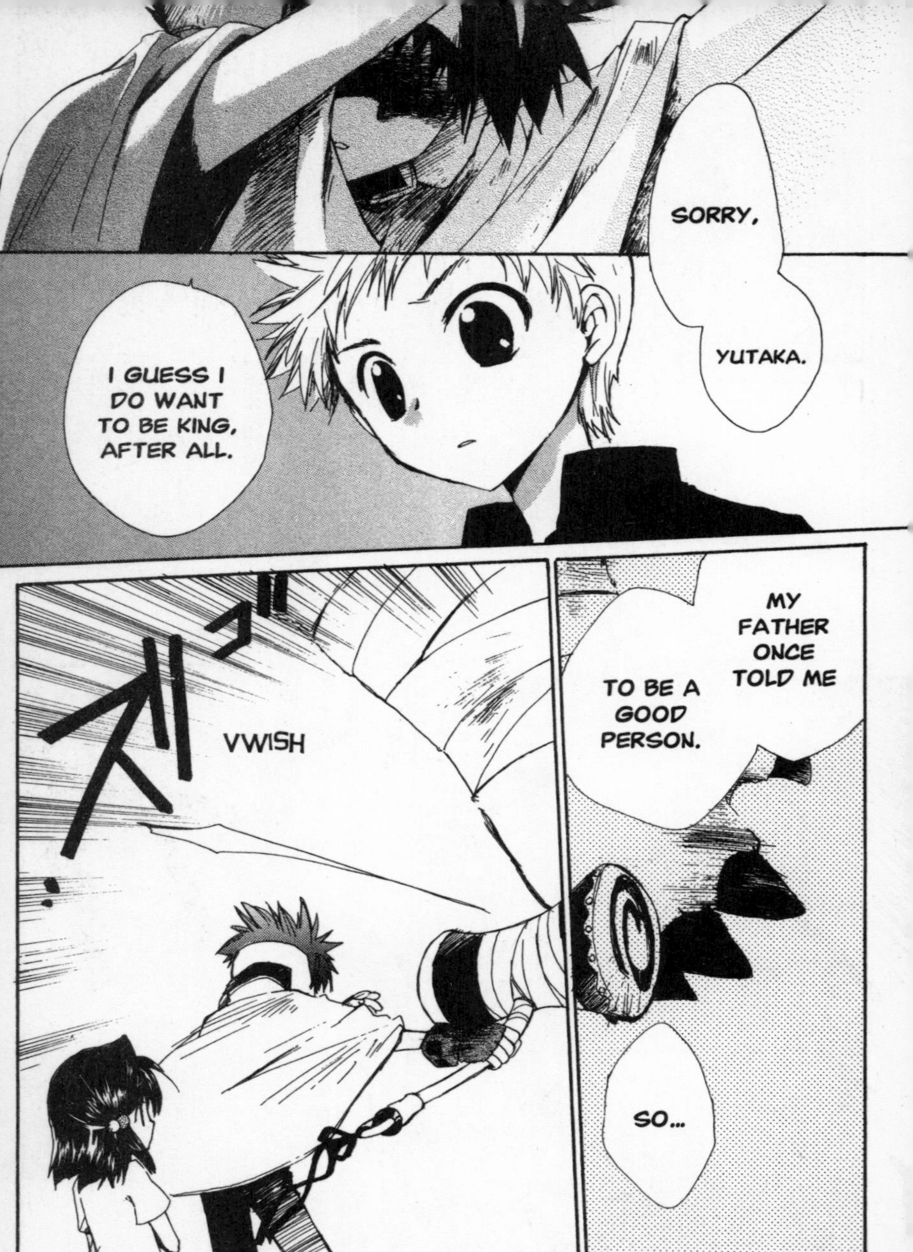
SORRY,
YUTAKA.
I GUESS I DO WANT TO BE KING, AFTER ALL.
MY FATHER ONCE TOLD ME
TO BE A GOOD PERSON.
SO...
VWISH

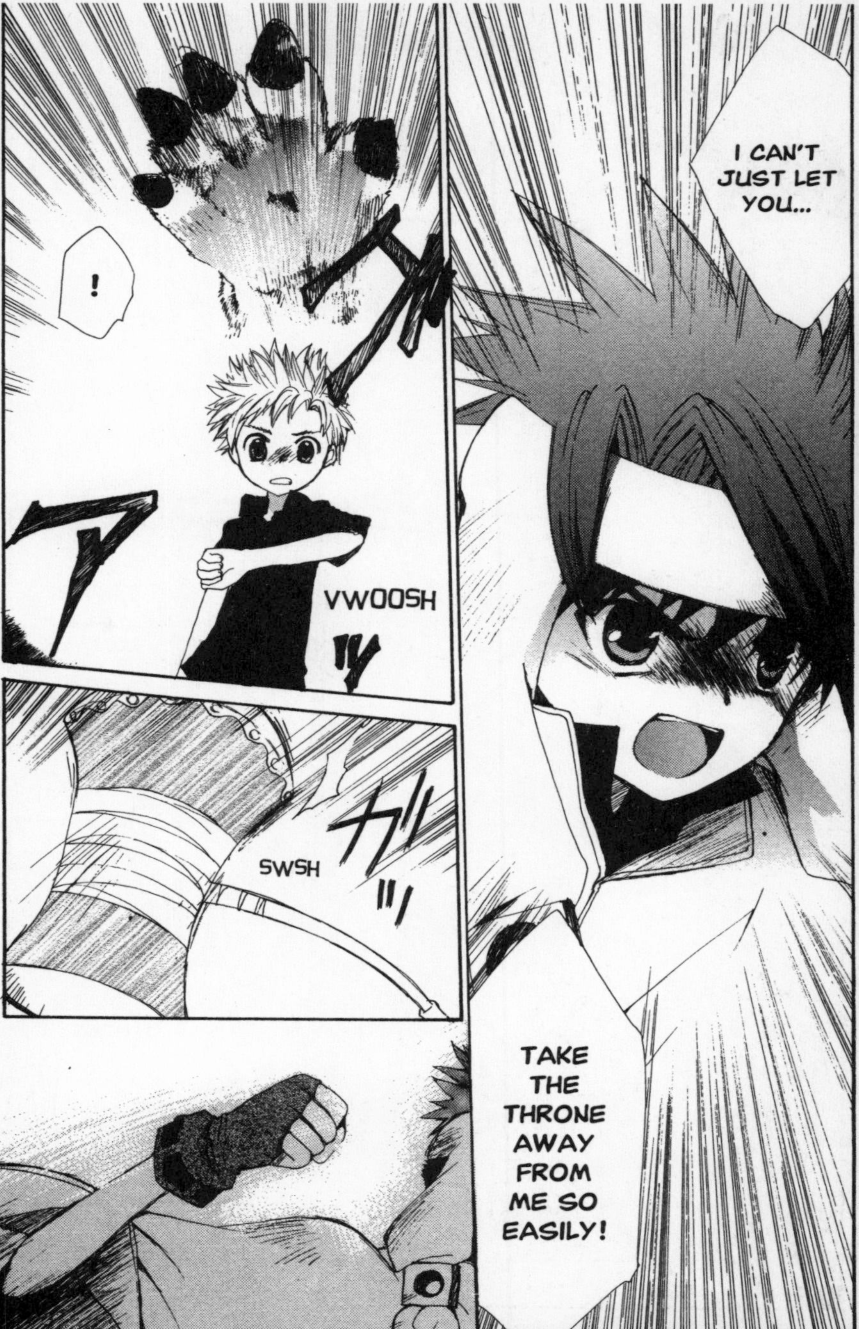
I CAN'T JUST LET YOU...
!
VWOOSH
SWSH
TAKE THE THRONE AWAY FROM ME SO EASILY!

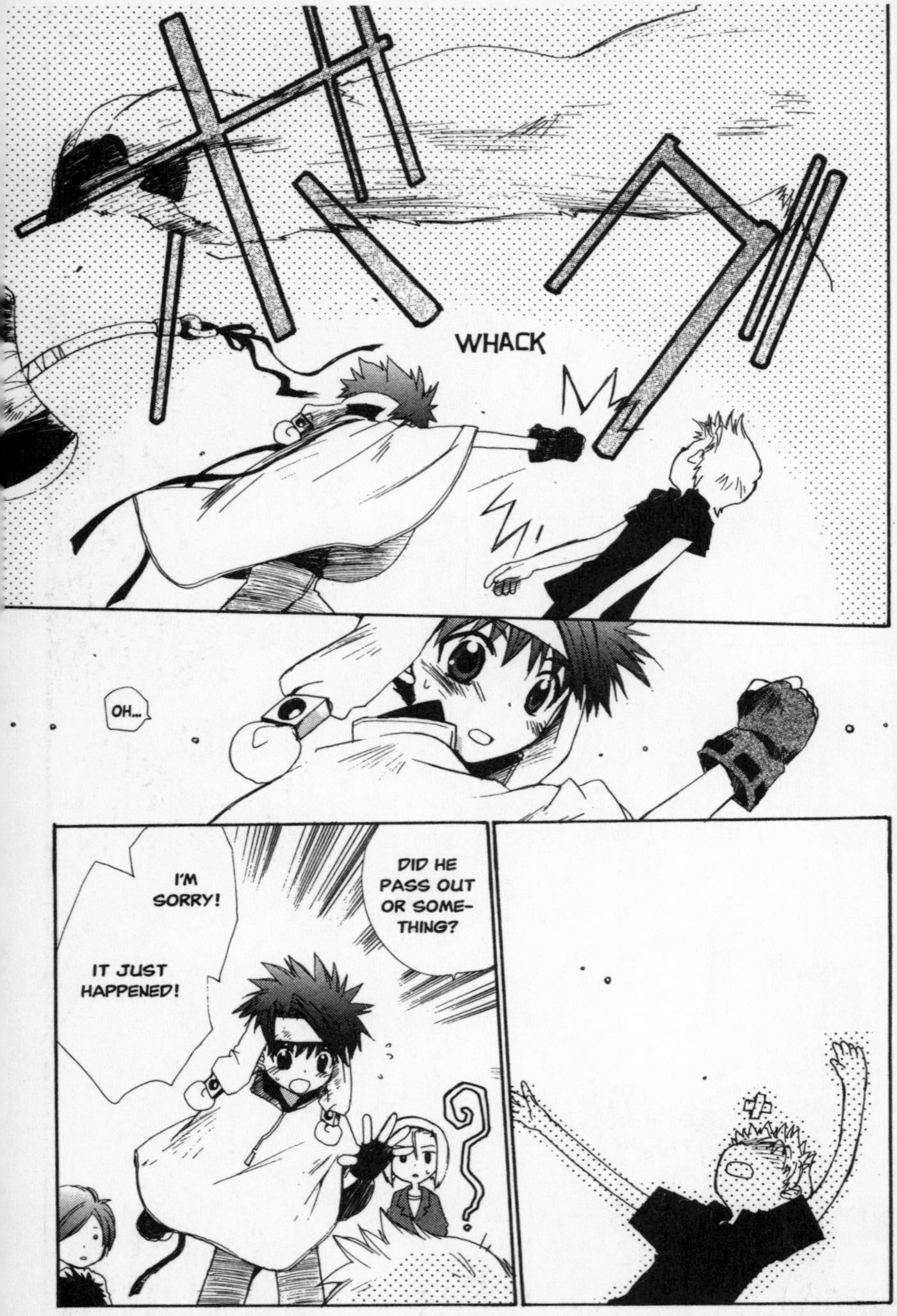
WHACK
OH...
DID HE PASS OUT OR SOME-THING?
I'M SORRY!
IT JUST HAPPENED!

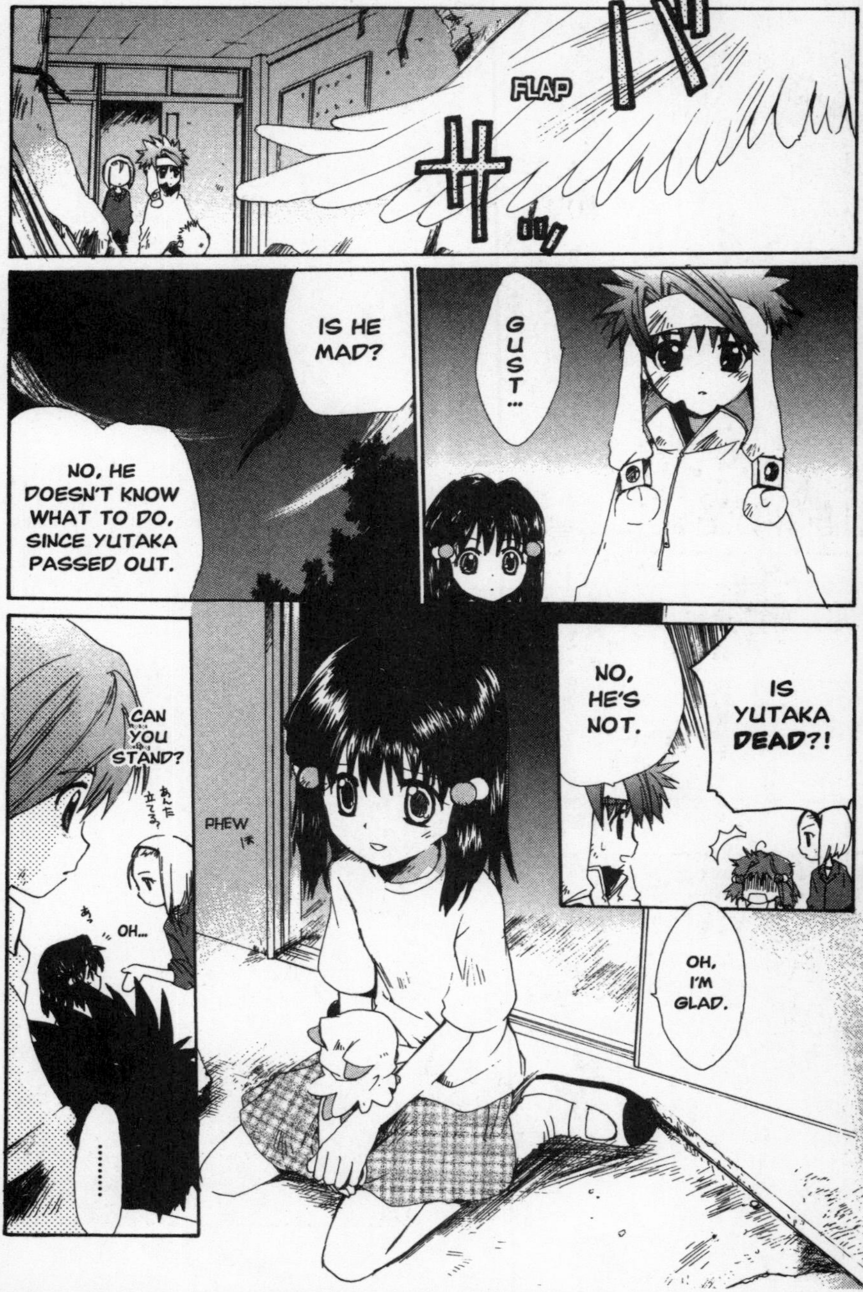

バ
サ
FLAP
GUST...
IS HE MAD?
NO, HE DOESN'T KNOW WHAT TO DO, SINCE YUTAKA PASSED OUT.
IS YUTAKA DEAD?!
NO, HE'S NOT.
OH, I'M GLAD.
PHEW
CAN YOU STAND?
あんた立てる?
あっ
OH...
....

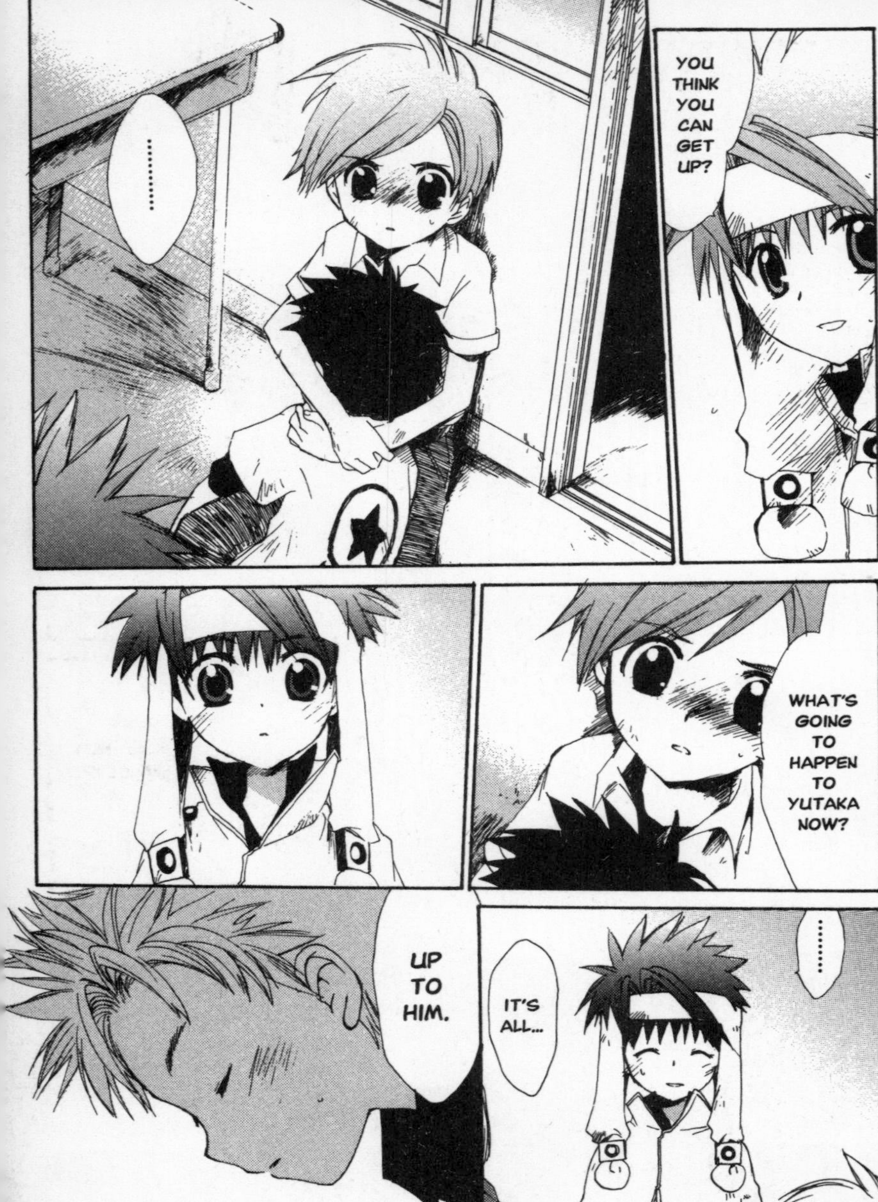
YOU THINK YOU CAN GET UP?
....
WHAT'S GOING TO HAPPEN TO YUTAKA NOW?
....
IT'S ALL...
UP TO HIM.

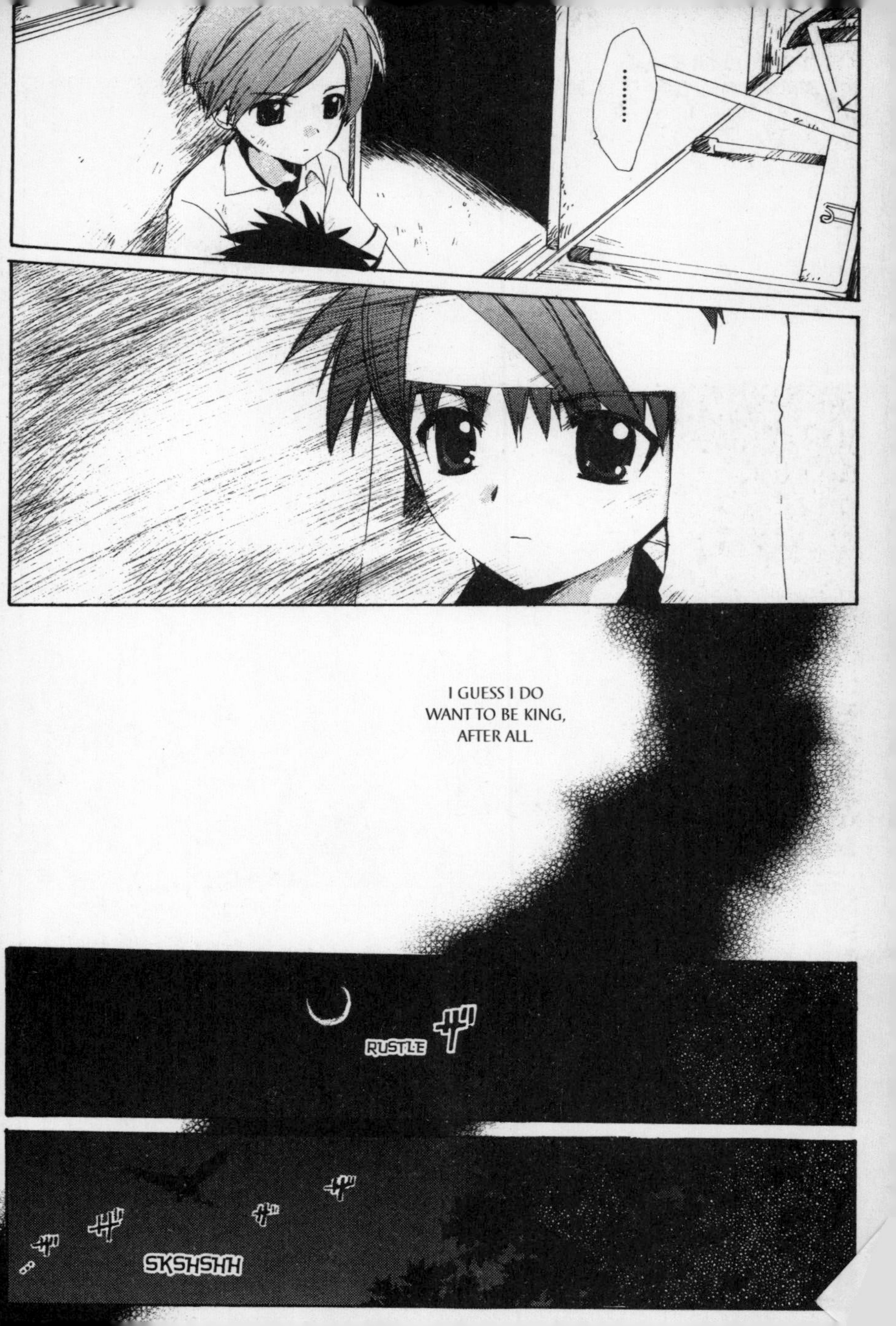
……
I GUESS I DO
WANT TO BE KING,
AFTER ALL.
RUSTLE
SKSHSHH

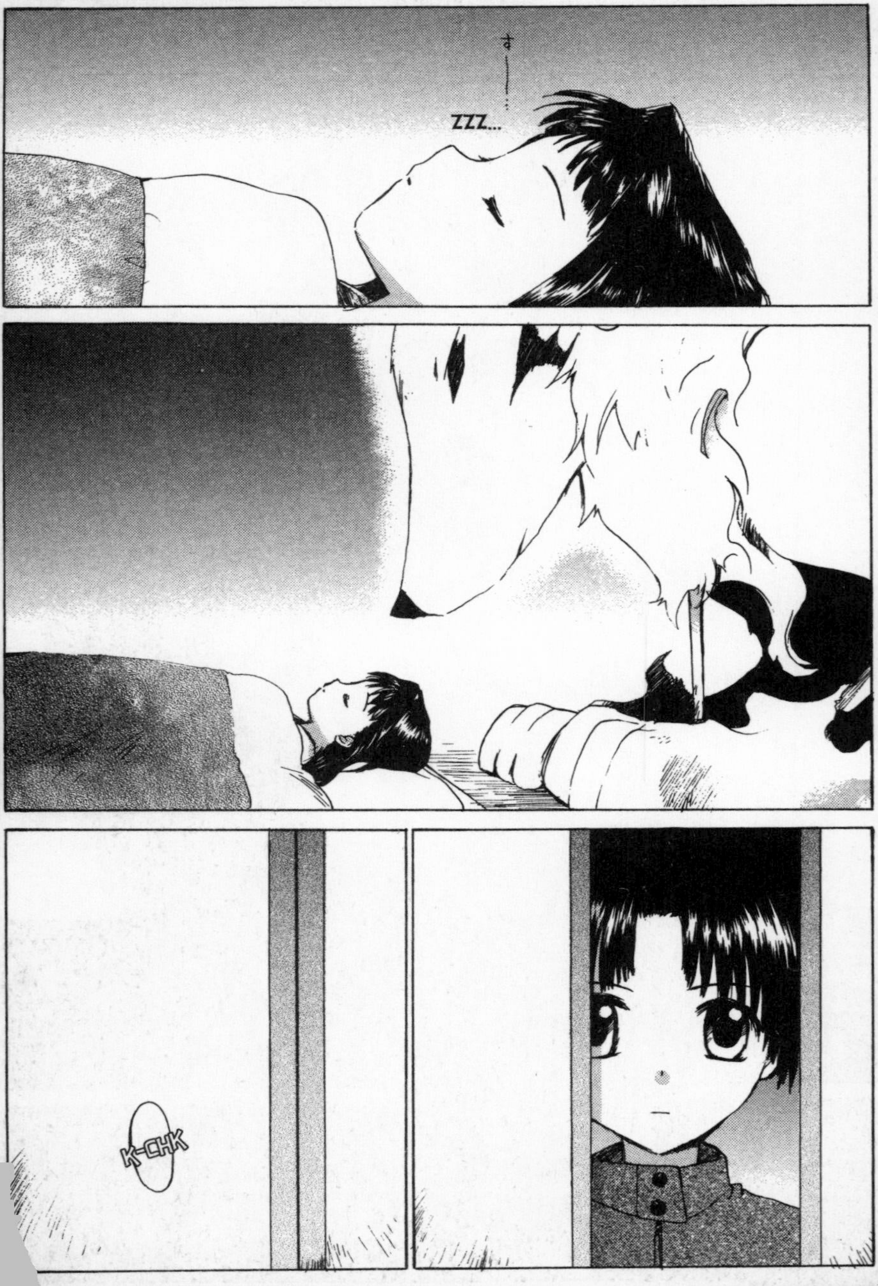
す—…
ZZZ...
K-CHK

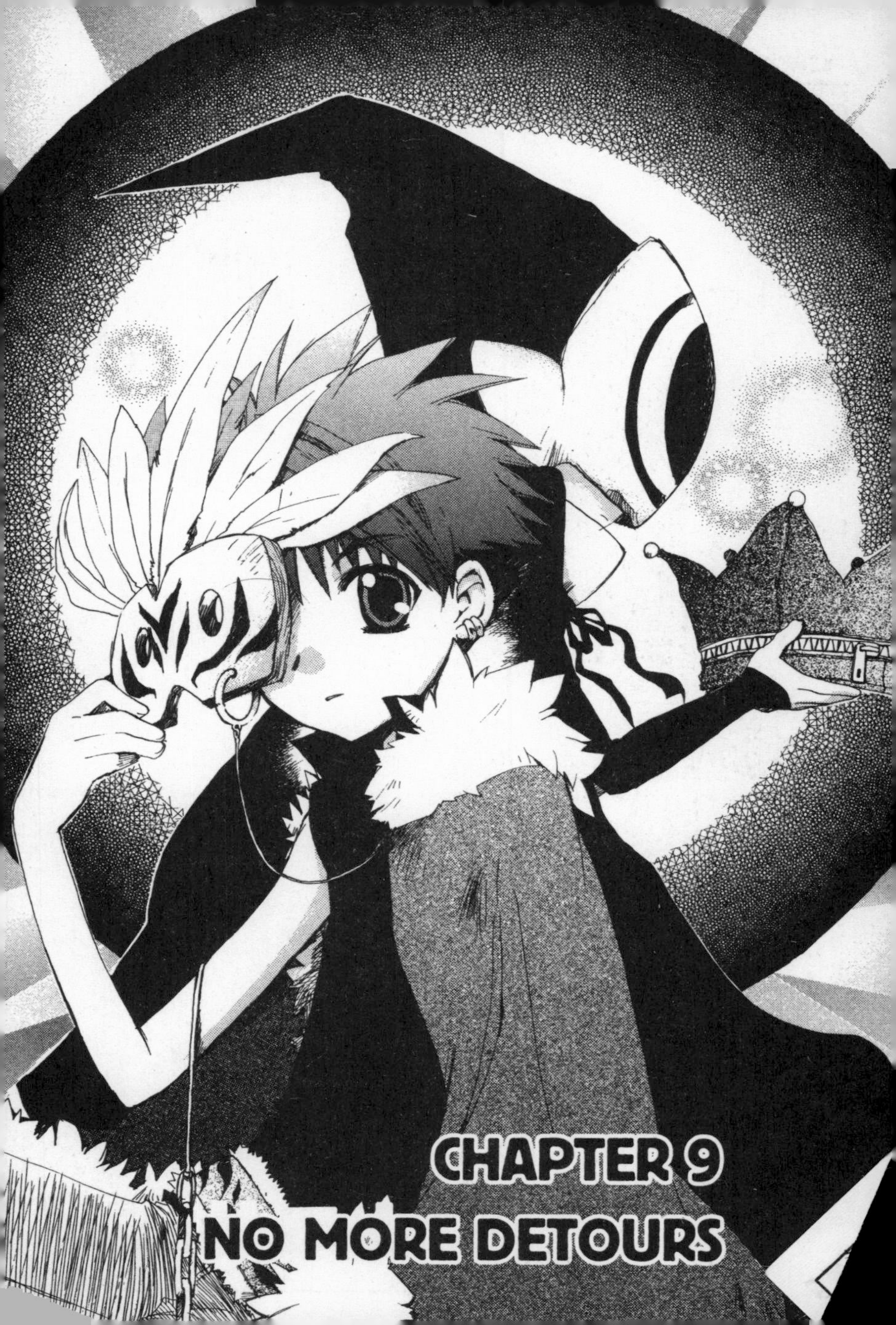
CHAPTER 9
NO MORE DETOURS

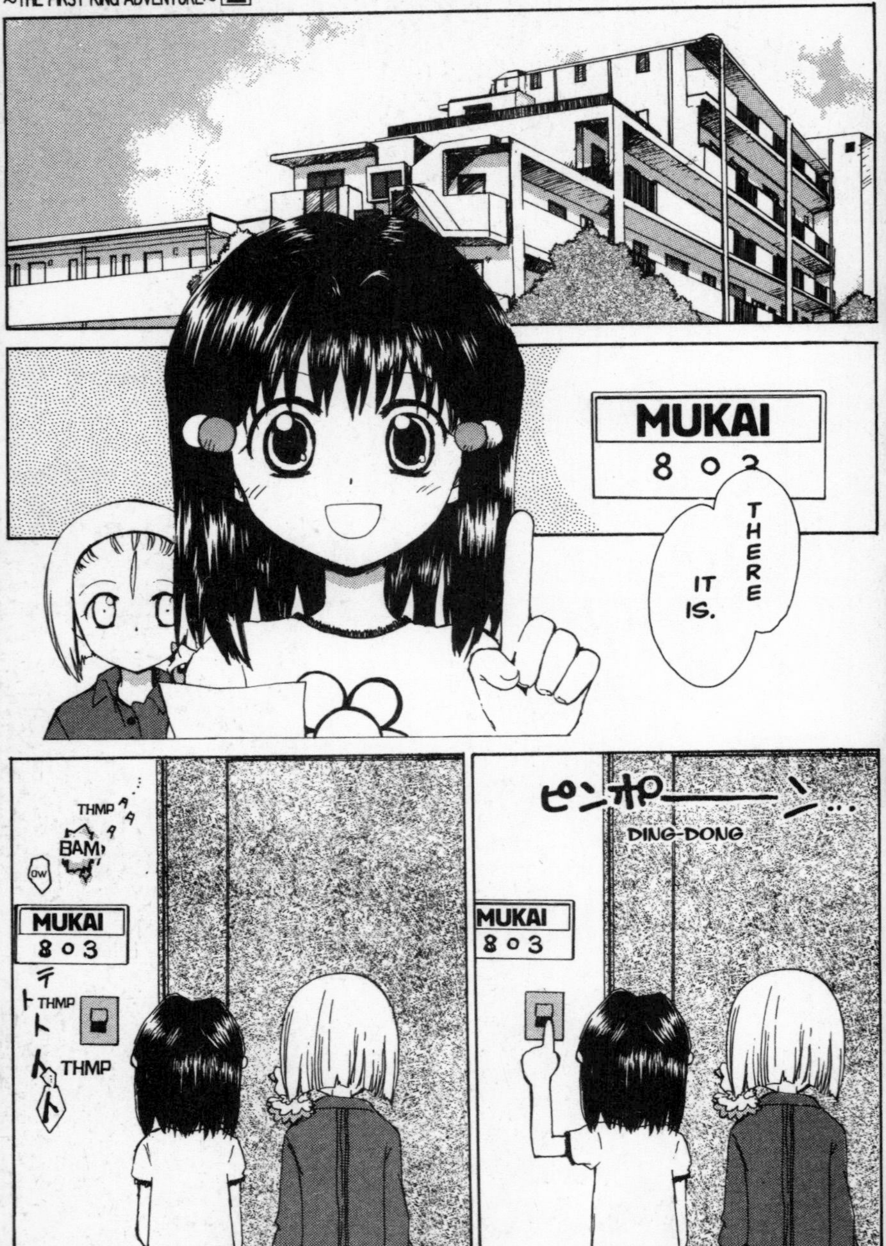
MUKAI
803
THERE IT IS.
ピンポーーーン…
DING-DONG
MUKAI
803
タタタ…
THMP
BAM
OW
MUKAI
803
テトトト…
THMP
THMP

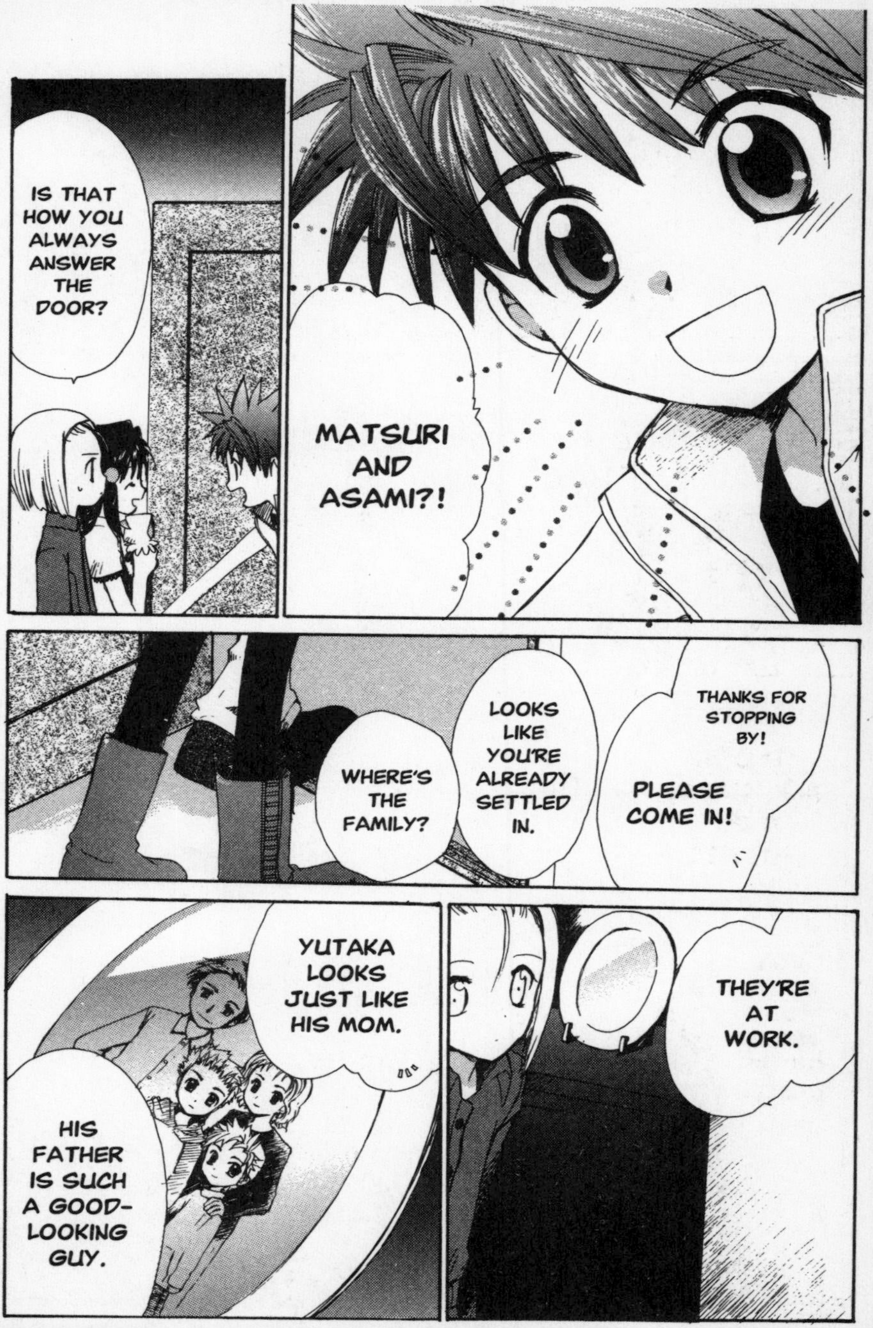
MATSURI AND ASAMI?!
IS THAT HOW YOU ALWAYS ANSWER THE DOOR?
THANKS FOR STOPPING BY!
PLEASE COME IN!
LOOKS LIKE YOU'RE ALREADY SETTLED IN.
WHERE'S THE FAMILY?
THEY'RE AT WORK.
YUTAKA LOOKS JUST LIKE HIS MOM.
HIS FATHER IS SUCH A GOOD-LOOKING GUY.

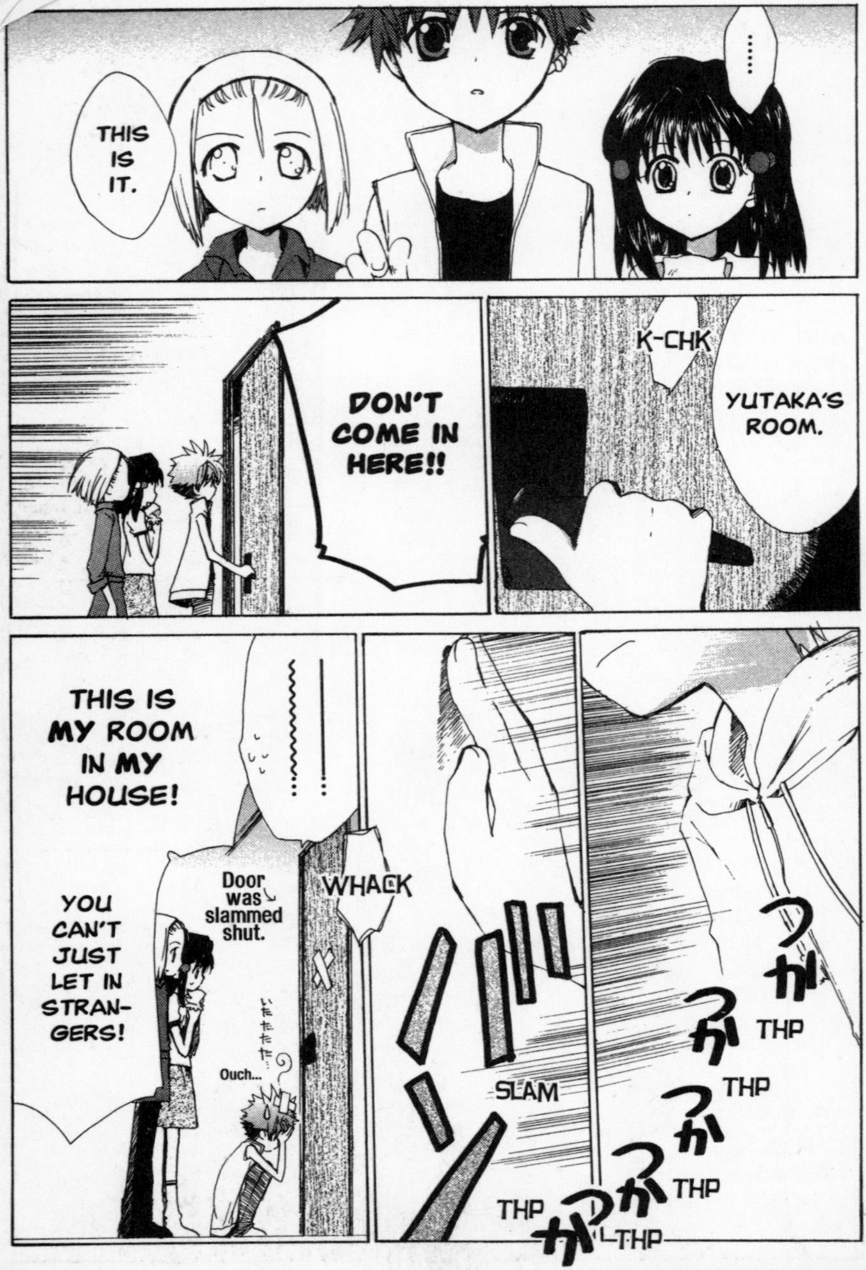
......
THIS IS IT.
K-CHK
YUTAKA'S ROOM.
DON'T COME IN HERE!!
つかつかつかつかつか
THP
THP
THP
THP
THP
SLAM
WHACK
......
THIS IS MY ROOM IN MY HOUSE!
Door was slammed shut.
YOU CAN'T JUST LET IN STRANGERS!
いたたた…
Ouch...

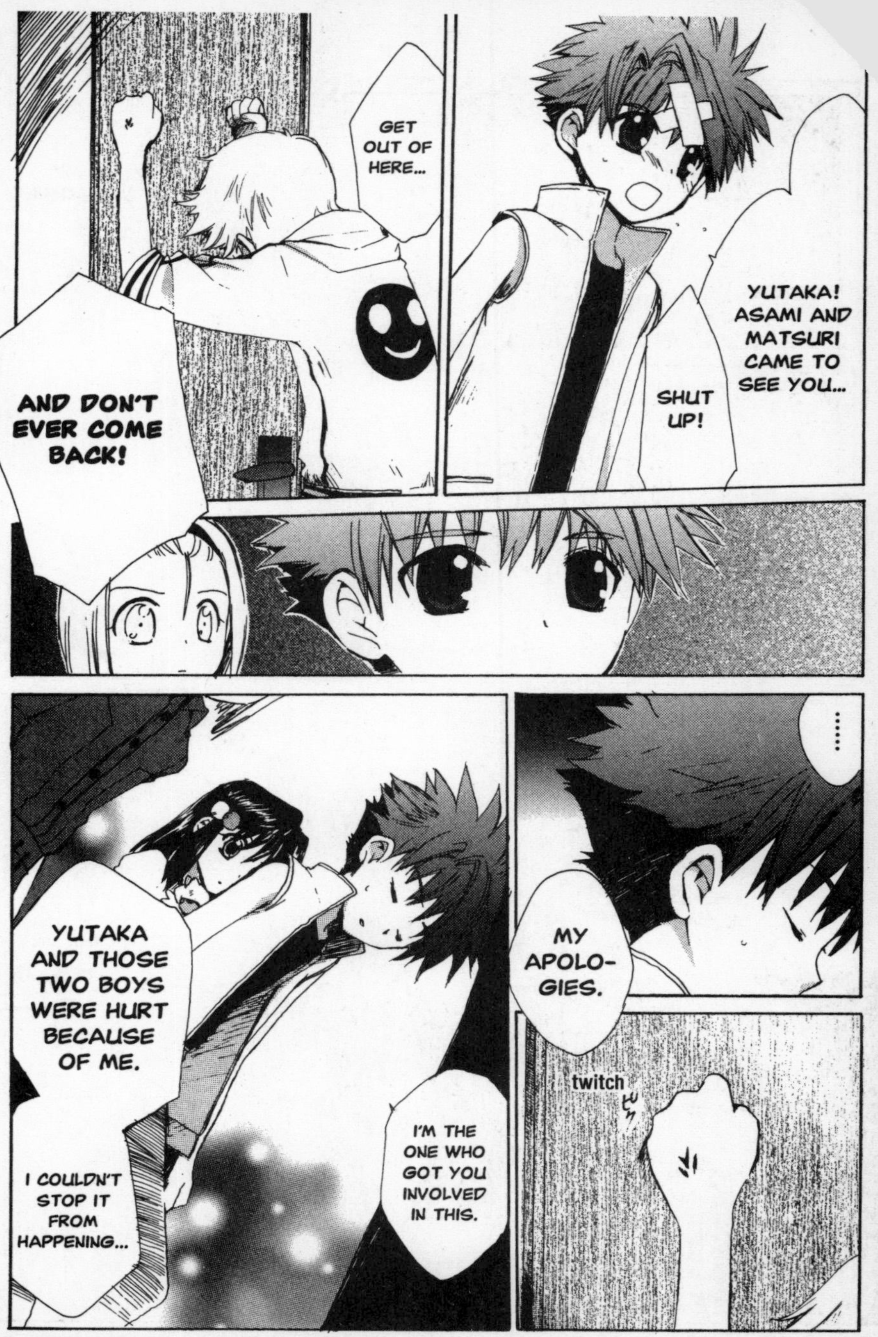
YUTAKA! ASAMI AND MATSURI CAME TO SEE YOU...
SHUT UP!
GET OUT OF HERE...
AND DON'T EVER COME BACK!
......
MY APOLO-GIES.
YUTAKA AND THOSE TWO BOYS WERE HURT BECAUSE OF ME.
I'M THE ONE WHO GOT YOU INVOLVED IN THIS.
I COULDN'T STOP IT FROM HAPPENING...
twitch

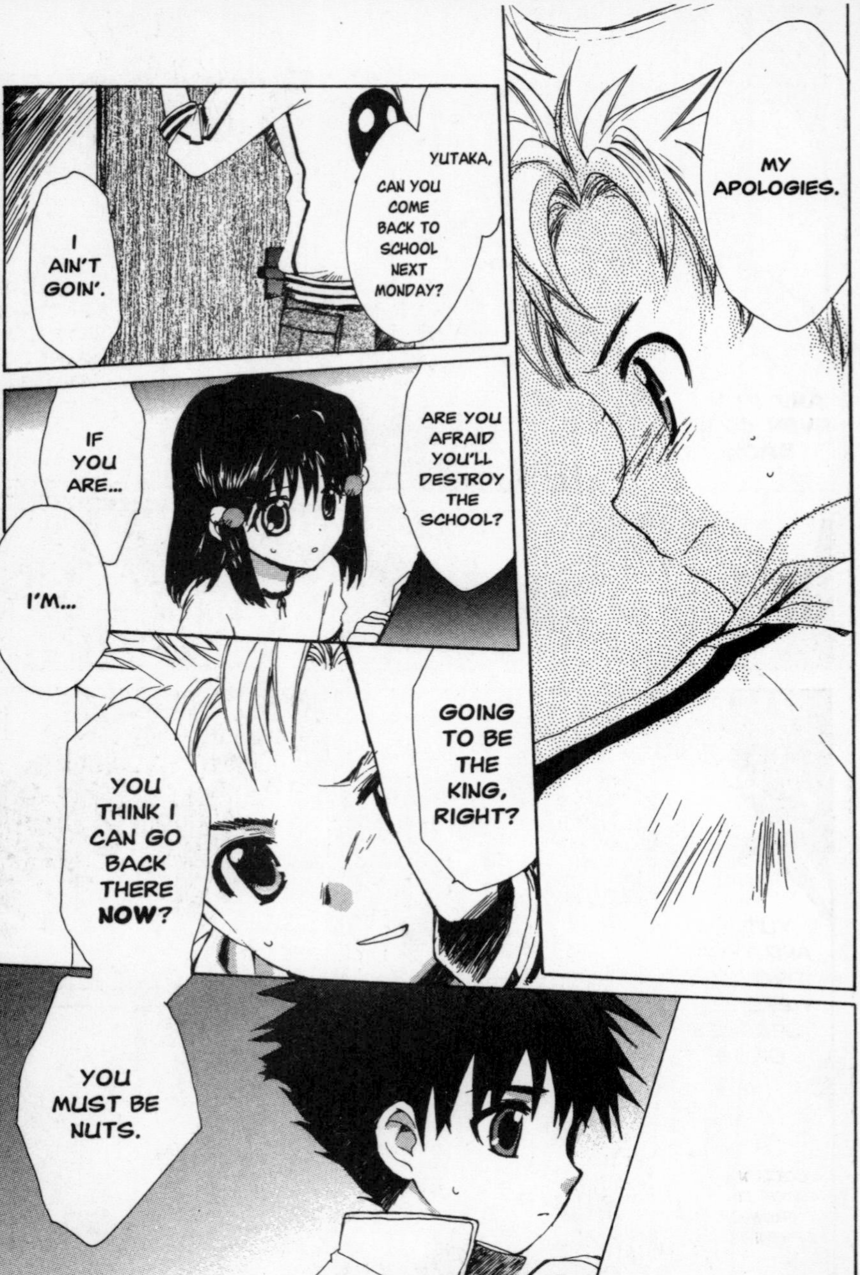

MY APOLOGIES.
YUTAKA,
CAN YOU COME BACK TO SCHOOL NEXT MONDAY?
I AIN'T GOIN'.
ARE YOU AFRAID YOU'LL DESTROY THE SCHOOL?
IF YOU ARE...
I'M...
GOING TO BE THE KING, RIGHT?
YOU THINK I CAN GO BACK THERE NOW?
YOU MUST BE NUTS.

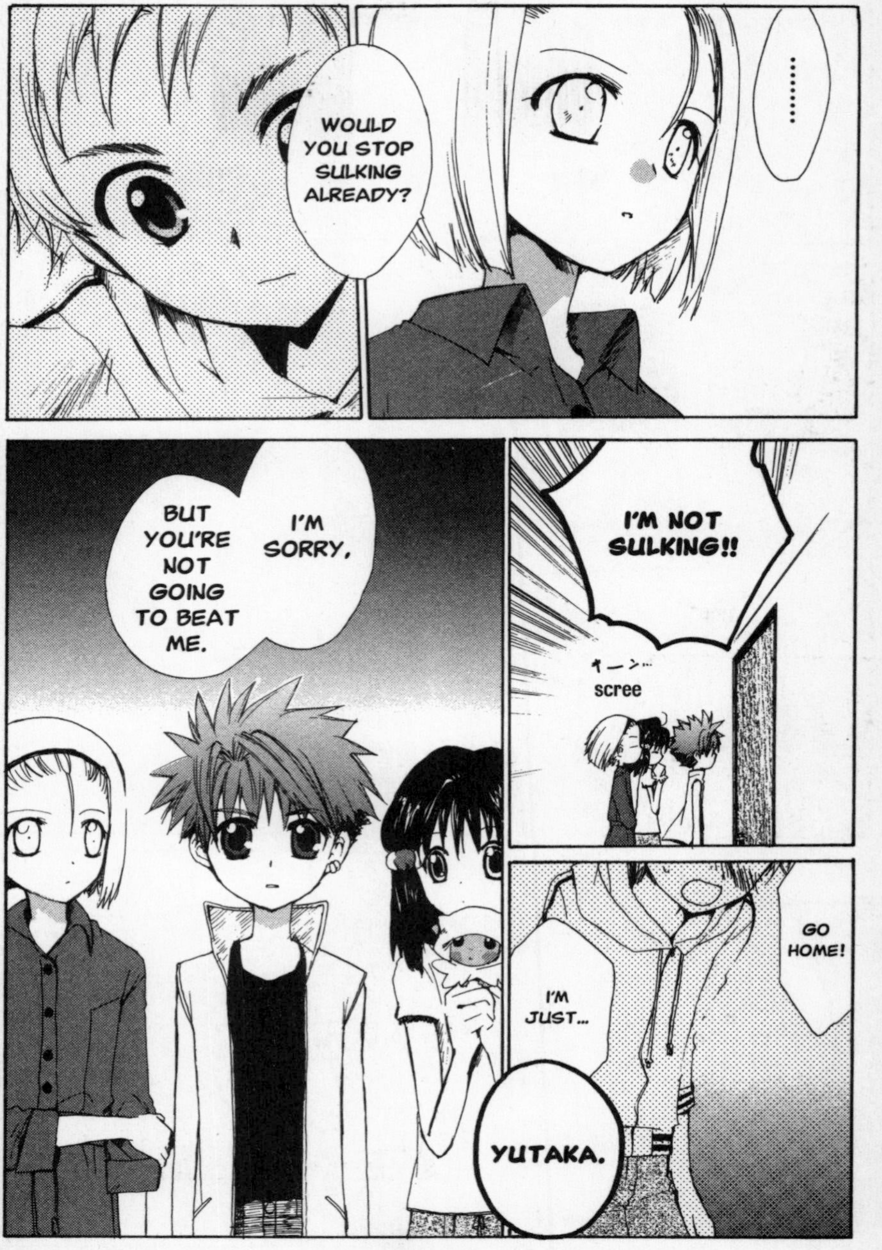

WOULD YOU STOP SULKING ALREADY?
......
I'M NOT SULKING!!
scree
I'M SORRY, BUT YOU'RE NOT GOING TO BEAT ME.
GO HOME!
I'M JUST...
YUTAKA.

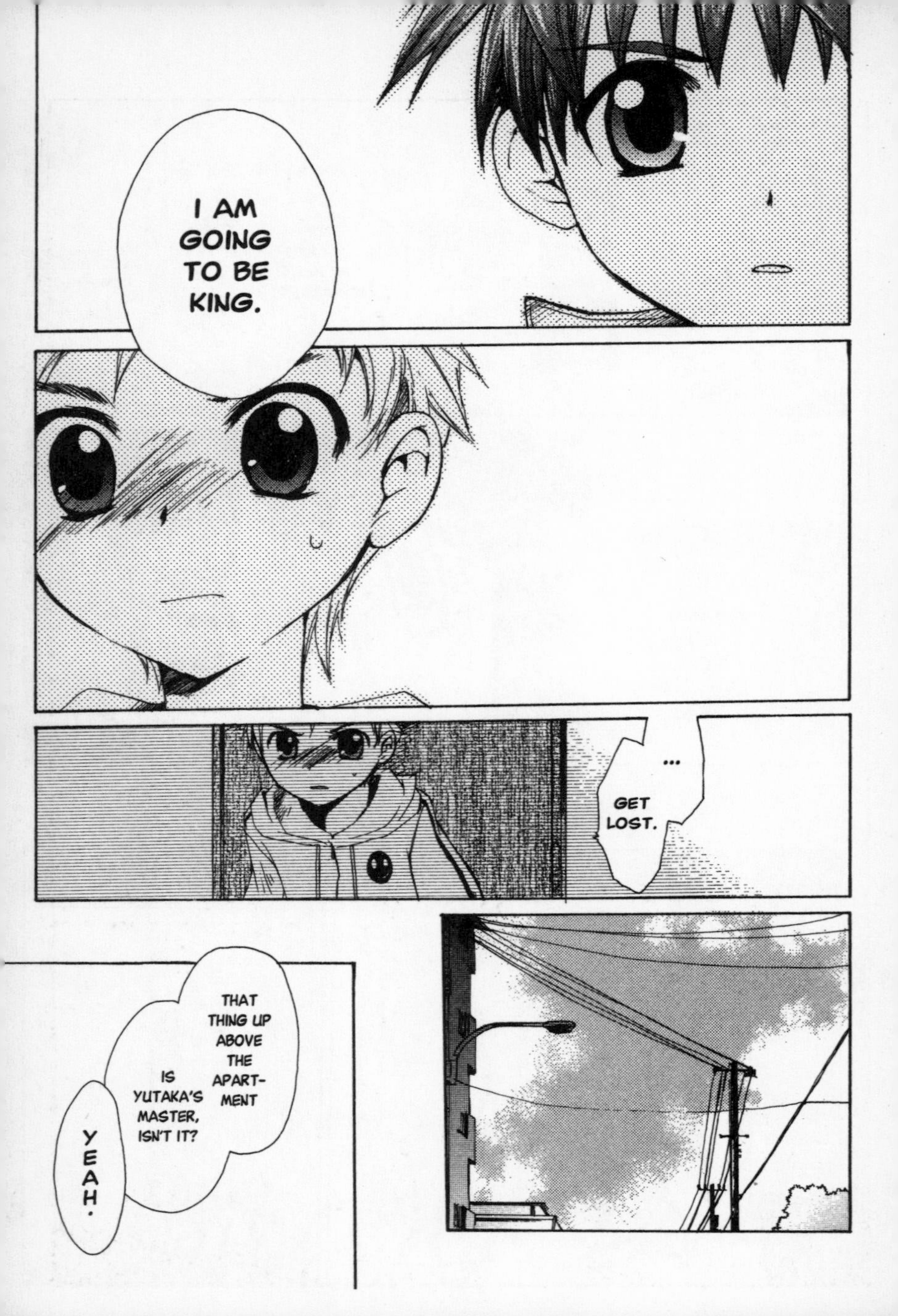
I AM GOING TO BE KING.
... GET LOST.
THAT THING UP ABOVE THE APARTMENT IS YUTAKA'S MASTER, ISN'T IT?
YEAH.

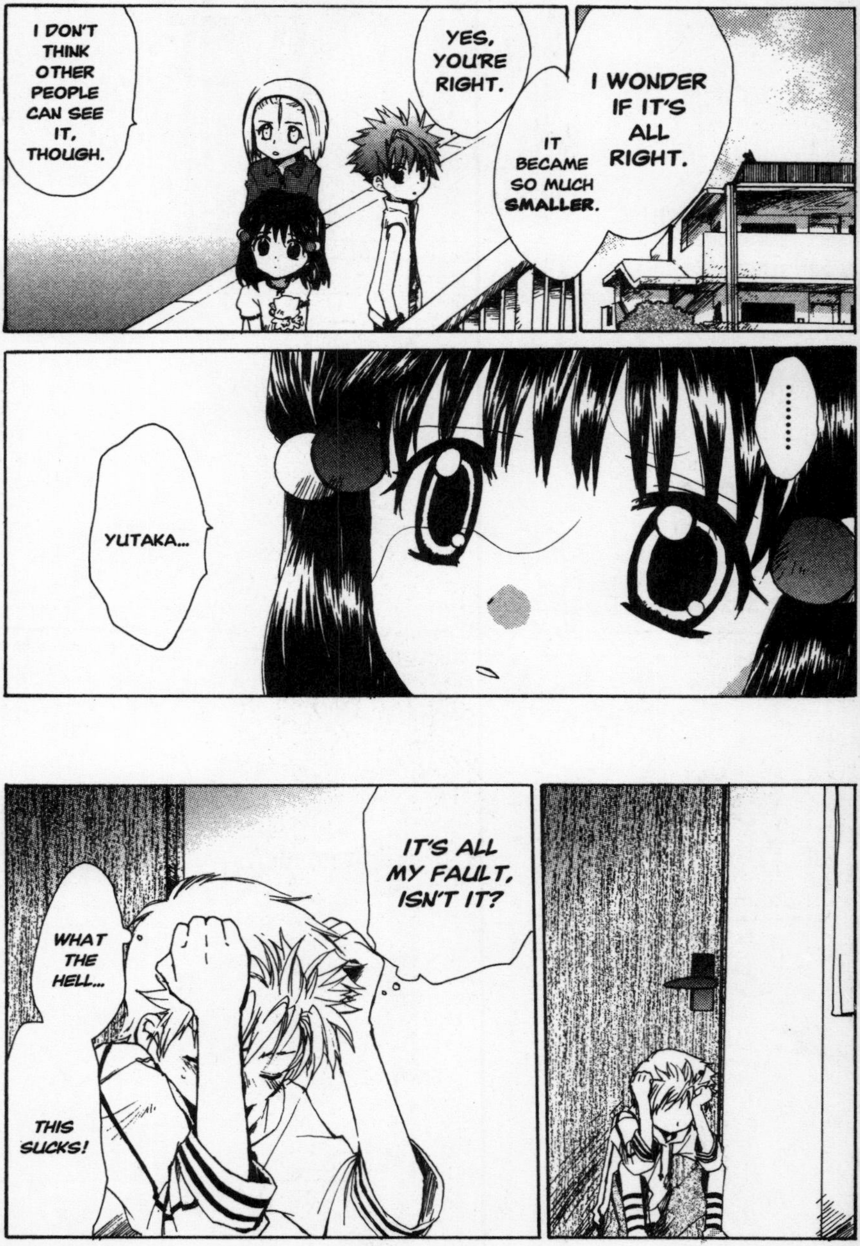
I WONDER IF IT'S ALL RIGHT.
IT BECAME SO MUCH SMALLER.
YES, YOU'RE RIGHT.
I DON'T THINK OTHER PEOPLE CAN SEE IT, THOUGH.
......
YUTAKA...
IT'S ALL MY FAULT, ISN'T IT?
WHAT THE HELL...
THIS SUCKS!

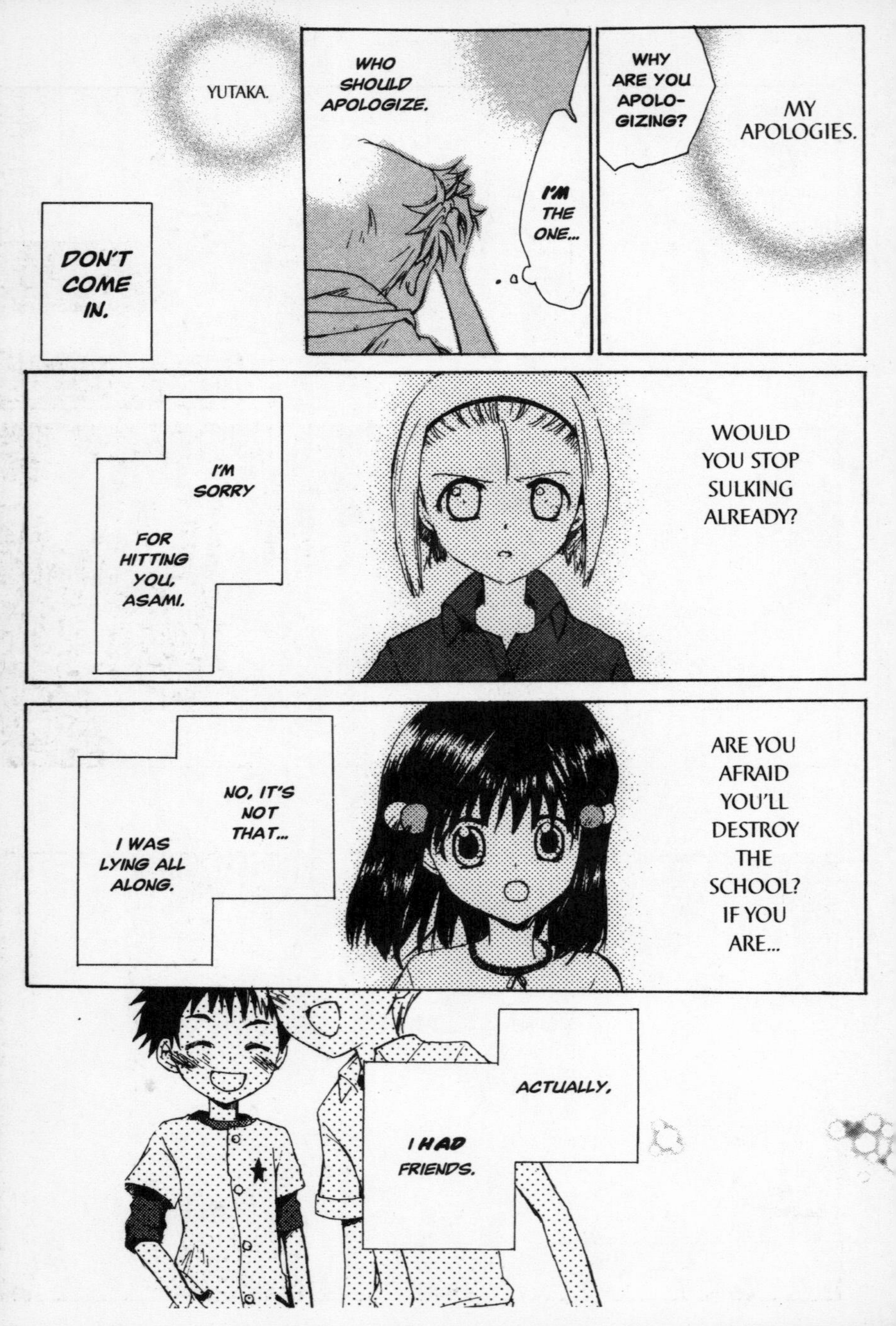
MY APOLOGIES.
WHY ARE YOU APOLOGIZING?
I'M THE ONE...
WHO SHOULD APOLOGIZE.
YUTAKA.
DON'T COME IN.
WOULD YOU STOP SULKING ALREADY?
I'M SORRY
FOR HITTING YOU, ASAMI.
ARE YOU AFRAID YOU'LL DESTROY THE SCHOOL? IF YOU ARE...
NO, IT'S NOT THAT...
I WAS LYING ALL ALONG.
ACTUALLY,
I HAD FRIENDS.

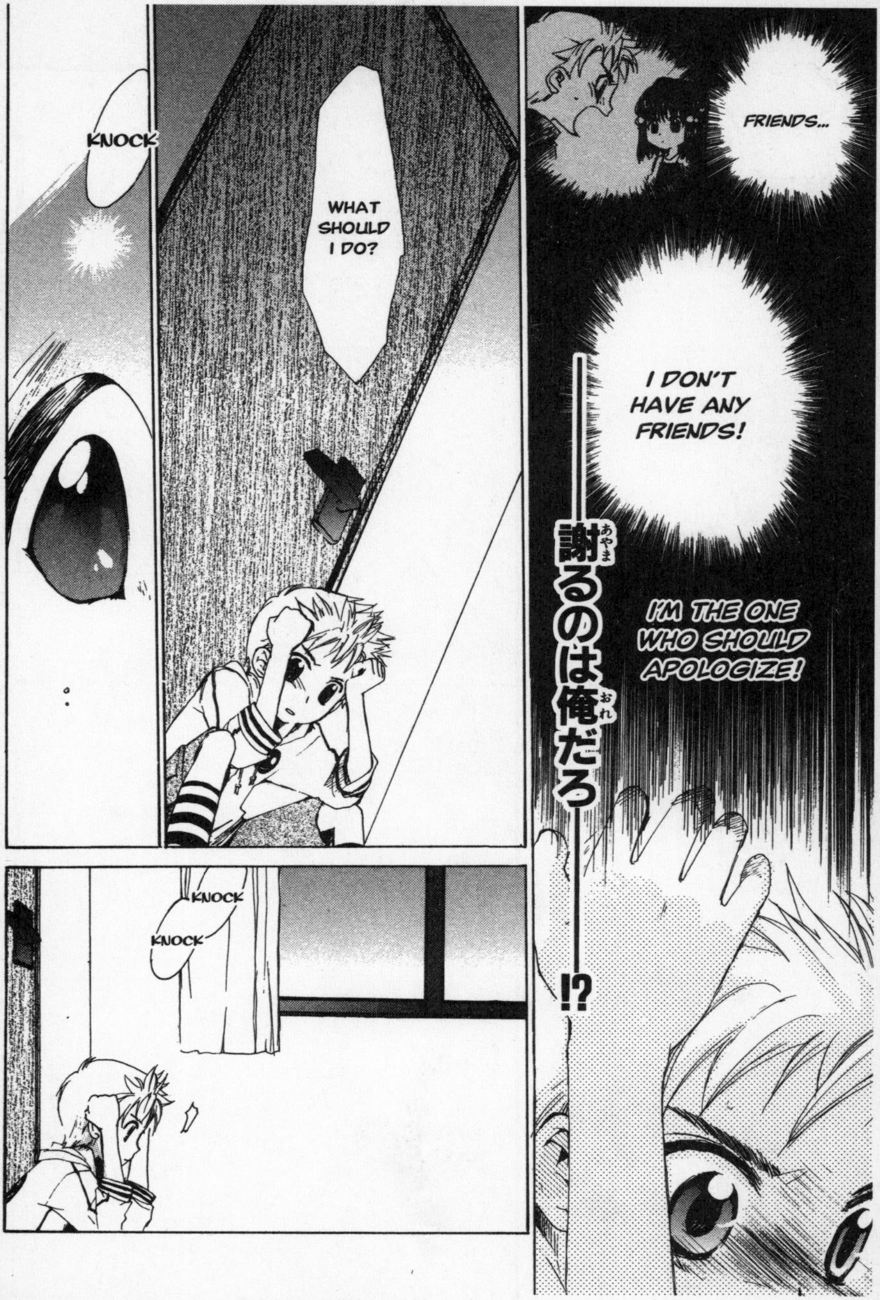
FRIENDS...
I DON'T HAVE ANY FRIENDS!
謝(あやま)るのは俺(おれ)だろ――!?
I'M THE ONE WHO SHOULD APOLOGIZE!
WHAT SHOULD I DO?
KNOCK
KNOCK
KNOCK

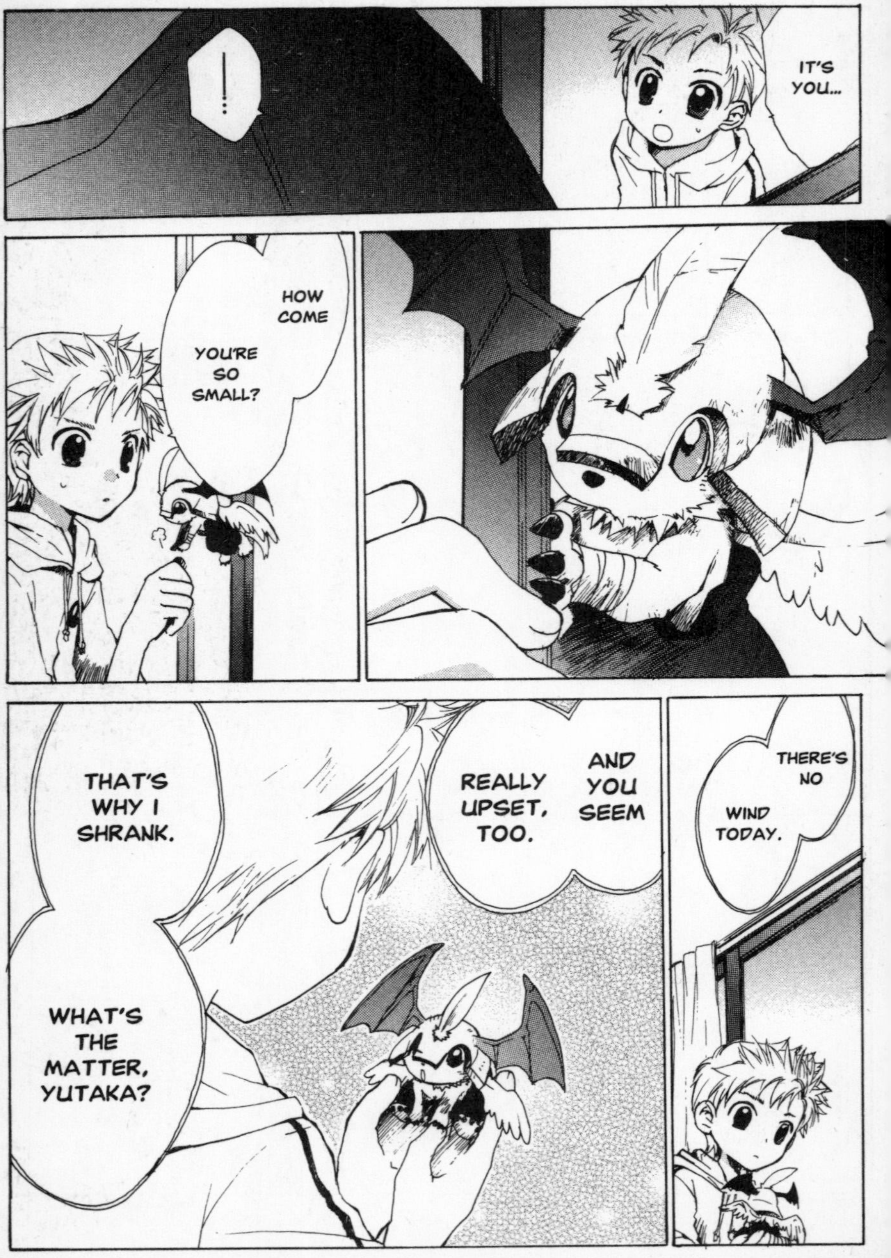
IT'S YOU...
!
HOW COME YOU'RE SO SMALL?
THERE'S NO WIND TODAY.
AND YOU SEEM REALLY UPSET, TOO.
THAT'S WHY I SHRANK.
WHAT'S THE MATTER, YUTAKA?

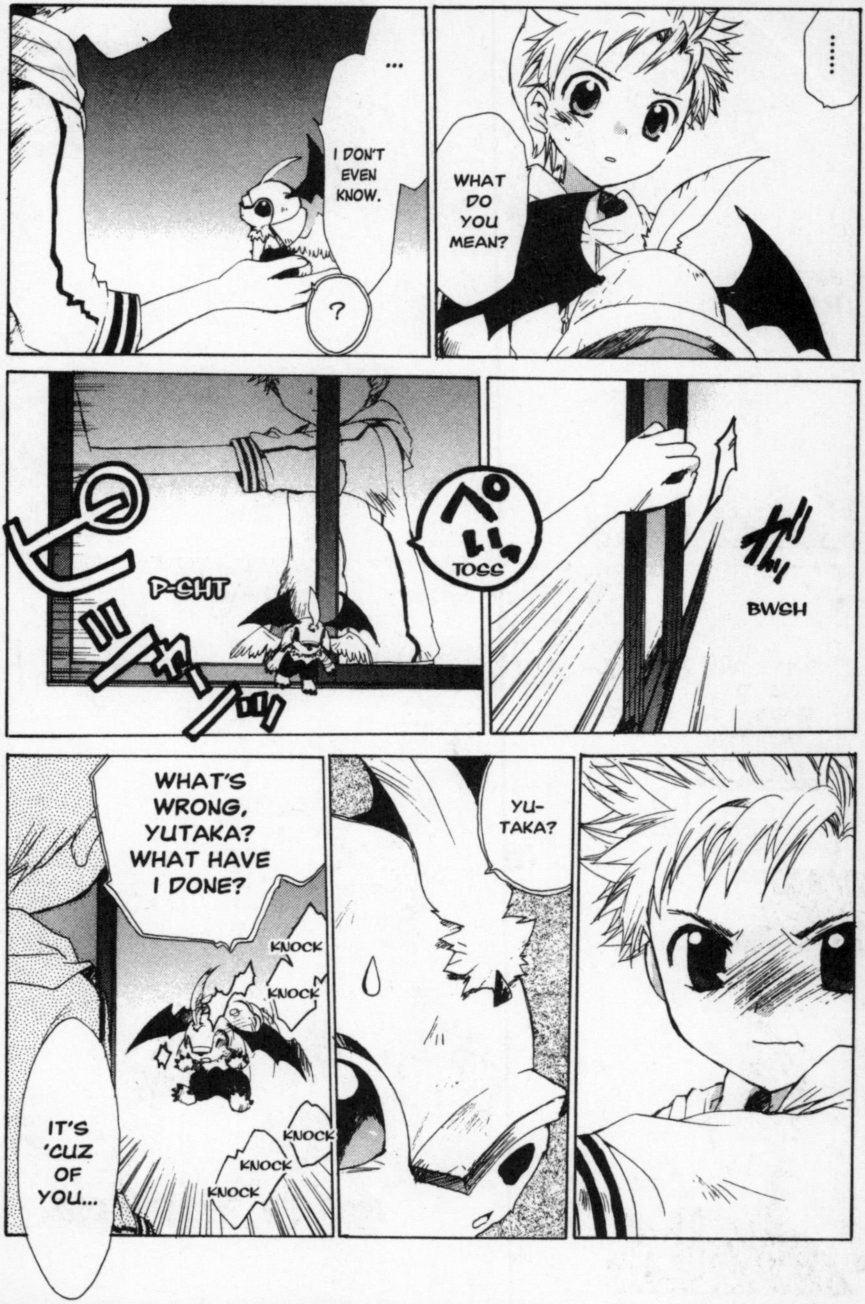
......
WHAT DO YOU MEAN?
...
I DON'T EVEN KNOW.
?
BWSH
TOSS
P-SHT
YU-TAKA?
WHAT'S WRONG, YUTAKA? WHAT HAVE I DONE?
KNOCK
KNOCK
KNOCK
KNOCK
KNOCK
IT'S 'CUZ OF YOU...

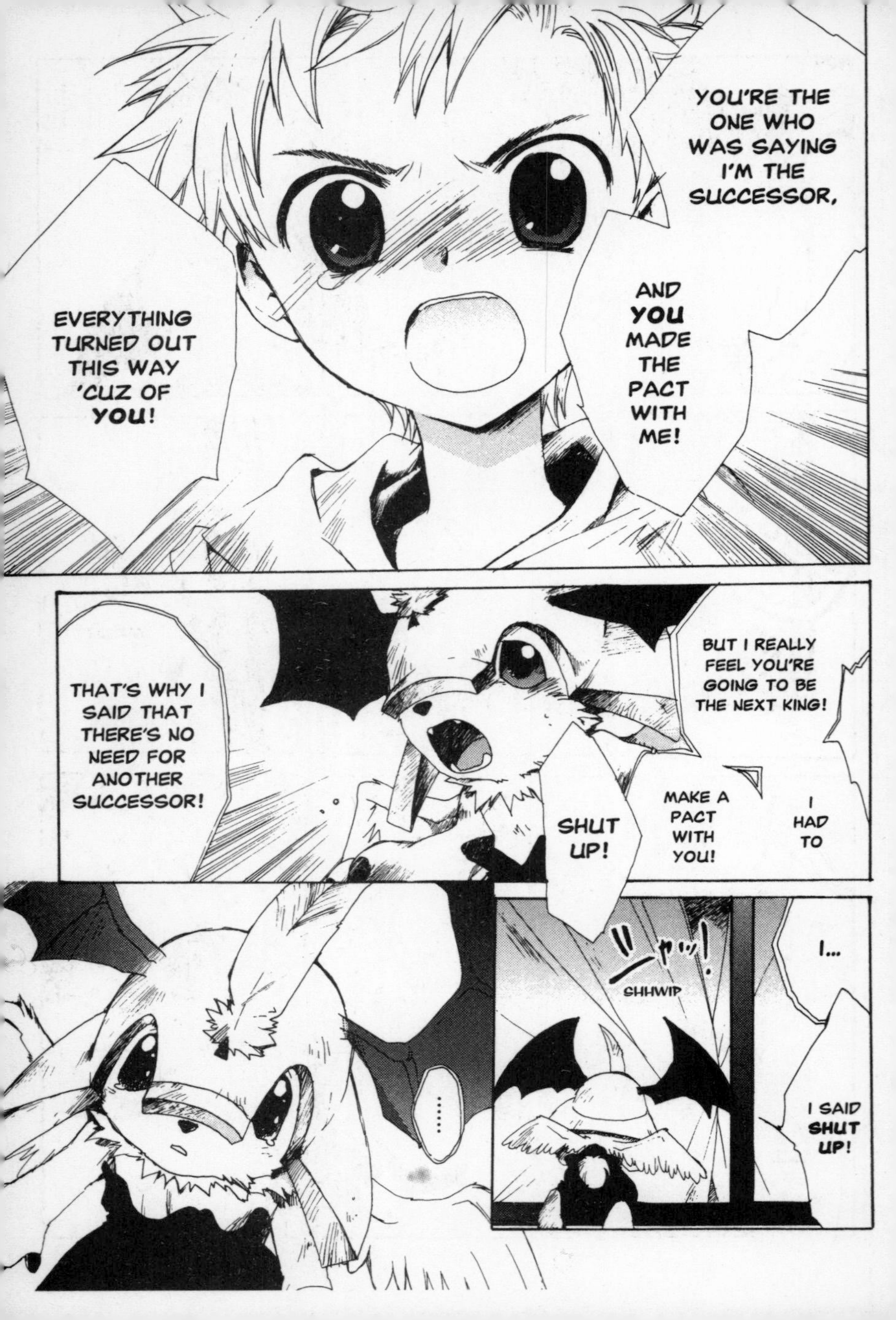
YOU'RE THE ONE WHO WAS SAYING I'M THE SUCCESSOR,
AND **YOU** MADE THE PACT WITH ME!
EVERYTHING TURNED OUT THIS WAY 'CUZ OF **YOU**!
BUT I REALLY FEEL YOU'RE GOING TO BE THE NEXT KING!
THAT'S WHY I SAID THAT THERE'S NO NEED FOR ANOTHER SUCCESSOR!
I HAD TO
MAKE A PACT WITH YOU!
SHUT UP!
I...
SHHWIP
I SAID **SHUT UP**!
......

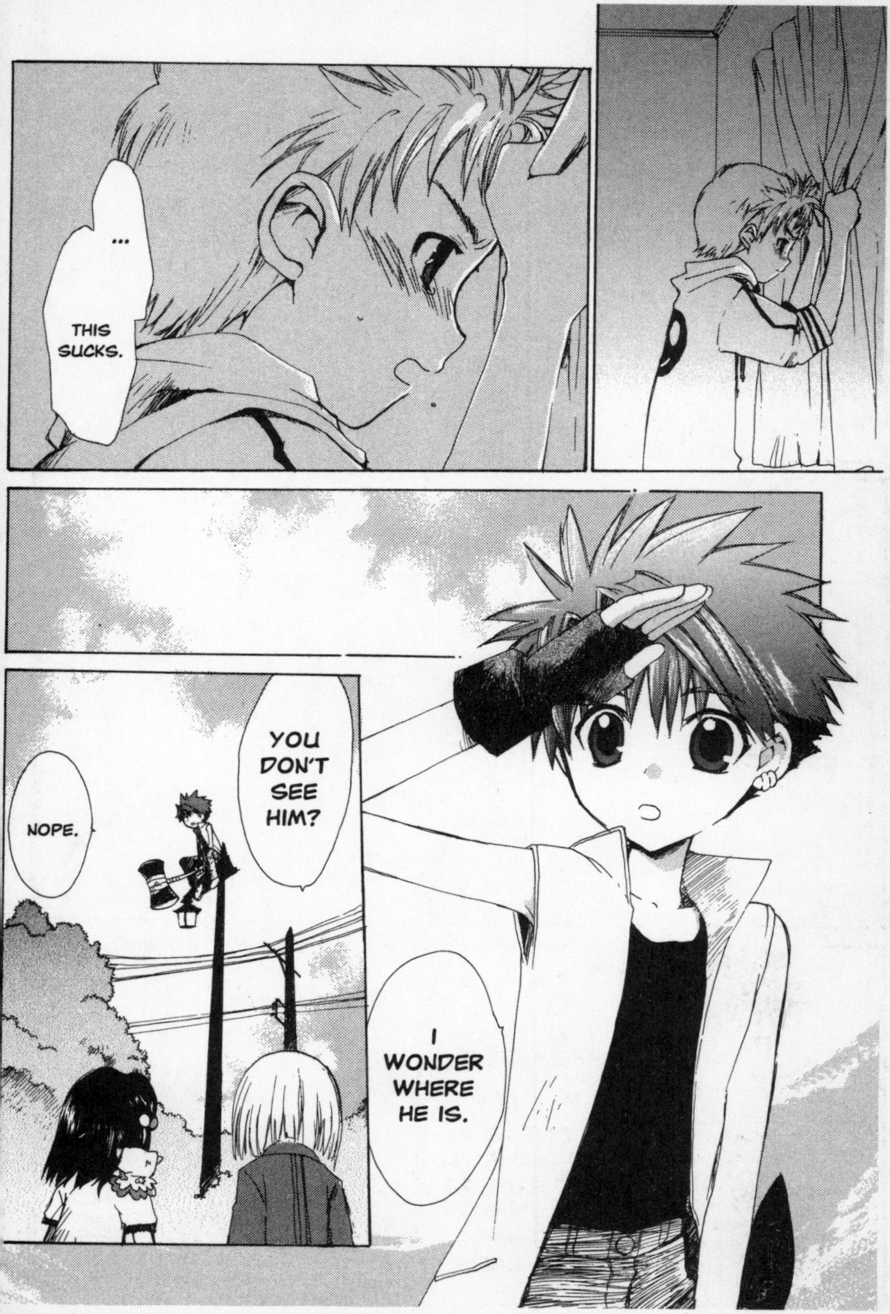
...
THIS SUCKS.
I WONDER WHERE HE IS.
YOU DON'T SEE HIM?
NOPE.

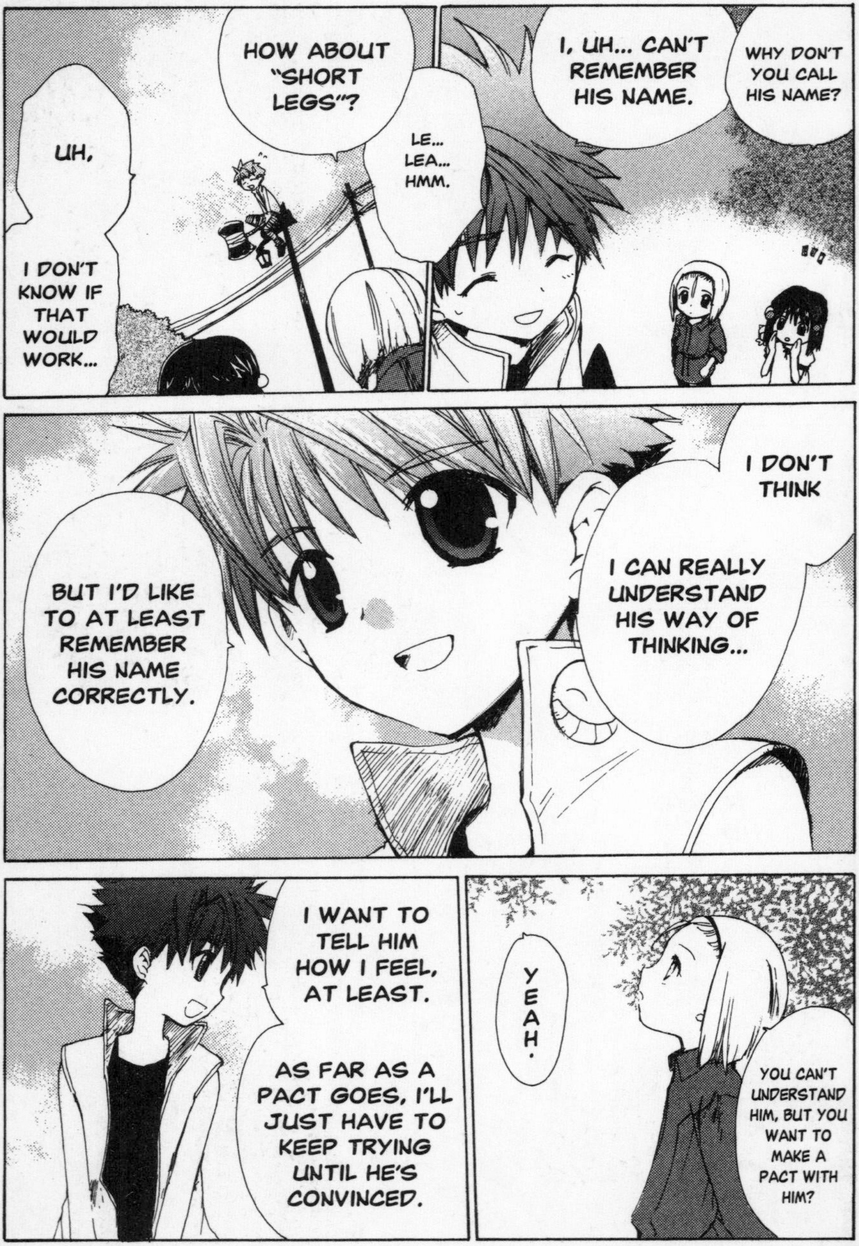
WHY DON'T YOU CALL HIS NAME?
I, UH... CAN'T REMEMBER HIS NAME.
LE... LEA... HMM.
HOW ABOUT "SHORT LEGS"?
UH,
I DON'T KNOW IF THAT WOULD WORK...
I DON'T THINK
I CAN REALLY UNDERSTAND HIS WAY OF THINKING...
BUT I'D LIKE TO AT LEAST REMEMBER HIS NAME CORRECTLY.
YOU CAN'T UNDERSTAND HIM, BUT YOU WANT TO MAKE A PACT WITH HIM?
YEAH.
I WANT TO TELL HIM HOW I FEEL, AT LEAST.
AS FAR AS A PACT GOES, I'LL JUST HAVE TO KEEP TRYING UNTIL HE'S CONVINCED.

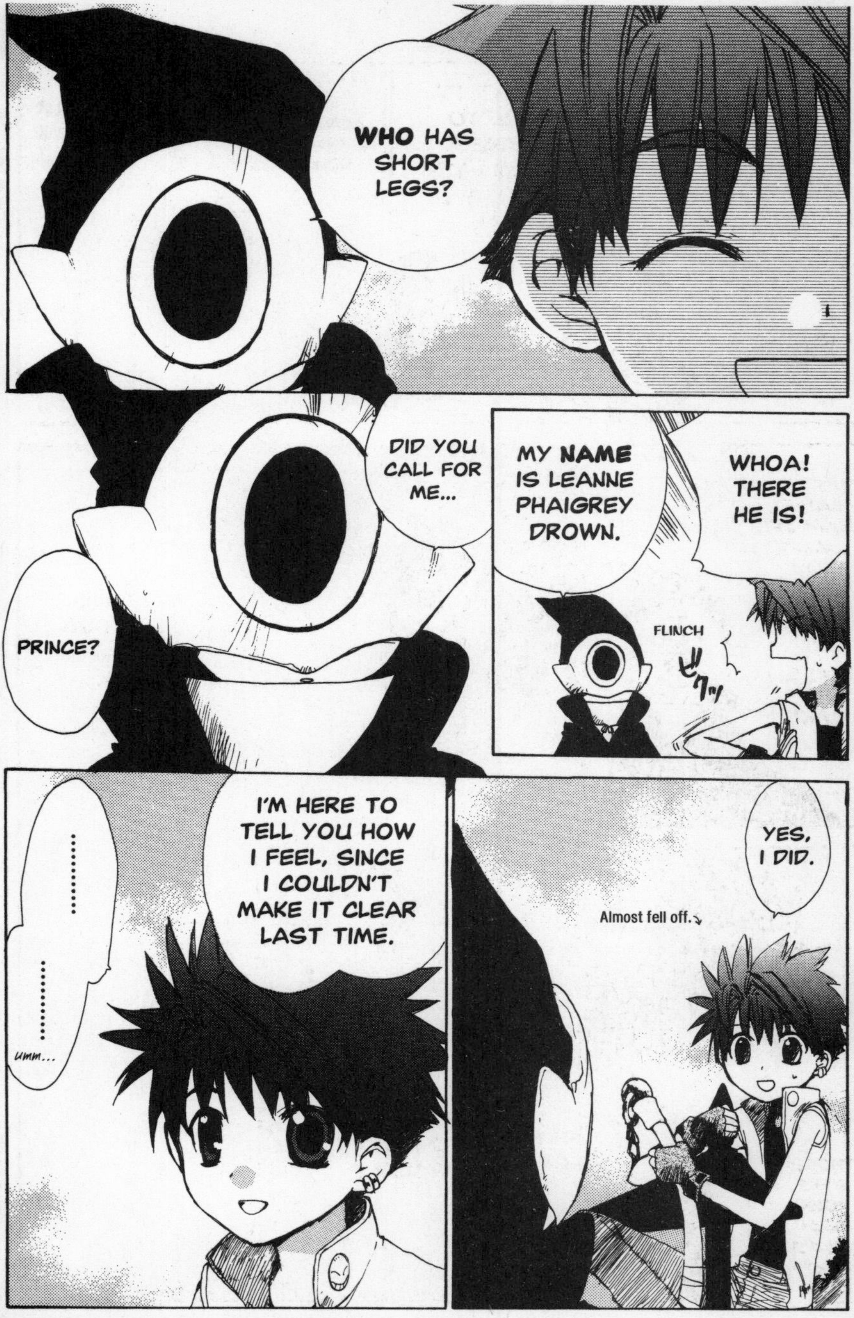
WHO HAS SHORT LEGS?
WHOA! THERE HE IS!
FLINCH
MY NAME IS LEANNE PHAIGREY DROWN.
DID YOU CALL FOR ME...
PRINCE?
YES, I DID.
Almost fell off.
I'M HERE TO TELL YOU HOW I FEEL, SINCE I COULDN'T MAKE IT CLEAR LAST TIME.
....
....
umm...

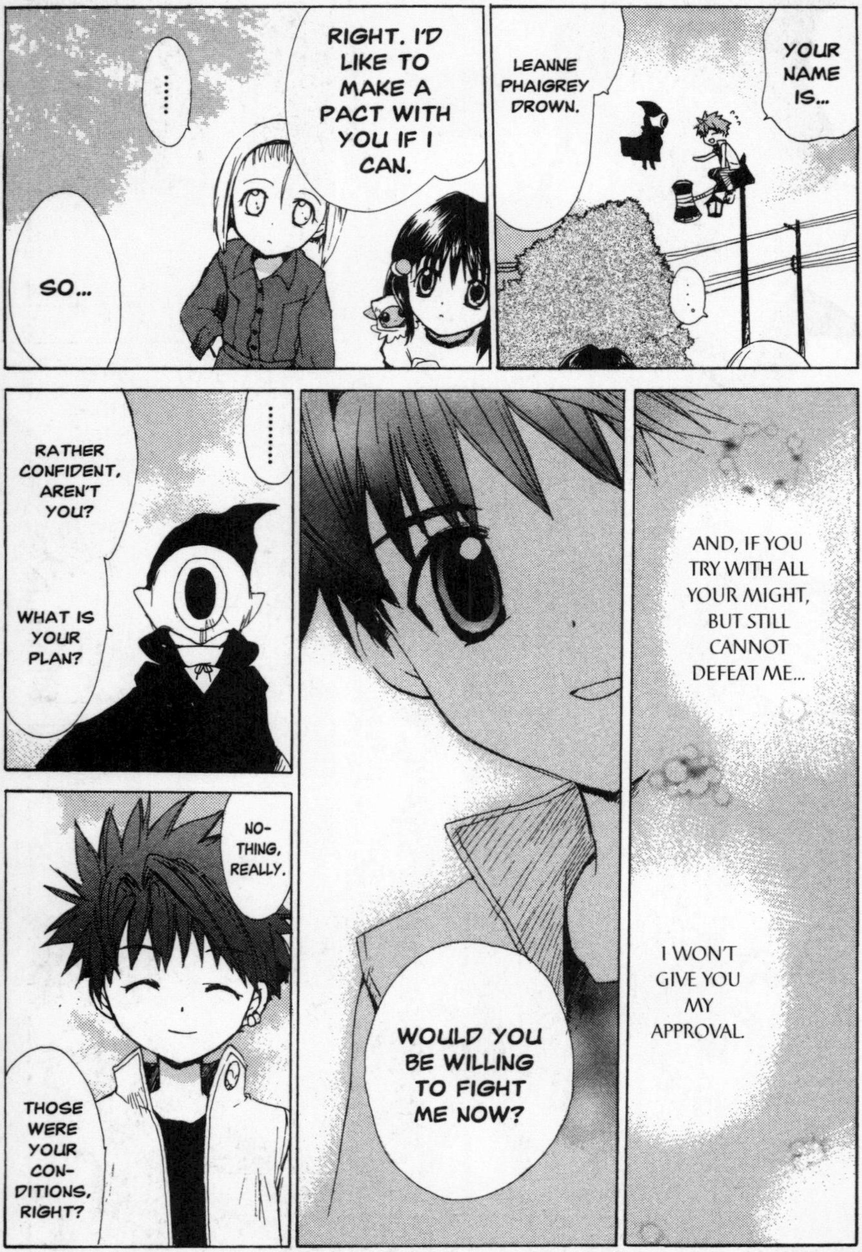

YOUR NAME IS...
LEANNE PHAIGREY DROWN.
...
RIGHT. I'D LIKE TO MAKE A PACT WITH YOU IF I CAN.
......
SO...
AND, IF YOU TRY WITH ALL YOUR MIGHT, BUT STILL CANNOT DEFEAT ME...
I WON'T GIVE YOU MY APPROVAL.
WOULD YOU BE WILLING TO FIGHT ME NOW?
....
RATHER CONFIDENT, AREN'T YOU?
WHAT IS YOUR PLAN?
NO-THING, REALLY.
THOSE WERE YOUR CON-DITIONS, RIGHT?

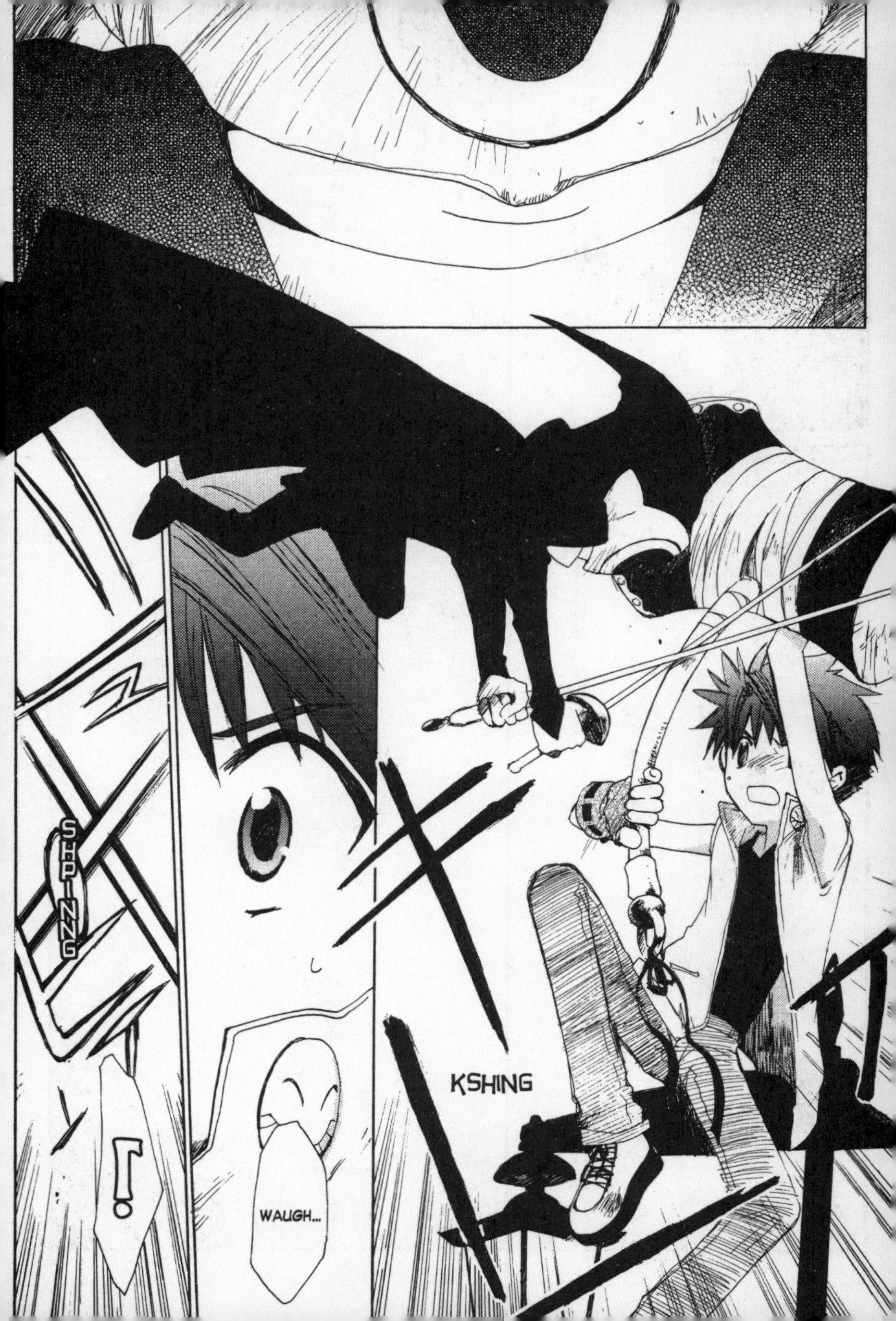
KSHING
WAUGH...
!
SHPING

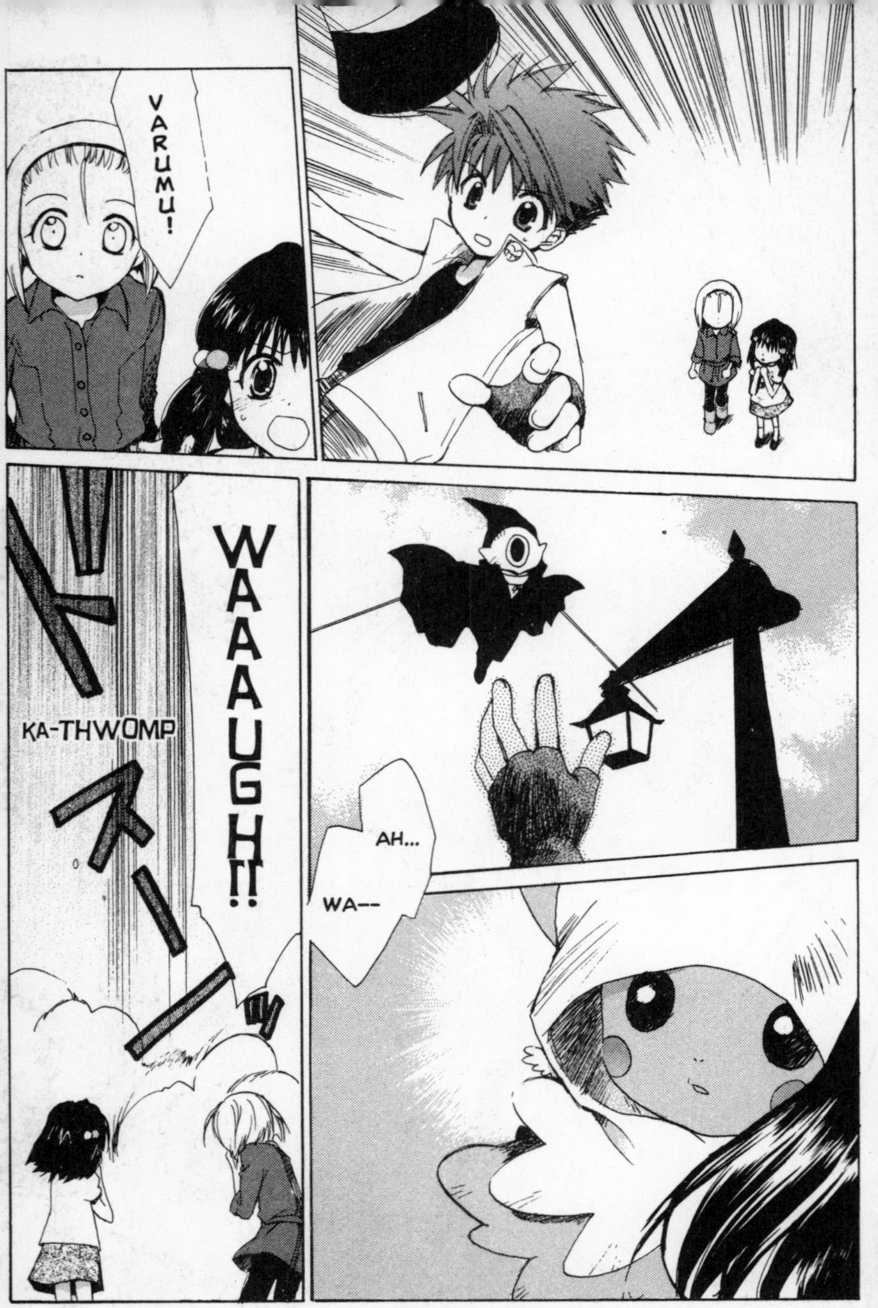
VARUMU!
AH...
WA--
WAAAAUGH!!
KA-THWOMP

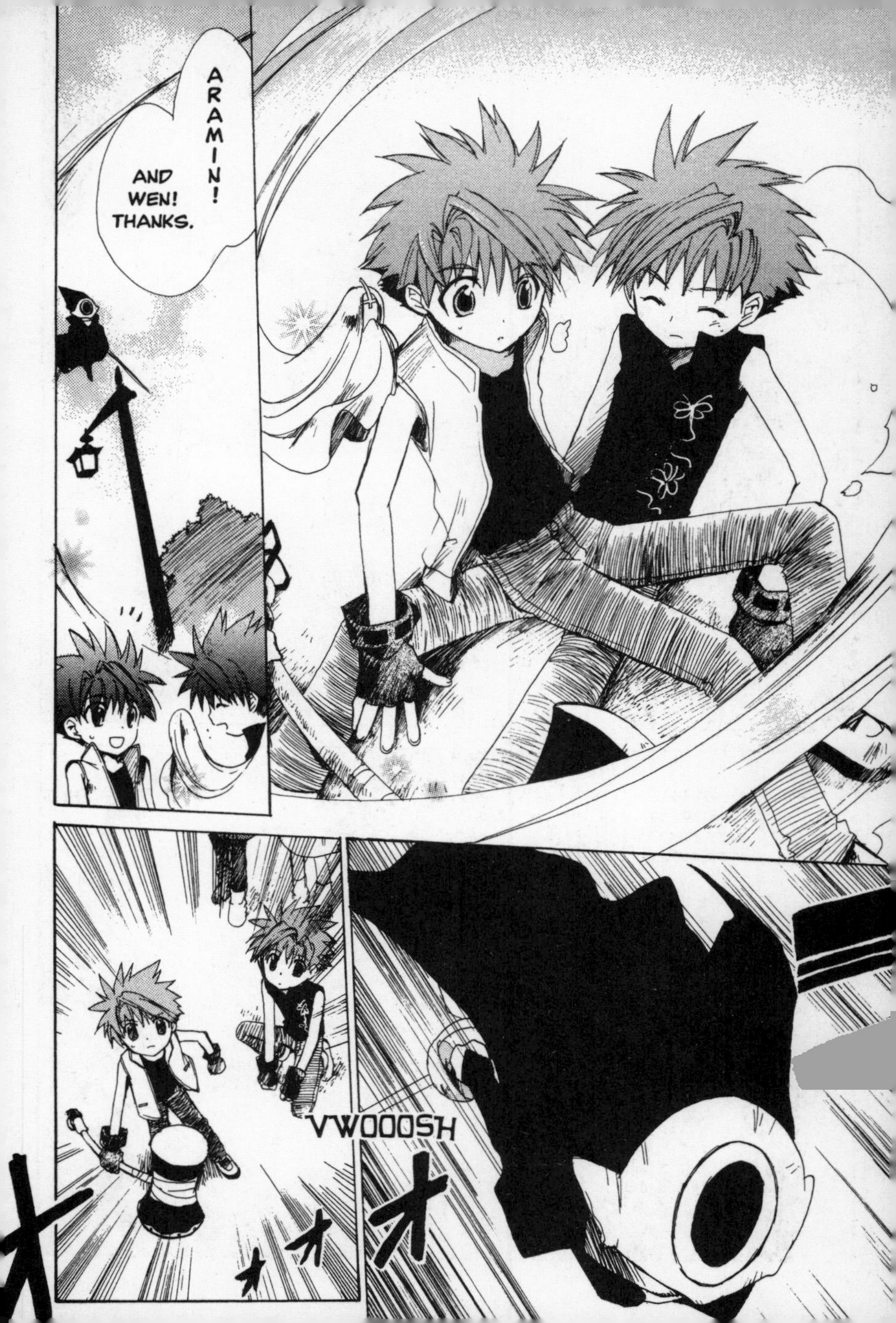
ARAMIN!
AND WEN! THANKS.
VWOOOSH

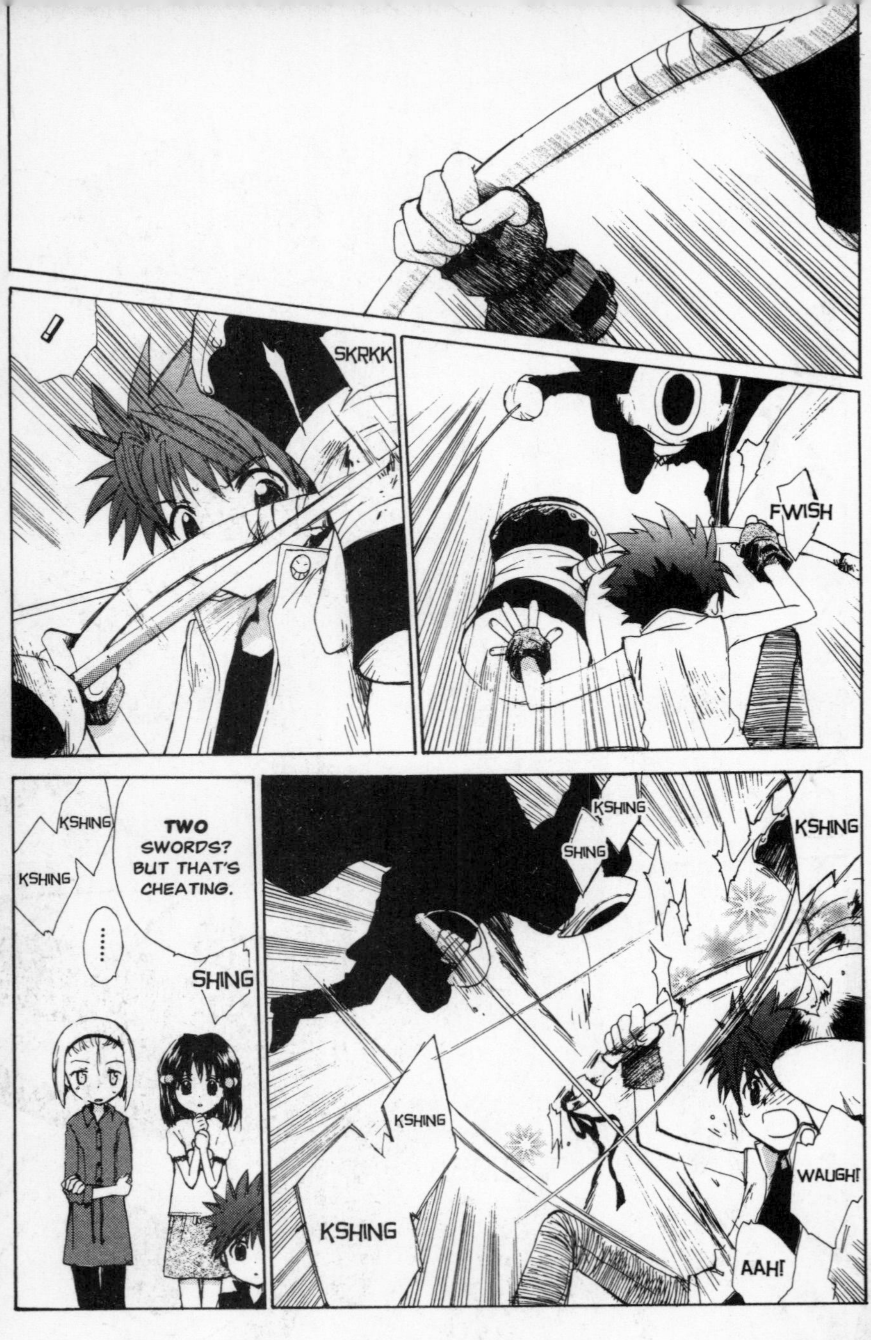

FWISH
!
SKRKK
KSHING
SHING
KSHING
WAUGH!
KSHING
KSHING
AAH!
TWO SWORDS? BUT THAT'S CHEATING.
KSHING
KSHING
......
SHING

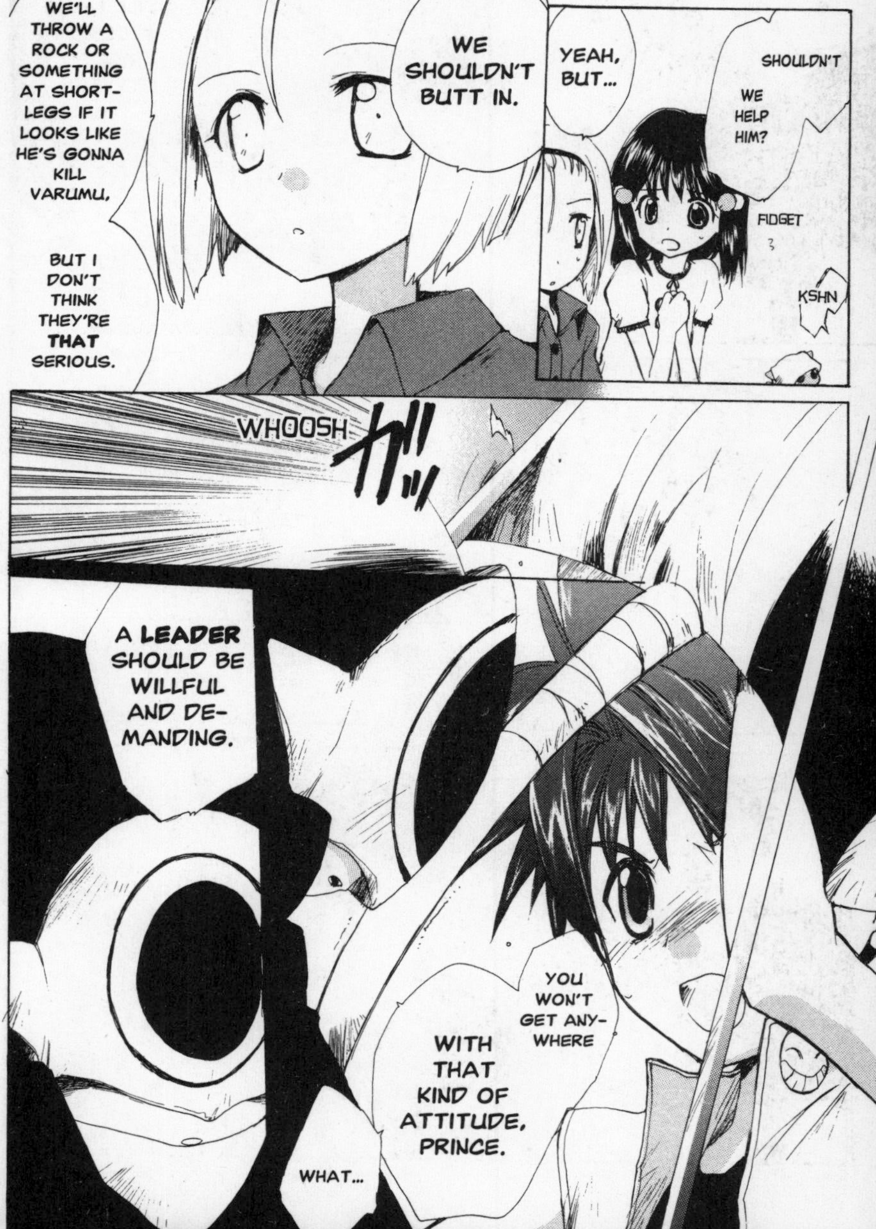

SHOULDN'T WE HELP HIM?
FIDGET
KSHN
YEAH, BUT...
WE SHOULDN'T BUTT IN.
WE'LL THROW A ROCK OR SOMETHING AT SHORT-LEGS IF IT LOOKS LIKE HE'S GONNA KILL VARUMU,
BUT I DON'T THINK THEY'RE **THAT** SERIOUS.
WHOOSH
YOU WON'T GET ANY-WHERE
WITH THAT KIND OF ATTITUDE, PRINCE.
A **LEADER** SHOULD BE WILLFUL AND DE-MANDING.
WHAT...

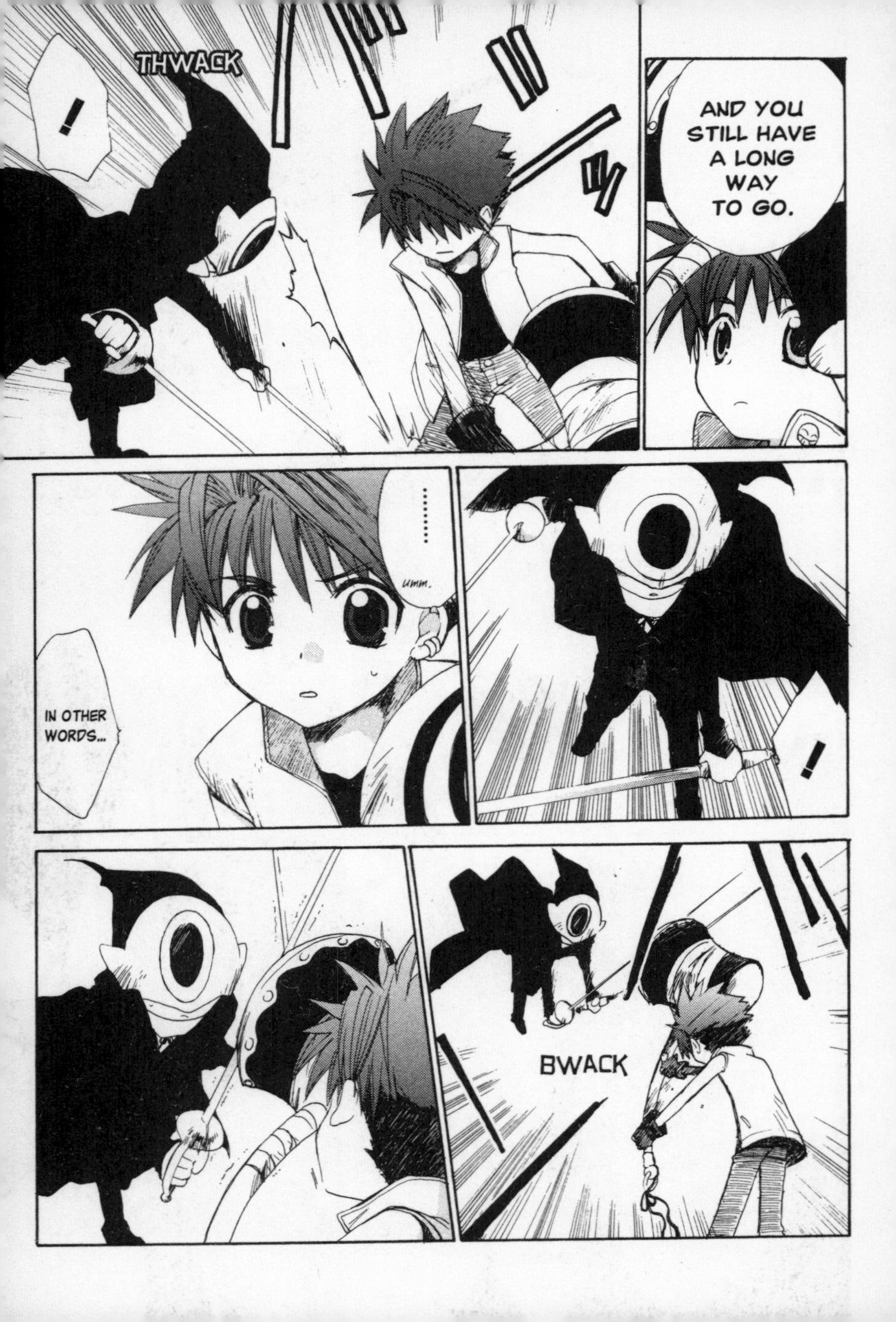
AND YOU STILL HAVE A LONG WAY TO GO.
THWACK
!
....
UMM.
IN OTHER WORDS...
!
BWACK

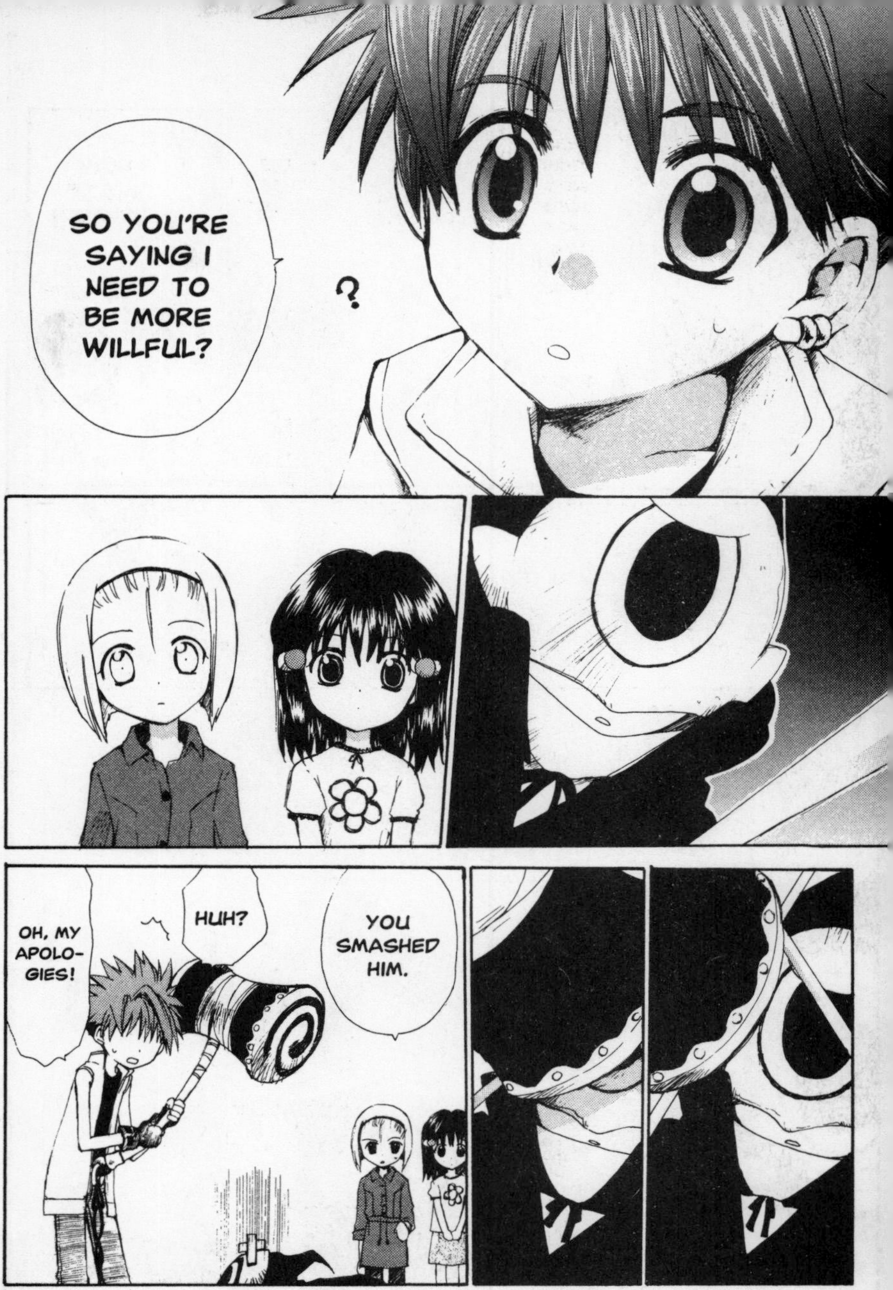
SO YOU'RE SAYING I NEED TO BE MORE WILLFUL?
?
YOU SMASHED HIM.
HUH?
OH, MY APOLOGIES!

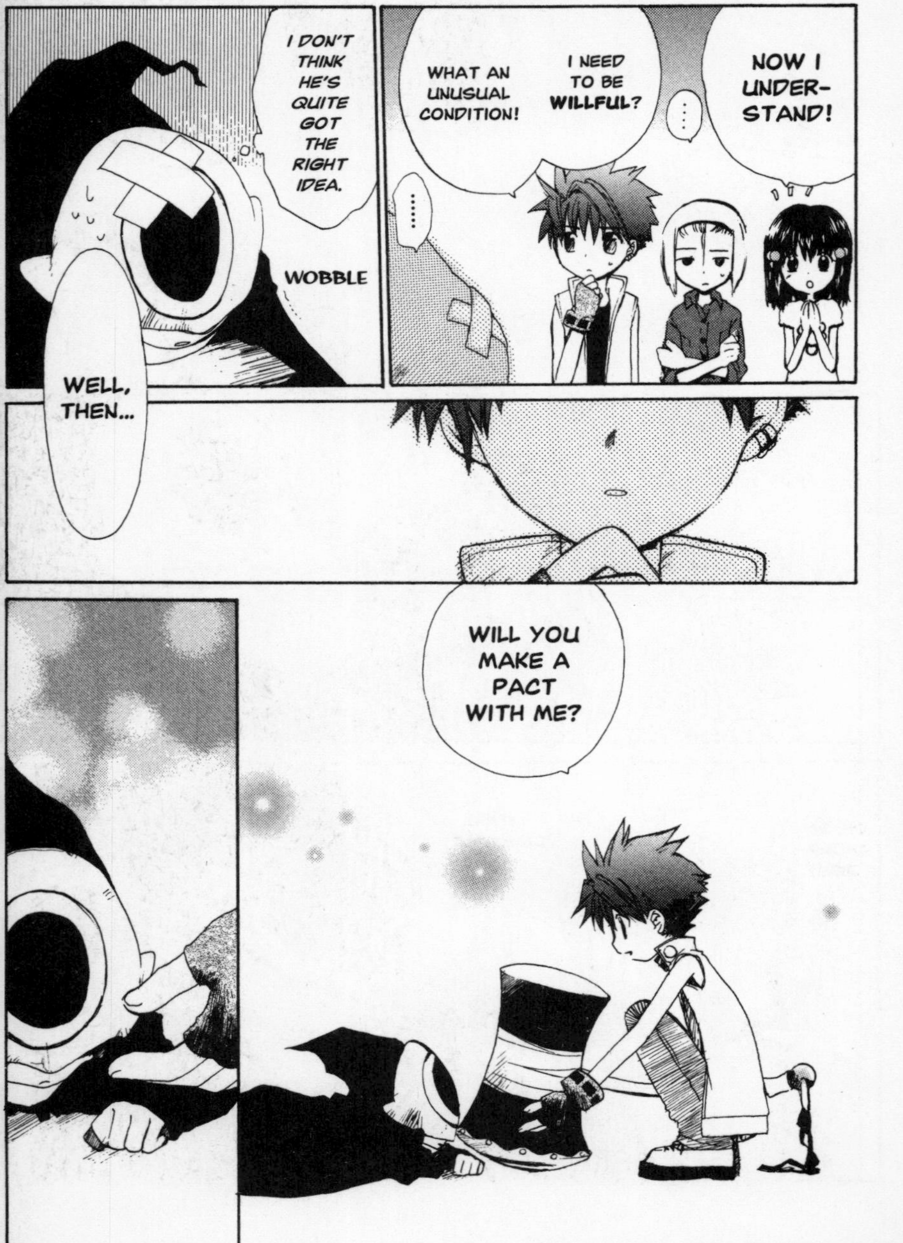

NOW I UNDERSTAND!
...
I NEED TO BE WILLFUL?
WHAT AN UNUSUAL CONDITION!
......
I DON'T THINK HE'S QUITE GOT THE RIGHT IDEA.
WOBBLE
WELL, THEN...
WILL YOU MAKE A PACT WITH ME?

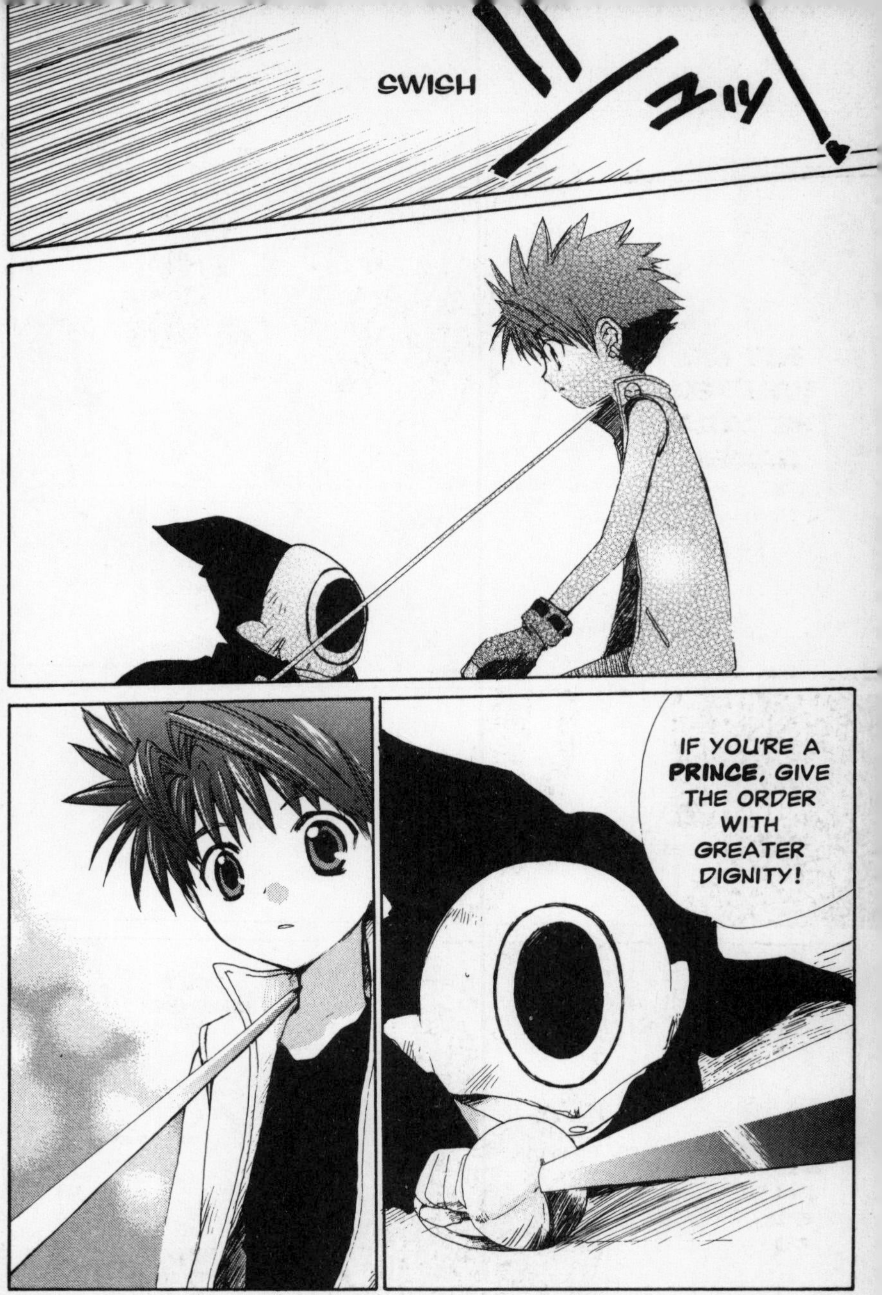
SWISH
IF YOU'RE A **PRINCE**, GIVE THE ORDER WITH GREATER DIGNITY!

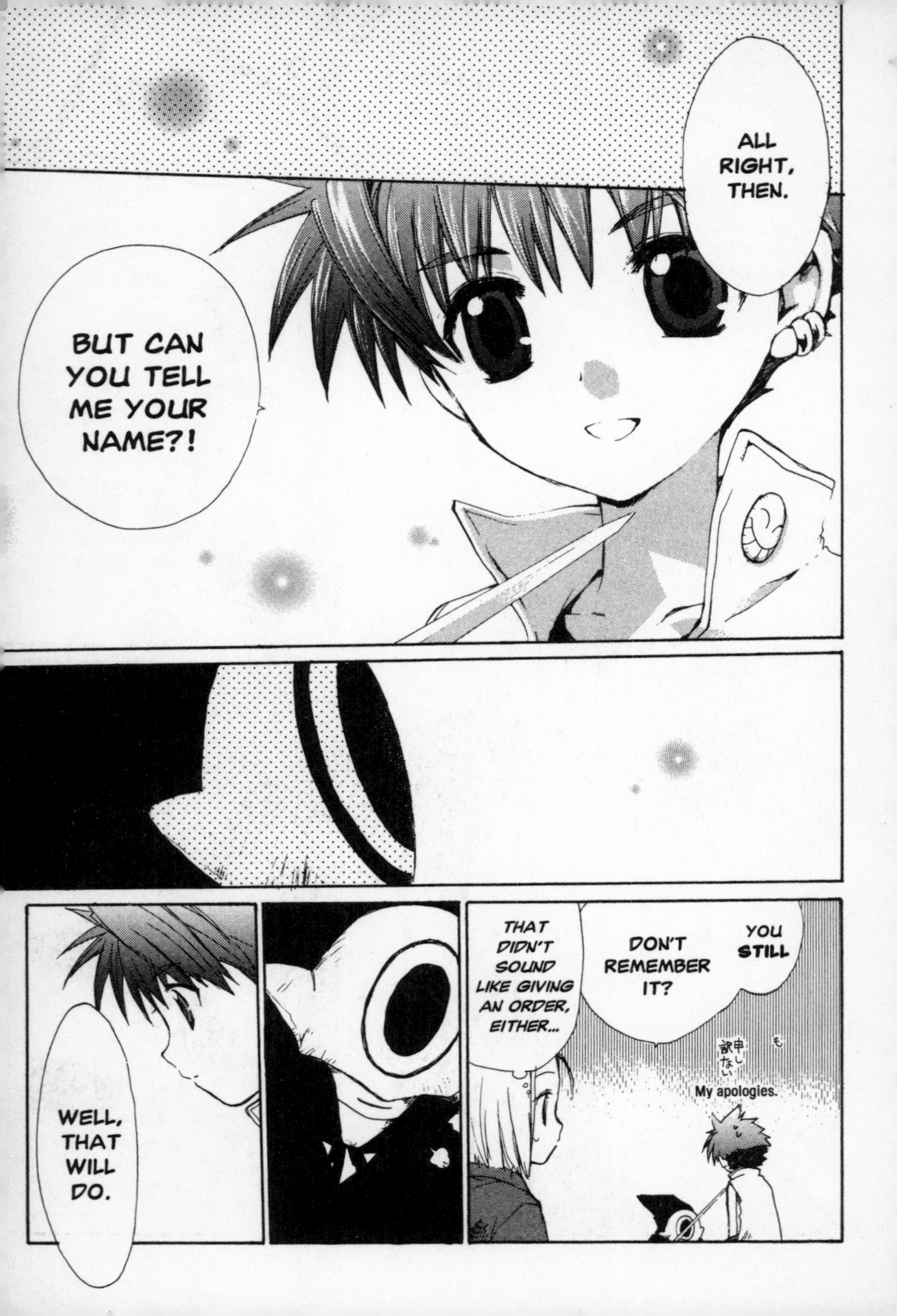
ALL RIGHT, THEN.
BUT CAN YOU TELL ME YOUR NAME?!
YOU STILL DON'T REMEMBER IT?
THAT DIDN'T SOUND LIKE GIVING AN ORDER, EITHER...
申し訳ない
My apologies.
WELL, THAT WILL DO.

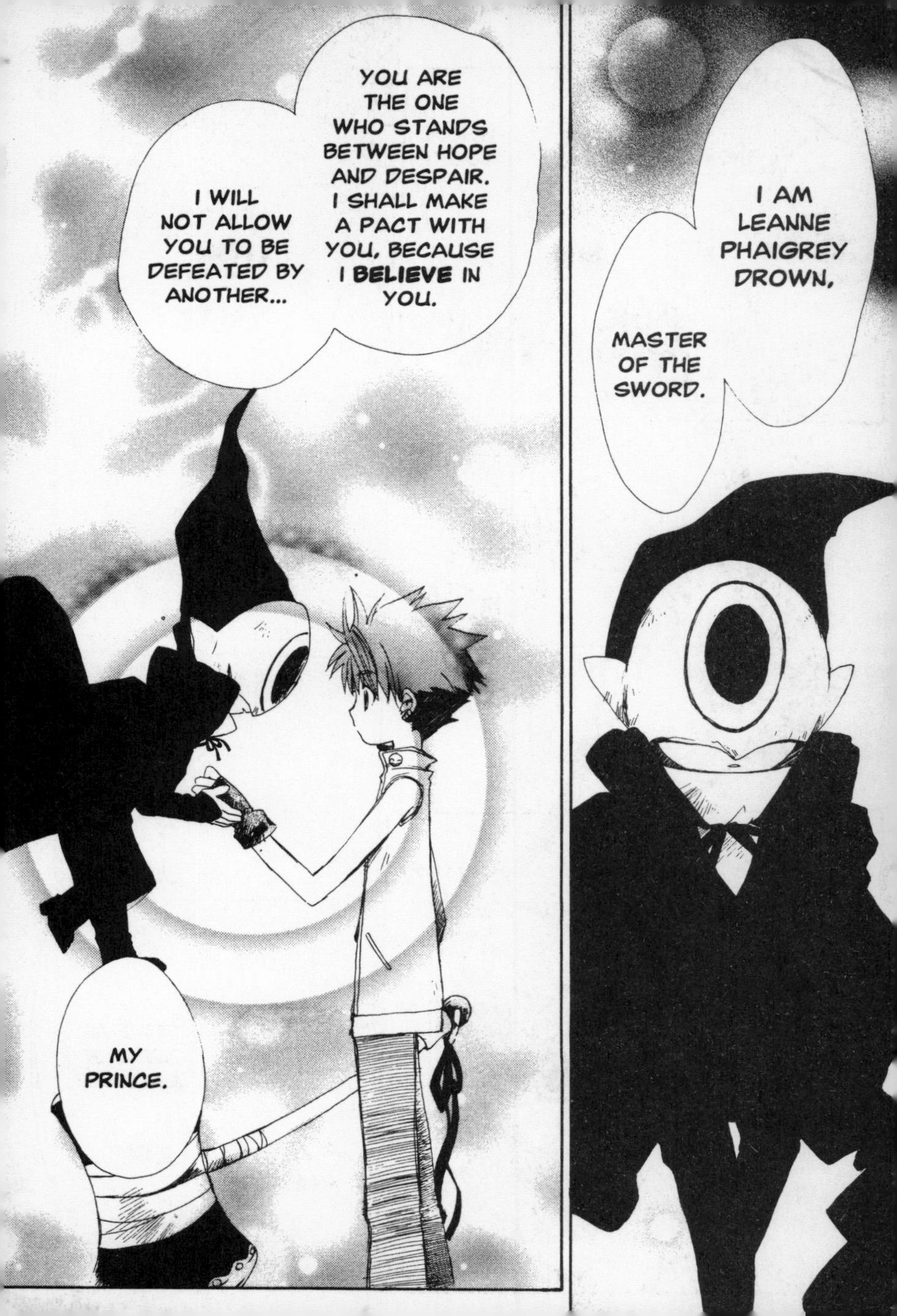
I AM LEANNE PHAIGREY DROWN,
MASTER OF THE SWORD.
YOU ARE THE ONE WHO STANDS BETWEEN HOPE AND DESPAIR. I SHALL MAKE A PACT WITH YOU, BECAUSE I BELIEVE IN YOU.
I WILL NOT ALLOW YOU TO BE DEFEATED BY ANOTHER...
MY PRINCE.

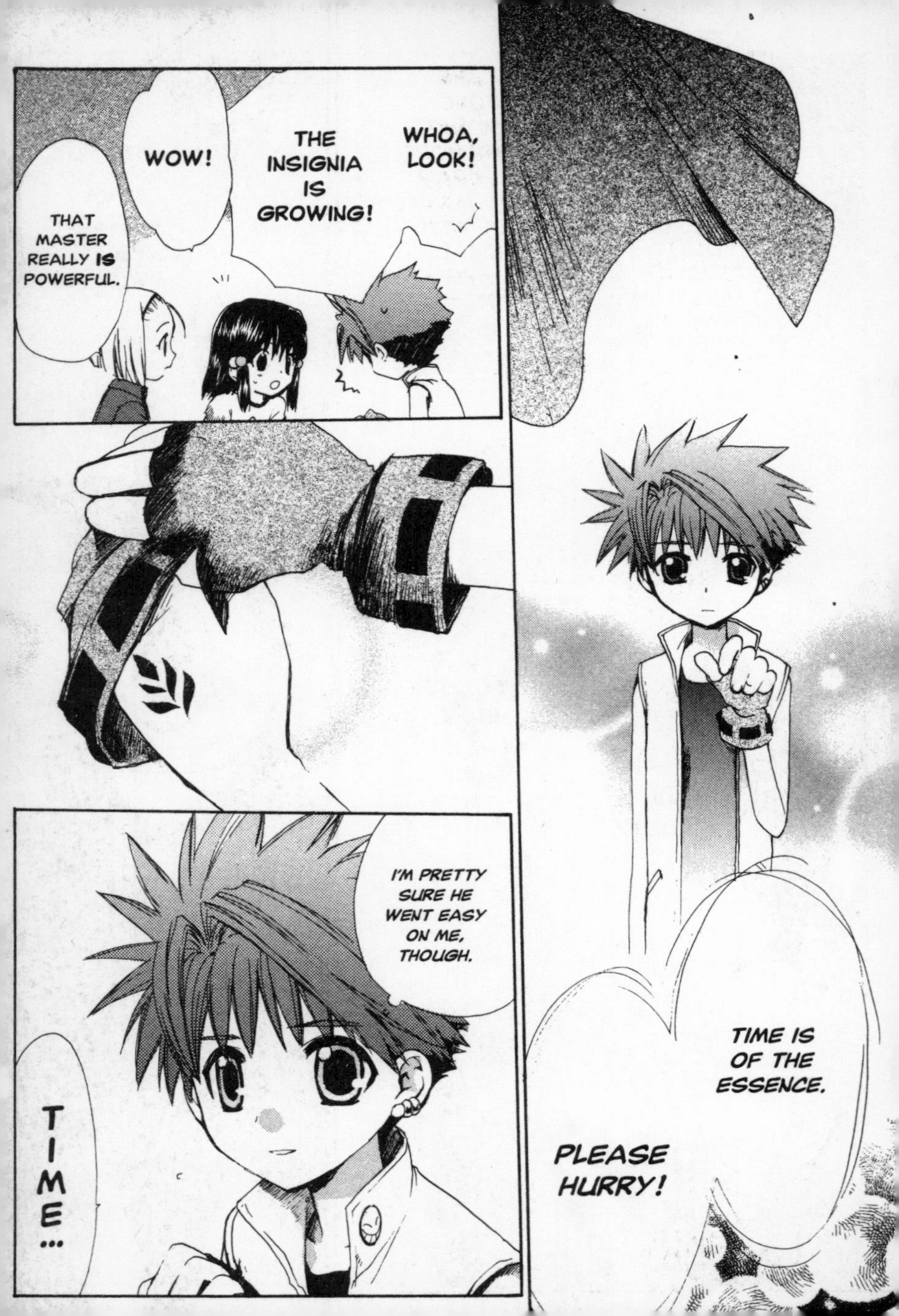
WHOA, LOOK!
THE INSIGNIA IS GROWING!
WOW!
THAT MASTER REALLY IS POWERFUL.
I'M PRETTY SURE HE WENT EASY ON ME, THOUGH.
TIME...
TIME IS OF THE ESSENCE.
PLEASE HURRY!

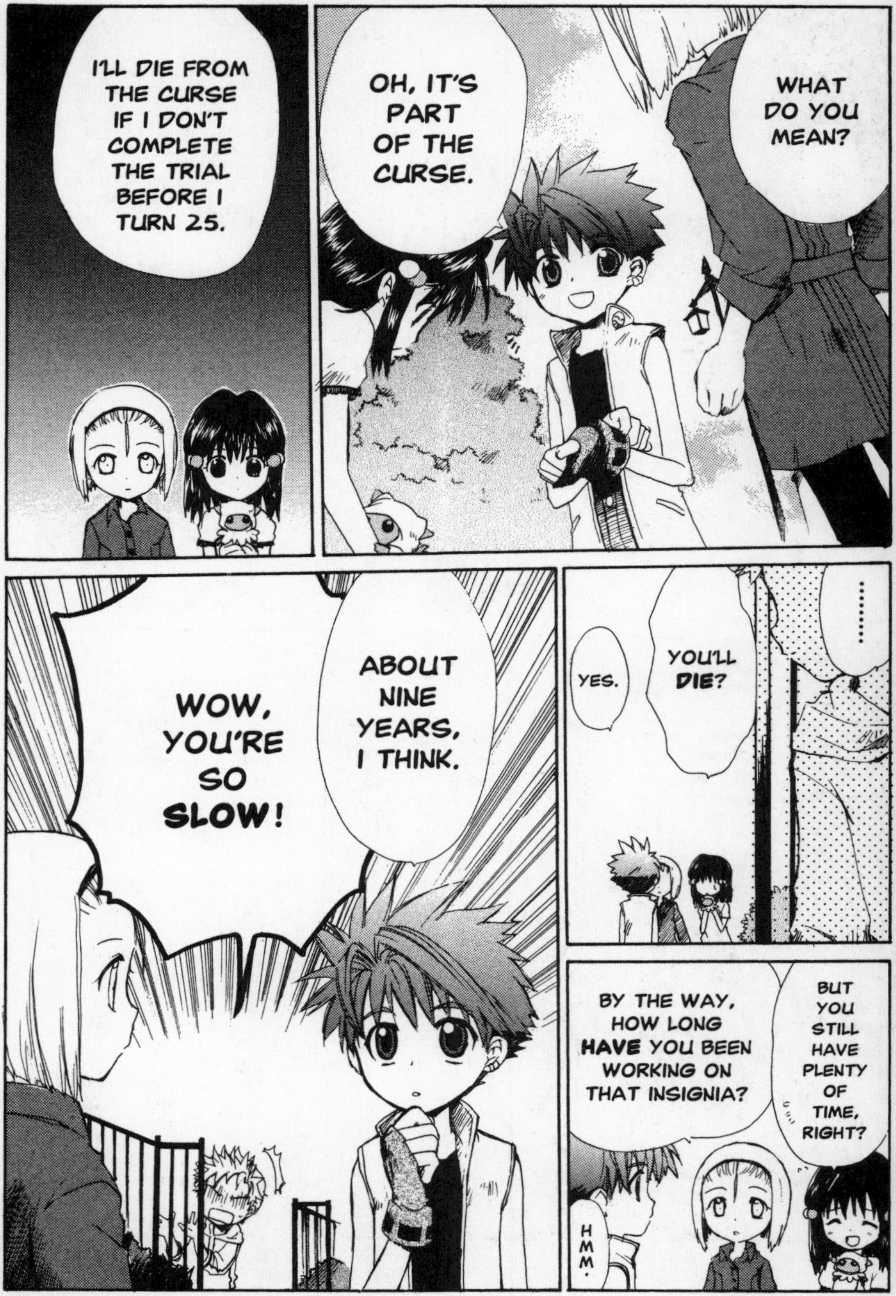
WHAT DO YOU MEAN?
OH, IT'S PART OF THE CURSE.
I'LL DIE FROM THE CURSE IF I DON'T COMPLETE THE TRIAL BEFORE I TURN 25.
......
YOU'LL **DIE**?
YES.
BUT YOU STILL HAVE PLENTY OF TIME, RIGHT?
BY THE WAY, HOW LONG **HAVE** YOU BEEN WORKING ON THAT INSIGNIA?
HMM.
ABOUT NINE YEARS, I THINK.
WOW, YOU'RE SO **SLOW**!

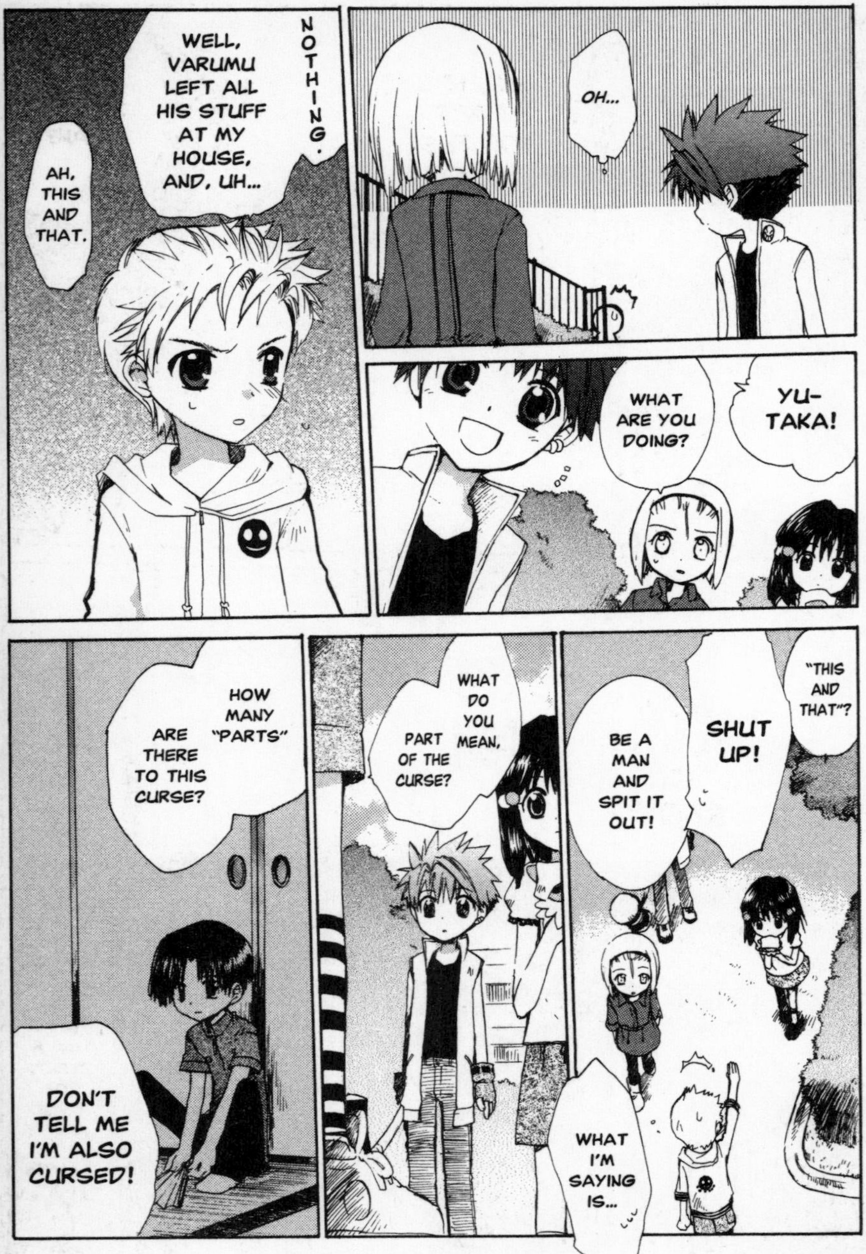
OH...
YU-TAKA!
WHAT ARE YOU DOING?
NOTHING.
WELL, VARUMU LEFT ALL HIS STUFF AT MY HOUSE, AND, UH...
AH, THIS AND THAT.
"THIS AND THAT"?
SHUT UP!
BE A MAN AND SPIT IT OUT!
WHAT I'M SAYING IS...
WHAT DO YOU MEAN, PART OF THE CURSE?
HOW MANY "PARTS" ARE THERE TO THIS CURSE?
DON'T TELL ME I'M ALSO CURSED!

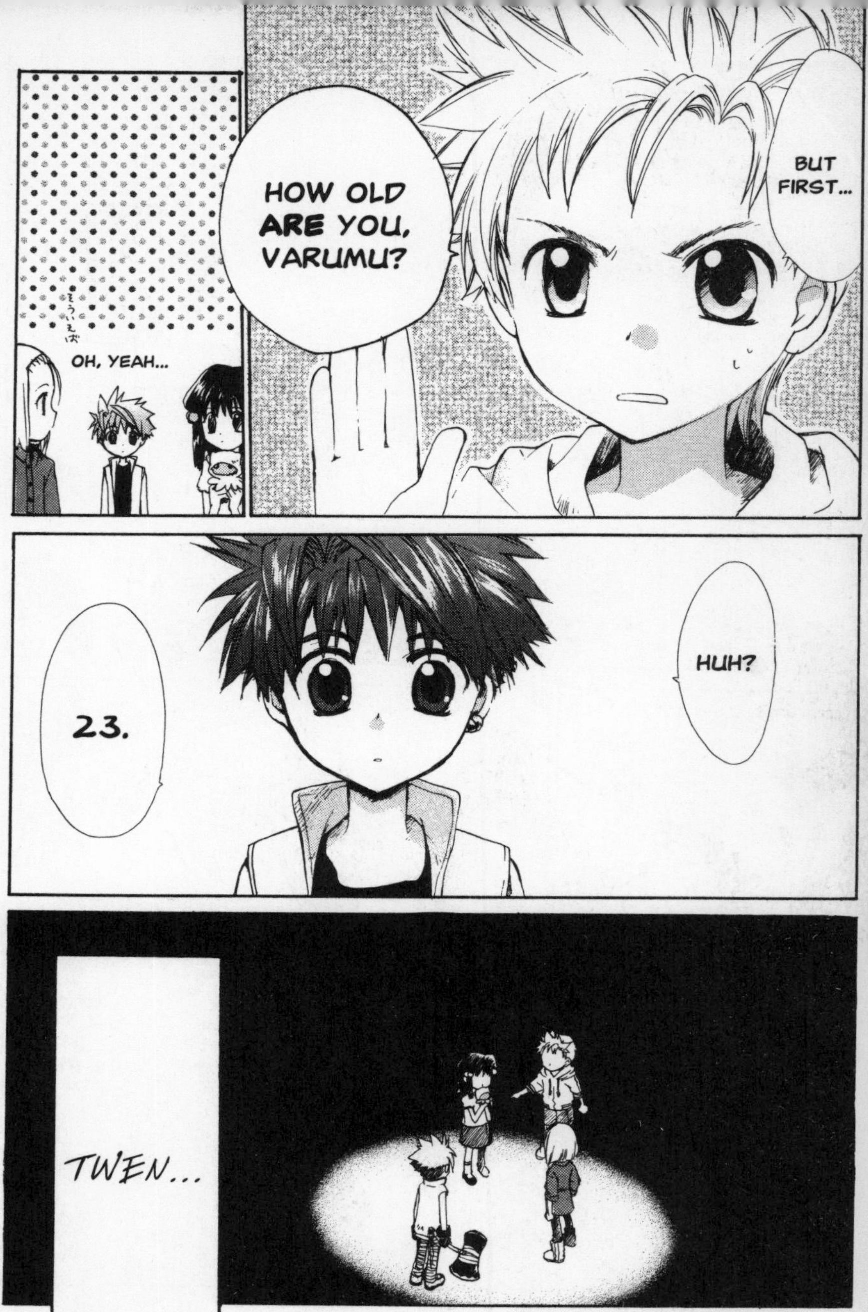
BUT FIRST...
HOW OLD ARE YOU, VARUMU?
そういえば
OH, YEAH...
HUH?
23.
TWEN...

THE FIRST KING ADVENTURE 2 /END

THE FIRST KING ADVENTURE 賢者の長き不在

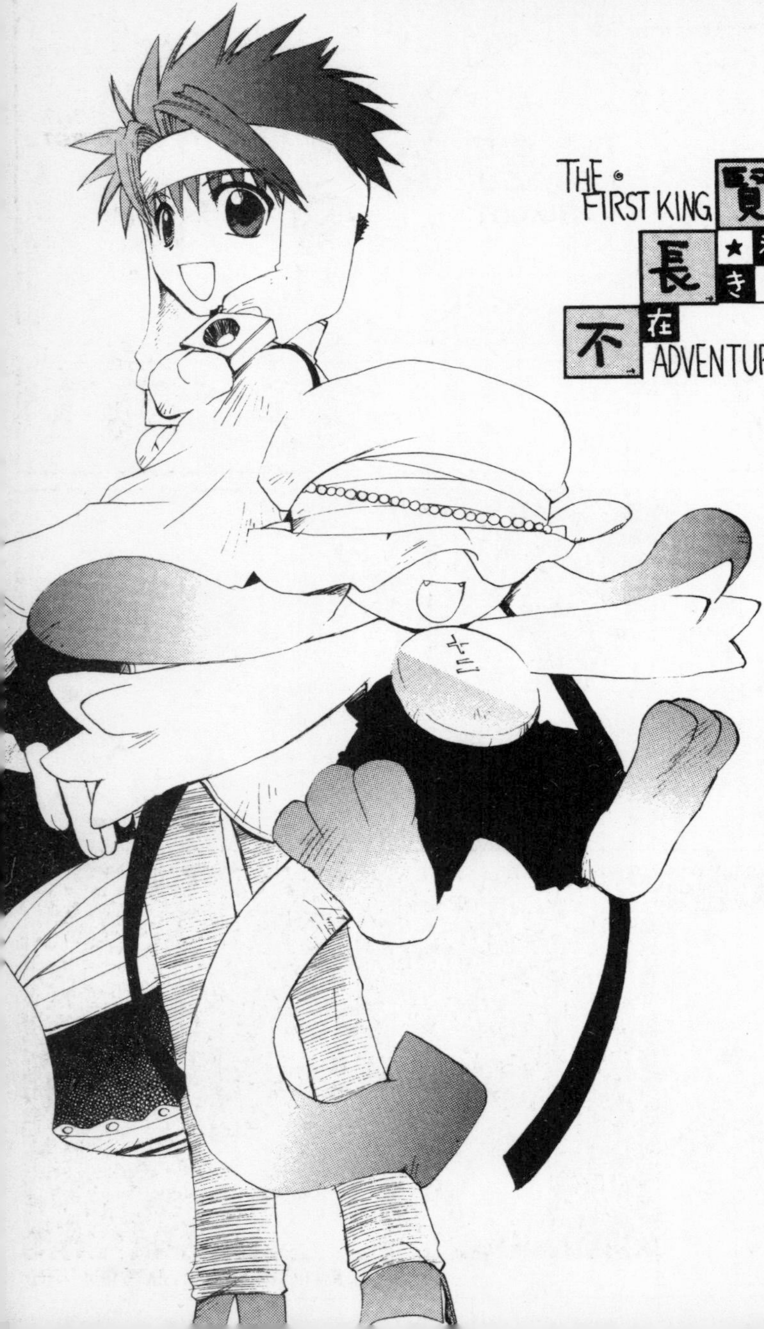
十二

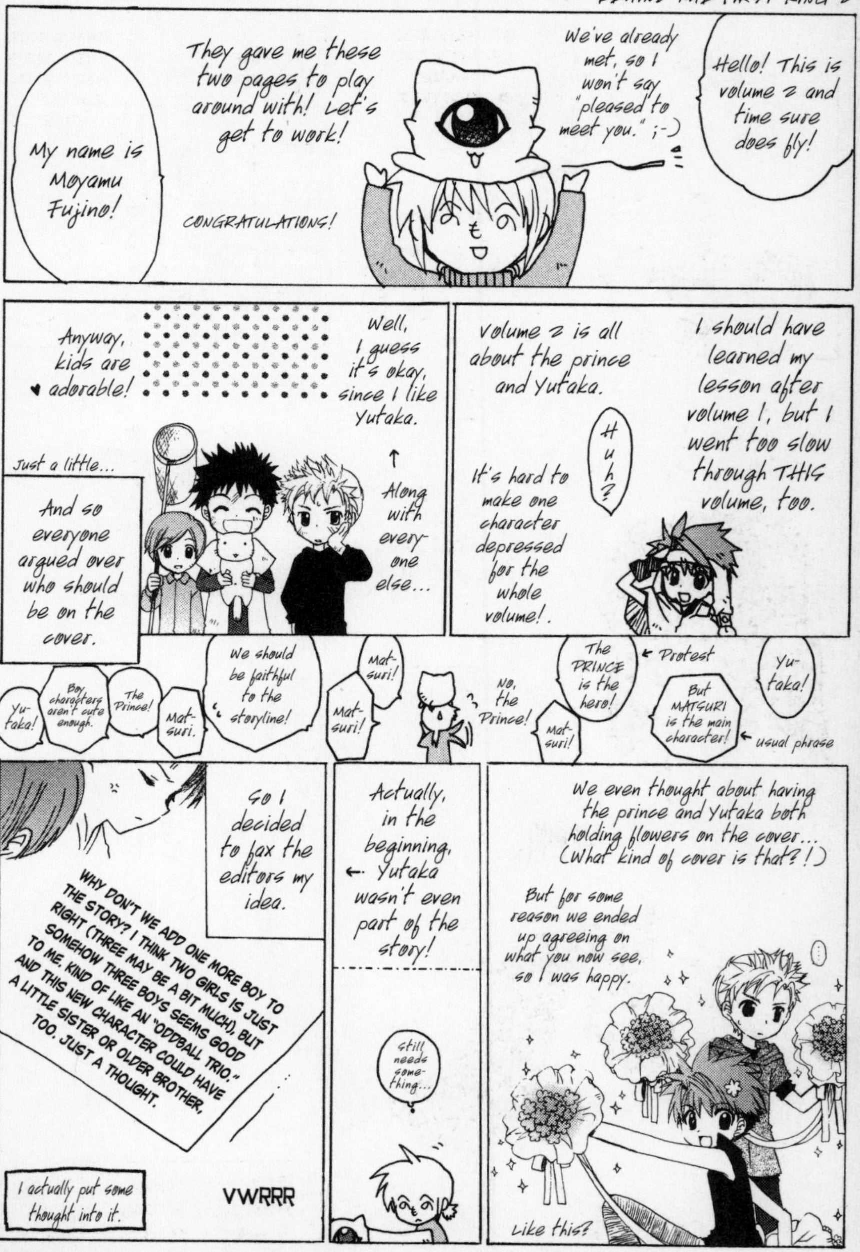
Hello! This is volume 2 and time sure does fly!
We've already met, so I won't say "pleased to meet you." ;-)
They gave me these two pages to play around with! Let's get to work!
My name is Moyamu Fujino!
CONGRATULATIONS!
I should have learned my lesson after volume 1, but I went too slow through THIS volume, too.
Volume 2 is all about the prince and Yutaka.
Huh?
It's hard to make one character depressed for the whole volume!.
Well, I guess it's okay, since I like Yutaka.
Anyway, kids are adorable!
Along with every-one else...
Just a little...
And so everyone argued over who should be on the cover.
Yu-taka!
Protest
The PRINCE is the hero!
But MATSURI is the main character!
usual phrase
Mat-suri!
No, the Prince!
Mat-suri!
Mat-suri!
We should be faithful to the storyline!
Mat-suri.
The Prince!
Boy characters aren't cute enough.
Yu-taka!
We even thought about having the prince and Yutaka both holding flowers on the cover... (What kind of cover is that?!)
But for some reason we ended up agreeing on what you now see, so I was happy.
...
Like this?
Actually, in the beginning, Yutaka wasn't even part of the story!
Still needs some-thing...
So I decided to fax the editors my idea.
WHY DON'T WE ADD ONE MORE BOY TO THE STORY? I THINK TWO GIRLS IS JUST RIGHT (THREE MAY BE A BIT MUCH), BUT SOMEHOW THREE BOYS SEEMS GOOD TO ME. KIND OF LIKE AN "ODDBALL TRIO." AND THIS NEW CHARACTER COULD HAVE A LITTLE SISTER OR OLDER BROTHER, TOO. JUST A THOUGHT.
I actually put some thought into it.
VWRRR